A CHRONOLOGICAL OUTLINE OF BRITISH LITERATURE

A CHRONOLOGICAL OUTLINE OF BRITISH LITERATURE

Samuel J. Rogal

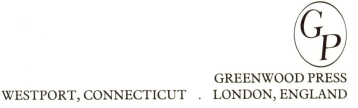

GREENWOOD PRESS
WESTPORT, CONNECTICUT · LONDON, ENGLAND

Library of Congress Cataloging in Publication Data

Rogal, Samuel J
    A chronological outline of British literature.

    Bibliography: p.
    Includes index.
    1. English literature--Outlines, syllabi, etc.
I. Title.
PR87.R57   1980   820'.9   79-8577
ISBN 0-313-21477-8 lib. bdg.

Copyright © 1980 by Samuel J. Rogal

All rights reserved. No portion of this book may be reproduced, by any process or technique, without the express written consent of the publisher.

Library of Congress Catalog Card Number: 79-8577
ISBN: 0-313-21477-8

First published in 1980

Greenwood Press
A division of Congressional Information Service, Inc.
51 Riverside Avenue, Westport, Connecticut 06880

Printed in the United States of America

10 9 8 7 6 5 4 3 2 1

Contents

Introduction	vii
Key to Symbols	xi
References	xiii
1. The Beginnings through the Fourteenth Century	3
2. The Fifteenth Century	22
3. The Sixteenth Century	30
4. The Seventeenth Century	52
5. The Eighteenth Century	88
6. The Nineteenth Century	130
7. The Twentieth Century	210
Index	311

Introduction

As the title indicates, the *Chronological Outline of British Literature* is intended, primarily, to assist scholars, students, and general readers of British literature in determining the extent of literary activity and literary related events in England, Scotland, Ireland, and Wales during a specific year, decade, or century. As such, this volume should not be considered a repository for trivia, in which mental gymnasts may leap over one another in an effort to memorize dates, authors, and titles that, by themselves, have little meaning and even less value. Rather, these entries enable the reader to comprehend the significance of events and activities within the overall context of British literary history. For example, consider 1859, the year embedded in the minds and notebooks of historians principally because of the publication of Charles Darwin's *On the Origin of Species by Means of Natural Selection*. Yet, neither we nor the historians can forget that Britons living in 1859 could have witnessed, if interested, the publication of *Chambers's Encyclopaedia*, Dickens' *Tale of Two Cities*, George Eliot's *Adam Bede*, Fitzgerald's *Omar Khayyam*, Meredith's *Richard Feverel*, J. S. Mill's essay on *Liberty*, Newman's *Lectures on Universities*, Tennyson's *Idylls of the King*, and the founding of four major literary periodicals: *Macmillan's Magazine, Household Words, The Cornhill Magazine,* and *All the Year Round*. In addition, the same year saw the births of Arthur Conan Doyle, Havelock Ellis, A. E. Housman, and Francis Thompson; while Thomas DeQuincey, Henry Hallam, Leigh Hunt, and Thomas Babington Macaulay all departed from the world of life and letters.

Thus, we may perceive a clear example of a year practically bursting with literary energy—a time in which political, scientific, and social controversy fired the imaginations of Britain's writers and fed the appetites of a newly formed and highly informed reading public. But there are other reasons for observing literary productivity from a chronological perspective, especially when a specific moment in history produces unexpected variety and identifies the complex alliance necessarily formed by transition and new developments. What are we to conclude, for instance, from an examination of 1930, when John Masefield received the honor as Poet Laureate of England and Stephen Spender published his volume of *Twenty Poems?* How do we focus, in that same year of 1930, on the appearance of T. S. Eliot's *Ash Wednesday* and Thomas Hardy's *Collected Poems?* How do we reconcile the common bond of chronology between Rudyard Kipling's *The Complete Stalky and Co.* and D. H. Lawrence's *Love among the Haystacks*, even though the two works bear the same date of publication? And how might we judge the impact on a readership that, within a single year, was asked to partake of such a varied menu as Siegfried Sassoon's *Memoirs of an Infantry Officer,* George Macaulay Trevelyan's third volume of *England under Queen Anne,* Somerset Maugham's *Cakes and Ale,* H. G. Wells' *Autobiography of Mr. Parkham,* Winston Churchill's *Early Life,* and George Bernard Shaw's *Apple Cart?* Surely those questions, and the almost endless possibilities for answering them, constitute the real purpose of examining literary and literary related events within the British Isles, year by year.

Nevertheless, the *Chronological Outline of British Literature* is in no way intended to function as a substitute for such standard references as The *Cambridge Bibliography of English Literature* (CBEL), *The Oxford Companion to English Literature,* the *Cambridge History of English Literature,* or even the *Annals of English Literature.* Thus, it contains neither a complete list of all British writers and their works nor a complete bibliography for any single writer whose name appears. Rather, the attempt has been to inject variety and representation into the literary events of a given year. Also, the term literature is used in its broadest definition, which means that writers from a large number of areas—imaginative literature, history, theology, science, philosophy, medicine, sport, fine arts, psychology, politics, economics, and so on—have been included in this outline.

Obviously, in a reference volume such as the *Chronological Outline,* readers may well wish to inquire about the selection process that determines what items will be included in the work. Simply, the selection criteria for this particular project have been significance and representativeness. Those two qualities pose no serious problems when considering *major* literary figures: the student of the Restoration and the eighteenth century, for example, will have little difficulty casting the likes of Dryden, Defoe, Addison, Steele, Swift, Pope, Johnson, Fielding, Sterne, Smollett, Goldsmith, or Sheridan into the major mold. Does that mean, though, that those *literati* of the period, who never quite reached their "majority," should be excluded from such reference projects as this *Outline?* Certainly not! What is does mean, however, is that the so-called lesser lights of a given literary period—the minor figures—need to be studied carefully, both in terms of their specific contributions to that period and the relationship of their efforts with the works of their major contemporaries.

INTRODUCTION

The labels secondary and minor need not necessarily be derogatory or synonymous with artistic obscurity or sterility. For instance, such purely religious poets of the eighteenth century as Isaac Watts, Philip Doddridge, Charles Wesley, and John Newton may be identified or stamped as minor figures not because they lacked poetic genius or artistic responsibility, but because their poetry—in their cases hymns and psalm paraphrases—was intentionally directed to a specialized and sometimes limited audience. Yet, that audience cannot be ignored if one is determined to consider the overall context of intellectual, literary, and even social history of the period between 1660 and 1789. The hymnodists represented a vital part of that history, and they contributed significantly to it.

Of course, the issue is not so simple (or clear) when one looks at the immediate present. The order and the neatness that literary historians seek (and usually find) in antiquity have not settled in on the 1950s, the 1960s, and the 1970s. Thus, the works of writers from those decades have not been tested by time, by the tastes of the reading public, or by the criteria of critical commentators—all necessary for final determination of their actual literary worth. The wide variety of literary exercises, in addition to an even wider variety of literary demands, causes problems whenever one attempts to make distinctions between artistry and pure popularity. Nevertheless, decisions must be made, for to turn one's back upon the present—to avoid the literature of Great Britain from 1950 to 1979—is to turn away from reality, to erase (without justification) three decades from the face of a nation's artistic productivity. Therefore, the criteria for including contemporary writers into this *Outline* remain the same, essentially, as for those of past literary periods. Significance and representativeness are still primary, but they have been seasoned with liberal doses of educated guesswork and the critical reactions of those competent to judge the literary activity flurrying about them.

The format for the *Chronological Outline* is simple and self-explanatory. Those symbols and abbreviations employed throughout the text are defined in the Key to Symbols.

Key to Symbols

auto = autobiography
bibl = bibliography
bio = biography
blt = built
c = ceased or closed
des = destroyed
dia = dialogue
dr = drama
e = essay
ed = edition
enl = enlarged edition
f = founded, begun, instituted
fic = fiction (other than novel)
his = history

n = novel
nar = narrative
op = opened
p = periodical (newspaper, magazine, journal)
po = poetry
pub = published
ref = reference work
rev = revision
s = satire
ser = sermon address
sp = speech
t = treatise
trans = translation
trav = travel work

References

Allen, Arthur B. *A Tale That Is Told: A Pageant of English Literature, 1900-1950.* London, 1960.
Allibone, Samuel Austin. *A Critical Dictionary of English Literature and British and American Authors.* 3 vols. Philadelphia, Pennsylvania, 1858, 1891; rpt. Detroit, Michigan, 1965.
Altick, Richard D. and Andrew Wright. *Selective Bibliography for the Study of English and American Literature.* 5th ed. New York and London, 1975.
Annals of English Literature: 1475-1950. The Principal Publications of Each Year . . . 2nd ed., rev. by Robert W. Chapman. Oxford, 1961.
Barnhart, Clarence L. *The New Century Handbook of English Literature.* rev. ed. New York, 1967.
Baugh, Albert C., et al. *A Literary History of England.* 2nd ed., rev. New York, 1967.
Brett-Jams, Antony, *The Triple Stream: Four Centuries of English, French, and German Literature, 1531-1930.* Cambridge, 1953.
Browning, David Clayton. *Everyman's Dictionary of Literary Biography: English and American.* 3rd ed., rev. with *Supplement.* London, 1969.
Butler, Audrey. *Everyman's Dictionary of Dates.* 6th ed. New York, 1971.
Chambers's Encyclopaedia of English Literature. 3 vols. rev. ed. by David Patrick and J. L. Geddie. London, 1922-1938.
Crosland, Margaret. *Literary Europe.* 2 vols. London, 1966.
Daiches, David. *The Present Age: After 1920.* London, 1958.
Dictionary of National Biography. ed. Leslie Stephen and Sidney Lee. 63 vols. London, 1885-1900.
Eagle, Dorothy and Hilary Carnell. *The Oxford Literary Guide to the British Isles.* Oxford, 1977.
Gillie, Christopher. *Longman Companion to English Literature.* London, 1972.

Harvey, Sir Paul. *The Oxford Companion to English Literature.* 4th ed. rev. by Dorothy Eagle. Oxford, 1967.

Haydn's Dictionary of Dates and Universal Information Relating to All Ages and Nations. ed. Benjamin Vincent. 25th ed. New York, 1911.

International Who's Who in Poetry, 1974-1975. 4th ed. Totowa, New Jersey, 1974.

Keller, Helen Rex. *The Dictionary of Dates.* 2 vols. New York, 1934.

Kunitz, Stanley J. and Howard Haycraft. *British Authors before 1800: A Biographical Dictionary.* New York, 1952.

———. *British Authors of the Nineteenth Century.* New York, 1936.

———. *Twentieth-Century Authors: A Biographical Dictionary of Modern Literature.* rev. ed. New York, 1955.

Langer, William L. *An Encyclopedia of World History.* 5th ed. Boston, 1972.

Little, Charles E. *Cyclopedia of Classified Dates.* New York, 1899.

Longaker, Mark and Edwin C. Bolles. *Contemporary English Literature.* New York, 1953.

Lowndes, William Thomas. *The Bibliographer's Manual of English Literature.* 4 vols. London, 1869-1914; rpt. 8 vols. Detroit, Michigan, 1967.

Mayer, Alfred. *Annals of European Civilization, 1501-1900.* London, 1949.

Millett, Fred B. *Contemporary British Literature: A Critical Survey and 232 Author-bibliographies.* 3rd ed., rev. and enlgd. ed. John M. Manly and Edith Rickert. New York, 1935.

Morris, Richard B. and Graham Irwin. *Harper Encyclopedia of the Modern World: 1760 to the Present.* New York, 1970.

Myers, Robin. *A Dictionary of Literature in the English Language, from Chaucer to 1940.* 2 vols. London, 1970-1971.

O'Donoghue, David. *The Poets of Ireland: A Biographical Dictionary.* London, 1892.

The Oxford History of English Literature. 14 vols. Oxford, 1945-

Pollard, Arthur. *Webster's New World Companion to English and American Literature.* New York, 1973.

Powicke, Sir F. Maurice and E. B. Fryde. *Handbook of British Chronology.* 2nd ed. London, 1961.

Russell, Josiah C. *Dictionary of Writers of Thirteenth-Century England.* London, 1936; rpt. New York, 1971.

Schweik, Robert C. and Dieter Riesner. *Reference Sources in English and American Literature: An Annotated Bibliography.* New York, 1977.

Spender, Stephen and Donald Hall, eds. *The Concise Encyclopedia of English and American Poets and Poetry.* New York, 1963.

Stark, John O. *Almanac of British and American Literature.* Littleton, Colorado, 1979.

Storey, R. L. *Chronology of the Medieval World, 800-1491.* London, 1973.

Vinson, James, ed. *Contemporary Poets.* London and New York, 1975.

———. *Contemporary Novelists,* 2nd ed. London and New York, 1976.

———. *Contemporary Dramatists,* 2nd ed. London and New York, 1977.

REFERENCES

Ward, A. C. *Longman Companion to Twentieth-Century Literature.* London, 1970.

Watt, Robert, *Bibliotheca Britannica; Or, a General Index to British and Foreign Literature.* 4 vols. Edinburgh, 1824; rpt. New York, 1965.

Williams, Neville. *Chronology of the Expanding World, 1492-1762.* London, 1969.

———. *Chronology of the Modern World, 1763 to the Present Time.* rev. ed. London, 1969.

Wright, Andrew H. *A Reader's Guide to English and American Literature.* Glenview, Illinois, 1970.

The Writer's Directory, 1974-1976. New York, 1976.

A CHRONOLOGICAL OUTLINE OF BRITISH LITERATURE

1 *The Beginnings through the Fourteenth Century*

516
BIRTHS
  Gildas

547
WORKS
  Gildas. De Excidio et Conquestu Britanniae

597
EVENTS
  Pope Gregory's missionaries reach England; the beginning of English history

600
WORKS
  Gododdin (po)

602
WORKS
  The laws of AEthelbert of Kent (t)

627
EVENTS
  Conversion of King Edwin of Northumbria

628
BIRTHS
  Benedict Biscop

640

BIRTHS
  Ealdhelm of Wessex (poet)

650

WORKS
  Beowulf (po), to 750
  Widsith (po, his,), to 700

657

EVENTS
  Beginning of Caedmon's literary activity

664

EVENTS
  Synod of Whitby

668

EVENTS
  Theodore of Tarsus, Archbishop of Canterbury, to 690

673

BIRTHS
  The Venerable Bede

674

EVENTS
  Benedictine monastery at Wearmouth (f)

677

EVENTS
  Monastery of St. Paul, Jarrow (f)

680

EVENTS
  End of Caedmon's literary activity

690

DEATHS
  Benedict of Biscop

698

WORKS
  Lindisfarne Gospels

BEGINNINGS THROUGH THE FOURTEENTH CENTURY

700

WORKS
  Daniel (tr, po)
  Exodus (tr, po)
  "Earlier" Genesis (tr, po)

709

DEATHS
  Ealdhelm of Wessex (poet)

731

WORKS
  Bede. Historia Ecclesiastica Gentis Anglorum (his)

735

BIRTHS
  Alcuin of York

DEATHS
  The Venerable Bede

750

WORKS
  The Finnisburg fragment (po)

775

EVENTS
  Beginning of Cynewulf's literary activity

781

WORKS
  The Wife's Lament, to 830 (po)

796

WORKS
  Nennius. Historia Brittonum (his)

797

WORKS
  Song of Ingeld (po)

800

WORKS
  Andreas (po)

804

DEATHS
  Alcuin of York

825

EVENTS
  End of Cynewulf's literary activities

849

BIRTHS
  King Alfred

WORKS
  Asser. Chronicle of English History, to 887

871

EVENTS
  Alfred, King of the West Saxons, to 901

875

WORKS
  Daniel (tr, po)

885

WORKS
  Dream of the Rood (po, rev)

887

WORKS
  Alfred's commonplace book begun

891

WORKS
  The Old English Annals (Anglo-Saxon Chronicle), to 1154 (his)

893

WORKS
  Asser. King Alfred (bio)

901

DEATHS
  King Alfred

EVENTS
  EAdward the Elder, King of England, to 924

BEGINNINGS THROUGH THE FOURTEENTH CENTURY 7

908

BIRTHS
  AEthewold

909

DEATHS
  Asser of St. David's, Bishop of Sherborne

925

EVENTS
  AEthelstan, King of England, to 940

937

WORKS
  The Battle of Brunanburh (po)

940

EVENTS
  EAdmund, King of England, to 946

946

EVENTS
  EAdred, King of England, to 955

950

WORKS
  The Lover's Message (po)

954

WORKS
  Annales Cambriae (his)

955

BIRTHS
  AElfric

EVENTS
  EAdwig, King of England, to 959

959

EVENTS
  EAdgar, King of England, to 975

960

WORKS
  AEthelwold. Rule of St. Benedict (trans)

970

WORKS
  Blickling Homilies (ser)

975

EVENTS
  EAdward the Martyr, King of England, to 979

WORKS
  The Exeter Book (po, ed)

979

EVENTS
  AEthelred, King of England, to 1016

980

WORKS
  Deor's Lament (po)

984

DEATHS
  AEthelwold

990

WORKS
  AElfric. Catholic Homilies, to 998 (ser, trans)

991

WORKS
  Battle of Malden (po)

993

WORKS
  AElfric. Lives of the Saints, to 996 (ser, po)

1000

WORKS
  West Saxon version of the Four Gospels (trans)

1016

EVENTS

BEGINNINGS THROUGH THE FOURTEENTH CENTURY 9

EAdmond Ironside, King of England
Canute, King of England, to 1035

1020

DEATHS
AElfric

1023

DEATHS
Wulfstan, Archbishop of York

1035

EVENTS
Harold I, King of England, to 1040

1040

EVENTS
Hardicanute, King of England, to 1042

1042

EVENTS
EAdward the Confessor, King of England, to 1066
Harold II, King of England, to 1066

1057

WORKS
Chronicle of Mont St. Michel (hist)

1065

BIRTHS
St. Godric of Durham

1066

EVENTS
William I, King of England, to 1087

1086

WORKS
The Doomsday Book (ref)

1087

EVENTS
William II, King of England, to 1100

1099

EVENTS
  The Hospitallers of St. John of Jerusalem (f)

                              1100

BIRTHS
  Geoffrey of Monmouth

EVENTS
  Henry I, King of England, to 1135

                              1104

BIRTHS
  Wace of Jersey

                              1108

WORKS
  Liber Eliensis, to 1131 (his, po)

                              1115

WORKS
  Phillippe de Thaun. Comput (po, t)

                              1116

WORKS
  Adelard of Bath. De EOdem et Diverso (t)

                              1118

EVENTS
  Order of Knights Templars (f)

WORKS
  Florence of Worcester. Chronicon ex Chronicis (his)

                              1120

BIRTHS
  John of Salisbury

                              1121

WORKS
  Benedict. Voyage of St. Brendan (trav)

                              1122

WORKS
  EAdmer. Historia Novorum in Anglia (his)

                              1125

WORKS
    William of Malmesbury. Gesta Pontificum Anglorum (his)

                            1128

WORKS
    William of Malmesbury. Gesta Regum Anglorum (his)

                            1129

EVENTS
    Osney Abbey (f)

                            1130

WORKS
    Simon of Durham. De Rebus a se Gestis (his)

                            1137

WORKS
    Geoffrey of Monmouth. Historia Regum Britanniae (his, fic)

                            1139

EVENTS
    Gilbertine Order (f)

WORKS
    William of Malmesbury. De Antiquitate Glastoniensis Ecclesiae (his)

                            1140

BIRTHS
    Walter Map

WORKS
    Samson de Nanteuil. Proverbs of Solomon (trans, po)

                            1141

WORKS
    Ordericus Vitalis. Ecclesiastical History (his)

                            1142

WORKS
    William of Malmesbury. Historia Novella (his)

                            1143

DEATHS
    William of Malmesbury

                            1146

BIRTHS
  Giraldus de Barri (Cambrensis)

                    1150

WORKS
  Geoffrey Gaimar. Estorie des Engles (his, po)
  _____. Histoire des Bretons (his, po)

                    1154

EVENTS
  Henry II, King of England, to 1189

WORKS
  Henry of Huntingdon. Historia Anglorum (his)
  The Peterborough Chronicle (his)

                    1155

DEATHS
  Geoffrey of Monmouth
  Henry of Huntingdon

WORKS
  Benoit de Sainte-More. Roman de Troie, to 1160 (po)
  Wace of Jersey. Roman de Brut (his, po)

                    1159

WORKS
  John of Salisbury. Metalogicon (t)
  _____. Policraticus (t)

                    1166

WORKS
  The Song of Canute (po)

                    1167

EVENTS
  Oxford University (f)

                    1170

DEATHS
  St. Godric of Durham

WORKS
  Denis Piramus. La Vie Seint Edmund le Rei (bio, po)
  Poema Morale (po)
  Thomas. Tristan (po)

                    1174

BEGINNINGS THROUGH THE FOURTEENTH CENTURY   13

DEATHS
  Wace of Jersey

WORKS
  Jordan Fantosme. Chronicle (his, po)

                              1175

BIRTHS
  Michael Scott

                              1180

DEATHS
  John of Salisbury

WORKS
  Thomas. Horn (po)
  Nigel Wireker. Speculum Stultorum (po)

                              1181

WORKS
  Walter Map. De Nugis Curialium (fic)

                              1184

WORKS
  Joseph of Exeter. De Bello Trojano (po)

                              1185

WORKS
  Giraldus de Barri. Expugnatio Hibernica (his)
  _____. Topographica Hibernica (e. his)
  Hugh of Rutland. Ipomedon (po)

                              1189

EVENTS
  Richard I, King of England, to 1199
  Henry Fitz Aylwin, Lord Mayor of London

                              1190

WORKS
  Hugh of Rutland. Protheselaus (po)

                              1191

WORKS
  Here Prophecy (po)

                              1195

WORKS

The Owl and the Nightingale (po)

1197

EVENTS
Priory and Hospital of St. Mary, London (f)

1198

WORKS
William of Newburgh. Historia Rerum Anglicarum (his)

1200

WORKS
Lambeth Homilies (ser)
Trinity Homilies (ser)

1202

WORKS
Jocelyn de Brakelond. Chronicle (his)

1205

WORKS
Layamon. Roman de Brut (po, trans)

1209

DEATHS
Walter Map

EVENTS
London Bridge (blt)

1211

WORKS
Gervase of Tilbury. Otia Imperialia (his, fic)

1214

BIRTHS
Roger Bacon

1216

EVENTS
Henry III, King of England, to 1272

1220

DEATHS
Giraldus de Barri (Cambrensis)

BEGINNINGS THROUGH THE FOURTEENTH CENTURY

1221

EVENTS
  Dominican Friars reach England

1224

EVENTS
  Franciscan Friars reach England

1230

EVENTS
  Cambridge University (f)

WORKS
  Bartholomeus Anglicus. De Proprietatibus Rerum (t)

1234

DEATHS
  Michael Scott

1235

WORKS
  Matthew Paris. Chronica Majora, to 1259 (his)
  Raymond of Pennafort. Summa Casuum Poenitentiae (t)

1237

WORKS
  Edmund Rich, Archbishop of Canterbury. Merure de Seinte Englise (t)

1240

WORKS
  Thomas de Hales. Luve Ron (po)
  Walter of Bibbesworth. Traite (po)

1245

WORKS
  Floris and Blauncheflour (po)
  Henry of Avranches. La Estorie de Seint AEdward le Rei (bio, po)
  When Holy Church Is under Foot (po)

1247

EVENTS
  The Priory of St. Mary of Bethlehem, London (f)

1249

EVENTS
  University College, Oxford (f)

1250

WORKS
Dame Sirith (po, fic)
Matthew Paris. Historia Anglorum (his)
Genesis and Exodus (po, trans)
The Harrowing of Hell (po)
Havelock the Dane, to c. 1300 (po, fic)
King Horn (po, fic)

1255

WORKS
Matthew Paris. Vitae Abbatum S. Albani (bio)

1259

DEATHS
Mathhew Paris

1263

EVENTS
Balliol College, Oxford (f)

1264

EVENTS
Merton College, Oxford (f)

WORKS
Song of Lewes

1267

WORKS
Peter of Peckham. Lumiere as Lais (po, ref)

1270

WORKS
Peter of Peckham. Vie de Saint Richard (bio)

1272

EVENTS
Edward I, King of England, to 1307

1275

WORKS
Liber Exemplorum (t)

1280

WORKS

BEGINNINGS THROUGH THE FOURTEENTH CENTURY

    Thomas of Kent. Roman de Toute Chevalerie (po)

                                 1281

WORKS
  John Peckham. Constitutions (t)

                                 1285

WORKS
  Speculum Laicorum (t)

                                 1294

DEATHS
  Roger Bacon

                                 1300

BIRTHS
  Richard Rolle

WORKS
  Arthur and Merlin (po)
  Bevis of Hampton (po)
  The Cuckoo Song (po)
  Guy of Warwick (po, fic)
  King Alisaunder (po)
  Northern Homily Cycle (po)
  Richard Coeur de Lion (po, fic)

                                 1303

WORKS
  Robert Mannyng of Brunne. Handlyng Synne (t)

                                 1307

EVENTS
  Edward II, King of England, to 1327

WORKS
  Peter Langtoft. Chronicle (his, po)

                                 1314

EVENTS
  Old St. Paul's Cathedral, London (blt)

                                 1320

WORKS
  Fascisulum Morum (t)

                                 1326

BIRTHS
  John de Trevisa

                    1327

EVENTS
  Edward III, King of England, to 1377

WORKS
  Ranulf Higden. Polychronicon (his)

                    1328

BIRTHS
  John Wycliffe

EVENTS
  The Chester Plays

                    1330

BIRTHS
  John Gower
  William Langland

                    1340

WORKS
  Dan Michel of Northgate. Ayenbite of Inwit (trans)

                    1343

BIRTHS
  Geoffrey Chaucer

                    1349

DEATHS
  Richard Rolle

                    1350

WORKS
  Athelston (po)
  Cloud of Unknowing (t)
  The Tale of Gamelyn (po)
  Joseph of Arimathie (po)
  The Pearl, to 1380 (po)
  Sir Perceval of Gales (po)
  Ywain and Gawain (po)

                    1352

EVENTS
  Corpus Christi College, Cambridge (f)

WORKS
  Laurence Minot. War Songs (po)
  Wynnere and Wastoure (po)

1357

WORKS
　John Thoresby, Archbishop of York. Lay Folks' Catechism (t)

1360

WORKS
　Morte Arthure (po)
　Speculum Christiani (t)

1362

WORKS
　William Langland. The Vision of William concerning Piers the Plowman,
　　　first version (po)

1366

BIRTHS
　John Shirley

WORKS
　Sir John Mandeville. Travels of Sir John Mandeville (trav)

1369

WORKS
　Geoffrey Chaucer. The Boke of the Duchesse (po)

1370

BIRTHS
　Thomas Hoccleve
　John Lydgate

1371

EVENTS
　The Charterhouse, London (blt)

1375

WORKS
　John Barbour. The Bruce (po)
　Sir Gawain and the Green Knight (po)

1376

WORKS
　John Gower. Mirour de l'Omme (po)
　John Wycliffe. De Domino Divino (t)

1377

EVENTS

Richard II, King of England, to 1399

WORKS
  William Langland. The Vision of William concerning Piers the Plowman, second version (po)

1378

EVENTS
  The York Plays

WORKS
  Geoffrey Chaucer. The Canterbury Tales, to 1400 (po, fic)
  Paternoster Play (dr)
  John Wycliffe. De Ecclesia (t)
  _____. De Officio Regis (t)
  _____. De Veritate Sacrae Scripturae (t)

1379

WORKS
  John Wycliffe. De Potestate Papae (t)

1382

WORKS
  John Gower. Vox Clamantis (po)

1384

DEATHS
  John Wycliffe

1386

EVENTS
  New College, Oxford (blt)

WORKS
  Geoffrey Chaucer. The Hous of Fame (po)
  _____. The Legende of Good Women (po)
  _____. The Parlement of Foules (po)
  _____. Troylus and Cryseyde (po)

1387

WORKS
  John de Trevisa. Polychronicon (trans)
  William Langland. The Vision of William concerning Piers the Plowman, third version (po)

1388

WORKS
  Thomas Usk. Testament of Love (auto, fic)

BEGINNINGS THROUGH THE FOURTEENTH CENTURY

1390

WORKS
  John Gower. Confessio Amantis (po)
  John of Bromyard. Summa Praedicanttium (ser, t)

1393

WORKS
  Juliana of Norwich. Revelations (auto)

1394

BIRTHS
  Sir John Fortesque

EVENTS
  Winchester College (blt)

WORKS
  Pierce the Ploughman's Creed (po)

1395

BIRTHS
  Reginald Peacock

WORKS
  John Purvey. Remonstrance against Romish Corruptions in the Church (t)
  The Wycliffe Bible (trans)

1397

EVENTS
  Richard Whittington, Lord Mayor of London, to 1398

1398

WORKS
  John de Trevisa. De Proprietatibus Rerum (trans)

1399

EVENTS
  Henry IV, King of England, to 1413

WORKS
  Richard the Redeless (po)

2 The Fifteenth Century

1400

DEATHS
  Geoffrey Chaucer
  William Langland

WORKS
  Laud Troy Book (po)
  Morte Arthur (po)
  The Pride of Life (dr)
  Titus and Vespasian (po)

1402

WORKS
  Sir Thomas Clanvowe. The Cuckoo and the Nightingale (po)

1403

WORKS
  Mum and the Sothsegger, to 1406 (po)

1405

WORKS
  Dives and Pauper, to 1410 (t)

1406

EVENTS
  Richard Whittington, Lord Mayor of London, to 1407

WORKS
  Thomas Hoccleve. La Male Regle (auto, po)

THE FIFTEENTH CENTURY

1408

DEATHS
  John Gower

WORKS
  John Lydgate. Life of Our Lady. Reason and Sensuality (po)
  John Walton. De Re Militari (trans)

1410

WORKS
  Nicholas Love. The Mirrour of the Blessed Lyf of Jesu Christ (t,trans)
  John Walton. Consolation of Philosophy (po, trans)

1411

WORKS
  Thomas Hoccleve. De Regimine Principum (po)

1412

DEATHS
  John de Trevisa

WORKS
  Thomas Hoccleve. Regiment of Princes (po)
  John Lydgate. Troy Book (po, trans)

1413

EVENTS
  Henry V, King of England, to 1422

WORKS
  Grace Dieu, or The Pilgrimage of the Soul (po, trans)

1419

EVENTS
  Richard Whittington, Lord Mayor of London, to 1420

1420

WORKS
  Andrew Wyntoun. Orygynale Cronykil (po, his)

1421

BIRTHS
  William Caxton

1422

EVENTS
  Henry VI, King of England, to 1461

WORKS
  Thomas Hoccleve. Complaint, and Dialogue with a Friend (po)
  John Lydgate. Siege of Thebes (po)

                            1424

WORKS
  James I of Scotland. The Kingis Quair (po)

                            1425

WORKS
  Jacob's Well (ser, t)
  Henry Lovelich. Merlin (po)

                            1430

BIRTHS
  Robert Henryson

WORKS
  Thomas Chestre. Sir Launfal (po)
  John Lydgate. The Pilgrimage of the Life of Man (po)

                            1436

WORKS
  The Libel of English Policy (po)

                            1438

EVENTS
  All Souls College, Oxford (f)

WORKS
  Margery Kempe of Lynn. The Book of Margery Kempe (auto)
  John Lydgate. The Fall of Princes (po)

                            1440

EVENTS
  Eton College (f)

                            1441

EVENTS
  King's College, Cambridge (f)

                            1443

WORKS
  Reginald Peacock. The Reule of Crysten Religioun (t)

                            1445

WORKS

THE FIFTEENTH CENTURY   25

        Osbern Bokenham. Legendys of Hooly Wummen (po)

                            1449

DEATHS
    John Lydgate

WORKS
    John Metham. Amoryus and Cleopes (po)

                            1450

DEATHS
    Thomas Hoccleve

WORKS
    Richard Holland. The Buke of the Howlat (po)

                            1455

WORKS
    Reginald Peacock. Repressor of Over Much Blaming of the Clergy (t)

                            1456

DEATHS
    John Shirley

WORKS
    Reginald Peacock. The Book of Faith (t)

                            1458

EVENTS
    Magdalen College, Oxford (f)

                            1460

BIRTHS
    John Skelton

DEATHS
    Reginald Peacock

WORKS
    The Castle of Perseverance (dr)

                            1461

EVENTS
    Edward IV, King of England, to 1483

WORKS
    Sir John Fortesque. De Natura Legis Naturae, to 1463 (t)

1463

WORKS
George Ashby. A Prisoner's Reflections (po)

1464

DEATHS
John Capgrave

WORKS
John Capgrave. Chronicle of England (his)

1465

BIRTHS
William Dunbar

WORKS
The Court of Sapience (po)

1466

EVENTS
Crosby Hall, Bishopsgate, London (blt)

1467

BIRTHS
John Bourchier Berners

1469

BIRTHS
John Major

1470

EVENTS
Henry VI, King of England, to 1471

WORKS
Sir Thomas Malory. Le Morte Darthur (trans)

1471

DEATHS
Sir Thomas Malory

WORKS
Sir John Fortesque. De Laudibus Legum Angliae (t)
_____. A Declaration upon Certain Wrytinges (e)
George Ripley. Compend of Alchemy (po)

1473

THE FIFTEENTH CENTURY

WORKS
  Richard de Bury. Philobiblon (bio)

                            1474

BIRTHS
  Gavin Douglas
  Stephen Hawes

WORKS
  William Caxton. Recuyell of the Historyes of Troye (trans, fic)

                            1475

BIRTHS
  Alexander Barclay

WORKS
  The Wallace (po)

                            1476

DEATHS
  Sir John Fortesque

EVENTS
  Establishment of the printing press in England

                            1477

WORKS
  Michael Scott. Liber Physiognomiae (pub)

                            1478

BIRTHS
  Sir Thomas More

WORKS
  Geoffrey Chaucer. The Canterbury Tales (po, pub)

                            1481

WORKS
  William Caxton. Godeffroy of Boloyne (trans)
  _____. Mirrour of the World (ref, trans)
  Reynard the Fox (trans, pub)

                            1483

EVENTS
  Edward V, King of England
  Richard III, King of England, to 1485
  Heralds' College (f)

WORKS

William Caxton. The Golden Legend (trans)

1484

WORKS
William Caxton. Book of the Knight of La Tour-Landry (trans)

1485

EVENTS
Henry VII, King of England, to 1509

WORKS
William Caxton. Charles the Great (trans)
_____. Paris and Vienne (trans)
Thomas Malory. Morte Darthur (pub)

1486

WORKS
The Book of St. Albans (e)
Henry Medwall. Fulgens and Lucrece (dr)

1488

BIRTHS
Miles Coverdale

WORKS
William Caxton. The Royal Book (fic, trans)

1490

BIRTHS
Sir David Lindsay

WORKS
William Caxton. Blanchardyn and Eglantine (trans)
_____. Fierabras; The Four Sonnes of Aymon (trans)
_____. Eneydos (trans)

1491

DEATHS
William Caxton

1494

BIRTHS
William Tyndale

WORKS
John Lydgate. Falls of Princes (po, pub)

1495

THE FIFTEENTH CENTURY   29

BIRTHS
  John Bale

WORKS
  Lytell Geste of Robyn Hoode (pub)

                    1496

WORKS
  Michael Scott. De Animalibus (trans, pub)

                    1497

BIRTHS
  John Heywood

WORKS
  Henry Medwell. Fulgens and Lucrece (dr, pub)

                    1499

BIRTHS
  Sir Thomas Elyot

3   The Sixteenth Century

1500

WORKS
  John Lydgate. The Story of Thebes (po, pub)

1501

WORKS
  Gavin Douglas. The Palace of Honour (po)

1503

BIRTHS
  Sir Thomas Wyatt

WORKS
  William Dunbar. The Thrissill and the Rois (po)

1504

BIRTHS
  Barnabe Googe

1505

BIRTHS
  John Knox

WORKS
  Alexander Barclay. The Castle of Labour, to 1506 (trans, po)

1506

BIRTHS
  John Leland

DEATHS

THE SIXTEENTH CENTURY   31

    Robert Henryson

                                    1508

WORKS
    William Dunbar. The Dance of the Sevin Deidly Synnis (po)
    _____. The Golden Targe (po)
    _____. Lament for the Makaris (po)
    _____. The Twa Maryit Women and the Wedo (po)
    Geoffrey of Monmouth. Historia Regum Britanniae (his, pub)
    Golagros and Gawain (po, pub)
    Robert Henryson. Tale of Orpheus (po, pub)

                                    1509

EVENTS
    Henry VIII, King of England, to 1547
    Brasenose College, Oxford (f)
    The Society of Doctors' Commons (f)

WORKS
    Alexander Barclay. The Ship of Fools (trans, po)
    Stephen Hawes. Passetyme of Pleasure; or, History of Graunde Amoure
            and la Bel Pucel (po)
    John Major. Commentary on the Sentences of Peter Lombard, to 1517 (e)

                                    1510

WORKS
    Sir Thomas More. Life of John Picus, Earl of Mirandula (bio)

                                    1512

EVENTS
    Guild, Fraternity, or Brotherhood of the Most Glorious and Undividable
        Trinity (f)
    St. Paul's School (f)
    Westminster Palace (des)

WORKS
    Gavin Douglas. Aeneid, to 1513 (trans)
    Stephen Hawes. Example of Virtue (po)

                                    1513

DEATHS
    Robert Fabyan

WORKS
    John Lydgate. Troy Book (po, pub)
    John Skelton. Ballad of the Scottish King (po)

                                    1515

BIRTHS
    Roger Ascham

WORKS
　　Alexander Barclay. Eclogues, to 1521 (po)

　　　　　　　　　　　　1516

BIRTHS
　　John Foxe

WORKS
　　Robert Fabyan. The Concordance of Histories (his, pub)
　　Sir Thomas More. Utopia (e)

　　　　　　　　　　　　1517

BIRTHS
　　Henry Howard, Earl of Surrey

　　　　　　　　　　　　1519

WORKS
　　William Horman. Vulgaria Puerorum (aphorisms)
　　John Skelton. Colin Clout (po)

　　　　　　　　　　　　1520

BIRTHS
　　Thomas Churchyard

　　　　　　　　　　　　1521

BIRTHS
　　Richard Eden

WORKS
　　Alexander Barclay. The Introductory to Write and to Pronounce French
　　　　　　　　　　(ref)
　　Henry VIII. A Defence of the Seven Sacraments (e)
　　John Major. History of Greater Britain, both England and Scotland
　　　　　　　　(his)
　　John Skelton. Speak Parrot (po)

　　　　　　　　　　　　1522

DEATHS
　　Gavin Douglas

WORKS
　　Mundus et Infans (dr)
　　John Skelton. Why Come Ye Not to Court (po)

　　　　　　　　　　　　1523

BIRTHS
　　Richard Edwards

DEATHS

THE SIXTEENTH CENTURY 33

Stephen Hawes

WORKS
John Bourchier Berners. The Chronicles of Froissart, to 1525 (trans)
John Skelton. The Doughty Duke of Albany (po)
_____. The Garland of Laurel (po)

1525

BIRTHS
George Gascoigne
John Stowe
Thomas Wilson

WORKS
William Tyndale. The New Testament (trans)

1527

BIRTHS
John Dee

WORKS
William Lily. Grammatices Rudimenta (ref, pub)

1528

WORKS
Sir David Lindsay. The Dreme (po)
Sir Thomas More. Dialogue (e)
John Skelton. Replication (po)

1529

DEATHS
John Skelton

WORKS
Simon Fish. Supplication for the Beggars (t)
Sir David Lindsay. Complaynt to the King (po)
Sir Thomas More. Supplycacyon of Soulys (t)

1530

BIRTHS
Richard Mulcaster

DEATHS
William Dunbar

WORKS
William Tyndale. The Pentateuch (trans)

1531

WORKS

Sir Thomas Elyot. The Boke Named the Governour (t)
William Tyndale. An Answere unto Sir Thomas Mores Dialoge (e)
_____. The Book of Jonah (trans)

1532

WORKS
Sir Thomas More. Confutacyon of Tyndale's Answere (e)

1533

DEATHS
John Bourchier Berners

WORKS
John Heywood. Play of the Wether (dr)
Sir Thomas More. An Apologye of Syr Thomas More (e)

1534

WORKS
John Bourchier Berners. Huon of Bordeaux (trans, pub)
Sir Thomas Elyot. The Doctrine of Princes (trans)
John Heywood. A Play of Love (dr)
The History of Richard the Thirde (pub)
Sir Thomas More. Dialogue of Comfort against Tribulation (e)

1535

BIRTHS
Sir Thomas North

DEATHS
Sir Thomas More

EVENTS
Miles Coverdale's complete English Bible

WORKS
John Bourchier Berners. The Golden Boke of Marcus Aurelius (trans,pub)
Robert Copland. The Highway to the Spital-house (po)
Thomas Starkey. Dialogue between Pole and Lupset (t)

1536

BIRTHS
Thomas Sackville

DEATHS
William Tyndale

WORKS
Reginald Pole. Pro Ecclesiasticae Unitatis Defensione (t)

THE SIXTEENTH CENTURY 35

Thomas Starkey. Exhortation to the People (t)

1537

EVENTS
Matthew's Bible (pub)

1538

WORKS
Sir Thomas Elyot. Dictionary (Latin-English) (ref)
Sir David Lindsay. Testament and Complaynt of Our Soverane Lordis
    Papyngo (po)

1539

EVENTS
The Great Bible (pub)
Taverner's Bible (pub)

WORKS
Sir Thomas Elyot. The Castle of Heath (pub)

1540

BIRTHS
George Turberville

EVENTS
Regius Professorships, Cambridge University (f)

WORKS
John Bourchier Berners. The Castell of Love (trans, pub)
Sir Thomas Elyot. The Image of Governance (trans)
Sir David Lindsay. Ane Pleasant Satyre of the Thrie Estaitis (po, dr)

1542

DEATHS
Sir Thomas Wyatt

WORKS
Andrew Borde. The First Book of the Introduction of Knowledge (fic)
Henry Brinkelow The Complaint of Roderick Mors (t)
_____. The Lamentation of a Christian against the City of
    London (t)
Edward Hall. Union of the Noble and Illustre Families of Lancaster and
    York (his)
Sir Thomas More. History of Richard III (pub)

1545

BIRTHS
Nicholas Breton
John Gerard
Gabriel Harvey

WORKS
  Roger Ascham. Toxophilus (t)
  John Foxe. Commentarii (t)
  John Heywood. The Four P's (dr)
  John Leland. A New Year's Gift (e, bibl)

                          1546

DEATHS
  Sir Thomas Elyot.

EVENTS
  Christ Church, Oxford (f)
  Trinity College, Cambridge (f)

WORKS
  John Heywood. A Dialogue containing the Number in Effect of All the
                Proverbs in the English Tongue, to 1561 (po)

                          1547

DEATHS
  Henry Howard, Earl of Surrey

EVENTS
  Edward VI, King of England, to 1553

WORKS
  Book of Homilies (pub)

                          1548

WORKS
  William Baldwin. A Treatise of Moral Philosophy, containing the Say-
                ings of the Wise (t)
  John Bale. Illustrium Maioris Britanniae Scriptorum Summarium (t)
  John Knox. Epistle on Justification by Faith (e)

                          1549

BIRTHS
  Giles Fletcher the elder
  Sir Henry Savile

WORKS
  John Leland and John Bale. The Laborious Journey and Search of John
                Leylande for England's Antiquities (his)
  Sir Thomas Wyatt. Certayne Psalmes drawn into Englyshe Meter (po, pub)

                          1550

BIRTHS
  John Davys
  John Napier

DEATHS

John Major

WORKS
  Roger Ascham. The Report of the Affairs and State of Germany, to 1553 (t)
  Henry Watson. The History of Two Valyannte Brethren, Valentyne and Orson (fic)

                                1551

BIRTHS
  William Camden

WORKS
  Thomas Wilson. Rule of Reason (t)

                                1552

BIRTHS
  Sir Edward Coke
  Philemon Holland
  Sir Walter Raleigh
  Edmund Spenser

DEATHS
  Alexander Barclay
  John Leland

WORKS
  The Book of Common Prayer (pub)

                                1553

BIRTHS
  Richard Hakluyt
  Anthony Munday

EVENTS
  Mary I, Queen of England, to 1558

WORKS
  Gavin Douglas. The Aeneid (trans, pub)
  _____. The Palice of Honour (po, pub)
  Richard Eden. Cosmography (trans)
  Sir David Lindsay. A Dialogue betwixt Experience and a Courtier of the Miserable Estate of the World (po)
  Nicholas Udall. Ralph Roister Doister (dr)
  _____. Respublica (dr)
  Thomas Wilson. Art of Rhetorique (t)

                                1554

BIRTHS
  Sir Fulke Greville
  Richard Hooker
  John Lyly

Sir Philip Sidney

WORKS
Sir David Lindsay. The Monarchie (po)
Henry Howard, Earl of Surrey. Aeneid, Book IV (trans, pub)

1555

DEATHS
Sir David Lindsay

WORKS
Richard Eden. Decades of the Newe Worlde, or West India (trans)

1556

BIRTHS
Alexander Montgomerie

WORKS
John Foxe. Christus Triumphans (t)
John Heywood. The Spider and the Fly (s)

1557

BIRTHS
Thomas Watson

EVENTS
Caius College, Cambridge (f)
The Stationers' Company (f)

WORKS
Sir Thomas North. Diall of Princes (trans)
Henry Howard, Earl of Surrey. Aeneid, Book II (trans, pub)
_____. "Poems," in Tottel's Miscellany (pub)
Richard Tottel and Nicholas Grimald. Songs and Sonnets (became known, popularly, as Tottel's Miscellany; po, ed)
Thomas Tusser. Hundreth Good Pointes of Husbandrie (po)
Sir Thomas Wyatt. "Poems," in Tottel's Miscellany (pub)

1558

BIRTHS
Thomas Kyd
Thomas Lodge
George Peele
William Warner

EVENTS
Elizabeth I, Queen of England, to 1603

WORKS
Thomas Becon. The Sick Man's Salve, to 1559 (t)
John Knox. The First Blast of the Trumpet Against the Monstrous Regiment of Women (t)

THE SIXTEENTH CENTURY   39

                                    1559

BIRTHS
   George Chapman

WORKS
   John Foxe. Rerum in Ecclesia Gestarum Commentarii (t)
   John Knox. First Book of Discipline (e)
   A Mirrour for Magistrates (po, nar, pub)

                                    1560

BIRTHS
   Robert Greene

EVENTS
   The Church of Scotland (f)
   Westminster School (f)

WORKS
   John Knox. Treatise on Predestination (t)
   Misogonus (dr)
   Nice Wanton (dr)

                                    1561

BIRTHS
   Francis Bacon
   Robert Southwell

WORKS
   John Awdeley. Fraternity of Vacabones (t)
   Richard Eden. The Arte of Navigation (trans)
   Godly Queen Hester (dr)
   Thomas Norton and Thomas Sackville. Gorboduc; or, Ferrex and Porrex
             (dr)
   John Stowe. The Woorkes of Geffrey Chaucer (ed)

                                    1562

BIRTHS
   Henry Constable
   Samuel Daniel

WORKS
   A New Interlude for Children To Play Named Jack Juggler (dr)
   Thomas Sternhold and John Hopkins. The Whole Booke of Psalmes (ed)

                                    1563

BIRTHS
   Michael Drayton

DEATHS
   John Bale

WORKS
  Book of Homilies (pub)
  Thomas Churchyard. Shore's Wife (po)
  John Foxe. Actes and Monuments of these Latter Perilous Times (his)
  Barnabe Googe. Eglogs, Epytaphes, and Sonnetes (po)
  A Mirrour for Magistrates, enl. ed. (po, nar, pub)
  Thomas Sackville. The Complaint of Buckingham (po)
  _____. Induction (po)

1564

BIRTHS
  Sir John Hayward
  Christopher Marlowe
  William Shakespeare

1565

BIRTHS
  John Davies

WORKS
  John Dee. De Trigono (t)
  The Geystes of Skoggan (nar)
  King Darius (dr)
  John Stowe. Summarie of Englyshe Chronicles (his)
  John Phillip. Patient and Meek Grissill (dr)

1566

DEATHS
  Richard Edwards

EVENTS
  The Royal Exchange (f, blt)

WORKS
  Richard Edwards. Palamon and Arcite (dr)
  George Gascoigne. Supposes (dr)
  William Painter. Palace of Pleasure, to 1567 (fic, ed)
  Lewis Wager. Life and Repentance of Mary Magdalene (dr)

1567

BIRTHS
  Sir William Alexander
  Thomas Nashe
  Thomas Parkinson

EVENTS
  Rugby School (f)

WORKS
  John Pickering. Interlude of Vice containing the History of Orestes (dr)
  John Stowe. Flores Historiarum (ed)

THE SIXTEENTH CENTURY   41

George Turberville. Epitaphs, Epigrams, Songs, and Sonnets (pub)

1568

BIRTHS
  Gervase Markham
  Sir Henry Wotton

DEATHS
  Roger Ascham
  Miles Coverdale

EVENTS
  The Bishops' Bible (pub)

WORKS
  Roger Ascham. The Scholemaster (t)
  Ulpian Fulwell. Like Will to Like (dr)
  John Skelton. Collected Poems (pub)
  George Turberville. Poems Describing Russia

1569

BIRTHS
  Barnabe Barnes
  Sir John Davies

WORKS
  Sir John Hawkins. A True Declaration of the Troublesome Voyage of Mr. John Hawkins to Guinea and the West Indies in 1567 and 1568 (trav, nar)
  The Marriage of Wit and Science (dr)
  Thomas Preston. Cambises, King of Persia (dr)
  _____. A Lamentable Tragedy Mixed full of Mirth, Conteyning the Life of Cambises, King of Persia (dr, pub)
  Edmund Spenser. Visions (po)

1570

BIRTHS
  Thomas Dekker
  Thomas Middleton
  Samuel Rowlands

WORKS
  John Foxe. On Christ Crucified (ser)
  Sir Thomas North. The Morall Philosophie of Doni (trans)

1571

WORKS
  Richard Edwards. An Excellent Comedie of Damon and Pithias (dr)
  John Foxe. Reformatio Legum (t)
  John Stowe. Matthew Paris's Chronicle (ed)

1572

BIRTHS
  John Donne
  Ben Jonson

DEATHS
  John Knox

EVENTS
  The Society of Antiquaries (f)

WORKS
    Matthew Parker. De Antiquitate Ecclesiae et Privilegiis Ecclesiae
              Cantauriensis cum Archiepiscopis ejusdem 70 (t,
              his)
  Rauf Coilyear (po, pub)

1573

BIRTHS
  Richard Johnson

1574

BIRTHS
  Richard Barnfield
  Joseph Hall
  Thomas Heywood

WORKS
  John Stowe. Thomas Walsingham's Chronicle (ed)

1575

BIRTHS
  John Marston
  Samuel Purchas
  Cyril Tourneur

WORKS
  Appius and Virginia (dr)
  George Gascoigne. Glasse of Government (dr)
  _____. The Poesies of George Gascoigne (po)
  Grammer Gurton's Needle (dr, pub)
  George Turberville. The Booke of Falconrie (po)
  _____. The Noble Art of Venerie, or Hunting (po)

1576

BIRTHS
  Henry Peacham

DEATHS
  Richard Eden

THE SIXTEENTH CENTURY 43

WORKS
Common Conditions
Richard Edwards. Paradise of Daynty Devises (po, ed, pub)
George Gascoigne. The Steele Glas (po)
Sir Humphrey Gilbert. Discourse of a Discoverie for a New Passage to Cataia (t, trav)
George Wapull. The Tide Tarrieth No Man (dr)

1577

BIRTHS
Robert Burton
Thomas Coryate

DEATHS
George Gascoigne

WORKS
George Gascoigne. Glasse of Government (dr, pub)
Barnabe Googe. Foure Bookes of Husbandrie (trans)

1578

BIRTHS
William Harvey
George Sandys

WORKS
Thomas Churchyard. Wofull Warres in Flaunders (po)
Thomas Garter. Most Virtuous and Godly Susanna (dr)
John Lyly. Euphues: the Anatomy of Wit (fic)
George Whetstone. Promos and Cassandra (dr)
Thomas Lupton. All for Money (dr)

1579

BIRTHS
John Fletcher

WORKS
Thomas Churchyard. General Rehearsall of Warres (po)
The Marriage of Wit and Wisdom (dr)
Sir Thomas North. Plutarch's Lives (trans)
Edmund Spenser. The Shepheards Calender (po)

1580

BIRTHS
John Webster

DEATHS
John Heywood

WORKS
John Dee. Navigationis ad Cathayam delineatio Hydrographica (t)
Thomas Lodge. A Defence of Plays (e)

John Lyly. Euphues and His England (fic)
Sir Philip Sidney. The Apologie for Poetry; or, Defence of Poesie (e)
_____. Astrophel and Stella, to 1584 (po)
John Stowe. The Chronicles of England (ed)

1581

BIRTHS
Sir Thomas Overbury

DEATHS
Thomas Wilson

WORKS
Richard Mulcaster. The Positions (e)
George Peele. The Arraignment of Paris (dr)
Barnabe Rich. Farewell to the Military Profession (fic)
Thomas Watson. Antigone (dr, po)
Nathaniel Woodes. The Conflict of Conscience (dr)

1582

BIRTHS
Richard Corbet
Phineas Fletcher

EVENTS
Rheims-Douai New Testament (pub)

WORKS
Richard Hakluyt. Divers Voyages Touching the Discovery of America (trav)
Sir David Lindsay. History of Squire Meldrum (po, pub)
Richard Mulcaster. The Elementarie (e)
Richard Watson. Passionate Centurie of Loue (po, trans)

1583

BIRTHS
Edward Herbert
Philip Massinger

EVENTS
Cambridge University Press (f)

WORKS
Philip Stubbes. The Anatomie of Abuses (t)

1584

BIRTHS
Francis Beaumont
John Selden

WORKS
Thomas Lodge. An Alarum Against Usurers (e)

THE SIXTEENTH CENTURY   45

    _____. The Delectable Historie of Forbonius and Priscilla (po)
John Lyly. Alexander and Campaspe (dr)
    _____. Sapho and Phao (dr)
George Peele. The Arraignment of Paris (po, dr, pub)
Reginald Scott. The Discoverie of Witchcraft (t)
Robert Wilson. Three Ladies of London (dr)

1585

BIRTHS
  William Drummond
  William Rowley

WORKS
  William Warner. Pan His Syrinx (fic)
  Richard Watson. Aminta (trans)

1586

DEATHS
  Sir Philip Sidney

WORKS
  William Camden. Britannia (his, trav)
  Edmund Spenser. Astrophel (po)
  William Warner. Albion's England, 1st ed (po)
  Richard Watson. Raptus Helenae (trans)

1587

BIRTHS
  Nathaniel Field

DEATHS
  John Foxe

WORKS
  Bp. John Bridges. A Defence of the Government Established in the
                Church of England for Ecclesiastical Matters (t)
  Thomas Churchyard. Worthines of Wales (po)
  Dudley Fenner. A Defence of the Godly Ministers Against the Slanders of
            Dr. Bridges (t)
  Robert Greene. Euphues, His Censure of Philautus (fic)
  Richard Hakluyt. De Orbe Novo (ed)
  _____. Notable History, containing Four Voyages Made by Cer-
          tain French Captains into Florida (trav)
  John Knox. History of the Reformation of Religion within the Realme of
          Scotland (his, e)

1588

BIRTHS
  Giles Fletcher the younger
  Thomas Hobbes
  George Wither

WORKS
  Robert Greene. Pondosto; or, Dorastus and Fawnia (fic)
  _____. Perimedes the Blacksmith (fic)
  Anthony Munday. Palladino of England (fic, trans)
  Sir Walter Ralegh. Farewell, False Love (po)
  Walter Travers. A Defense of the Ecclesiastical Discipline (t)

1589

WORKS
  Robert Greene. Menaphon (fic)
  Richard Hakluyt. Principall Navigations, Voiages, and Discoveries of
                the English Nation (his, trav)
  John Lyly. Pappe with an Hatchet (e)
  Thomas Nashe. Anatomie of Absurditie (e)
  _____. The Return of the Renouned Cavaliero Pasquil of England
                (s)
  Richard Puttenham. The Arte of English Poesie (e)
  Edmund Spenser. The Faerie Queene, I-III (po)

1590

WORKS
  Robert Greene. Greene's Mourning Garment (fic, e)
  _____. Never Too Late (fic, e)
  Thomas Lodge. Rosalynde. Euphues Golden Legacie (po)
  Christopher Marlowe. Tamburlaine the Great (dr)
  Anthony Munday. Amadis of Gaule (fic, trans)
  Thomas Nashe. The First Parte of Pasquils Apology (s)
  George Peele. Polyhymnia (po)
  William Shakespeare. 1 Henry VI (dr)
  _____. 2 Henry VI (dr)
  _____. 3 Henry VI (dr)
  Sir Philip Sidney. The Arcadia (fic, pub)
  Richard Watson. Eglogue (po)
  _____. The First Sette of Italian Madrigalls Englished (trans)
  Robert Wilson. Three Lords and Three Ladies of London (dr)

1591

BIRTHS
  William Browne
  Robert Herrick

WORKS
  Michael Drayton. Harmonie of the Church (po)
  Robert Greene. Farewell to Folly (fic, e)
  John Lyly. Endimion (dr)
  Thomas Nashe. A Wonderful, Strange, and Miraculous Astrologicall Prog-
                nostication (s)
  Sir Walter Ralegh. A Report of the Truth of the Fight about the Isles
                of the Azores (nar)
  Sir Henry Savile. Histories of Tacitus (trans)
  William Shakespeare. The Comedy of Errors (dr)
  _____. Titus Andronicus (dr)
  Sir Philip Sidney. Astrophel and Stella (po)

THE SIXTEENTH CENTURY   47

Edmund Spenser. Complaints, Containing Sundrie Small Poems of the
            Worlds Vanitie (po)
_____. Daphnaida (po)
Robert Wilmot. The Tragedie of Tancred and Gismund (dr)

                            1592

BIRTHS
  Francis Quarles

DEATHS
  Robert Greene
  Thomas Watson

EVENTS
  The Rose Theatre, Bankside, Southwark (op)

WORKS
  Nicholas Breton. The Countess of Pembrooke's Love (po)
  Henry Chettle. Groatsworth of Wit (ed)
  _____. Kind-Hart's Dreame (s)
  Henry Constable. Diana (po)
  Chronicon ex Chronicis (his, pub)
  Samuel Daniel. Complaynt of Rosamond (po)
  _____. Delia (po)
  Robert Greene. A Groatsworth of Wit Bought with a Million of Repen-
            tance (fic, e)
  _____. Philomela (fic)
  _____. A Quip for an Upstart Courtier (fic, e)
  Gabriel Harvey. Foure Letters (po)
  Richard Johnson. The Nine Worthies of London (fic)
  John Lyly. Midas (dr)
  Thomas Nashe. Pierce Pennilesse: His Supplication to the Devil (s)
  Sir Walter Ralegh. The Lie (po)
  William Shakespeare. Richard III (dr)
  The Tragedy of Mr. Arden of Feversham (dr)
  Richard Watson. Amyntae Gaudia (po, pub)

                            1593

BIRTHS
  George Herbert
  Izaac Walton

DEATHS
  Christopher Marlowe

EVENTS
  Marischal College, Aberdeen (f)

WORKS
  Barnabe Barnes. Parthenophil and Parthenophe, Sonnettes, Madrigals,
            Elegies, and Odes (po)
  Michael Drayton. Idea, the Shepheards Garland (po)
  _____. Piers Gaveston (po)
  Giles Fletcher the elder. Licia, or Poems of Love (po)

Gabriel Harvey. *Pierce's Supererogation* (po)
Robert Henryson. *Testament of Cresseid* (po, pub)
Thomas Lodge. *Phillis* (po)
Gervase Markham. *A Discourse of Horsemanshippe* (e)
Thomas Nashe. *Christes Teares over Jerusalem* (t)
_____. *Strange Newes of the Intercepting Certaine Letters* (e)
George Peele. *The Honour of the Garter* (po)
The Phoenix Nest (po, ed)
William Shakespeare. *The Taming of the Shrew* (dr)
_____. *Venus and Adonis* (po)
Richard Watson. *The Tears of Fancie* (po, pub)

1594

BIRTHS
  James Howell

DEATHS
  Barnabe Googe
  Thomas Kyd
  Richard Tottel

WORKS
  Richard Barnfield. *The Affectionate Shepherd* (po)
  George Chapman. *The Shadow of Night* (po)
  Samuel Daniel. *Cleopatra* (dr, po)
  John Davys. *The Seaman's Secrets* (e)
  Michael Drayton. *Ideas Mirrour* (po)
  _____. *Matilda* (po)
  Robert Greene. *The Honourable Historie of Friar Bacon and Friar Bungay* (dr, pub)
  Richard Hooker. *Of the Laws of Ecclesiastical Politie*, Books I-IV (t)
  A Knack To Know a Knave (dr)
  Thomas Kyd. *The Spanish Tragedy* (dr, pub)
  John Lyly. *Mother Bombie* (dr)
  Christopher Marlowe. *Edward II* (dr, pub)
  _____ and Thomas Nashe. *The Tragedy of Dido* (dr, pub)
  Anthony Munday. *John a Kent and John a Cumber* (dr)
  Thomas Nashe. *The Terrors of the Night* (e)
  _____. *The Unfortunate Traveller, or the Life of Jack Wilton* (fic)
  George Peele. *The Battle of Alcazar* (dr)
  William Shakespeare. *Love's Labour Lost* (dr)
  _____. *The Rape of Lucrece* (po)
  _____. *Two Gentlemen of Verona* (dr)
  Robert Wilson. *Cobbler's Prophecy* (dr)

1595

BIRTHS
  Thomas May

DEATHS
  Robert Southwell

WORKS

THE SIXTEENTH CENTURY 49

    Barnabe Barnes. A Divine Centurie of Spirituall Sonnets (po)
    Richard Barnfield. Cynthia, with Certaine Sonnets (po)
    Thomas Campion. Poemata (po)
    George Chapman. Ovid's Banquet of Sence (po)
    Henry Chettle. Pierce Plainnes Prentiship (s)
    Samuel Daniel. Civil Wars between the Two Houses of York and Lancaster,
        Books I-IV (po)
    John Davys. The Worldes Hydrographical Description (e)
    Michael Drayton. Endimion and Phoebe (po)
    Thomas Kyd. Pompey the Great, His Faire Corneliaes Tragedy (dr, pub)
    The Lamentable Tragedies of Locrine (dr, pub)
    Thomas Lodge. A Fig for Momus (po)
    Gervase Markham. The Most Honourable Tragedie of Sir Richard Grinvile,
        Knight (dr)
    George Peele. The Old Wives' Tale (dr)
    William Shakespeare. A Midsummer Night's Dream (dr)
    _____. Richard II (dr)
    _____. Romeo and Juliet (dr)
    Sir Philip Sidney. The Aplogie for Poetrie (e, pub)
    Sir Thomas More (dr)
    Robert Southwell. Maeoniae (po, pub)
    _____. St. Peter's Complaint (po)
    Edmund Spenser. Amoretti (po)
    _____. Colin Clouts Come Home Againe (po, pub)
    _____. Epithalamion (po)
    William Warner. Menaechmi (trans)

                1596

BIRTHS
    James Shirley

WORKS
    The Croyland History (his, pub)
    Sir John Davies. Orchestra (po)
    Michael Drayton. The Tragicall Legend of Robert, Duke of Normandie (po)
    Sir John Harington. Metamorphosis of Ajax (s)
    Sir Henry Knyvett. The Defence of the Realme (e)
    Thomas Lodge. A Margarite of America (po)
    _____. Wits Miserie and Worlds Madnesse (po)
    Thomas Nashe. Haue with You to Suffron-Walden (s)
    The Raigne of Edward III (dr)
    Sir Walter Ralegh. The Discovery of the Empyre of Guiana (nar)
    William Shakespeare. King John (dr)
    _____. The Merchant of Venice (dr)
    Edmund Spenser. Foure Hymnes (po)
    _____. The Faerie Queene, IV-VI (po)
    _____. Hymnes in Honour of Love and Beautie (pub)
    _____. Prothalamion (po)
    _____. View of the Present State of Ireland (e)

                1597

DEATHS
    George Peele

WORKS
  Francis Bacon. The Essays, or Counsels, Civill and Morall (e)
  Nicholas Breton. Wits Trenchmour (fic, nar)
  Michael Drayton. England's Heroicall Epistles (po)
  John Gerard. Herball, or Generall Historie of Plantes (t, ref)
  Joseph Hall. Virgidemiarum Sex Libri, vol 1 (s)
  Gabriel Harvey. The Trimming of Thomas Nashe (po)
  Richard Hooker. Of the Laws of Ecclesiastical Politie, Book V (t)
  Richard Johnson. The Famous Historie of the Seven Champions of Christendom (fic)
  John Lyly. The Woman in the Moone (dr)
  Alexander Montgomerie. The Cherry and the Slae (po)
  Thomas Nashe. The Isle of Dogs (dr)
  William Shakespeare. 1 Henry IV (dr)
  _____. 2 Henry IV (dr)

1598

BIRTHS
  Thomas Carew

WORKS
  Richard Barnfield. The Ecomion of Lady Pecunia (po)
  George Chapman. The Blind Beggar of Alexandria (dr)
  _____, and Christopher Marlowe. Hero and Leander (po)
  _____. The Iliad (trans)
  The Comedie of Mucedorus (dr, pub)
  Joseph Hall. Virgidemiarum Sex Libri, vol 2 (s)
  Ben Jonson. Every Man in His Humour (dr)
  John Marston. The Metamorphosis of Pigmalion's Image (po)
  Francis Meres. Palladis Tamia, Wit's Treasury (ed)
  Thomas Nashe. A Countercuffe Given to Martin Junior (s)
  Samuel Rowlands. The Betraying of Christ (po)
  William Shakespeare. The Merry Wives of Windsor (dr)
  _____. Much Ado about Nothing (dr)
  John Stowe. A Survey of London, to 1603 (his)

1599

DEATHS
  Edmund Spenser

EVENTS
  The Globe Theatre (op)

WORKS
  George Chapman. An Humourous Day's Mirth (dr)
  Samuel Daniel. Musophilus, or Defence of All Learning (po)
  Sir John Davies. Astraea (po)
  _____. Nosce Teipsum (po)
  Sir John Hayward. First Part of the Life and Raigne of Henrie the III (his, bio)
  Thomas Heywood. Edward IV (dr)
  William Jaggard. The Passionate Pilgrim (po, ed)
  Ben Jonson. Every Man Out of His Humour (dr)
  Christopher Marlowe. Come live with me and be my love (po, pub)

THE SIXTEENTH CENTURY

Thomas Nashe. Lenten Stuffe (s)
George Peele. David and Bethsabe (dr, pub)
William Shakespeare. As You Like It (dr)
_____. Henry V (dr)
_____. Julius Caesar (dr)
Sir Clyomon and Sir Clamides (dr)

4 The Seventeenth Century

1600

BIRTHS
  Peter Heylyn
  William Prynne

DEATHS
  Richard Hooker

EVENTS
  The East India Company (f)

WORKS
  Sir Edward Coke. Reports, to 1615 (t)
  John Day and Henry Chettle. The Blind Beggar of Bednal Green (dr)
  Thomas Dekker. Old Fortunatus (dr)
  _____. The Shoemaker's Holiday (dr)
  England's Helicon (po, ed)
  England's Parnassus (po, ed)
  The First Part of Sir John Oldcastle (dr, pub)
  William Gilbert. De Magnete (t)
  Thomas Heywood. The Four Prentices of London (dr)
  Ben Jonson. Cynthia's Revels (dr)
  William Kemp. Kemps Nine Daies Wonder (nar)
  Christopher Marlowe. Massacre at Paris (dr, pub)
  Thomas Nashe. Summers Last Will (dr)
  The Parnassus Plays (dr)
  Sir Walter Ralegh. To His Son (po)
  Samuel Rowlands. The Letting of Humours Blood in the Head-Vaine (s)
  William Shakespeare. Hamlet (dr)
  _____. Twelfth Night (dr)
  Cyril Tourneur. The Transformed Metamorphosis (po)

1601

THE SEVENTEENTH CENTURY

DEATHS
  Thomas Nashe
  Sir Thomas North

WORKS
  Nicholas Breton. The Soules Heavenly Exercise (po)
  Philemon Holland. Natural History (trans)
  Ben Jonson. The Poetaster (dr)
  Anthony Munday. The Downfall of Robert, Earle of Huntington (dr)
  William Shakespeare. The Phoenix and the Turtle (po)
  ──────────────. Troilus and Cressida (dr)

1602

WORKS
  Thomas Campion. Observations on the Art of English Poesy (e)
  Henry Chettle. The Tragedy of Hoffman (dr)
  Francis and Walter Davison. Poetical Rhapsody, 1st ed (ed)
  Thomas Dekker. Satiromastix (dr)
  Thomas Lodge. The Famous and Memorable Workes of Josephus (ed)
  John Marston. Antonio and Mellida (dr)
  Samuel Rowlands. Greene's Ghost (s)
  ──────────────. 'Tis Merrie when Gossips Meete (fic)
  The True Chronicle Historie of the Whole Life and Death of Thomas Lord
      Cromwell (dr)

1603

BIRTHS
  Sir Kenelm Digby
  Shackerley Marmion

EVENTS
  James I, King of England, to 1625
  The Society of Antiquaries (c)

WORKS
  John Barclay. Euphormionis Satyricon (s)
  Nicholas Breton. A Mad World, My Masters (dia)
  Henry Chettle. Englande's Mourning Garment (po)
  John Davies. Microcosmos (po)
  Thomas Dekker. The Wonderful Yeare (nar)
  ──────────── and Henry Chettle. Patient Grissil (dr)
  Michael Drayton. The Barrons Wars (po)
  John Florio. Essays of Montaigne (trans)
  Thomas Heywood. A Woman Kilde with Kindnesse (dr)
  Philemon Holland. Moralia (trans)
  James I of England. The True Law of Free Monarchies (t)
  Ben Jonson. Sejanus (dr)
  Richard Knolles. General Historie of the Turkes (his)
  Thomas Lodge. A Treatise of the Plague (t)
  Samuel Rowley. When you see me, You know Me; or, The Famous Chronicle
              Historie of King Henry VIII (dr)
  William Shakespeare. All's Well That Ends Well (dr)

1604

DEATHS
  Thomas Churchyard

WORKS
  Sir William Alexander. Aurora (po)
  Nicholas Breton. The Passionate Shepherd (po)
  Thomas Dekker. The Honest Whore, Part I (dr)
  Michael Drayton. The Owle (po)
  Christopher Marlowe. Tragedy of Dr. Faustus (dr, pub)
  John Marston and John Webster. The Malcontent (dr)
  William Shakespeare. Measure for Measure (dr)
  _____. Othello (dr)

1605

BIRTHS
  Sir Thomas Browne
  Sir William Dugdale
  William Habington
  Thomas Rudolph

DEATHS
  John Davys
  John Stowe

WORKS
  Francis Bacon. The Advancement of Learning (t)
  Nicholas Breton. The Honour of Valour (po)
  George Chapman. All Fools (dr)
  Samuel Daniel. Philotas (dr, po)
  John Davies. Honours Heau'n on Earth. . .As also the Triumph of Death
          (po)
  Michael Drayton. Poemes Lyrick and Pastorall (po)
  Ben Jonson. Masque of Blackness (dr)
  _____, John Marston, and George Chapman. Eastward hoe! (dr)
  The London Prodigal (dr, pub)
  John Marston. The Dutch Courtezan (dr)
  Samuel Rowlands. Hell's Broke Loose (s)
  William Shakespeare. King Lear (dr)
  _____. Macbeth (dr)

1606

BIRTHS
  Sir William D'Avenant
  Sir William Killigrew
  Edmund Waller

DEATHS
  John Lyly

WORKS
  George Chapman. The Gentleman Usher (dr)
  _____. Monsieur D'Olive (dr)
  John Day. The Isle of Gulls (dr)
  Ben Jonson. Volpone (dr)

THE SEVENTEENTH CENTURY   55

    John Marston. The Parasitaster (dr)
    _____. Saphonsiba (dr)
    Henry Peacham. Graphica (t)
    William Shakespeare. Antony and Cleopatra (dr)
    Robert Southwell. Fourefould Meditation of the Foure Last Things (pub)
    William Warner. Albion's England, 2nd ed (po)

                                      1607

DEATHS
    Henry Chettle

WORKS
    Francis Beaumont. The Woman-Hater (dr)
    William Camden. Britannia, 6th ed, enl (his, trav)
    George Chapman. Bussy D'Ambois (dr)
    John Day. The Parliament of Bees (dr, po)
    Richard Johnson. Pleasant Conceites of Old Hobson (fic)
    Gervase Markham. Cavelarice; or, the English Horseman (e)
    John Marston. What You Will (dr)
    Thomas Middleton. Michaelmas Term (dr)
    The Puritan, or the Widow of Watling-Street (dr, pub)
    Samuel Rowlands. Democritus, or Doctor Merryman, His Medicines against
            Melancholy Humours (e)
    William Shakespeare. Coriolanus (dr)
    _____. Timon of Athens (dr)
    Thomas Tomkis. Lingua; or, the Combat of the Tongue and the Five Sen-
            ses for Superiority (dr)
    Cyril Tourneur. The Revenger's Tragedy (dr)

                                      1608

BIRTHS
    Thomas Fuller
    John Milton

DEATHS
    John Dee
    Thomas Sackville

WORKS
    Francis Beaumont and John Fletcher. Four Plays in One (dr)
    George Chapman. The Conspiracy and Tragedy of Byron (dr)
    John Day. Humour out of Breath (dr)
    _____. Law Trickes (dr)
    Joseph Hall. Characters of Virtues and Vices (nar)
    Thomas Heywood. The Rape of Lucrece (dr)
    The Merry Devil of Edmonton (dr, pub)
    Thomas Middleton. The Familie of Love (dr)
    _____. A Mad World, My Masters (dr)
    _____. A Trick To Catch the Old-One (dr)
    Samuel Rowlands. Humours Looking Glasse (s)
    William Shakespeare. Pericles (dr)
    John Webster. The White Divel (dr)
    A Yorkshire Tragedy (dr, pub)

1609

BIRTHS
　Edward Hyde, Earl of Clarendon
　Sir Matthew Hale
　Sir John Suckling

DEATHS
　Barnabe Barnes
　William Warner

EVENTS
　Rheims-Douai Old Testament, to 1610 (pub)

WORKS
　Francis Bacon. De Sapientia Veterum (e)
　Francis Beaumont and John Fletcher. The Knight of the Burning Pestle (dr)
　Samuel Daniel. Civil Wars between the Two Houses of York and Lancaster, Books V-VIII (po)
　John Davies. Holy Roode (po)
　Thomas Dekker. Fowre Birds of Noahs Arke (t)
　_____. The Guls Hornebooke (e)
　Sir Fulke Greville. Mustapha (dr)
　Ben Jonson. Epicoene, or the Silent Woman (dr)
　_____. Masque of Queens (dr)
　Pimlyco, or Runne Red-Cap (s, po)
　William Shakespeare. Cymbeline (dr)
　_____. Sonnets (pub)
　John Webster. Appius and Virginia (dr)

1610

DEATHS
　Alexander Montgomerie
　George Turberville

EVENTS
　Bodleian Library (f)
　Kensington Palace (blt)

WORKS
　Francis Beaumont and John Fletcher. The Scornful Lady (dr)
　Thomas Campion. Books of Ayers, to 1612 (po)
　Samuel Daniel. Tethys Festival (po, dr)
　Michael Drayton. Legend of Great Cromwell (po)
　Giles Fletcher the younger. Christ's Victorie and Triumph in Heaven and Earth (po)
　John Fletcher. The Faithful Shepherdess (dr)
　Philemon Holland. Britannia (trans)
　Ben Jonson. The Alchemist (dr)
　Samuel Rowlands. Martin Mark-all (s)
　Sir Henry Savile. Works of St. Chrysostom, to 1613 (ed)
　William Shakespeare. The Winter's Tale (dr)

1611

BIRTHS
  William Cartwright
  Sir Thomas Urquhart

DEATHS
  Giles Fletcher the elder
  Richard Mulcaster

EVENTS
  Authorized Version of the Bible (pub)

WORKS
  Francis Beaumont and John Fletcher. A King and No King (dr)
  _____. The Maid's Tragedy (dr)
  _____. Philaster (dr)
  George Chapman. The Iliad (trans)
  _____. May-Day (dr)
  Thomas Coryate. Coryats Cramb (trav)
  _____. Coryats Crudities (trav)
  _____. The Odcombian Banquet (po)
  Randle Cotgrave. French-English Dictionary (ref)
  John Davies. Wittes Pilgrimage (po)
  Francis and Walter Davison. Poetical Rhapsody, 2nd ed (ed)
  Thomas Dekker and Thomas Middleton. The Roaring Girl (dr)
  John Donne. An Anatomy of the World: The First Anniversary (po)
  William Shakespeare. The Tempest (dr)
  John Speed. Historie of Great Britaine (his)
  Cyril Tourneur. The Atheist's Tragedy (dr)

                        1612

BIRTHS
  Samuel Butler
  Richard Crashaw

DEATHS
  John Gerard

WORKS
  Francis Beaumont and John Fletcher. The Captain (dr)
  _____. The Coxcomb (dr)
  _____. Cupid's Revenge (dr)
  George Chapman. The Widow's Tears (dr)
  John Davies. The Muse's Sacrifice (po)
  John Donne. The Progress of the Soul: The Second Anniversary (po)
  Nathaniel Field. A Woman's a Weathercock (dr)
  Thomas Heywood. An Apology for Actors (e)
  Richard Johnson. The Crowne Garland of Golden Roses (fic)
  Ben Jonson. Love Restored (dr)
  Sir Walter Ralegh. What is our Life? (po)
  William Shakespeare. Henry VIII (dr)

                        1613

BIRTHS
  Jeremy Taylor

DEATHS
  Henry Constable
  Sir Thomas Overbury

EVENTS
  The Globe Theatre (des)
  The Hope Theatre, Bankside, Southwark (op)

WORKS
  William Browne. Britannia's Pastorals, to 1615 (po)
  George Chapman. The Revenge of Bussy D'Ambois (dr)
  William Drummond. Tears on the Death of Moeliades (po)
  Sir John Hayward. Lives of the III Normans, Kings of England (bio)
  Thomas Middleton. The Triumphs of Truth (dr)
  Samuel Purchas. Purchas His Pilgrimage; or, Relations of the World and the Religions observed in All Ages (trav, t)
  Sir Henry Savile. Cyropaedia (ed)
  George Wither. Abuses Stript and Whipt (s)
  _____. The Shepherd's Hunting (po)

1614

BIRTHS
  Henry More

EVENTS
  The Globe Theatre (blt)

WORKS
  Sir William Alexander. Doomsday (po)
  William Browne and George Wither. Shepherd's Pipe (po)
  George Chapman. The Odyssey, to 1615 (trans)
  Ben Jonson. Bartholomew Fayre (dr)
  Thomas Lodge. The Workes, both Morall and Naturall, of Lucius Annaeus Seneca (ed)
  John Napier. Mirifici Logarithmorum Canonis Descriptio (t, pub)
  Sir Thomas Overbury. Characters (fic, pub)
  _____. A Wife (po, pub)
  Sir Walter Ralegh. History of the World (his)
  John Selden. Titles of Honour (t)
  John Webster. The Duchess of Malfi (dr)

1615

BIRTHS
  Richard Baxter
  Sir John Denham

WORKS
  William Camden. Annales. . .Regnante Elizabetha. . .ad annum 1589, Part I (nar, t)
  Samuel Daniel. Hymen's Triumph (po, dr)
  Ben Jonson. Mercury Vindicated from the Alchemists (dr)
  Simon Latham. Latham's Falconry (ref)
  John Napier. Rabdologia (t)
  Samuel Rowlands. The Melancholie Knight (s)

THE SEVENTEENTH CENTURY 59

George Ruggle. Ignoramus (dr)
Thomas Tomkis. Albumazar (dr)
George Wither. Fidelia (po)

1616

BIRTHS
Sir Roger L'Estrange

DEATHS
Francis Beaumont
Richard Hakluyt
William Shakespeare

WORKS
Thomas Coryate. Thomas Coriate. Traveller for the English Wits: Greeting (nar, trav)
Ben Jonson. The Devil Is an Ass (dr)
_____. The Forrest (po)
Gervase Markham. Markham's Method, or Epitome (e)
Thomas Middleton. Civitatis Amor (dr)

1617

BIRTHS
Ralph Cudworth

DEATHS
Thomas Coryate
John Napier

WORKS
John Davies. Wit's Bedlam (po)
Thomas Middleton. The Triumphs of Honour and Industry (dr)
_____ and William Rowley. A Faire Quarrell (dr)
John Selden. De Diis Syris (t)

1618

BIRTHS
Abraham Cowley
Richard Lovelace

DEATHS
John Davies
Sir Walter Ralegh

WORKS
George Chapman. Gerogicks of Hesiod (trans)
Nathaniel Field. Amends for Ladies (dr)
John Fletcher. The Loyal Subject (dr)
Ben Jonson. Pleasure Reconciled to Vertue (dr)
John Selden. History of Tythes (t)
James Shirley. Eccho (po)
John Tradescant. A Voiag of Ambasad (trav)

1619

BIRTHS
  William Chamberlayne

DEATHS
  Samuel Daniel
  Thomas Campion

WORKS
  Francis Beaumont and John Fletcher. The Knight of Malta (dr)
  Robert Carliell. Britaines Glorie (po)
  Michael Drayton. Pastorals (po)
  John Fletcher. The Humorous Lieutenant (dr)
  _____. The Mad Lover (dr)
  _____. Monsieur Thomas (dr)
  _____. Sir John van Olden Barnavelt (dr)
  _____. Valentinian (dr)
  Thomas Middleton. The Inner Temple Masque (dr)
  _____. The Triumphs of Love and Antiquity (dr)
  John Napier. Constructio (t, pub)
  Samuel Purchas. Purchas His Pilgrim, Microcosmus or the Histories of Man (t)
  George Wither. Shall I, Wasting in Despair (po)

1621

BIRTHS
  Andrew Marvell

WORKS
  Francis Beaumont and John Fletcher. Thierry and Theodoret (dr)
  Robert Burton. The Anatomy of Melancholy (t)
  Francis and Walter Davison. Poetical Rhapsody, 3rd ed (ed)
  John Fletcher. The Island Princess (dr)
  _____. The Pilgrim (dr)
  _____. The Wild Goose Chase (dr)
  Robert Henryson. Morall Fables of Esope the Phrygian (po, pub)
  Ben Jonson. Newes from the New World (dr)
  Alexander Montgomerie. Flyting Betwixt Montgomerie and Polwart (pub)
  George Sandys. Metamorphoses (po, trans)
  George Wither. Motto, Nec habeo, nec Careo, nec Curo (po)

1622

BIRTHS
  Henry Vaughan

DEATHS
  Sir Henry Savile

WORKS
  Francis Bacon. The History of Henry the Seventh (his)
  Thomas Dekker and Philip Massinger. The Virgin Martyr (dr)
  Michael Drayton. Polyolbion (po)
  Sir Richard Hawkins. Observations. . .in His Voiage into the South Sea, A.D. 1593 (trav, nar)

THE SEVENTEENTH CENTURY   61

Thomas Middleton. The Triumphs of Honour and Virtue (dr)
Henry Peacham. The Compleat Gentleman (ref)
Michael Scott. Quaestio Curiosa de Natura Solis et Lunae (pub)
George Wither. Juvenilia (pub)
_____. Mistress of Phil'Arete (po)

1623

DEATHS
  William Camden
  Giles Fletcher the younger

EVENTS
  First Shakespeare Folio (pub)
  Sion College, London (f)

WORKS
  Francis Bacon. De Augmentis (t)
  Richard Brome. A Fault in Friendship (dr)
  Thomas Dekker, John Ford, and William Rowley. The Witch of Edmonton (dr)
  Henry Drummond. The Cypress Grove (t)
  _____. Flowers of Zion (po)
  Philip Massinger. The Duke of Milan (dr)
  Thomas Middleton. The Triumphs of Integrity (dr)
  _____, and William Rowley. The Changeling (dr)
  _____. The Spanish Gypsy (dr)
  John Webster. The Devil's Law Case (dr)
  George Wither. Hymnes and Songs of the Church (po)

1624

BIRTHS
  George Fox

WORKS
  Francis Bacon. Apophthegms New and Old (e)
  John Donne. Devotions upon Emergent Occasions (pub)
  John Fletcher. Rule a Wife and Have a Wife (dr)
  _____. A Wife for a Month (dr)
  Edward Herbert. De Veritate (e)
  Thomas Heywood. The Captives (dr)
  Philip Massinger. The Bondman (dr)
  _____. The Parliament of Love (dr)
  Thomas Middleton. A Game of Chesse (dr)
  John Selden. Marmora Arundelliana (t)
  Sir Henry Wotton. Elements of Architecture (e)

1625

DEATHS
  John Fletcher
  Thomas Lodge
  John Webster

EVENTS

Charles I, King of England, to 1649

WORKS
John Fletcher. The Woman's Prize; or, the Tamer Tamed (dr)
Ben Jonson. The Staple of Newes (dr)
Thomas Lodge. A Learned Summary upon the Famous Poeme of William of
               Saluste, Lord of Bartas, Translated out of the French
               (e, trans)
John Milton. On the Death of a Fair Infant (po)
Samuel Purchas. Hakulytus Posthumus; or, Purchas His Pilgrims, Contayn-
               ing a History of the World in Sea Voyages and Land
               Travell by Englishmen and Others (trav, ed)
Edmund Waller. His Majesty's Escape at St. Andere (po)

1626

BIRTHS
John Aubrey

DEATHS
Francis Bacon
Nicholas Breton
Sir John Davies
Samuel Purchas
Cyril Tourneur

WORKS
Francis Bacon. The New Atlantis (t)
Thomas May. Antigone (dr)
_____. Cleopatra (dr)
Thomas Middleton. The Triumphs of Health and Prosperity (dr)
James Shirley. The Maid's Revenge (dr)

1627

BIRTHS
John Ray
John Wilson

DEATHS
Richard Barnfield
Sir John Hayward
Thomas Middleton

WORKS
William Camden. Annales. . .regnante Elizabetha. . .ad annum 1589,
               Part II (nar, t)
Michael Drayton. Nimphidia (po)
_____. To Henry Reynolds (po)
Phineas Fletcher. The Locusts, or Apollyonists (po)
John Milton. At a Vacation Exercise (po)

1628

BIRTHS
John Bunyan

THE SEVENTEENTH CENTURY   63

Sir William Temple

DEATHS
  Sir Fulke Greville

WORKS
  John Clavell. Recantation of an Ill-Led Life (po, auto)
  Sir Edward Coke. Institutes, to 1644 (t)
  Abraham Cowley. Pyramus and Thisbe (po)
  John Earle. Microcosmographie (nar,e)
  William Harvey. Exercitatio Anatomica de Motu Cordis et Sanguinis in
                Animalibus (t)
  Thomas May. Julia Agrippina (dr)

                              1629

WORKS
  Sir William D'Avenant. The Tragedy of Albovine (dr)
  John Ford. Lover's Melancholy (dr)
  Ben Jonson. The New Inn (dr)
  Philip Massinger. The Roman Actor (dr)
  John Milton. Ode on the Morning of Christ's Nativity (po)
  John Parkinson. Paradisi in sole Paradisus terrestris; or, A Garden of
                All Sorts of Pleasant Flowers (t, ref)

                              1630

BIRTHS
  Isaac Barrow

DEATHS
  Gabriel Harvey
  Samuel Rowlands

WORKS
  Abraham Cowley. Constantia and Philetus (po)
  Sir William D'Avenant. The Cruel Brother (dr)
  Thomas Dekker. The Honest Whore, Part II (dr)
  Sir John Hayward. Life and Raigne of King Edward the Sixth (bio, his,
                pub)
  Ben Jonson. Chloridia (dr)
  Philip Massinger. The Picture (dr)
  _____. The Renegado (dr)
  Thomas Middleton. A Chaste Maid in Cheapside (dr, pub)
  John Milton. On Shakespeare (po)
  Thomas Randolph. Aristippus; or, The Joviall Philosopher (dr)
  John Taylor. All the Workes of John Taylor, the Water Poet (pub)

                              1631

BIRTHS
  John Dryden

DEATHS
  John Donne
  Michael Drayton

WORKS
  George Chapman. Caesar and Pompey (dr)
  Thomas Dekker. Match Mee (dr)
  Thomas Heywood. The Fair Maid of the West (dr, pub)
  Gervase Markham. A Way To Get Wealth, to 1638 (t)
  John Selden. De Seccessionibus (t)
  James Shirley. Love's Cruelty (dr)
  _____. The Traitor (dr)

1632

BIRTHS
  John Locke
  Anthony Wood

DEATHS
  Thomas Dekker

EVENTS
  Second Shakespeare Folio (pub)

WORKS
  Richard Brome. The Northern Lass (dr)
  Philemon Holland. Cyropaedia (trans)
  Ben Jonson. The Magnetic Lady (dr)
  Philip Massinger. The Emperour of the East (dr)
  _____. The Maid of Honour (dr)
  _____ and Nathaniel Field. The Fatal Dowry (dr)
  John Milton. Il Penseroso (po)
  _____. L'Allegro (po)
  William Prynne. Histriomastix (t)
  William Rowley. A New Wonder (dr)
  James Shirley. Changes; or, Love in a Maze (dr)
  _____. Hyde Park (dr)
  The True Tale of Robin Hood (po, pub)

1633

BIRTHS
  Samuel Pepys
  Samuel Pordage
  Wentworth Dillon, Earl of Roscommon
  George Savile

DEATHS
  Nathaniel Field
  George Herbert
  Anthony Munday

WORKS
  Abraham Cowley. Poetical Blossoms (po)
  John Davies. Anatomy of Fair Writing (t)
  John Donne. Songs and Sonnets (pub)
  Phineas Fletcher. Elisa (po)
  _____. The Purple Island (po)
  John Ford. The Broken Heart (dr)

THE SEVENTEENTH CENTURY 65

    _____. Love's Sacrifice (dr)
    _____.'Tis a Pity She's a Whore (dr)
    Fulke Greville. Alaham, a Tragedy (dr)
    George Herbert. The Temple (po)
    Thomas Heywood. The English Traveller (dr, pub)
    Ben Jonson. A Tale of a Tub (dr)
    Christopher Marlowe. The Jew of Malta (dr, pub)
    Philip Massinger. A New Way To Pay Old Debts (dr)
    John Milton. Arcades, Part of an Entertainment Presented to the Countess-Dowager of Derby, at Harefield (po)
    William Rowley. All's Lost by Lust, a Tragedy (dr)
    _____. A Match at Midnight (dr)
    James Shirley. The Gamester (dr)

1634

BIRTHS
  Sir George Etherege

DEATHS
  George Chapman
  Sir Edward Coke
  John Marston

WORKS
  Thomas Carew. Coelum Britannicum (dr)
  William D'Avenant. Love and Honour (dr)
  John Ford. Perkin Warbeck (dr)
  William Habington. Castara, 1st ed (po)
  John Milton. Comus (po, dr)

1635

BIRTHS
  Thomas Betterton
  Thomas Sprat
  Edward Stillingfleet

DEATHS
  Richard Corbet
  Thomas Randolph

EVENTS
  The French Academy (f)
  St. Paul's, Covent Garden, London (blt)

WORKS
  Richard Brome. The Sparagus Garden (dr)
  William Habington. Castara, 2nd ed (po)
  Thomas Heywood. Hierarchy of the Blessed Angels (po)
  Gervase Markham. The Faithful Farrier (e)
  Francis Quarles. Emblems (po)
  John Selden. Mare Clausum (t)
  James Shirley. The Coronation (dr)
  _____. The Lady of Pleasure (dr)

1636

BIRTHS
Joseph Glanvill

WORKS
William Cartwright. The Royal Slave (dr)
Sir William D'Avenant. The Platonick Lovers (dr)
_____. The Wits (dr)
Sir John Hayward. The Beginning of the Reign of Elizabeth (his, pub)
Philip Massinger. The Great Duke of Florence (dr)
George Sandys. Paraphrase upon the Psalmes (po)

1637

BIRTHS
Thomas Ken

DEATHS
Philemon Holland
Ben Jonson
Gervase Markham

EVENTS
Sir William D'Avenant, Poet Laureate of England, to 1668

WORKS
Thomas Heywood. The Royal King and the Loyal Subject (dr)
Jonsonus Virbius (po, pub)
Thomas Killigrew the elder. The Parson's Wedding (dr)
Shackerley Marmion. Cupid and Psyche (po)
John Milton. Lycidas (po)
Sir John Suckling. Aglaura (dr)
_____. Session of the Poets (fic, nar)

1638

BIRTHS
Charles Sackville

WORKS
William Chillingworth. The Religion of the Protestants a Safe Way to Salvation (t)
Abraham Cowley. Love's Riddle (po)
_____. Naufragium Jocular (dr)
William D'Avenant. The Unfortunate Lovers (dr)
John Ford. The Ladies Triall (dr)
Henry Killigrew. The Conspiracy (dr)
Thomas Randolf. The Muse's Looking-Glasse (dr, pub)
William Rowley. A Shoemaker a Gentleman (dr)
Sir John Suckling. The Goblins (dr)

1639

BIRTHS

THE SEVENTEENTH CENTURY   67

   Sir Charles Sedley

DEATHS
   Thomas Carew
   Shackerley Marmion
   Sir Henry Wotton

WORKS
   George Chapman. The Tragedy of Chabot (dr)
   John Fletcher. Wit without Money (dr)
   Thomas Fuller. History of the Holy Warre (his)
   Philip Massinger. The Unnatural Combat (dr)

                              1640

BIRTHS
   Aphra Behn
   John Crowne
   William Wycherley

DEATHS
   Sir William Alexander
   Robert Burton
   Philip Massinger

WORKS
   Thomas Carew. An Elegy upon the Death of John Donne (po)
   John Donne. LXXX Sermons (pub)
   William Habington. Castara, 3rd ed (po)
   _____. The Queene of Arragon (dr)
   Ben Jonson. Timber; or, Discoveries Made upon Men and Matter (e, pub)
   _____. Underwoods (po, pub)
   John Parkinson. Theatrum Botanicum (t)
   George Sandys. Christ's Passion, a Tragedy (po, trans)
   John Selden. De Jure Naturali (t)
   _____. Judicature in Parliament (t)
   James Shirley. The Arcadia (dr)
   _____. The Imposture (dr)
   Sir John Suckling. The Discontented Colonell (dr)
   Izaak Walton. John Donne (bio)

                              1641

BIRTHS
   Thomas Rymer
   William Sherlock

DEATHS
   Thomas Heywood

EVENTS
   The Court of Star-Chamber (c)

WORKS
   Richard Brome. The Joviall Crew (dr)
   George Cavendish. The Life and Death of Thomas Woolsey (bio)

Abraham Cowley. The Cutter of Coleman Street (dr)
Shackerley Marmion. The Antiquary (dr, pub)
John Milton. Of Reformation in England (t)
James Shirley. The Cardinall (dr)
George Wither. Heleluiah (po)

1642

BIRTHS
Sir Isaac Newton
Thomas Shadwell

DEATHS
William Rowley
Sir John Suckling

WORKS
Sir John Denham. Cooper's Hill (po)
Thomas Fuller. The Holy State and the Profane State (e)
Thomas Hobbes. De Cive (t)
James Howell. Instructions for Forreine Travel (e)
John Milton. Apology against a Pamphlet. . .Against Smectymnuus (t)
_____. The Reason of Church Government Urged Against Prelaty (e)
Henry More. Platonica; or, A Platonical Song of the Soul (po)
John Selden. Privileges of Baronage (t)
James Shirley. The Sisters (dr)

1643

BIRTHS
Gilbert Burnet

DEATHS
William Browne
William Cartwright
Henry Peacham

WORKS
Sir Thomas Browne. Religio Medici (e)
Sir Kenhelm Digby. Of Bodies (t)
_____. Of the Immortality of Man's Soul (t)
John Milton. On the Doctrine and Discipline of Divorce (t)

1644

BIRTHS
William Penn

DEATHS
Francis Quarles
George Sandys

WORKS
John Cleveland. The Rebel Scot (po)
John Milton. Aeropagitica: A Speech for the Liberty of Unlicensed Printing (e)

THE SEVENTEENTH CENTURY   69

    _____. The Doctrine and Discipline of Divorce, enl ed (t)
    _____. Of Education (e)

1645

EVENTS
  The Philosophical Society (f)

WORKS
  Edward Fisher. The Marrow of Modern Divinity (t)
  Thomas Fuller. Good Thoughts in Bad Times (e, nar)
  John Milton. Colasterion (t)
  _____. Poems (pub)
  _____. Tetrachordon (t)
  Edmund Waller. Go, Lovely rose! (po)
  _____. Poems (pub)

1646

WORKS
  Sir Thomas Browne. Pseudodoxia Epidemica (e)
  Richard Crashaw. Steps to the Temple (po)
  Sir John Suckling. Brennoralt (dr, pub)
  _____. Fragmenta Aurea (pub)
  Jeremy Taylor. Liberty of Prophesying (t)
  Henry Vaughan. Poems (pub)

1647

BIRTHS
  John Wilmot, second Earl of Rochester

WORKS
  Francis Beaumont and John Fletcher. The Honest Man's Fortune (dr, pub)
  _____. Love's Cure (dr, pub)
  Richard Corbet. Certaine Elegant Poems (po)
  Abraham Cowley. The Mistress (po)
  Thomas Fuller. Good Thoughts in Worse Times (e, nar)
  Joseph Hall. Hard Measure (t)
  Robert Herrick. Noble Numbers (po)
  Matthew Hopkins. Discovery of Witches
  Thomas May. History of the Long Parliament (his)
  Henry More. Philosophical Poems (pub)
  John Selden. Fleta (t)

1648

BIRTHS
  Elkanah Settle

DEATHS
  Edward Herbert

EVENTS
  The Society of Friends (f)

WORKS
  Richard Corbet. Poetica Stromata; or, A Collection of Sundry Pieces in
              Poetry (pub)
  Robert Herrick. Hesperides (po)

1649

DEATHS
  Richard Crashaw
  William Drummond

WORKS
  John Donne. Fifty Sermons (pub)
  John Dryden. Upon the Death of Lord Hastings (po)
  Edward Herbert. Life of Henry VIII (his, pub)
  James Howell. Perfect Description of the Country of Scotland (s)
  Richard Lovelace. To Althea, from Prison (po)
  _____. To Lucasta, Going to the Wars (po)
  John Milton. Eikonoklastes (t)
  _____. The Tenure of Kings and Magistrates (t)

1650

BIRTHS
  Jeremy Collier
  Archbishop William King

DEATHS
  Phineas Fletcher
  Thomas May
  John Parkinson

WORKS
  Richard Baxter. The Saint's Everlasting Rest (e)
  Thomas Fuller. A Pisgah-Sight of Palestine (e)
  Thomas Hobbes. Human Nature (t)
  James Howell. Epistolae Howelianae: Familiar Letters (e)
  Andrew Marvell. Horatian Ode upon Cromwell's Return from Ireland (po)
  Jeremy Taylor. Holy Living (t)
  Henry Vaughan. Silex Scintillans, Part I (po)

1651

WORKS
  William Cartwright. Comedies, Tragedies, with Other Poems (pub)
  Sir William D'Avenant. Gondibert (po)
  William Harvey. Exercitationes de Generatione Animalium (t)
  Thomas Hobbes. Leviathan (t)
  William Lilly. A True History of King James I and King Charles I (his,
              bio)
  John Milton. Pro Populo Anglicano Defensio (t)
  Thomas Randolph. Hey for Honesty (dr, pub)
  Jeremy Taylor. Holy Dying (t)
  Henry Vaughan. Olar Iscanus (po, pub)
  Izaak Walton. Sir Henry Wooton (bio)
  Sir Henry Wooton. Reliquiae Wootonianae (ed, pub)

THE SEVENTEENTH CENTURY 71

1652

BIRTHS
　William Dampier
　Thomas Otway
　Nahum Tate

DEATHS
　Richard Brome

WORKS
　Edward Benlowes. Theophila; or, Love's Sacrifice (po)
　Richard Crashaw. Carmen Deo Nostro (po)
　Nathanael Cilverwel. Light of Nature (t)
　Sir Fulke Greville. Life of Sidney (bio, pub)
　George Herbert. A Priest to the Temple (e, pub)
　Peter Heylyn. Cosmographie (trav)
　Thomas Middleton, Ben Jonson, and John Fletcher. The Widdow (dr, pub)
　Lodowicke Muggleton and John Reeve. Transcendent Spirituall Treatise (t)

1653

BIRTHS
　Thomas D'Urfey
　Nathaniel Lee
　John Oldham

WORKS
　Richard Brome. The City Witt (dr, pub)
　Philip Massinger. Believe as You List (dr, pub)
　Henry More. An Antidote against Atheism (t)
　_____. Conjectura Cabbalistica (t)
　Jeremy Taylor. Eniautos (ser)
　Sir Thomas Urquhart. Pantagruel, Gargantua (trans)
　Izaak Walton. The Compleat Angler, 1st ed (t)

1654

DEATHS
　John Selden

WORKS
　Appius and Virginia (dr)
　John Milton. Second Defence of the English People (t)
　Brian Walton. The Polygot Bible, to 1657 (ed)

1655

WORKS
　Isaac Barrow. Euclidis Elementa (t)
　Henry Drummond. History of Scotland (his, pub)
　Sir William Dugdale. Monasticon Anglicanum, to 1673 (trav, e)
　Thomas Fuller. Church History of Britain (his)
　_____. History of Cambridge University (his)
　Thomas Hobbes. De Corpore (t)

Philip Massinger. The Guardian (dr, pub)
John Milton. On the Late Massacre in Piedmont (po)
_____. Pro Se Defensio (t)
John Phillips. Satyr against Hypocrites (s)
Thomas Stanley. History of Philosophy, to 1662 (his, e)
Jeremy Taylor. The Golden Grove (prayers)
Henry Vaughan. Silex Scintillans, Part II (po)
John Wallis. Arithmetica Infinitorum (t)
Izaak Walton. The Compleat Angler, 2nd ed (t)

                              1656

DEATHS
  Joseph Hall

WORKS
  John Bunyan. Some Gospel Truths Opened (t)
  Abraham Cowley. Miscellanies (po)
  Sir William D'Avenant. The Siege of Rhodes (dr)
  Sir William Dugdale. The Antiquities of Warwickshire (his)
  Richard Flecknoe. A Relation of Ten Years' Travel in Europe, Asia,
              Affrique, and America (trav)
  James Harington. The Commonwealth of Oceana (fic)
  Henry More. Enthusiasmus Triumphatus (t)

                              1657

BIRTHS
  John Dennis

DEATHS
  William Harvey

WORKS
  Richard Baxter. Call to the Unconverted (e)
  Richard Brome. The Queen's Exchange (dr, pub)
  John Bunyan. A Vindication of Some Gospel Truths Opened (e)
  James Howell. Londonopolis; An Historical Discourse or Perlustration
              of the City of London (e)
  Thomas Middleton. More Dissemblers with Women (dr, pub)
  _____. No Wit, No Help Like a Woman's (dr, pub)
  _____. Women Beware Women (dr, pub)

                              1658

DEATHS
  Richard Lovelace

WORKS
  Sir Thomas Browne. Urn Burial (t)
  _____. Garden of Cyprus (t)
  William Chamberlayne. Love's Victory (dr)
  John Dryden. Heroic Stanzas (po)
  Sir William Dugdale. History of St. Paul's Cathedral (his)
  Thomas Hobbes. De Homine (t)
  Philip Massinger. The City Madam (dr, pub)

THE SEVENTEENTH CENTURY 73

John Milton. Methought I Saw My Late Espoused Saint (po)
Edward Phillips. New World of Words (ref)
The Whole Duty of Man (t, pub)

1659

BIRTHS
Thomas Southerne

DEATHS
Richard Johnson

EVENTS
Mercurius Publicus (p, f)
The Parliamentary Intelligencer (p, f)

WORKS
Richard Brome. The Queen and Concubine (dr, pub)
William Chamberlayne. Pharonnida (po)
John Milton. Considerations Touching the Likeliest Means To Remove Hirelings out of the Church (t)
_____. A Treatise of Civil Power in Ecclesiastical Causes (t)
Henry More. The Immortality of the Soul (t)
John Pearson. Exposition of the Creed (ser)
James Shirley. The Contention of Ajax and Ulysses (dr)
Thomas Sprat. To the Happy Memory of the Most Renowned Prince Oliver, Lord Protector (po)
Edward Stillingfleet. The Irenicum (t)

1660

BIRTHS
Daniel Defoe

DEATHS
Sir Thomas Urquhart

EVENTS
Charles II, King of England, to 1685
St. James's Square, Londpn (op)

WORKS
John Donne. XXVI Sermons (pub)
John Dryden. Astraea Redux (po)
Thomas Fuller. Mixt Contemplations in Better Times (e, nar)
Joseph Hall. The Shaking of the Olive Tree (t, pub)
John Milton. The Ready and Easy Way To Establish a Free Commonwealth (t)
Henry More. An Explanation of the Grand Mystery of Godliness (t)
John Smith. Selected Discourses (pub)
Jeremy Taylor. Ductor Dubitantium (t)
_____. The Worthy Communicant (t)

1661

BIRTHS

Sir Samuel Garth
Anne Finch, Countess of Winchelsea

DEATHS
Thomas Fuller

WORKS
Abraham Cowley. The Advancement of Experimental Philosophy (t)
_____. Discourse by Way of Vision Concerning Oliver Cromwell (e)
John Dryden. Panegyric (po)
John Evelyn. Fumifugium; or, The Inconvenience of the Air and Smoke of London Dissipated (e)
Joseph Glanvill. The Vanity of Dogmatizing (e, nar)
Peter Heylyn. Ecclesia Restaurata; or, History of the Reformation (his)
Thomas Middleton. The Mayor of Quinborough (dr, pub)
John Selden. On the Nativity of Christ (pub)

1662

BIRTHS
Francis Atterbury

DEATHS
Peter Heylyn

EVENTS
The Royal Society (f)

WORKS
John Dryden. To My Lord Chancellor (po)
Sir William Dugdale. The History of Imbanking and Drayning of Divers Fenns and Marshes (his)
John Evelyn. Sculptura (e)
Thomas Fuller. The Worthies of England (bio, trav)
Joseph Glanvill. Lux Orientalis (e)
Thomas Middleton. Anything for a Quiet Life (dr, pub)
Poor Robin's Almanack (pub)
William Prynne. Brevia Parliamentaria Rediviva (t)
Edward Stillingfleet. Origines Sacrae (t)

1663

BIRTHS
William King
William Walsh

EVENTS
The Intellingencer (p, f)
The News (p, f)
Third Shakespeare Folio (pub)

WORKS
Samuel Butler. Hudibras, Part I (po)
Abraham Cowley. Verses on Several Occasions (pub)
John Dryden. The Wild Gallant (dr)

THE SEVENTEENTH CENTURY   75

   Thomas Ken. Ichabod (po)

                              1664

BIRTHS
   Matthew Prior
   Sir John Vanbrugh

DEATHS
   William Habington

EVENTS
   The London Hay Market, Haymarket (op)

WORKS
   Samuel Butler. Hudibras, Part II (po)
   John Dryden. The Rival Ladies (dr)
   Sir George Etherege. The Comical Revenge; or, Love in a Tub (dr)
   John Evelyn. Sylva (e)
   Richard Flecknoe. A Short Discourse on the English Stage (e)
   Sir William Killigrew. Ormasdes; or, Love and Friendship (dr)
   _____. Pandora (dr)
   _____. Selindra (dr)
   Henry More. The Mystery of Iniquity (t)
   John Wilson. Andronicus Comenius (dr)
   _____. The Cheats (dr)

                              1665

DEATHS
   Sir Kenhelm Digby

EVENTS
   The Oxford Gazette (p, f)

WORKS
   John Crowne. Pandion and Amphigenia (po)
   John Dryden. The Indian Emperor (dr)
   _____. Verses to Her Royal Highness the Duchess of York (pub)
   The Philosophical Transactions of the Royal Society (pub)
   Izaak Walton. Richard Hooker (bio)
   John Wilson. The Projectors (dr)

                              1666

DEATHS
   James Howell
   James Shirley

EVENTS
   The Great Fire of London
   The Intelligencer (p, c)
   The News (p, c)
   Old St. Paul's Cathedral, London (des)
   The Royal Exchange (des)

WORKS
  John Bunyan. Grace Abounding to the Chief of Sinners (nar)
  _____. The Holy City; or, The New Jerusalem (t)
  Sir William Dugdale. Origines Juridicales (t)
  Sir William Killigrew. The Siege of Urbin (dr)

                                1667

BIRTHS
  John Arbuthnot
  Abel Boyer
  Susannah Centlivre
  Jonathan Swift
  Edward Ward

DEATHS
  Abraham Cowley
  Jeremy Taylor
  George Wither

WORKS
  John Dryden. Annus Mirabilis (po)
  John Milton. Paradise Lost (po)
  Henry More. Enchiridion Ethicum (t)
  Thomas Sprat. The History of the Royal Society of London (his)

                                1668

DEATHS
  Sir William D'Avenant

WORKS
  John Dryden. An Essay of Dramatick Poesie (e)
  _____. The Mock Astrologer (dr)
  _____. Secret Love, or the Maiden-Queen (dr)
  _____. Sir Martin Mar-all, or the Feign'd Innocence (dr)
  Sir George Etherege. She Would If She Could (dr)
  Peter Heylyn. Cyprianus Anglicus (his, pub)
  Henry More. Divine Dialogues (e)
  _____. Enchiridion Metaphysicum (t)
  William Penn. The Sandy Foundation Shaken (e)
  Sir Charles Sedley. The Mulberry Garden (dr)
  Thomas Shadwell. Sullen Lovers (dr)
  Sir William Temple. Essay on the Present State of Ireland (e)

                                1669

DEATHS
  Sir John Denham
  William Prynne

EVENTS
  The Sheldonian Theatre, Oxford (blt)

WORKS
  Isaac Barrow. Exposition of the Creed, Decalogue, and Sacraments (t)

THE SEVENTEENTH CENTURY   77

   Edward Chamberlayne. Angliae Notitia; or, The Present State of Eng-
                  land (e)
   John Dryden. Tyrannic Love; or, The Royal Martyr (dr)
   William Penn. No Cross, No Crown (t)

                              1670

BIRTHS
   William Congreve
   Bernard Mandeville

EVENTS
   John Dryden, Poet Laureate of England, to 1689
   Hudson's Bay Company (f)

WORKS
   Thomas Betterton. The Amorous Widow (dr)
   _____. The Roman Virgin (dr)
   Sir William D'Avenant and John Dryden. The Tempest (dr)
   John Dryden. Almanzor and Almahide; or, the Conquest of Grenada (dr)
   Peter Heylyn. Aerius Redivivus, or History of Presbyterianism (his,
                  pub)
   John Milton. History of Britain (pub)
   John Ray. A Collection of English Proverbs (ed)
   Robin Hood's Garland (pub)
   Izaak Walton. George Herbert (bio)

                              1671

BIRTHS
   Colley Cibber
   Anthony Ashley Cooper, third Earl of Shaftesbury

WORKS
   George Villiers, second Duke of Buckingham. The Rehearsal (dr)
   John Bunyan. A Confession of My Faith, and a Reason of My Practice (t)
   John Milton. Paradise Regained (po)
   _____. Samson Agonistes (po, dr)
   Sir William Temple. Upon the Original and Nature of Government (e)
   William Wycherley. Love in a Wood (dr)

                              1672

BIRTHS
   Joseph Addison
   Edmund Hoyle
   Sir Richard Steele

WORKS
   John Dryden. The Assignation, or Love in a Nunnery (dr)
   John Milton. Artis Logicae Plenior Institutio (t)
   Sir William Temple. Observations upon the Netherlands (e)

                              1673

BIRTHS

John Oldmixon

WORKS
John Dryden. Amboyna (dr)
_____. Marriage a-la-Mode (dr)
John Milton. Of True Religion (t)
_____. Poems (pub)
Thomas Shadwell. Enchanted Island (dr)
_____. Epsom Wells (dr)
Sir William Temple. The Advancement of Trade in Ireland (e)
William Wycherley. The Gentleman Dancing-Master (dr)

1674

BIRTHS
Nicholas Rowe
Isaac Watts

DEATHS
Edward Hyde, Earl of Clarendon
Robert Herrick
John Milton

EVENTS
Drury Lane Theatre, London (blt)

WORKS
John Evelyn. Navigation and Commerce (e)
Thomas Flatman. Poems and Songs (pub)
Andrew Marvell. On Paradise Lost (po, pub)
John Milton. Paradise Lost, 2nd ed (po)
Anthony Wood. Historia et Antiquitates Univ. Oxon. (his)

1675

BIRTHS
William Somerville

EVENTS
The City Mercury (p, f)
Hospital of St. Mary of Bethlehem, London (f)

WORKS
Isaac Barrow. Archimedis Opera (t)
John Crowne. The Country Wit (dr)
Sir William Dugdale. The Baronage of England, to 1676 (his)
Nathaniel Lee. Nero (dr)
Thomas Otway. Alcibiades (dr)
Thomas Traherne. Christian Ethics (t)
William Wycherley. The Country Wife (dr)

1676

BIRTHS
John Philips

THE SEVENTEENTH CENTURY 79

DEATHS
  Sir Matthew Hale

WORKS
  John Dryden. Aureng-Zebe (dr)
  Sir George Etherege. The Man of Mode; or, Sir Fopling Flutter (dr)
  Nathaniel Lee. Gloriana (dr)
  _____. Sophonisba (dr)
  Thomas Otway. Don Carlos (dr, po)
  Izaak Walton. The Compleat Angler, 5th ed (t)

1677

DEATHS
  Isaac Barrow

EVENTS
  The London Monument (blt)

WORKS
  Aphra Behn. The Rover, to 1681 (dr)
  Gilbert Burnet. Memoires of the Duke of Hamilton (bio, nar)
  John Dryden. The State of Innocence, and Fall of Man (dr)
  Thomas D'Urfey. Madame Fickle (dr)
  Nathaniel Lee. The Rival Queens; or, The Death of Alexander the Great
        (dr)
  Thomas Otway. The Cheats of Scapin (dr)
  _____. Titus and Berenice (dr)
  William Wycherley. The Plain Dealer (dr)

1678

BIRTHS
  Henry St. John, Viscount Bolingbroke
  George Farquhar

DEATHS
  Richard Flecknoe
  Andrew Marvell

WORKS
  Robert Barclay. An Apology for the People Called Quakers (e)
  Aphra Behn. Oroonoko; or, The Royal Slave (n)
  John Bunyan. The Pilgrim's Progress, to 1679 (fic)
  Samuel Butler. Hudibras, Part III (po)
  Ralph Cudworth. The True Intellectual System of the Universe (t)
  John Dryden. All for Love; or, The World Well Lost (dr)
  Nathaniel Lee. Mithridates (dr)
  Thomas Otway. Friendship in Fashion (dr)
  Thomas Rymer. Edgar; or, The English Monarch (dr, po)
  _____. Tragedies of the Last Age Considered (e)
  Thomas Shadwell. Timon of Athens (dr)
  Henry Vaughan. Thalia Rediviva (po)
  Nathaniel Wanley. The Wonders of the Little World (t)

1679

BIRTHS
    Thomas Parnell

DEATHS
    Thomas Hobbes

WORKS
    Gilbert Burnet. History of the Reformation in England, vol I (his)
    John Dryden. Troilus and Cressida (dr)
    _____ and Nathaniel Lee. Oedipus (dr)
    John Wilmot, second Earl of Rochester. A Satyr Against Mankind (po)

                            1680

DEATHS
    Samuel Butler
    Joseph Glanvill
    John Wilmot, second Earl of Rochester

EVENTS
    Mercurius Librarius; or, A Faithful Account of All Books and Pamphlets
       (p, f)

WORKS
    Isaac Barrow. The Pope's Supremacy (t)
    John Bunyan. The Life and Death of Mr. Badman (fic)
    John Dryden. The Kind Keeper, or Mr. Limberham (dr)
    Thomas D'Urfey. The Virtuous Wife (dr)
    Thomas Hobbes. Behemoth; or, The Long Parliament (e, pub)
    Nathaniel Lee. Theodosius (dr)
    Sir Roger L'Estrange. Colloquies (trans)
    Thomas Otway. The Orphan (dr, po)
    John Wilmot, second Earl of Rochester. Poems on Several Occasions (pub)
    Wentworth Dillon, Earl of Roscommon. Ars Poetica (trans, po)
    Sir William Temple. Miscellanies, to 1701 (pub)

                            1681

EVENTS
    The Observator (p, f)

WORKS
    Gilbert Burnet. History of the Reformation in England, vol II (his)
    John Crowne. Thyestes (dr)
    John Dryden. Absalom and Achitophel (po)
    _____. The Spanish Fryar (dr)
    Joseph Glanvill. Saducismus Triumphatus (e)
    Nathaniel Lee. Lucius Junius Brutus (dr)
    Andrew Marvell. A Dialogue between the Soul and the Body (po, pub)
    _____. The Garden (po, pub)
    _____. Bermudas (po, pub)
    _____. Mourning (po, pub)
    _____. To His Coy Mistress (po, pub)
    John Oldham. Satire Against Virtue (po)
    _____. Satires Against Jesuits (po)
    Thomas Otway. The Soldier's Fortune (dr)

THE SEVENTEENTH CENTURY   81

                                    1682

DEATHS
    Sir Thomas Browne

WORKS
    Aphra Behn. The City Heiress (dr)
    John Bunyan. The Holy War (fic)
    Gilbert Burnet. The Life of Sir Matthew Hale (bio)
    John Dryden. Mac Flecknoe (po)
    _____. The Medal (po)
    _____. Religio Laici (po)
    _____ and Nathaniel Lee. The Duke of Guise (dr)
    John Milton. Brief History of Moscovia (pub)
    Thomas Otway. Venice Preserv'd (dr, po)
    Samuel Pordage. Azaria and Hushai (po)
    _____. The Medal Revers'd (po)
    Edward Ravenscroft. The London Cuckolds (dr)
    Elkanah Settle. Absalom Senior, or Achitophel Transpos'd (s)
    Thomas Shadwell. The Medal of John Bayes (s)
    Nahum Tate and John Dryden. Absalom and Achitophel, Part II (po)

                                    1683

BIRTHS
    Conyers Middleton
    Edward Young

DEATHS
    John Oldham
    Izaak Walton

WORKS
    John Chalkhill. Thealma and Clearchus (po, pub)
    John Crowne. City Politiques (dr)
    John Dryden and Nathaniel Lee. The Duke of Guise (dr, pub)
    Joseph Moxon. Mechanick Exercises, or the Doctrine of Handy-Works (ref)
    John Oldham. Poems and Translations (pub)

                                    1684

WORKS
    Thomas Burnet. The Second Theory of the Earth, to 1690 (fic)
    John Dryden. The History of the League (trans)
    Thomas Otway. The Atheist (dr)
    Wentworth Dillon, Earl of Roscommon. Essay on Translated Verse (po)

                                    1685

BIRTHS
    George Berkeley
    John Gay

DEATHS
    Thomas Otway
    Wentworth Dillon, fourth Earl of Roscommon

EVENTS
    James II, King of England, to 1688
    Fourth Shakespeare Folio (pub)

WORKS
    Richard Baxter. Paraphrase of the New Testament (trans)
    John Crowne. Sir Courtly Nice (dr)
    John Dryden. Albion and Albanius (dr)
    _____. Threnodia Augustalis (po)
    Thomas Ken. The Practice of Divine Love (t)
    Edward Stillingfleet. Origines Britannicae (t, his)
    Edmund Waller. Of Divine Love (po)

1686

BIRTHS
    William Law
    Allan Ramsay
    Thomas Tickell

DEATHS
    Sir William Dugdale

WORKS
    John Dryden. The Life of St. Francis Xavier (trans)
    _____. Ode to the Memory of Mrs. Anne Killigrew (po)
    John Ray. Historia Plantarum, to 1704 (t)
    George Savile. A Letter to a Dissenter upon Occasion of His Majesties Late Gracious Declaration of Indulgence (e)
    Edmund Waller. Of the Last Verses in the Book (po)
    _____. Poems Written upon Several Occasions (pub)

1687

BIRTHS
    William Stukeley

DEATHS
    Henry More
    Edmund Waller

EVENTS
    The Observator (p, c)

WORKS
    John Dryden. The Hind and the Panther (po)
    _____. Song for St. Cecelia's Day (po)
    Sir Isaac Newton. Philosophiae Naturalis Principia Methematica (t)
    Matthew Prior and Charles Montagu. The Hind and the Panther Transvers'd to the Story of the Country and City Mouse (s)
    Sir Charles Sedley. Bellamira (dr)
    Elkanah Settle. Reflections on Several of Mr. Dryden's Plays (e)
    Thomas Shadwell. Tenth Satire of Juvenal (s)

1688

THE SEVENTEENTH CENTURY   83

BIRTHS
  Alexander Pope
  Lewis Theobald

DEATHS
  John Bunyan
  Ralph Cudworth

WORKS
  John Dryden. Britannia Rediviva: a Poem on the Birth of the Prince (po)
  George Savile. The Anatomy of an Equivalent (e)
  _____. Character of a Trimmer (e)
  _____. A Lady's Gift, or Advice to a Daughter (e)
  Thomas Shadwell. Squire of Alsatia (dr)

                              1689

BIRTHS
  Lady Mary Wortley Montagu
  Samuel Richardson

DEATHS
  Aphra Behn
  William Chamberlayne

EVENTS
  William III, King of England, to 1702
  Mary II, Queen of England, to 1694
  Thomas Shadwell, Poet Laureate of England, to 1692
  The Advocates' Library, Edinburgh (f)
  The Tory Party (f)
  The Whig Party (f)

WORKS
  John Locke. A Letter Concerning Toleration (e)
  Andrew Marvell. Last Instructions to a Painter (po, pub)
  Matthew Prior. An Epistle to Fleetwood Shephard (po)
  John Selden. Table Talk (pub)
  Thomas Shadwell. Bury Fair (dr)
  William Sherlock. A Practical Discourse Concerning Death (t)

                              1690

BIRTHS
  Arthur Collins

EVENTS
  The Athenian Gazette (p, f)
  Oxford University Press (f)

WORKS
  Thomas Betterton. The Prophetess (dr)
  John Crowne. The English Frier (dr)
  John Dryden. Amphitryon, a Comedy (dr)
  _____. Don Sebastian (dr)
  William King. Dialogue concerning the Way to Modern Preferment (s)

Nathaniel Lee. The Massacre of Paris (dr)
John Locke. Essay concerning Human Understanding (e)
_____. A Second Letter concerning Toleration (e)
_____. Treatises of Government (t)
Sir William Petty. Political Arithmetic (t)

1691

BIRTHS
  Thomas Amory

DEATHS
  Richard Baxter
  Sir George Etherege
  George Fox
  Samuel Pordage

EVENTS
  Elkanah Settle, City Poet of London
  Gentleman's Journal (p, f)

WORKS
  John Dryden. King Arthur (dr)
  William King. State of the Protestants in Ireland under the Late King
          James's Government (e)
  John Wilson. Belphegor, or the Marriage of the Devil (dr)
  Anthony Wood. Athenae Oxonienses, to 1692 (ref)

1692

BIRTHS
  Joseph Butler.

DEATHS
  Nathaniel Lee
  Thomas Shadwell

EVENTS
  Nahum Tate, Poet Laureate of England, to 1715

WORKS
  William Congreve. Incognita (fic)
  John Dryden. Character of St. Evremont (e)
  _____. Cleomenes (dr)
  _____. Eleonora; a Panegyrical Poem to the Memory of the Coun-
          tess of Abingdon (po)
  Sir Roger L'Estrange. Aesop's Fables (trans)
  John Locke. A Third Letter concerning Toleration (e)
  Thomas Rymer. A Short View of Tragedy (e)
  William Sherlock. A Practical Discourse concerning a Future Judgment
          (t)
  Jonathan Swift. Ode to the Athenian Society (po)
  Sir William Temple. Of Ancient and Modern Learning (e)

1693

THE SEVENTEENTH CENTURY   85

BIRTHS
  Eliza Haywood
  George Lillo

WORKS
  William Congreve. The Old Bachelor (dr)
  John Dennis. The Impartial Critic (nar)
  John Dryden. The Satires of Juvenal (trans)
  John Locke. On Education (e)
  William Penn. Some Fruits of Solitude (ed)
  Sir Thomas Urquhart. The Third Book (trans, pub)

                            1694

BIRTHS
  Philip Dormer Stanhope, fourth Earl of Chesterfield
  Francis Hutcheson

EVENTS
  Gentleman's Journal (p, c)

WORKS
  William Congreve. The Double Dealer (dr)
  John Crowne. The Married Beau (dr)
  John Dryden. Love Triumphant (dr)
  George Fox. Journal (nar, pub)
  Thomas Southerne. The Fatal Marriage (dr)

                            1695

DEATHS
  Sir William Killigrew
  George Savile
  Henry Vaughan
  Anthony Wood

EVENTS
  The Bank of England (f)

WORKS
  William Congreve. Love for Love (dr)
  John Dryden. De Arte Graphica (trans)
  Thomas Ken. Manual of Prayers for Winchester Scholars (ed)
  John Locke. Reasonableness of Christianity (e)
  Thomas Southerne. Oroonoko (dr)

                            1696

BIRTHS
  Henry Home, Lord Kames

DEATHS
  John Wilson

EVENTS
  The Athenian Gazette (p, c)

WORKS
  John Aubrey. Miscellanies (fic)
  Richard Baxter. Reliquiae Baxterianae (bio)
  Colley Cibber. Love's Last Shift (dr)
  John Dryden. Life of Lucian (bio, e)
  _____. An Ode, on the Death of Mr. Henry Purcell (po)
  Nahum Tate and Nicholas Brady. The Psalmes of David in Metre (po, ed)

1697

BIRTHS
  Charles Macklin

DEATHS
  John Aubrey

EVENTS
  White's Chocolate-House, St. James's Street, London (op)

WORKS
  Edward Barnard and Humfry Wanley. Catalogi Librorum Manuscriptorum Angliae et Hiberniae (bibl, ref)
  William Congreve. The Mourning Bride (dr)
  William Dampier. Voyages (trav)
  Daniel Defoe. An Essay upon Projects (e)
  John Dryden. Alexander's Feast (po)
  _____. Virgil (trans)
  Sir John Vanbrugh. The Provok'd Wife (dr)
  _____. The Relapse, or Virtue in Danger (dr)

1698

BIRTHS
  William Warburton

EVENTS
  The Society for Promoting Christian Knowledge (f)
  Whitehall Palace (des)

WORKS
  Francis Atterbury. Discourse Occasion'd by the Death of Lady Cutts (e)
  Jeremy Collier. A Short View of the Immorality and Profaneness of the English Stage (e)
  John Dennis. The Usefulness of the Stage (e)
  Thomas D'Urfey. The Campaigners (dr)
  George Fox. A Collection of Epistles (pub)
  Edmund Ludlow. Memoirs, to 1699 (pub)
  Algernon Sidney. Discourses concerning Government (t, pub)
  Edward Ward. The London Spy, to 1709 (fic)

1699

BIRTHS
  Robert Blair
  John Dyer

THE SEVENTEENTH CENTURY							87

DEATHS
  Edward Stillingfleet
  Sir William Temple

WORKS
  Gilbert Burnet. Exposition of the Thirty-nine Articles (t)
  William Dampier. Voyages and Descriptions (trav)
  George Farquhar. Love and a Bottle (dr)
  Sir Samuel Garth. The Dispensary (po)
  William King. Dialogues of the Dead (s)
  Anthony Ashley Cooper, third Earl of Shaftesbury. Enquiry concerning
                                                            Virtue (t)

5 The Eighteenth Century

1700

BIRTHS
  James Thomson

DEATHS
  John Dryden

EVENTS
  The Kit-Kat Club (f)

WORKS
  Thomas Betterton. King Henry IV (dr)
  Thomas Brown. Amusements Serious and Comical (s)
  William Congreve. The Way of the World (dr)
  John Dryden. Fables, Ancient and Modern (ed, trans)
  George Farquhar. The Constant Couple, or a Trip to the Jubilee (dr)
  Francis Moore. Vox Stellarum, an Almanack for 1701, with Astrological Observations (ref)
  John Pomfret. The Choice (po)
  Matthew Prior. Carmen Saeculare (po)
  Nicholas Rowe. The Ambitious Step-mother (dr)
  Nahum Tate. Panacea, a Poem on Tea (po)

1701

DEATHS
  Sir Charles Sedley

WORKS
  John Arbuthnot. An Essay on the Usefulness of Mathematical Learning (e)
  Daniel Defoe. The True-Born Englishman (po)
  John Dennis. The Advancement and Reformation of Modern Poetry (e)
  George Farquhar. Sir Harry Wildair (dr)

THE EIGHTEENTH CENTURY   89

    John Norris. <u>An Essay towards the Theory of an Ideal and Intelligible World</u>, to 1704 (e)
    Charles Sackville. <u>To all you Ladies now at Land</u> (po)
    Sir Richard Steele. <u>The Christian Hero</u> (t)
    _____. <u>The Funeral</u> (dr)
    Jonathan Swift. <u>Discourse of the Contests and Dissensions in Athens and Rome</u> (t)
    Anne Finch, Countess of Winchelsea. <u>The Spleen</u> (po)

                              1702

BIRTHS
    Philip Doddridge

EVENTS
    Anne, Queen of England, to 1714
    <u>The Daily Courant</u> (p, f)

WORKS
    Abel Boyer. <u>History of William III</u> (his, bio)
    Edward Hyde, Earl of Clarendon. <u>The True Historical Narrative of the Rebellion and Civil Wars in England</u>, to 1704 (his)
    Daniel Defoe. <u>The Shortest Way with the Dissenters</u> (t)
    George Farquhar. <u>The Inconstant</u> (dr)
    _____. <u>The Twin Rivals</u> (dr)
    Archbishop William King. <u>De Origine Mali</u> (t)
    Sir Roger L'Estrange. <u>The Works of Josephus</u> (trans)
    Nicholas Rowe. <u>Tamerlane</u> (dr)

                              1703

BIRTHS
    Henry Brooke
    Robert Dodsley
    John Wesley

DEATHS
    John Crowne
    Samuel Pepys

WORKS
    William Dampier. <u>A Voyage to New Holland</u> (trav)
    Daniel Defoe. <u>Hymn to the Pillory</u> (po)
    Thomas Hearne. <u>Reliquiae Bodleianae</u> (his, e)
    Nicholas Rowe. <u>The Fair Penitent</u> (dr)
    Sir Richard Steele. <u>The Lying Lover</u> (dr)
    William Walsh. <u>The Golden Age Restored</u> (po)

                              1704

BIRTHS
    Soame Jenyns

DEATHS
    Sir Roger L'Estrange

John Locke

EVENTS
The Review of the Affairs of France (p, f)

WORKS
Joseph Addison. The Campaign (po)
John Dennis. The Grounds of Criticism in Poetry (e)
Daniel Defoe. Giving No Alms No Charity (e)
George Farquhar and Peter Motteaux. The Stage Coach (dr)
Sir Isaac Newton. Method of Fluxions (t)
_____. Optics (t)
Nicholas Rowe. The Biter (dr)
Thomas Rymer and Robert Sanderson. Foedera, Conventiones, et Cujus-cunque generis Acta Publica (ed)
Jonathan Swift. The Battle of the Books (s)
_____. A Tale of a Tub (s)
William Walsh. The Despairing Lover (po)
William Wycherley. Miscellany Poems (pub)

1705

BIRTHS
Stephen Duck
David Hartley
David Mallet

DEATHS
John Ray

EVENTS
Her Majesty's Theatre, Haymarket, London (op)

WORKS
Colley Cibber. The Careless Husband (dr)
John Dunton. The Life and Errors of John Dunton (auto)
Bernard Mandeville. The Grumbling Hive, or Knaves Turned Honest (po)
John Philips. Blenheim, a Poem (po)
_____. The Splendid Shilling (po)
Sir Richard Steele. The Tender Husband (dr)
Sir John Vanbrugh. The Confederacy (dr)
_____. The Country House (dr)
_____. The Mistake (dr)
William Walsh. Ode III, Book III [of Horace]. Imitated (po)
Edward Ward. Hudibras Redivivus, to 1707 (po)

1706

DEATHS
John Evelyn
Charles Sackville

WORKS
John Arbuthnot. A Sermon Preached to the People at the Mercat Cross, Edinburgh (e)
Daniel Defoe. The True Relation of the Apparition of One Mrs. Veal (nar)

THE EIGHTEENTH CENTURY   91

George Farquhar. The Recruiting Officer (dr)
George Fox. Gospel Truth (pub)
John Philips. Cerealia (po)
Nicholas Rowe. Ulysses (dr)
Edmund Smith. Phaedra and Hippolitus (trans)
Isaac Watts. Horae Lyricae (po)

                             1707

BIRTHS
  Henry Fielding
  Charles Wesley

DEATHS
  George Farquhar
  William Sherlock

WORKS
  George Farquhar. The Beaux' Stratagem (dr)
  John Philips. Ode to Henry St. John (po)
  Matthew Prior. Poems on Several Occasions (pub)
  Nicholas Rowe. Royal Convert (dr)
  Sir Hans Sloane. Voyage to the West Indies, to 1725 (trav)
  Isaac Watts. Hymns and Spiritual Songs (po)

                             1708

DEATHS
  William Walsh

WORKS
  Joseph Bingham. Origines Ecclesiasticae, or the Antiquities of the
       Christian Church (e)
  Jeremy Collier. Ecclesiastical History of Great Britain (his)
  John Gay. Wine (po)
  William King. The Art of Cookery (po)
  John Oldmixon. The British Empire in America (his)
  John Philips. Cyder (po)
  Jonathan Swift. Argument against Abolishing Christianity (t)
  _____. Letter concerning the Sacramental Test (t)

                             1709

BIRTHS
  John Cleland
  Samuel Johnson
  George Lyttelton

DEATHS
  John Philips

EVENTS
  Copyright Act
  The Tatler (p, f)

WORKS

92 CHRONOLOGICAL OUTLINE OF BRITISH LITERATURE

    Joseph Addison. Contributions to The Tatler, to 1711 (e)
    George Berkeley. Essay towards a New Theory of Vision (e)
    Susannah Centlivre. The Busybody (dr)
    Arthur Collins. The Peerage of England (ref, his)
    William King. Miscellanies in Prose and Verse (pub)
    _____. Useful Transactions in Philosophy (s)
    Ambrose Philips. Pastorals (po)
    Alexander Pope. Pastorals (po)
    Nicholas Rowe. The Works of William Shakespeare (ed)
    Sir Richard Steele. Contributions to The Tatler, to 1711 (e)
    Jonathan Swift. Baucis and Philemon (po)
    _____. Description of a City Shower (po)
    _____. Description of the Morning (po)

1710

BIRTHS
    Sarah Fielding
    Thomas Reid

DEATHS
    Thomas Betterton

EVENTS
    The Examiner (p, f)
    The Whig Examiner (p, f, c)

WORKS
    George Berkeley. Principles of Human Knowledge (e)
    John Leland. Leland's Itinerary, 9 vols (nar, trav, pub)
    Jonathan Swift. Journal to Stella, to 1713 (nar)

1711

BIRTHS
    David Hume

DEATHS
    Thomas Ken

EVENTS
    The Examiner (p, c)
    South Sea Company (f)
    The Spectator (p, f)
    The Tatler (p, c)

WORKS
    Joseph Addison. Contributions to The Spectator, to 1712, 1714 (e)
    Abel Boyer. The Political State of Great Britain, to 1729 (p)
    John Dennis. Reflections, Critical and Satirical (e)
    Alexander Pope. Essay on Criticism (po)
    Anthony Ashley Cooper, Earl of Shaftesbury. Characteristics of Men, Manners, Opinions, Times (t)
    Sir Richard Steele. Contributions to The Spectator, to 1712 (e)
    Jonathan Swift. The Conduct of the Allies (t)
    _____. Some Remarks on the Barrier Treaty (t)

THE EIGHTEENTH CENTURY   93

                                1712

BIRTHS
   Richard Glover
   Edward Moore

DEATHS
   William King

EVENTS
   The Spectator (p, c)

WORKS
   John Arbuthnot. The History of John Bull (s)
   Sir Richard Blackmore. The Creation (po)
   John Dennis. An Essay on the Genius and Writings of Shakespeare (e)
   William Diaper. Nereides: or, Sea-Eclogues (po)
   William King. Useful Miscellanies (pub)
   John Oldmixon. The Secret History of Europe, to 1715 (his)
   Alexander Pope. Messiah (po)
   _____. The Rape of the Lock, 1st version (po)
   Woodes Rogers. A Cruizing Voyage round the World (trav)
   Thomas Tickell. On the Prospect of Peace (po)

                                1713

BIRTHS
   Laurence Sterne

DEATHS
   Thomas Rymer
   Anthony Ashley Cooper, third Earl of Shaftesbury
   Thomas Sprat

EVENTS
   The Englishman (p, f)
   The Guardian (p, f, c)
   The Mercator (p, f)
   The Review of the Affairs of France (p, c)
   The Scriblerus Club (f)

WORKS
   Joseph Addison. Cato (dr)
   _____. Contributions to The Guardian (e)
   George Berkeley. Dialogues between Hylas and Philonous (e)
   John Gay. Rural Sports (po)
   Sir Matthew Hale. History of the Common Law of England (his, pub)
   Anthony Hamilton. Memoires de la Vie du Comte de Gramont (bio)
   Alexander Pope. Ode for Music on St. Cecelia's Day (po)
   _____. Windsor Forest (po)
   Jonathan Swift. Cadenus and Vanessa (po)
   _____. The Importance of the Guardian Considered (t)
   Anne Finch, Countess of Winchelsea. A Nocturnal Reverie (po)
   _____. To the Nightingale (po)
   Edward Young. The Last Day (po)

1714

BIRTHS
  James Burnett, Lord Monboddo
  William Shenstone
  George Whitefield

EVENTS
  George I, King of England, to 1727
  The Englishman (p, c)
  The Lover (p, f, c)
  The Mercator (p, c)
  New Theatre, Lincoln's Inn Fields (op)
  The Spectator (p, f, c)

WORKS
  Gilbert Burnet. History of the Reformation in England, vol III (his)
  Susannah Centlivre. The Wonder! a Woman Keeps a Secret (dr)
  John Gay. The Shepherd's Week (po)
  Narcissus Luttrell. A Brief Historicall Relation of State Affairs, 1678-1714 (his, e)
  Bernard Mandeville. The Fable of the Bees, or Private Vices, Publick Benefits (po)
  Alexander Pope. The Rape of the Lock, enl version (po)
  Nicholas Rowe. Jane Shore (dr)
  Sir Richard Steele. Apology for Himself and His Writings (e)
  _____. The Crisis (e)
  Jonathan Swift. The Public Spirit of the Whigs (t)

1715

BIRTHS
  Richard Graves
  William Whitehead

DEATHS
  Gilbert Burnet
  William Dampier
  Nahum Tate

EVENTS
  Nicholas Rowe, Poet Laureate of England, to 1718

WORKS
  Joseph Addison. The Drummer (dr)
  _____. The Freeholder, to 1716 (p)
  Colin Campbell. Vitruvius Brittanicus, vol I (ref)
  John Gay. What D'ye Call It (dr)
  John Leland. Collectanea (pub)
  Alexander Pope. The Iliad, to 1720 (trans, po)
  Nicholas Rowe. Lady Jane Grey (dr)
  Thomas Tickell. The Iliad, Book I (trans, po)
  Isaac Watts. Divine and Moral Songs for Children (po)

1716

THE EIGHTEENTH CENTURY   95

BIRTHS
  Thomas Gray

DEATHS
  William Wycherley

EVENTS
  Mercurius Politicus (p, f)
  The Vinegar Bible, to 1717 (pub)

WORKS
  Sir Thomas Browne. Christian Morals (e)
  John Gay. Trivia (po)
  Lady Mary Wortley Montagu. Court Poems by a Lady of Quality (pub)
  _____. Town Eclogues (po)

                                1717

BIRTHS
  David Garrick
  Horace Walpole

WORKS
  John Arbuthnot, John Gay, and Alexander Pope. Three Hours after Mar-
                                riage (dr)
  Henry St. John, Viscount Bolingbroke. Letter to Sir William Wyndham (e)
  Colin Campbell. Vitruvius Brittanicus, vol II (ref)
  William Law. Three Letters to the Bishop of Bangor, to 1719 (e)
  Thomas Parnell. Homer's Battle of the Frogs and Mice, with the Remarks
                       of Zoilus (s)
  Alexander Pope. Eloisa to Abelard (po)
  _____. Verses to the Memory of an Unfortunate Lady (po)
  _____. Works (pub)

                                1718

BIRTHS
  Hugh Blair

DEATHS
  Thomas Parnell
  William Penn
  Nicholas Rowe

EVENTS
  Lawrence Eusden, Poet Laureate of England, to 1730
  The Society of Antiquaries (f)
  The Theatre (p, f)

WORKS
  Susannah Centlivre. A Bold Stroke for a Wife (dr)
  Matthew Prior. Alma: or, the Progress of the Mind (po)
  _____. Poems on Several Occasions (pub)
  _____. Solomon on the Vanity of the World (po)

                                1719

BIRTHS
  Sir John Hawkins

DEATHS
  Joseph Addison
  Sir Samuel Garth

WORKS
  Joseph Addison. The Old Whig (p)
  John Aubrey. Perambulation of Surrey (e)
  Thomas Betterton. The Bondman (dr)
  Daniel Defoe. The Life and Adventures of Robinson Crusoe (n)
  _____. The Farther Adventures of Robinson Crusoe (n)
  Thomas D'Urfey. Wit and Mirth, or Pills To Purge Melancholy (po)
  Thomas Killigrew, the younger. Chit Chat (dr)
  Thomas Salmon. Collection of State Trials (ed)
  Isaac Watts. The Psalms of David Imitated (po)
  Edward Young. Busiris (dr)
  _____. Paraphrase of Job (po)

1720

BIRTHS
  Samuel Foote
  Richard Hurd
  Charlotte Lennox
  Gilbert White

DEATHS
  Anne Finch, Countess of Winchelsea

EVENTS
  Mercurius Politicus (p, c)
  The Theatre (p, c)

WORKS
  Arthur Collins. The Baronetage of England (ref, his)
  Daniel Defoe. Adventures of Captain Singleton (fic)
  _____. The Life and Adventures of Mr. Duncan Campbell (n)

1721

BIRTHS
  Mark Akenside
  William Collins
  William Robertson
  Tobias George Smollett

DEATHS
  Matthew Prior

WORKS
  Nathaniel Bailey. An English Dictionary (ref)
  Edward Hyde, Earl of Clarendon. The History of the Irish Rebellion and
                      Civil Wars in Ireland (his)
  Thomas Parnell. Poems (pub)

THE EIGHTEENTH CENTURY 97

Alexander Pope. Epistle to Addison (po)
Thomas Tickell. To the Earl of Warwick on the Death of Mr. Addison (po)
Edward Young. The Revenge (dr)

1722

BIRTHS
  Sir John Burgoyne
  Christopher Smart
  Joseph Warton

WORKS
  Abel Boyer. History of Queen Anne (his, bio)
  Daniel Defoe. The History and Remarkable Life of Colonel Jack (fic)
  _____. The Fortunes and Misfortunes of the Famous Moll Flanders (n)
  _____. A Journal of the Plague Year (nar, his, fic)
  Sir Richard Steele. The Conscious Lovers (dr)

1723

BIRTHS
  Sir William Blackstone
  Sir Joshua Reynolds
  Adam Smith

DEATHS
  Susannah Centlivre
  Thomas D'Urfey

WORKS
  William Law. Remarks on the Fable of the Bees (e)
  Matthew Prior. Down-Hall, a Ballad (pub)

1724

BIRTHS
  Christopher Anstey
  William Gilpin
  Frances Sheridan

DEATHS
  Elkanah Settle

WORKS
  Gilbert Burnet. The History of My Own Times, to 1734 (his)
  Daniel Defoe. Roxana, or the Fortunate Mistress (n)
  _____. Tour through the Whole Island of Great Britain, to 1727 (trav)
  David Mallet. WIlliam and Margaret (po)
  Memoirs of a Cavalier (fic, pub)
  John Oldmixon. Critical History of England (his)
  Allan Ramsay. The Evergreen (po, ed)
  _____. Tea-table Miscellany, to 1732 (ed)
  William Stukeley. Itinerarium Curiosum (his)
  Jonathan Swift. Drapier's Letters (s)

1725

WORKS
  Colin Campbell. Vitruvius Brittanicus, vol III (ref)
  Thomas Hearne. The Story of England, by Robert Mannyng of Brun (his, trans)
  Francis Hutcheson. An Inquiry into the Original of Our Ideas of Beauty and Virtue (e)
  Alexander Pope. The Odyssey, to 1726 (trans, po)
  _____. The Works of Shakespeare (ed)
  Allan Ramsay. The Gentle Shepherd (dr)
  Edward Young. The Universal Passion (s)

1726

BIRTHS
  Thomas Pennant

DEATHS
  Jeremy Collier
  Sir John Vanbrugh

EVENTS
  The Craftsman (p. f)

WORKS
  Joseph Butler. Fifteen Sermons (ser, pub)
  John Dyer. Grongar Hill (po)
  Francis Hutcheson. An Essay on the Nature and Conduct of the Passions and Affections (e)
  William Law. A Practical Treatise on Christian Perfection (t)
  Jonathan Swift. Gulliver's Travels (s)
  Lewis Theobald. Shakespeare Restored (e)
  James Thomson. Winter (po)

1727

BIRTHS
  Arthur Murphy
  John Wilkes

DEATHS
  Sir Isaac Newton

EVENTS
  George II, King of England, to 1760

WORKS
  Edward Dorrington. Adventures of Philip Quarll (n)
  John Gay. Fables, 1st series (po)
  John Oldmixon. Essay on Criticism (pub)
  Alexander Pope. Martinus Scriblerus. . .or the Art of Sinking in Poetry (e, s)
  _____, and Jonathan Swift. Miscellanies, I-II (pub)
  James Thomson. A Poem Sacred to the Memory of Sir Isaac Newton (po)

THE EIGHTEENTH CENTURY   99

　　　　——————. Summer (po)

                              1728

BIRTHS
　Robert Adam
　Robert Bage
　James Cook
　Thomas Warton the younger

WORKS
　Ephraim Chambers. Cyclopaedia (ref)
　John Gay. The Beggar's Opera (dr)
　Memoirs of Captain Carleton (fic)
　Alexander Pope. The Dunciad. In Three Books (s, po)
　——————— and Jonathan Swift. Miscellanies, III (pub)
　Richard Savage. The Bastard (po)
　James Thomson. Spring (po)
　Sir John Vanbrugh and Colley Cibber. The Provok'd Husband (dr)
　William Wycherley. Posthumous Works (pub)

                              1729

BIRTHS
　Edmund Burke
　John Cunningham
　John Moore
　Thomas Percy
　Clara Reeve

DEATHS
　Abel Boyer
　William Congreve
　Archbishop William King
　Sir Richard Steele

WORKS
　Robert Dodsley. Servitude, a Poem (po)
　John Gay. Polly (dr)
　William Law. A Serious Call to a Devout and Holy Life (e)
　Alexander Pope. The Dunciad Variorum (s, po)
　Robert Samber. The Sleeping Beauty (trans)
　Richard Savage. The Wanderer (po)
　Thomas Sherlock. The Tryal of the Witnesses of the Resurrection of
　　　　　　　　　　　　Jesus (t)
　Jonathan Swift. The Grand Question Debated (po)
　——————. A Modest Proposal (s)

                              1730

BIRTHS
　Oliver Goldsmith
　Thomas Tyrwhitt

EVENTS
　Colley Cibber, Poet Laureate of England, to 1757

The Grub Street Journal (p, f)

WORKS
   Henry St. John, Viscount Bolingbroke. Remarks on the History of Eng-
         land, to 1731 (his, e)
   Henry Fielding. The Tragedy of Tragedies, or Tom Thumb (dr)
   James Thomson. Autumn (po)
   _____. Hymn to the Seasons (po)
   _____. Sophonisba (dr)

                              1731

BIRTHS
   Charles Churchill
   William Cowper
   Erasmus Darwin

DEATHS
   Daniel Defoe
   Edward Ward

EVENTS
   The Gentleman's Magazine (p, f)

WORKS
   John Arbuthnot. An Essay concerning the Nature of Aliments (e)
   Ralph Cudworth. Treatise concerning Eternal and Immutable Morality (t)
   Samuel Johnson. Messiah (trans)
   William Law. The Case for Reason (e)
   George Lillo. The London Merchant, or the History of George Barnwell
         (dr)
   Alexander Pope. Epistle to the Earl of Burlington (po)
   Jonathan Swift. Directions to Servants (s)

                              1732

BIRTHS
   George Coleman the elder
   Richard Cumberland

DEATHS
   Francis Atterbury
   John Gay

EVENTS
   Covent Garden Theatre (op)
   The London Magazine (p, f)
   The Society of Dilettanti (f)

WORKS
   George Berkeley. Alciphron, or the Minute Philosopher (t)
   Daniel Neal. History of the Puritans (his)
   Alexander Pope and Jonathan Swift. Miscellanies, IV (pub)

                              1733

THE EIGHTEENTH CENTURY   101

BIRTHS
   Joseph Priestley

DEATHS
   Bernard Mandeville

WORKS
   John Arbuthnot. An Essay concerning the Effect of Air on Human
                     Bodies (e)
   George Berkeley. Theory of Vision (e)
   Alexander Pope. Epistle to Bathurst (po)
   _____. Essay on Man, I-III (po)
   _____. First Satire of the Second Book of Horace Imitated
                   (po)

                              1734

DEATHS
   John Dennis

WORKS
   John Arbuthnot. Know Thyself (po)
   George Berkeley. The Analyst (e)
   Henry Carey. Chrononhotonthologos (dr)
   _____. The Dragon of Wantley (dr)
   Alexander Pope. Epistle to Cobham (po)
   _____. Essay on Man, IV (po)
   Lewis Theobald. The Workes of Shakespeare (ed)
   James Thomson. Liberty, to 1736 (po)

                              1735

DEATHS
   John Arbuthnot

BIRTHS
   James Beattie

EVENTS
   The Sublime Society of Beef Steaks (f)
   Calves' Head Club (f)
   The Daily Courant (p, c)

WORKS
   George Berkeley. The Querist, to 1737 (e)
   Henry Brooke. Universal Beauty (po)
   Arthur Collins. The Peerage of England (ref, his)
   Henry St. John, Viscount Bolingbroke. A Dissertation upon Parties (e)
   Robert Dodsley. The Toyshop, a Dramatic Satire (dr)
   Samuel Johnson. Voyage to Abyssinia (trans, trav)
   George Lillo. The Christian Hero (dr)
   Alexander Pope. The Characters of Women, to a Lady (po)
   _____. Epistle to Dr. Arbuthnot (po)
   William Popple. The Double Deceit (dr)
   William Somerville. The Chase (po)
   Jonathan Swift. Works, 4 vols (pub)

1736

BIRTHS
   James Macpherson
   George Steevens

EVENTS
   The Craftsman (p, c)

WORKS
   Henry St. John, Viscount Bolingbroke. A Letter on the Spirit of Patri-
               otism (e)
   Joseph Butler. The Analogy of Religion, Natural and Revealed, to the
               Constitution and Course of Nature (t)
   Stephen Duck. The Thresher's Labour (po)
   Henry Fielding. Pasquin (dr)
   Sir Matthew Hale. Historia Placitorum Coronae (his, pub)
   George Lillo. Fatal Curiosity (dr)
   William Warburton. The Alliance between Church and State (e)

1737

BIRTHS
   Edward Gibbon
   Thomas Paine
   Richard Watson.

WORKS
   Alexander Cruden. Biblical Concordance (ref)
   Henry Fielding. The Historical Register for 1736 (dr)
   Richard Glover. The Athenaid (po)
   _____. Leonidas (po)
   Matthew Green. The Spleen (po)
   Alexander Pope. The First Epistle of the Second Book of Horace, to
               Augustus (po)
   William Warburton. The Divine Legation of Moses (e)

1738

BIRTHS
   John Wolcot ("Peter Pindar")

EVENTS
   The Grub Street Journal (p, c)

WORKS
   John Gay. Fables, 2nd ser (po, pub)
   Samuel Johnson. London (po)
   Alexander Pope. One Thousand Seven Hundred and Thirty-Eight (po)
   Jonathan Swift. A Complete Collection of Polite and Ingenious Conver-
               sation (s)
   James Thomson. Agamemnon (dr)

1739

BIRTHS

THE EIGHTEENTH CENTURY   103

   Hugh Kelly

DEATHS
   George Lillo

EVENTS
   The Champion (p, f)

WORKS
   Henry Brooke. Gustavus Vasa (dr)
   David Hume. Treatise on Human Nature, vols I-II (t)
   Samuel Johnson. A Compleat Vindication of the Licensers of the Stage
               (e)
   _____. Marmor Norfolciense: or, an Essay on the Ancient Pro-
               phetical Inscription (e)
   Jonathan Swift. Verses on the Death of Dr. Swift (po, pub)
   James Thomson. Edward and Eleanore (dr)

                               1740

BIRTHS
   Peter Beckford
   James Boswell
   Susannah Minifie Gunning

DEATHS
   Thomas Tickell

WORKS
   Francis Atterbury. Sermons (pub)
   Colley Cibber. An Apology for the Life of Mr. Colley Cibber, Comedian
               (auto)
   John Dyer. The Ruins of Rome (po)
   David Garrick. Lethe (dr)
   David Hume. Treatise on Human Nature, vol III (t)
   William Law. An Appeal to All That Doubt (e)
   George Lillo. Elmerick, or Justice Triumphant (dr, pub)
   Christopher Pitt. Aeneid (trans)
   Samuel Richardson. Pamela, vols I-II (n)
   William Somerville. Hobbinol (po)
   William Stukeley. Stonehenge (his)
   James Thomson and David Mallet. Alfred (po, dr)

                               1741

BIRTHS
   William Combe
   Edmund Malone
   Arthur Young

EVENTS
   The Champion (p, c)

WORKS
   John Arbuthnot and Alexander Pope. The Memoirs of Martinus Scriblerus
               (s)

Robert Dodsley. The Blind Beggar of Bethnal Green (dr)
Henry Fielding. Shamela (n, s)
David Garrick. The Lying Valet (dr)
David Hume. Essays Moral and Political, to 1742 (e)
Conyers Middleton. Life of Cicero (bio)
Alexander Pope. Works (pub)
Samuel Richardson. Pamela, vols III-IV (n)

1742

DEATHS
John Oldmixon
William Somerville

EVENTS
Ranelagh Gardens, Chelsea (op)

WORKS
William Collins. Persian Eclogues (po)
Henry Fielding. The History of the Adventures of Joseph Andrews (n)
Thomas Gray. On Adversity (po)
_____. On a Distant Prospect of Eton College (po)
_____. Spring (po)
_____. Sonnet on the Death of West (po)
Edmund Hoyle. Short Treatise on Whist (e)
Alexander Pope. The New Dunciad (po)
William Shenstone. The Schoolmistress (po)
William Somerville. Field Sports (po)
Charles Viner. Abridgment of Law and Equity, 23 vols, to 1753 (ref)
Edward Young. The Complaint, or Night Thoughts on Life, Death, and Immortality, to 1745 (po)

1743

BIRTHS
Hannah Cowley
William Paley

DEATHS
Henry Carey
Richard Savage

WORKS
Robert Blair. The Grave (po)
Henry Fielding. A Journey from This World to the Next (fic)
_____. The Life of Jonathan Wild the Great (n)
Alexander Pope. The Dunciad in Four Books (po, s)

1744

DEATHS
Alexander Pope
Lewis Theobald

EVENTS
The Female Spectator (p, f)

THE EIGHTEENTH CENTURY 105

WORKS
  Mark Akenside. Pleasures of Imagination (po)
  John Armstrong. The Art of Preserving Health (po)
  George Berkeley. Siris (e)
  Robert Dodsley. A Select Collection of Old Plays (ed)
  Sarah Fielding. The Adventures of David Simple (n)
  Samuel Johnson. Life of Mr. Richard Savage (bio, e)
  Thomas Osborne. Harleian Miscellany (e, ed)
  Jonathan Swift. Sermons (pub)
  Joseph Warton. The Enthusiast (po)

1745

BIRTHS
  Thomas Holcroft
  Henry Mackenzie
  Hannah More
  Lindley Murray
  John Nichols

DEATHS
  Jonathan Swift

EVENTS
  Hell-fire Club (f)

WORKS
  Philip Doddridge. The Rise and Progress of Religion in the Soul (t)
  Samuel Johnson. Miscellaneous Observations on the Tragedy of Macbeth (e)
  James Thomson. Tancred and Sigismunda (dr)
  Thomas Warton the younger. The Pleasures of Melancholy (po)

1746

DEATHS
  Robert Blair
  Francis Hutcheson
  Thomas Southerne

EVENTS
  The Female Spectator (p, c)

WORKS
  Mark Akenside. Hymn to the Naiads (po)
  Tobias George Smollett. The Tears of Scotland (po)
  Joseph Warton. Ode to Fancy (po)

1747

BIRTHS
  John O'Keefe

EVENTS
  The Parrot (p, f, c)

WORKS
   William Collins. Odes (po)
   John Cunningham. Love in a Mist (dr)
   Philip Doddridge. Some Remarkable Passages in the Life of Col. James
                     Gardiner (bio)
   David Garrick. Miss in Her Teens (dr)
   Hannah Glasse. The Art of Cookery Made Plain and Easy (e)
   Thomas Gray. Ode on the Death of a Favourite Cat (po)
   Benjamin Hoadly. The Suspicious Husband (dr)
   Samuel Johnson. Plan of an English Dictionary (e)
   Samuel Richardson. Clarissa Harlowe, to 1748 (n)
   William Warburton. The Works of Shakespeare (ed)

1748

BIRTHS
   Jeremy Bentham

DEATHS
   James Thomson
   Isaac Watts

WORKS
   John Cleland. Fanny Hill: Memoirs of a Woman of Pleasure, to 1749 (n)
   Robert Dodsley. A Collection of Poems by Several Hands, to 1758 (ed)
   David Hume. Enquiry concerning Human Understanding (e)
   Samuel Johnson. The Vision of Theodore, the Hermit of Teneriffe (e)
   Conyers Middleton. Free Inquiry into Miracles (e)
   Tobias George Smoblett. Roderick Random (n)
   James Thomson. The Castle of Indolence (po)

1749

BIRTHS
   Joseph Strutt

EVENTS
   The Monthly Review (p, f)

WORKS
   Henry St. John, Viscount Bolingbroke. The Idea of a Patriot King (e)
   _____. Some Reflections on the Present State of the Nation
                 (e)
   William Collins. Ode on the Popular Superstitions of the Highlands
                    (po)
   Henry Fielding. Tom Jones, a Foundling (n)
   David Hartley. Observations on Man, His Frame, Duty, and Expectations
                  (e)
   Richard Hurd. Ars Poetica (ed)
   _____. The Polite Arts: or, a Dissertation on Poetry, Painting,
                 and Music (e)
   Samuel Johnson. Irene (dr)
   _____. The Vanity of Human Wishes (po)
   James Thomson. Coriolanus (dr, pub)

THE EIGHTEENTH CENTURY   107

                                    1750

DEATHS
   Conyers Middleton

EVENTS
   The Jockey Club, Newmarket (f)

WORKS
   William Collins. Ode on the Music of the Grecian Theatre (po)
   Thomas Gray. Elegy in a Country Churchyard (po)
   Thomas Gurney. Brachygraphy (ref)
   Samuel Johnson. Rambler essays, to 1752 (e)
   George Savile. A Character of King Charles II (pub)
   William Whitehead. The Roman Father (dr)
   Christopher Wren the younger. Parentalia, or Memories of the Family of
                                   the Wrens (ed)

                                    1751

BIRTHS
   Thomas Sheraton
   Richard Brinsley Sheridan

DEATHS
   Henry St. John, Viscount Bolingbroke
   Philip Doddridge

WORKS
   John Cleland. Memoirs of a Coxcomb (n)
   Francis Coventry. History of Pompey the Little (s)
   Henry Fielding. Amelia (n)
   Eliza Haywood. The History of Betsy Thoughtless (n)
   David Hume. Enquiry concerning the Principles of Morals (e)
   Richard Hurd. Epistola ad Augustum (ed)
   Edward More. Gil Blas (n)
   Robert Paltock. The Life and Adventures of Peter Wilkins
   Tobias George Smollett. Peregrine Pickle (n)
   William Warburton. The Works of Pope (ed)

                                    1752

BIRTHS
   Frances Burney
   Thomas Chatterton
   Vicesimus Knox
   Joseph Ritson

DEATHS
   Joseph Butler

EVENTS
   New Style (ns) Calendar
   The Adventurer (p, f)
   Covent Garden Journal (p, f)
   The Public Advertiser (p, f)

WORKS
  Henry St. John, Viscount Bolingbroke. Letters on the Study and Use of
                History (e, pub)
  _____. Philosophical Works (pub)
  William Dodd. The Beauties of Shakespeare (e)
  Samuel Foote. Taste (dr)
  David Hume. Political Discourses (e)
  Soame Jenyns. Poems (pub)
  William Law. The Way to Divine Knowledge (e)
  Charlotte Lennox. The Female Quixote, or the Adventures of Arabella
                (n)
  Christopher Smart. Poems (pub)

1753

BIRTHS
  George Ellis
  Elizabeth Inchbald
  William Roscoe
  Dugald Stewart

DEATHS
  George Berkeley

EVENTS
  The British Museum (op)
  The World (p, f)

WORKS
  Richard Glover. Boadicea (dr)
  Eliza Haywood. The History of Jemmy and Jenny Jessamy (n)
  William Hogarth. The Analysis of Beauty (e)
  Samuel Johnson. Contributions to The Adventurer, to 1754 (e)
  Edward Moore. The Gamester (n)
  Samuel Richardson. Sir Charles Grandison, to 1754 (n)
  Christopher Smart. Hilliad (s)
  Tobias George Smollett. Ferdinand Count Fathom (n)

1754

BIRTHS
  George Crabbe

DEATHS
  Henry Fielding

EVENTS
  The Adventurer (p, c)
  The Select Society, Edinburgh (f)

WORKS
  Thomas Chippendale. The Gentleman and Cabinet-Maker's Director (ref)
  Patrick Delany. Observations upon Lord Orrery's Remarks on the Life
                and Writings of Dr. Jonathan Swift (e)
  Thomas Gray. The Progress of Poesy (po)
  David Hume. History of Great Britain, to 1761 (his)

THE EIGHTEENTH CENTURY 109

Thomas Warton the younger. Observations on the Faerie Queene of Spenser (e)
William Whitehead. Creusa (dr)

1755

EVENTS
The Edinburgh Review (p, f, c)
The Monitor (p, f)

WORKS
Thomas Amory. Memoirs of Several Ladies of Great Britain (fic)
Francis Hutcheson. System of Moral Philosophy (e, pub)
Samuel Johnson. A Dictionary of the English Language (ref)
William Shenstone. Pastoral Ballad (po)
Tobias George Smollett. Don Quixote (trans)

1756

BIRTHS
William Gifford
William Godwin
Gilbert Wakefield

DEATHS
Stephen Duck
Eliza Haywood

EVENTS
The Con-test (p, f)
The Critical Review (p, f)
The Literary Magazine, or Universal Review (p, f)
The Test (p, f)
The World (p, c)

WORKS
Thomas Amory. The Life of John Buncle, Esq., to 1766 (fic)
Edmund Burke. A Philosophical Inquiry into the Sublime and Beautiful (e)
_____. A Vindication of Natural Society (e)
Alban Butler. The Lives of the Principal Saints (bio)
Arthur Collins. The Peerage of England (ref, his)
John Home. Douglas (dr)
Samuel Johnson. Christian Morals (ed)
Richard Price. Review of the Principal Questions in Morals (e)
Joseph Warton. Essay on the Genius and Writings of Pope, I (e)

1757

BIRTHS
William Blake

DEATHS
Colley Cibber
David Hartley
Edward More

EVENTS
  William Whitehead, Poet Laureate of England, to 1785
  Strawberry Hill Press, London (f)

WORKS
  Mark Akenside. The Pleasures of the Imagination (po)
  John Dyer. The Fleece (po)
  Thomas Gray. The Bard (po)
  David Hume. The Natural History of Religion (e)
  Soame Jenyns. A Free Enquiry into the Nature and Origin of Evil (e)
  Tobias George Smollett. The Reprisal (dr)
  William Stukeley. De Situ Britanniae (ed)

                             1758

DEATHS
  John Dyer
  Allan Ramsay

EVENTS
  The Annual Register (pub)

WORKS
  Elizabeth Carter. Epictetus (trans)
  Robert Dodsley. Cleone (dr)
  Oliver Goldsmith. The Memoirs of a Protestant, Condemned to the Galleys of France for His Religion (trans)
  Samuel Johnson. Contributions to The Idler, to 1760 (e)
  Tobias George Smollett. Peregrine Pickle, rev ed (n)
  Horace Walpole. Catalogue of Royal and Noble Authors (bibl)

                             1759

BIRTHS
  William Beckford
  Robert Burns
  Richard Porson
  Mary Wollstonecraft

DEATHS
  William Collins

EVENTS
  The British Magazine (p, f)
  The Public Ledger (p, f)

WORKS
  Edward Hyde, Earl of Clarendon. Life of Clarendon (auto)
  Oliver Goldsmith. The Bee (p, e)
  _____. A City Night-Piece (po)
  _____. Elegy on Mrs. Mary Blaize (po)
  _____. Enquiry into the Present State of Polite Learning (e)
  Samuel Johnson. Rassalas, Prince of Abyssinia (fic)
  Charles Macklin. Love a la Mode (dr)
  William Robertson. History of Scotland during the Reigns of Queen Mary and of James VI (his)

THE EIGHTEENTH CENTURY   111

  Adam Smith. Theory of the Moral Sentiments (e)
  James Townley. High Life below Stairs (dr)
  Edward Young. Conjectures on Original Composition (e)

                              1760

DEATHS
  Arthur Collins

EVENTS
  George III, King of England, to 1820

WORKS
  The Ballad of Chevy Chase (po, pub)
  Guiseppe Marc' Antonio Baretti. An Italian and English Dictionary (ref)
  Henry Brooke. The Fool of Quality, to 1772 (n)
  George Coleman the elder. Polly Honeycombe (dr)
  Samuel Foote. The Minor (dr)
  Oliver Goldsmith. Adventures of a Strolling Player (nar)
  Edmund Hoyle. The Laws of Whist (e)
  Charles Johnstone. Chrysal, or the Adventures of a Guinea, to 1765 (s)
  George Lyttelton. Dialogues of the Dead, fic, e)
  James Macpherson. Fragments of Ancient Poetry Collected in the High-
                lands of Scotland, and Translated from the Gaelic
                or Erse Language (po)
  Arthur Murphy. The Way To Keep Him (dr)
  Tobias George Smollett. Sir Launcelot Greaves, to 1762 (n)
  Laurence Sterne. The Life and Opinions of Tristram Shandy, I-II (n)
  _____. Sermons of Mr. Yorick, to 1769 (e)

                              1761

DEATHS
  William Law
  Samuel Richardson

EVENTS
  The Whiteboys (Society), Ireland (f)

WORKS
  Charles Churchill. The Rosciad (po)
  George Coleman the elder. The Jealous Wife (dr)
  Edward Gibbon. Essai sur l'etude de la Litterature (e)
  Oliver Goldsmith. The Life of Voltaire (bio)
  Thomas Gray. The Descent of Odin (po)
  _____. The Fatal Sisters (po)
  Henry Home, Lord Kames. Introduction to the Art of Thinking (e)
  Frances Sheridan. Memoirs of Miss Sidney Bidulph, to 1767 (n)
  Laurence Sterne. The Life and Opinions of Tristram Shandy, III-VI, to
                1762 (n)

                              1762

BIRTHS
  Joanna Baillie
  Sir Samuel Egerton Brydges

George Coleman the younger
Helen Maria Williams

DEATHS
Lady Mary Wortley Montagu

EVENTS
The Briton (p, f)
The North Briton (p, f)

WORKS
Isaac Bickerstaffe. Love in a Village (dr)
Sir William Blackstone. Law Tracts (t)
William Falconer. The Shipwreck (po)
Sarah Fielding. Apologia (trans)
_____. Memorabilia (trans)
Samuel Foote. The Liar (dr)
Oliver Goldsmith. The Citizen of the World (s)
_____. Life of Richard Nash, Esq. (bio)
Henry Home, Lord Kames. Elements of Criticism (e)
Richard Hurd. Letters on Chivalry and Romance (nar, e)
James Macpherson. Fingal, an Ancient Epic Poem, in Six Books (po)
John Boyle, fifth Earl of Orrery. Remarks on the Life and Writings of Dr. Jonathan Swift (e)
John Hall Stevenson. Crazy Tales (fic)
Horace Walpole. Anecdotes of Painting in England, to 1780 (ed)
William Warburton. Doctrine of Grace (e)
William Whitehead. The School for Lovers (dr)
Edward Young. Resignation (po)

1763

BIRTHS
William Cobbett
Samuel Rogers

DEATHS
William Shenstone

WORKS
Charles Churchill. The Author (po)
_____. The Duellist (po)
_____. The Epistle to William Hogarth (po)
_____. The Prophecy of Famine (po)
Richard Glover. Medea (dr)
Susannah Minifie Gunning and Margaret Minifie. The Histories of Lady Frances S----- and Lady Caroline S----- (n)
James Macpherson. Temora (po)
Lady Mary Wortley Montagu. Turkish Letters (pub)
Thomas Percy. Five Pieces of Runic Poetry (ed)
Frances Sheridan. The Discovery (dr)
Christopher Smart. Poems (pub)
_____. A Song to David (po)

1764

BIRTHS
　Sir John Barrow
　Thomas Morton
　Ann Radcliffe

DEATHS
　Charles Churchill
　Robert Dodsley

EVENTS
　The Literary Club (f)

WORKS
　Charles Churchill. The Candidate (po)
　_____. The Times (po)
　Thomas Chatterton. Apostate Will (po)
　Samuel Foote. The Mayor of Garret (dr)
　Oliver Goldsmith. History of England in a Series of Letters (his, e)
　_____. The Traveller (po)
　Arthur Murphy. Three Weeks after Marriage (dr)
　John Newton. An Authentic Narrative (auto)
　Thomas Reid. Inquiry into the Human Mind (e)
　Horace Walpole. The Castle of Otranto (n)
　Thomas Warton the younger. The Oxford Sausage (po, ed)

1765

BIRTHS
　Sir James Mackintosh

DEATHS
　David Mallet
　William Stukeley
　Edward Young

EVENTS
　Sadler's Wells Theatre (op)

WORKS
　Isaac Bickerstaffe. The Maid of the Mill (dr)
　Sir William Blackstone. Commentaries on the Laws of England, to 1769 (t)
　Samuel Johnson. The Works of William Shakespeare (ed)
　Thomas Percy. Reliques of Ancient English Poetry (ed)
　Laurence Sterne. The Life and Adventures of Tristram Shandy, VII-VIII (n)
　_____. A Sentimental Journey through France and Italy, by Mr. Yorick (nar)
　Horace Walpole. Catalogue of Engravers in England (ref)

1766

BIRTHS
　Isaac Disraeli
　Thomas Malthus
　John Thomas Smith

DEATHS
  Frances Sheridan

EVENTS
  Tattersall's Auction-Room for Horses, Hyde Park Corner, London (op)

WORKS
  Christopher Anstey. The New Bath Guide (po, s)
  George Coleman the elder and David Garrick. The Clandestine Marriage (dr)
  James Cook. Sailing Directions (ref)
  John Cunningham. Poems, Chiefly Pastoral (pub)
  Oliver Goldsmith. The Vicar of Wakefield (n)
  Samuel Johnson. Considerations on the Corn Laws (e)
  Tobias George Smollett. Travels in France and Italy (nar, trav)
  George Steevens. Twenty of the Plays of Shakespeare, 4 vols (ed)
  Jonathan Swift. Journals to Stella, 1, 41-65 (pub)
  Thomas Tyrwhitt. Observations upon Shakespeare (e)

1767

BIRTHS
  Maria Edgeworth

WORKS
  George Lyttelton. The History of the Life of Henry the Second, to 1771 (bio)
  Joseph Priestley. The History and Present State of Electricity (e)
  Frances Sheridan. History of Nourjahad (pub)
  Laurence Sterne. The Life and Opinions of Tristram Shandy, IX (n)
  Sir James Steuart. Inquiry into the Principles of Political Economy (e)

1768

DEATHS
  Sarah Fielding
  Laurence Sterne

EVENTS
  The Royal Academy of Arts (f)

WORKS
  Isaac Bickerstaffe. Lionel and Clarissa (dr)
  _____. The Padlock (dr)
  James Boswell. An Account of Corsica (trav, his)
  Edward Capell. The Works of William Shakespeare (ed)
  Encyclopaedia Britannica, 1st ed, to 1771 (ref, pub)
  Oliver Goldsmith. The Good-Natur'd Man (dr)
  Susannah Gunning. Barford Abbey (n)
  Hugh Kelly. False Decency (dr)
  Thomas Pennant. British Zoology, to 1770 (t)
  Joseph Priestley. Essay on the First Principles of Government (e)
  Jonathan Swift. Journal to Stella, 2-40 (pub)
  Abraham Tucker. The Light of Nature Pursu'd, to 1778 (t)
  Horace Walpole. Historic Doubts on Richard III (his)

THE EIGHTEENTH CENTURY   115

_____. The Mysterious Mother (dr)

                               1769

BIRTHS
  John Frere
  Amelia Opie

DEATHS
  Edmund Hoyle

EVENTS
  The Morning Chronicle, London (p, f)

WORKS
  Isaac Bickerstaffe. The Hypocrite (dr)
  James Boswell. Essays in Favour of the Brave Corsicans (e)
  Edmund Burke. Observations on "The Present State of the Nation" (e)
  Thomas Chatterton. Elinoure and Juga (po)
  Richard Cumberland. The Brothers (dr)
  Oliver Goldsmith. A History of Rome (his)
  James Granger. Biographical History of England (bio, his)
  Charlotte Lennox. The Sister (dr)
  Elizabeth Montagu. Essays on the Writings and Genius of Shakespeare
                     (e)
  Sir Joshua Reynolds. Fifteen Discourses, to 1790 (e)
  William Robertson. History of Charles V (his)
  Tobias George Smollett. The Adventures of an Atom (s)

                               1770

BIRTHS
  James Hogg
  William Wordsworth

DEATHS
  Mark Akenside
  Thomas Chatterton
  George Whitefield

EVENTS
  The Mirror (p, f, c)

WORKS
  Edmund Burke. Thoughts on the Present Discontents (e)
  Thomas Chatterton. The Revenge (dr)
  Hannah Glasse. The Compleat Confectioner (e)
  _____. The Servant's Directory, or House-keeper's Companion
                (e, ref)
  Oliver Goldsmith. The Deserted Village (po)
  _____. Life of Henry, Lord Bolingbroke (bio)
  _____. Life of Thomas Parnell (bio)
  Samuel Johnson. The False Alarm (e)
  Hugh Kelly. A Word for the Wise (dr)

                               1771

BIRTHS
  John Lingard
  Robert Owen
  Sir Walter Scott

DEATHS
  Thomas Gray
  Christopher Smart
  Tobias George Smollett

WORKS
  James Beattie. The Minstrel, Book I (po)
  Richard Cumberland. The West Indian (dr)
  Samuel Foote. The Maid of Bath (dr)
  Oliver Goldsmith. The History of England (his)
  Samuel Johnson. Thoughts Respecting Falkland's Islands (e)
  Lady Anne Lindsay. Auld Robin Gray (po)
  Henry Mackenzie. The Man of Feeling (n)
  Thomas Pennant. Tour in Scotland (trav)
  Tobias George Smollett. The Expedition of Humphry Clinker (n)
  John Wesley. Works, to 1774 (pub)

1772

BIRTHS
  Henry Francis Cary
  Samuel Taylor Coleridge
  Pierce Egan
  David Ricardo

EVENTS
  The Morning Post, London (p, f)

WORKS
  Mark Akenside. Poems (pub)
  Samuel Foote. The Nabob (dr)
  David Garrick. The Irish Widow (dr)
  Richard Graves. The Spiritual Quixote (n)
  Richard Hurd. An Introduction to the Study of Prophecies concerning
           the Christian Church (e)
  The Letters of Junius (e, pub)

1773

BIRTHS
  James Mill

DEATHS
  Philip Dormer Stanhope, fourth Earl of Chesterfield
  John Cunningham
  George Lyttelton

EVENTS
  Unitarian Church (f)

WORKS

THE EIGHTEENTH CENTURY 117

Robert Fergusson. Poems (pub)
Oliver Goldsmith. The Grumbler (dr)
──────────────. She Stoops to Conquer (dr)
Hugh Kelly. The School for Wives (dr)
Henry Mackenzie. The Man of the World (n)
──────────────. The Prince of Tunis (dr)
James Burnett, Lord Monboddo. Of the Origin and Progress of Language, to 1792 (e)
Hannah More. The Search after Happiness (dr)
George Steevens. The Complete Works of William Shakespeare, 11 vols, to 1780 (ed)
The Works in Architecture of Robert and James Adam, to,1799, 1822 (ed)

1774

BIRTHS
 Robert Southey

DEATHS
 Oliver Goldsmith

WORKS
 James Beattie. The Minstrel, Book II (po)
 William Bowyer. Origin of Printing (his)
 Henry Brooke. Juliet Grenville (n)
 Sir John Burgoyne. The Maid of the Oaks (dr)
 Edmund Burke. On American Taxation (sp)
 Hester Mulso Chapone. Letters on the Improvement of the Mind (e)
 Philip Dormer Stanhope, fourth Earl of Chesterfield. Letters, to his natural son (pub)
 Oliver Goldsmith. History of Greece (his)
 ──────────────. Retaliation (po)
 The House of Commons' Journals (p, pub)
 Samuel Johnson. The Patriot (e)
 The Newgate Calendar, or Malefactors' Bloody Register (pub)
 Thomas Pennant. A Tour in Scotland and Voyage to the Hebrides, to 1776 (trav)
 Joseph Priestley. Examination of Scottish Philosophy (e)
 Thomas Warton the younger. History of Poetry, to 1781 (e, his)
 Arthur Young. Political Arithmetic (e)

1775

BIRTHS
 Jane Austen
 Charles Lamb
 Walter Savage Landor
 Matthew Gregory Lewis
 Mary Martha Sherwood
 Joseph White

WORKS
 Edmund Burke. On Conciliation with the Colonies (sp)
 David Garrick. Bon Ton, or High Life above Stairs (dr)
 Samuel Johnson. Journey to the Western Islands of Scotland (trav)
 ──────────────. Taxation No Tyranny (e)

James Macpherson. History of Great Britain, from the Restoration till
    the Accession of George I (his)
Richard Brinsley Sheridan. The Duenna (dr)
_____. The Rivals (dr)
_____. St. Patrick's Day (dr)
Augustus Montague Toplady. Rock of Ages, cleft for me (po)
Thomas Tyrwhitt. The Canterbury Tales, to 1778 (ed)

1776

BIRTHS
    Thomas Dibdin
    Jane Porter

DEATHS
    David Hume

WORKS
    Jeremy Bentham. Fragment on Government (e)
    Charles Burney. A History of Music, to 1789 (his)
    William Combe. The Diaboliad (po)
    Hannah Cowley. The Runaway (dr)
    Samuel Foote. A Trip to Calais (dr)
    Edward Gibbon. The Decline and Fall of the Roman Empire, vol I (his)
    Oliver Goldsmith. The Haunch of Venison (po, pub)
    Richard Graves. Columella, the Distressed Anchoret (n)
    Sir John Hawkins. History of Music, 5 vols (his)
    Soame Jenyns. View of the Internal Evidence of the Christian Religion
        (e)
    Thomas Paine. Common Sense (e)
    _____. The Crises, to 1783 (e)
    Adam Smith. An Enquiry into the Nature and Causes of the Wealth of
        Nations (e)
    Richard Watson. Apology for Christianity (e)

1777

BIRTHS
    Thomas Campbell
    Henry Hallam

DEATHS
    Samuel Foote
    Hugh Kelly

WORKS
    Hugh Blair. Sermons, to 1801 (pub)
    Edmund Burke. Letter to the Sheriffs of Bristol (e)
    Thomas Chatterton. Poems, Supposed To Have Been Written at Bristol, by
        Thomas Rowley (po, pub)
    James Cook. A Voyage towards the South Pole and round the World in
        1772-1775 (nar, trav)
    Encyclopaedia Britannica, 2nd ed, to 1784 (ref, pub)
    David Hume. On the Origin of Government (e, pub)
    Henry Mackenzie. Julia de Roubigne (n)
    Hannah More. Percy (dr)

THE EIGHTEENTH CENTURY   119

   Maurice Morgann. Essay on the Dramatic Character of Sir John Falstaff
                    (e)
   Clara Reeve. The Champion of Virtue, a Gothic Story (n)
   William Robertson. History of America (his)
   Richard Brinsley Sheridan. The School for Scandal (dr)
   _____. A Trip to Scarborough (dr)
   Joseph Strutt. Chronicle of England, to 1778 (his)
   Thomas Warton the younger. The Crusade (po)
   _____. Poems (pub)

                              1778

BIRTHS
   Henry Peter Brougham
   William Hazlitt

WORKS
   Edmund Burke. Two Letters. . .to Gentlemen in the City of Bristol (e)
   Frances Burney. Evelina (n)
   George Coleman the elder. The Dramatic Works of Beaumont and Fletcher
                             (ed)
   George Ellis. Poetical Tales of Sir Gregory Gander (po)
   Vicesimus Knox. Essays Moral and Literary (e)
   Edmund Malone. Attempt to Ascertain the Order in which the Plays of
                  Shakespeare Were Written (e)
   Thomas Middleton. The Witch (dr, pub)
   John O'Keefe. Tony Lumpkin in Town (dr)
   Thomas Pennant. A Tour in Wales, to 1781 (trav)

                              1779

BIRTHS
   Henry Thomas Cockburn
   Mountstuart Elphinstone
   John Galt
   Thomas Moore
   Horatio Smith

DEATHS
   James Cook
   David Garrick
   William Warburton

WORKS
   William Cowper. Olney Hymns (po)
   Edward Gibbon. A Vindication of Some Passages in the Fifteenth and Six-
                  teenth Chapters [of the Decline and Fall] (e)
   David Hume. Dialogues concerning Natural Religion (e, pub)
   Samuel Johnson. Lives of the Poets, to 1781 (bio, e)
   James Burnett, Lord Monboddo. Antient Metaphysics, to 1779 (e)
   John Moore. A View of Society and Manners in France, Switzerland, and
               Germany (trav)
   Hannah More. The Fatal Falsehood (dr)
   Richard Brinsley Sheridan. The Critic (dr)

                              1780

BIRTHS
  John Wilson Croker
  George Croly
  James Morier
  Frances Trollope

DEATHS
  Sir William Blackstone

EVENTS
  The Morning Herald, London (p, f)
  Newgate Prison (des)

WORKS
  Edmund Burke. Speech at the Guildhall, in Bristol (sp)
  Hannah Cowley. The Belle's Stratagem (dr)
  Susannah Gunning. Count de Poland (n)
  Thomas Holcroft. Alwyn, or the Gentleman Comedian (n)
  John Nichols. Bibliotheca Topographica, to 1790 (ref)
  _____. Collection of Miscellaneous Poems, to 1782 (ed)
  _____. Royal Wills (ed)
  Arthur Young. Tour in Ireland (trav)

                    1781

BIRTHS
  Ebenezer Elliott
  Robert Landor

WORKS
  Robert Bage. Mount Henneth (n)
  Peter Beckford. Thoughts upon Hare and Fox Hunting (e)
  George Crabbe. The Library (po)
  Edward Gibbon. The Decline and Fall of the Roman Empire, vols II-III
             (his)
  Charles Macklin. The Man of the World (dr)
  John Nichols. Biographical Anecdotes of Hogarth (ed)
  Thomas Pennant. History of Quadrupeds (t)

                    1782

BIRTHS
  Susan Ferrier
  Charles Maturin
  Ann Taylor

DEATHS
  Henry Home, Lord Kames

WORKS
  Edmund Burke. To a Peer of Ireland on the Penal Laws (e)
  Frances Burney. Cecelia (n)
  William Cowper. Charity (po)
  _____. Conversation (po)
  _____. Expostulation (po)
  _____. Hope (po)

THE EIGHTEENTH CENTURY   121

    _____. John Gilpin (po)
    _____. The Progress of Error (po)
    _____. Retirement (po)
    _____. Table Talk (po)
    _____. Truth (po)
William Gilpin. The Wye and South Wales (trav)
John O'Keefe. The Castle of Andalusia (dr)
Thomas Pennant. The Journey from Chester to London (trav)
Peter Pindar. Lyric Odes to the Royal Academicians, to 1785 (po)
Joseph Warton. Essay on the Genius and Writings of Pope, II (e)

1783

BIRTHS
  Lady Sydney Morgan
  Jane Taylor

DEATHS
  Henry Brooke

EVENTS
  Tyburn Gallows (c)

WORKS
  William Beckford. Dreams, Waking Thoughts, and Incidents (trav)
  Hugh Blair. Lectures on Rhetoric and Belles Lettres (e)
  William Blake. Poetical Sketches (po)
  Edward Capell. Notes and Various Readings to Shakespeare (e)
  George Coleman the elder. Horace. The Art of Poetry (trans)
  Hannah Cowley. A Bold Stroke for a Husband (dr)
  George Crabbe. The Village (po)
  Thomas Day. The History of Sandford and Merton, to 1789 (fic)
  Samuel Johnson. On the Death of Dr. Levett (po)
  Joseph Ritson. A Select Collection of English Songs (ed)

1784

BIRTHS
  Allan Cunningham
  Leigh Hunt
  James Knowles
  William Yarrell

DEATHS
  Samuel Johnson

EVENTS
  The Esto Perpetua Club (f)

WORKS
  Robert Bage. Barham Downs (n)
  James Cook and Thomas King. A Voyage to the Pacific Ocean in 1776-1780
       (nar, trav)
  William Cowper. The Task (po)
  Criticisms on the Rolliad (s)
  George Bubb Dodington. Diary (pub)

William Whitehead. Plays and Poems (pub)

1785

BIRTHS
Thomas DeQuincey
Lady Caroline Lamb
Thomas Love Peacock
John Wilson

DEATHS
Richard Glover
William Whitehead

EVENTS
Thomas Warton, Poet Laureate of England, to 1790
The Daily Universal Register (p, f)
The London Magazine (p, c)
The Lounger (p, f)

WORKS
James Boswell. Journal of a Tour to the Hebrides, with Samuel Johnson (trav, nar)
Edmund Burke. On the Nabob of Arcot's Private Debts (sp)
Richard Graves. Eugenius, or Anecdotes of the Golden Vale (n)
Francis Grose. Classical Dictionary of the Vulgar Tongue (ref)
Elizabeth Inchbald. I'll Tell You What (dr)
Samuel Johnson. Prayers and Meditations (pub)
William Mitford. History of Greece, to 1810 (his)
William Paley. Moral and Political Philosophy (e)
Peter Pindar. The Louisiad (po, s)
Clara Reeve. The Progress of Romance through Times, Centuries, and Manners (e)
Thomas Reid. Intellectual Powers (e)

1786

BIRTHS
John Poole

DEATHS
Thomas Tyrwhitt

EVENTS
The Lounger (p, c)
The Microcosm (p, f)
Sir William Jones' Indo-European language hypothesis

WORKS
William Beckford. Vathek, An Arabian Tale (n)
Sir John Burgoyne. The Heiress (dr)
Robert Burns. Poems, Chiefly in the Scottish Dialect (pub)
Gawin Douglas. King Hart (po, pub)
John Moore. Zeluco (n)
Peter Pindar. Bozzy and Piozzi (s)
Hester Lynch Thrale Piozzi. Anecdotes of the Late Samuel Johnson (bio, (ed)

THE EIGHTEENTH CENTURY   123

    Sarah Trimmer. Fabulous Histories (or, The History of the Robbins)
               (fic)

                            1787

BIRTHS
  Mary Mitford
  Richard Whately

DEATHS
  Soame Jenyns

EVENTS
  The Microcosm (p, c)

WORKS
  Robert Bage. The Fair Syrian (n)
  Jeremy Bentham. Defence of Usury (e)
  Robert Burns. Poems (pub)
  George Coleman the younger. Inkle and Yarico (dr)
  Sir John Hawkins. Life of Samuel Johnson (bio)
  James Johnson. Scots Musical Museum, to 1803 (po, ed)

                            1788

BIRTHS
  George Gordon, Lord Byron
  Theodore Hook
  Sir Francis Palgrave

DEATHS
  Thomas Amory
  Charles Wesley

EVENTS
  The Daily Universal Register (p, c)
  The Linnean Society (f)
  The Times, London (p, f)

WORKS
  Robert Bage. James Wallace (n)
  William Crowe. Lewesdon Hill (po)
  Encyclopaedia Britannica, 3rd ed, to 1797 (pub)
  Edward Gibbon. The Decline and Fall of the Roman Empire, vols IV-VI
               (his)
  George Hepplewhite. The Cabinet Maker and Upholsterer's Guide (ref,
               pub)
  James Hurdis. The Village Curate and Other Poems (pub)
  Samuel Johnson. Sermons, to 1789 (pub)
  Hannah More. Thoughts on the Importance of the Manners of the Great
        (e)
  Richard Porson. Letters to Archdeacon Travis, to 1789 (e)
  Thomas Reid. Active Powers (e)
  Gilbert Wakefield. Georgics (ed)
  William Whitehead. Poems (pub)

1789

BIRTHS
  John Payne Collier
  Michael Scott
  Sir James Stephen

DEATHS
  John Cleland
  Sir John Hawkins

WORKS
  Francis Atterbury. Miscellaneous Works, to 1798 (pub)
  Jeremy Bentham. Introduction to the Principles of Morals and Legislation (e)
  William Blake. The Book of Thel (po)
  Richard Cumberland. Arundel (n)
  Erasmus Darwin. The Botanic Garden: The Loves of the Plants (po)
  William Gilpin. The Lakes (trav)
  Vicesimus Knox. Elegant Extracts (ed)
  Gilbert White. Natural History and Antiquities of Selborne (his)

1790

BIRTHS
  Nassau Senior
  Thomas Smith

DEATHS
  Adam Smith
  Thomas Warton the younger

EVENTS
  Henry James Pye, Poet Laureate of England, to 1813

WORKS
  Joanna Baillie. Fugitive Verses (po)
  James Bruce. Travels to Discover the Source of the Nile (trav)
  Edmund Burke. Reflections on the Revolution in France (e)
  Richard Graves. Plexippus, or the Aspiring Plebeian (n)
  Edmund Malone. The Works of Shakespeare (ed)
  William Paley. Horae Paulinae (e)
  Ann Radcliffe. A Sicilian Romance (n)
  Helen Maria Williams. Letters on the French Revolution (e)

1791

BIRTHS
  Henry Milman
  Patrick Tytler

DEATHS
  John Wesley

WORKS
  William Blake. The French Revolution (po)

THE EIGHTEENTH CENTURY 125

James Boswell. Life of Samuel Johnson, LL.D. (bio, nar)
Edmund Burke. An Appeal from the New to the Old Whigs (e)
_____. A Letter. . .to a Member of the National Assembly (e)
_____. Thoughts on French Affairs (e)
Robert Burns. Tam O'Shanter (po)
William Cowper. Yardley Oak (po)
Erasmus Darwin. The Botanic Garden: The Economy of Vegetation (po)
Isaac Disraeli. Curiosities of Literature, to 1793 (nar)
William Gilpin. Forest Scenery (trav)
Elizabeth Inchbald. A Simple Story (n)
Sir James Mackintosh. Vindiciae Gallicae (e)
John O'Keefe. Wild Oats (dr)
Thomas Paine. The Rights of Man, Part I (e)
Ann Radcliffe. An Italian Romance (n)
_____. Romance of the Forest (n)
William Robertson. Disquisition concerning the Knowledge Which the Ancients Had of India (e)
Thomas Sheraton. The Cabinet-Maker and Upholsterer's Drawing Book (ref)

1792

BIRTHS
  Sir Archibald Alison
  John Keble
  Frederick Marryat
  Lord John Russell
  Percy Bysshe Shelley
  Edward Trelawny

DEATHS
  Robert Adam
  Sir John Burgoyne
  Sir Joshua Reynolds

EVENTS
  The Observer (p, f)
  The Pantheon, Oxford Street, London (des)

WORKS
  Robert Bage. Man As He Is (n)
  Edmund Burke. To Sir Hercules Langrishe (e)
  Thomas Holcroft. Anna St. Ives (n)
  _____. The Road to Ruin (dr)
  Thomas Paine. The Rights of Man, Part II (e)
  Samuel Rogers. The Pleasures of Memory (po)
  John Spalding. Memorials of the Troubles in Scotland and England from 1624 to 1645 (pub)
  Dugald Stewart. Elements of the Philosophy of the Human Mind, to 1827 (e)
  Mary Wollstonecraft. Vindication of the Rights of Woman (e)
  Arthur Young. Travels in France (trav)

1793

BIRTHS
  John Clare

DEATHS
  William Robertson
  Gilbert White

WORKS
  William Blake. America (po)
  _____. The Marriage of Heaven and Hell (po)
  _____. Visions of the Daughters of Albion (po)
  Edmund Burke. Remarks on the Policy of the Allies (e)
  William Godwin. Enquiry concerning Political Justice (e)
  Susannah Gunning. Memoirs of Mary (n)
  Thomas Paine. The Age of Reason (e)
  Dugald Stewart. Outlines of Moral Philosophy (e)
  William Wordsworth. Descriptive Sketches (po)
  _____. An Evening Walk (po)

1794

BIRTHS
  William Carleton
  George Grote
  John Lockhart
  William Whewell

DEATHS
  George Coleman the elder
  Edward Gibbon

EVENTS
  The English Opera House, London (op)
  The Morning Advertiser, London (p, f)

WORKS
  William Blake. The Book of Ahania (po)
  _____. The Book of Urizen (po)
  _____. Europe (po)
  _____. Songs of Innocence and Songs of Experience (po)
  Samuel Taylor Coleridge and Robert Southey. The Fall of Robespierre (dr)
  Erasmus Darwin. Zoonomia, or the Laws of Organic Life, to 1796 (e)
  William Gifford. The Baviad (po)
  William Godwin. The Adventures of Caleb Williams (n)
  Thomas Holcroft. Hugh Trevor (n)
  Thomas Mathias. Pursuits of Literature (s)
  John Moore. Journal during a Residence in France (nar)
  William Paley. Evidences of Christianity (e)
  Ann Radcliffe. Mysteries of Udolpho (n)
  Gilbert Wakefield. Horace (ed)
  Helen Maria Williams. Letters containing a Sketch of the Politics of France, 2 vols (e)

1795

BIRTHS
  Thomas Arnold
  Thomas Carlyle

THE EIGHTEENTH CENTURY   127

   George Darley
   Julius Hare
   John Keats

DEATHS
   James Boswell

EVENTS
   St. Paul's, Covent Garden, London (des)

WORKS
   William Blake. The Book of Los (po)
   _____. The Song of Los (po)
   Edmund Burke. Letters on a Regicide Peace (e)
   Samuel Taylor Coleridge. The Eolian Harp (po)
   Richard Cumberland. Henry (n)
   Charles Dibdin. History of the Stage (his)
   William Gifford. The Maeviad (po)
   Matthew Gregory Lewis. Ambrosio (n)
   Lindley Murray. English Grammar (ref)
   John Nichols. The History and Antiquities of Leicester, to 1815 (his)
   Thomas Paine. The Age of Reason (e)
   William Roscoe. Life of Lorenzo de Medici (bio)
   Gilbert White. A Naturalist's Calendar, Extracted from the Papers of
                  the Late Rev. Gilbert White (pub)
   William Wordsworth. The Borderers, to 1796 (dr)
   Andrew Wyntoun. Orygynale Cronykil (po, his, pub)

                              1796

BIRTHS
   Hartley Coleridge
   Richard Ford
   James Planche
   Agnes Strickland

DEATHS
   Robert Burns
   James Macpherson
   Thomas Reid

EVENTS
   The Watchman (p, f, c)

WORKS
   Robert Bage. Hermsprong, or Man As He Is Not (n)
   Edmund Burke. Letter to a Noble Lord (e)
   Frances Burney. Camilla (n)
   George Coleman the younger. The Iron Chest (dr)
   Maria Edgeworth. The Parents' Assistant, to 1801 (fic)
   Edward Gibbon. Memoirs (nar, pub)
   _____. Miscellaneous Works, to 1815 (pub)
   Elizabeth Inchbald. Nature and Art (n)
   Matthew Gregory Lewis. The Monk (n)
   John Moore. Edward (n)
   Thomas Morton. The Way To Get Married (dr)

    Sir Walter Scott. Der Wilde Jager (trans)
    _____. Lenore (trans)
    Joseph Strutt. Dresses and Habits of the English People, to 1799 (his)
    Gilbert Wakefield. Lucretius (ed)
    Richard Watson. Apology for the Bible (e)

                             1797

BIRTHS
    Emily Eden
    Samuel Lover
    Sir Charles Lyell
    William Motherwell
    Mary Shelley
    Connop Thirlwall

DEATHS
    Edmund Burke
    Charles Maklin
    Mary Wollstonecraft
    Horace Walpole
    John Wilkes

EVENTS
    Strawberry Hill Press, London (c)

WORKS
    William Blake. Vala (po)
    George Coleman the younger. The Heir-at-Law (dr)
    Erasmus Darwin. A Plan for the Conduct of Female Education (e)
    Thomas Morton. A Cure for Heartache (dr)
    Richard Porson. Hecuba (dr, ed)
    Ann Radcliffe. The Italian (n)
    Gilbert Wakefield. Diatribe Extemporalis (t)
    William Wilberforce. A Practical View of the Prevailing Religious System of Professed Christians (e)
    William Wordsworth. The Old Cumberland Beggar (po)

                             1798

BIRTHS
    Thomas Croker

DEATHS
    Thomas Pennant

EVENTS
    The Anti-Jacobin (p, c)
    The Public Advertiser (p, c)

WORKS
    Joanna Baillie. Plays on the Passions (dr)
    Samuel Taylor Coleridge. France, an Ode (po)
    _____. The Rime of the Ancient Mariner (po)
    Maria Edgeworth and Richard Lovell Edgeworth. Practical Education (e)
    William Gilpin. The West of England and the Isle of Wight (trav)

THE EIGHTEENTH CENTURY   129

   William Godwin. Memoirs of the Author of a "Vindication of the Rights
               of Women" (nar, bio)
   Charles Lamb. The Old Familiar Faces (po)
   _____. The Tale of Rosamund Gray and Old Blind Margaret (n)
   Walter Savage Landor. Gebir (po)
   Matthew Gregory Lewis. The Castle Spectre (n)
   Thomas Malthus. An Essay on the Principle of Population, 1st ed (e)
   Thomas Morton. Speed the Plough (dr)
   Richard Porson. Orestes (dr, ed)
   George Vancouver. Voyage of Discovery to the North Pacific (trav, pub)
   Horace Walpole. Collected Works (pub)
   Helen Maria Williams. A Tour in Switzerland, 2 vols (trav)
   William Wordsworth. Lines Composed a Few Miles above Tintern Abbey (po)
   _____. The Ruined Cottage (po)
   _____ and Samuel Taylor Coleridge. Lyrical Ballads (po)

                                 1799

BIRTHS
   Catherine Gore
   Thomas Hood
   George James

DEATHS
   James Burnett, Lord Monboddo

WORKS
   Robert Burns. Holy Willie's Prayer (po, pub)
   _____. The Jolly Beggars (po, pub)
   Thomas Campbell. The Pleasures of Hope (po)
   Samuel Taylor Coleridge. Piccolomini (trans)
   William Cowper. The Castaway (po)
   William Godwin. St. Leon (n)
   Kelly's Post Office London Directory (pub)
   Lindley Murray. English Reader (ref)
   Mungo Park. Travels in the Interior of Africa (trav)
   Richard Porson. Phoenissae (dr, ed)
   Sir Walter Scott. Goetz von Berlichingen (trans)
   Richard Brinsley Sheridan. Pizarro (dr)
   Sharon Turner. History of the Anglo-Saxons, from the Earliest Period
               to the Norman Conquest, to 1805 (his)
   William Wordsworth. The Fountain (po)
   _____. Lucy Gray, or Solitude (po)
   _____. The Prelude, to 1805 (po)

6 *The Nineteenth Century*

1800

BIRTHS
  Kenelm Digby
  Thomas Babington Macaulay
  Edward Pusey
  Sir Henry Taylor
  Charles Wells

DEATHS
  Hugh Blair
  William Cowper
  Susannah Minifie Gunning
  George Steevens
  Joseph Warton

WORKS
  Robert Bloomfield. The Farmer Boy (po)
  Samuel Taylor Coleridge. The Death of Wallenstein (trans)
  Maria Edgeworth. Castle Rackrent (n)
  William Gilpin. The Highlands (trav)
  John Moore. Mordaunt (n)
  Dugald Stewart. Lectures on Political Economy (e)
  William Wordsworth. Michael (po)

1801

BIRTHS
  Jane Carlyle
  William Barnes
  Abraham Hayward
  John Henry Newman

DEATHS
  Robert Bage

THE NINETEENTH CENTURY   131

    Gilbert Wakefield

WORKS
    Maria Edgeworth. Belinda (n)
    _____. Early Lessons (fic)
    _____. Moral Tales (fic)
    Encylopaedia Britannica, 4th ed, to 1810 (ref, pub)
    Thomas Moore. Poetical Works (pub)
    John Nichols. The Works of Jonathan Swift, 19 vols (ed)
    Richard Porson. Medea (dr, ed)
    Robert Southey. Thalaba the Destroyer (po)
    Joseph Strutt. Sports and Pastimes of the People of England (his)
    Helen Maria Williams. Sketches on the State of Manners and Opinions in
                         the French Republic, 3 vols (nar, e)

                                    1802

BIRTHS
    Robert Chambers
    Harriet Martineau
    Hugh Miller

DEATHS
    Erasmus Darwin
    John Moore
    Joseph Strutt

EVENTS
    Cobbett's Political Register (p, f)
    Madam Tussaud's Wax Museum, London (op)

WORKS
    Samuel Taylor Coleridge. Dejection: an Ode (po)
    John Debrett. Peerage of England, Scotland, and Ireland, containing an
                  Account of All the Peers (ref)
    Thomas Dibdin. Introduction to the Knowledge of Rare and Valuable Edi-
                   tions of the Greek and Latin Classics (ref, bibl)
    Charles Lamb. John Woodvil (dr)
    William Paley. Natural Theology (e)
    Joseph Ritson. Bibliographia Poetica (bibl)
    Sir Walter Scott. Minstrelsy of the Scottish Border (po, ed)
    Thomas Sheraton. The Cabinet Dictionary, to 1803 (ref)
    Mary Martha Sherwood. Susan Gray (fic)
    Dugald Stewart. Account of the Life and Writings of Thomas Reid (bio,
                    e)
    William Wordsworth. My heart leaps up when I behold (po)
    _____. Ode: Intimations of Immortality, to 1804 (po)
    _____. Resolution and Independence (po)

                                    1803

BIRTHS
    Thomas Lovell Beddoes
    George Borrow
    Edward G.E. Bulwer-Lytton
    Gerald Griffin

Richard Horne
  Douglas Jerrold
  William Thoms

DEATHS
  James Beattie
  Joseph Ritson

WORKS
  George Coleman the younger. John Bull (dr)
  William Godwin. Life of Chaucer (e, bio)
  Charles Lamb. Hester (po)
  Joseph Lancaster. Improvements in Education (e)
  Thomas Malthus. An Essay on the Principles of Population, 2nd ed (e)
  Jane Porter. Thaddeus of Warsaw (n)

1804

BIRTHS
  Benjamin Disraeli
  Rowland Warburton
  Charles Whitehead

DEATHS
  William Gilpin
  Richard Graves
  Charlotte Lennox
  Joseph Priestley

EVENTS
  Ranelagh Gardens, Chelsea (c)

WORKS
  John Wilson Croker. An Intercepted Letter from Canton (s)
  Maria Edgeworth. Popular Tales (fic)
  Lindley Murray. English Spelling Book (ref)
  Amelia Opie. Adeline Mowbray (n)
  Thomas Sheraton. Cabinet-Maker, Upholsterer and General Artist's Encyclopaedia (ref)
  Ann Taylor and Jane Taylor. Original Poems for Infant Minds (ed)
  William Wordsworth. I wandered lonely as a cloud (po)
  _____. Ode to Duty (po)
  _____. She was a phantom of delight (po)

1805

BIRTHS
  Sarah Flower Adams
  William Harrison Ainsworth
  James Martineau
  John Maurice
  Philip Stanhope
  Robert Smith Surtees

DEATHS
  Christopher Anstey

Arthur Murphy
William Paley

EVENTS
  Newdigate Prize for English Verse, Oxford (f)

WORKS
  Peter Beckford. Familiar Letters from Italy (e)
  Sir Samuel Egerton Brydges. Censura Literaria, to 1809, 1815 (bibl)
  Henry Francis Cary. Inferno, to 1806 (trans)
  George Ellis. Specimens of Early English Romances in Metre (ed)
  William Roscoe. Life and Pontificate of Leo the Tenth (bio, his)
  Sir Walter Scott. The Lay of the Last Minstrel (po)
  Robert Southey. Madoc (po)
  William Wordsworth. The Solitary Reaper (po)
  _____. Vaudracour and Julia (po)

                    1806

BIRTHS
  Elizabeth Barrett Browning
  Charles Lever
  Sir George Lewis
  John Stuart Mill

DEATHS
  Thomas Sheraton

WORKS
  Lucy Hutchinson. The Memoirs of the Life of Colonel Hutchinson (bio,
          his, pub; re: John Hutchinson)
  Elizabeth Inchbald. The British Theatre, to 1809 (dr, ed)
  Charles Lamb. Mr. H---- (dr)
  John Lingard. The Antiquities of the Anglo-Saxon Church (his)
  Lady Sydney Morgan. The Wild Irish Girl (n)
  Amelia Opie. Simple Tales (fic)
  Ann Taylor and Jane Taylor. Rhymes for the Nursery (pub)

                    1807

BIRTHS
  John Kemble
  Robert Montgomery
  Frederick Tennyson
  Richard Trench
  Samuel Warren

DEATHS
  Clara Reeve

WORKS
  George Gordon, Lord Byron. Hours of Idleness (po)
  George Crabbe. The Parish Register (po)
  _____. Sir Eustace Grey (po)
  James Hogg. The Mountain Bard (po)
  Charles Lamb and Mary Lamb. Tales from Shakespeare (fic)

Charles Maturin. The Fatal Revenge, or the Family of Montorio (n)
Anna Maria Porter. The Hungarian Brothers (n)
William Roscoe. The Butterfly's Ball and the Grasshopper's Feast (po)
Sydney Smith. The Letters of Peter Plymley, to 1808 (e)
Robert Southey. Letters of Espriella (e)
_____. Palmerin of England (trans)

1808

BIRTHS
James Ferrier
Charles Merivale

DEATHS
Richard Hurd
Richard Porson

EVENTS
Covent Garden Theatre, London (des)
The Examiner (p, f)

WORKS
John Jamieson. Etymological Dictionary of the Scottish Language (ref)
Charles Lamb. The Adventures of Ulysses (fic)
_____. Specimens of English Dramatic Poets Contemporary with Shakespeare, with Notes (ed)
Charles Maturin. The Wild Irish Boy (n)
Sir Walter Scott. The Life of John Dryden (bio)
_____. Marmion, a Tale of Flodden Field (po)
_____. The Works of Dryden (ed)
Robert Southey. Chronicle of the Cid (trans)

1809

BIRTHS
John Hill Burton
Charles Darwin
Edward Fitzgerald
William Gladstone
Frances Kemble
Alexander William Kinglake
Alfred Lord Tennyson

DEATHS
Hannah Cowley
Thomas Holcroft
Thomas Paine

EVENTS
The Friend (p, f)
The Quarterly Review (p, f)

WORKS
George Gordon, Lord Byron. English Bards and Scotch Reviewers (po)
Thomas Campbell. Gertrude of Wyoming (po)
Cobbett's Complete Collection of State Trials, to 1826 (ed, pub)

THE NINETEENTH CENTURY   135

>   William Combe. Dr. Syntax in Search of the Picturesque (po)
>   Thomas Dibdin. Bibliomania (fic)
>   Charles Lamb and Mary Lamb. Mrs. Leicester's School (fic)
>   Hannah More. Coelebs in Search of a Wife (n)
>   Legh Richmond. The Dairyman's Daughter (t, fic)
>   William Wordsworth. Concerning the Relations of Great Britain, Spain,
>   and Portugal (e)

                                    1810

BIRTHS
  Robert Curzon
  Sir Samuel Ferguson
  Elizabeth Gaskell
  Martin Tupper
  Thomas Wright

WORKS
  Joanna Baillie. The Family Legend (dr)
  Sir Samuel Egerton Brydges. The British Bibliographer, to 1814 (bibl)
  George Crabbe. The Borough (po)
  James Hogg. The Forest Minstrel (po)
  Jane Porter. The Scottish Chiefs (n)
  Samuel Rogers. Columbus (po)
  Sir Walter Scott. The Lady of the Lake (po)
  Percy Bysshe Shelley. St. Irvyne (fic)
  _____ and Elizabeth Shelley. Original Poetry by Victor
                        and Cazire (pub)
  Robert Southey. The Curse of Kehama (po)
  _____. History of Brazil, to 1819 (his)
  Ann Taylor and Jane Taylor. Hymns for Infant Minds (pub)
  William Wordsworth. A Description of the Scenery of the Lakes in the
                      North of England (e)

                                    1811

BIRTHS
  Alfred Domett
  John Morton
  William Thackeray

DEATHS
  Peter Beckford
  Richard Cumberland
  Thomas Percy

EVENTS
  George, Prince of Wales, Regent of England, to 1820

WORKS
  Jane Austen. Sense and Sensibility (n)
  Charles Lamb. On the Genius and Character of Hogarth (e)
  _____. The Tragedies of Shakespeare (e)
  Charles Maturin. The Milesian Chief (n)

1812

BIRTHS
  Robert Browning
  Charles Dickens
  John Forster
  Geraldine Jewsbury
  Edward Lear
  Henry Mayhew
  Augustus Pugin
  Samuel Smiles

DEATHS
  Isaac Bickerstaffe
  Edmund Malone

EVENTS
  Drury Lane Theatre, London (blt)

WORKS
  George Gordon, Lord Byron. Childe Harold's Pilgrimage, I-II (po)
  Isaac Disraeli. Calamities of Authors, to 1813 (nar)
  Maria Edgeworth. The Absentee (n)
  Pierce Egan. Boxiana; or Sketches of Antient and Modern Pugilism, to 1813, 1815-1819 (nar, his)
  Walter Savage Landor. Count Julian (po, dr)
  James Morier. A Journey through Persia in 1808 and 1809 (trav)
  John Nichols. Literary Anecdotes of the Eighteenth Century, 9 vols, to 1815 (bio, ed)
  Horatio Smith and James Smith. Rejected Addresses (s)
  William Tennant. Anster Fair (po, s)
  John Wilson. The Isle of Palms (po)

1813

BIRTHS
  Sir Arthur Helps
  David Livingstone
  Mark Pattison
  Sir William Smith
  William Torrens

EVENTS
  Robert Southey, Poet Laureate of England, to 1843

WORKS
  John Aubrey. Lives of Eminent Persons (bio, pub)
  Jane Austen. Pride and Prejudice (n)
  George Gordon, Lord Byron. The Bride of Abydos (po)
  _____. The Giaour (po)
  Samuel Taylor Coleridge. Osorio (dr)
  James Hogg. The Queen's Wake (po)
  John Keats. Imitation of Spenser (po)
  Thomas Moore. The Twopenny Post Bag (po)
  Robert Owen. A New View of Society (e)
  Sir Walter Scott. The Bridal of Triermain (po)

THE NINETEENTH CENTURY 137

_____. Rokeby (po)
Horatio Smith and James Smith. Horace in London (s)
Robert Southey. The Life of Nelson (bio)
Edward Thurlow. Poems on Several Occasions (pub)

1814

BIRTHS
  John Colenso
  Aubrey DeVere
  Joseph LeFanu
  Charles Reade
  Ellen Wood

EVENTS
  The New Monthly Magazine (p, f)
  Regent's Park, London (op)
  The Thatched House Club, St. James's Street, London (des)

WORKS
  Jane Austen. Mansfield Park (n)
  Sir Samuel Egerton Brydges. Restitua: or, Titles, Extracts, and Characters of Old Books in English Literature, to 1816 (bibl)
  Frances Burney. The Wanderer (n)
  George Gordon, Lord Byron. The Corsair (po)
  _____. Lara (po)
  Henry Francis Cary. Paradiso (trans)
  _____. Purgatorio (trans)
  Isaac Disraeli. Quarrels of Authors (nar)
  John Keats. To Byron (po)
  Lady Sydney Morgan. O'Donnel (n)
  Samuel Rogers. Jacqueline (po)
  Sir Walter Scott. Waverley (n)
  _____. The Works of Swift (ed)
  Robert Southey. Roderick, the Last of the Goths (po)
  William Wordsworth. The Excursion (po)
  _____. Laodamia (po)

1815

BIRTHS
  Richard William Church
  Henry Huth
  Sir Thomas Erskine May
  Arthur Stanley
  Anthony Trollope

DEATHS
  George Ellis

WORKS
  Jane Austen. Emma (n)
  George Gordon, Lord Byron. Hebrew Melodies (po)
  James Hogg. Pilgrims of the Sun (po)
  James Knowles. Caius Gracchus (dr)

Sir James Mackintosh. On the State of France (e)
Thomas Malthus. An Inquiry into the Nature and Progress of Rent (e)
Henry Milman. Fazio (dr)
Sir Walter Scott. Guy Mannering (n)
_____. The Lord of the Isles (po)
Mary Martha Sherwood. Little Henry and His Bearer (fic)
Jane Taylor. Display, a Tale for Young People (fic)
Helen Maria Williams. A Narrative of the Events in France from March 1815)nar)

1816

BIRTHS
Philip James Bailey
Charlotte Bronte
Sir Charles Duffy
Sir Theodore Martin
Sir Daniel Wilson

DEATHS
Richard Brinsley Sheridan
Richard Watson

WORKS
Jeremy Bentham. Chrestomathia (e)
George Gordon, Lord Byron. Childe Harold's Pilgrimage, III (po)
_____. The Dream (po)
_____. Parisina (po)
_____. The Siege of Corinth (po)
Samuel Taylor Coleridge. Kubla Khan (po)
_____. Christabel (po)
Leigh Hunt. The Story of Rimini (po)
John Keats. On First Looking into Chapman's Homer (po)
Lady Caroline Lamb. Glenarvon (n)
Charles Maturin. Bertram (dr)
Thomas Love Peacock. Headlong Hall (n)
Sir Walter Scott. The Antiquary (n)
_____. The Black Dwarf (n)
_____. Old Mortality (n)
Percy Bysshe Shelley. Alastor, or the Spirit of Solitude (po)
_____. Hymn to Intellectual Beauty (po)
_____. Mont Blanc (po)
Robert Surtees. History of Durham, to 1840 (his)
Helen Maria Williams. On the Late Persecution of the Protestants in the South of France (e, nar)
John Wilson. The City of the Plague (po)

1817

BIRTHS
Sir George Dasent
Benjamin Jowett
George Lewes
Tom Taylor

DEATHS

THE NINETEENTH CENTURY   139

   Jane Austen

EVENTS
   Blackwood's Edinburgh Magazine (p, f)
   The Critical Review (p, c)

WORKS
   Jane Austen. Sanditon (fic; pub 1925)
   George Gordon, Lord Byron. The Lament of Tasso (po)
   _____. Manfred (po, dr)
   William Cobbett. An English Grammar (ref)
   Samuel Taylor Coleridge. Biographia Literaria (e)
   _____. Zapolya (dr)
   Maria Edgeworth. Ormond (n)
   William Hazlitt. Characters of Shakespeare's Plays, to 1818 (e)
   _____ and Leigh Hunt. The Round Table, a Collection of
                  Essays on Literature, Men, and Manners, 2 vols (e)
   Charles Maturin. Manuel (dr)
   Thomas Moore. Lalla Rookh (po, fic)
   John Nichols. Illustrations of the Literary History of the Eighteenth
                  Century, to 1831, 6 vols (his)
   Thomas Love Peacock. Melincourt (n)
   David Ricardo. Principles of Political Economy and Taxation (e)
   Sir Walter Scott. Harold the Dauntless (po)
   _____. Rob Roy (n)
   Robert Southey. Wat Tyler (dr, pub)
   Charles Wolfe. The Burial of Sir John Moore (po)

                               1818

BIRTHS
   Alexander Bain
   Emily Bronte
   Eliza Cook
   James Froude
   Mary Anne Green
   John Mitchel
   John Mason Neale
   Thomas Mayne Reid
   Francis Smedley

DEATHS
   Matthew Gregory Lewis

EVENTS
   The Old Vic Theatre, Waterloo Bridge Road, London (op)

WORKS
   Jane Austen. Northanger Abbey (n, pub)
   _____. Persuasion (n, pub)
   Sir John Barrow. A History of Voyages into the Arctic Region (trav)
   Thomas Bowdler. The Family Shakespeare (ed)
   George Gordon, Lord Byron. Beppo (po)
   _____. Childe Harold's Pilgrimage, IV (po)
   Samuel Taylor Coleridge. The Friend (p, e)
   John Evelyn. Diary (pub)

Susan Ferrier. Marriage (n)
Henry Hallam. A View of the State of Europe during the Middle Ages (his)
William Hazlitt. Lectures on the English Poets, to 1819 (e)
_____. A View of the English Stage, to 1821 (e)
John Keats. Endymion (po)
Charles Maturin. Women, or Pour et Contre (n)
James Mill. History of British India (his)
Thomas Moore. The Fudge Family in Paris (po)
James Morier. A Second Journey through Persia (trav)
Thomas Love Peacock. Nightmare Abbey (n)
Sir Walter Scott. The Heart of Midlothian (n)
Mary Shelley. Frankenstein, or the Last Modern Prometheus (n)
Percy Bysshe Shelley. Julian and Maddalo, a Conversation (po)
_____. Lines Written in the Euganean Hills (po)
_____. The Revolt of Islam (po)
_____. Rosalind and Helen (po)
_____. Stanzas Written in Dejection, near Naples (po)
_____. Symposium (trans)
Mary Martha Sherwood. The History of the Fairchild Family, to 1847 (n)

1819

BIRTHS
Arthur Hugh Clough
Mary Ann Evans ("George Eliot")
Alexander Fraser
Samuel Hole
Charles Kingsley
John Westland Marston
Hugh Munro
John Ruskin

DEATHS
John Wolcot ("Peter Pindar")

EVENTS
The Indicator (p, f)
Watier's Club, Piccadilly, London (c)

WORKS
George Gordon, Lord Byron. Don Juan, to 1820 (po)
_____. Mazeppa (po)
William Hazlitt. English Comic Writers (e)
_____. Letter to William Gifford (e)
James Hogg. The Jacobite Relics of Scotland (po)
Thomas Hope. Anastasius (n)
Leigh Hunt. Hero and Leander (po)
John Keats. La Belle Dame Sans Merci (po)
_____. The Fall of Hyperion (po)
_____. The Eve of St. Agnes (po)
_____. Hyperion (po)
_____. Lamia (po)
_____. Ode on Melancholy (po)
_____. Ode on a Grecian Urn (po)
_____. Ode to Psyche (po)

THE NINETEENTH CENTURY   141

　　　　　　　　　. Ode to a Nightingale (po)
John Lingard. A History of England, to 1830 (his)
John Lockhart. Peter's Letters to His Kinfolk (fic)
Charles Maturin. Fredolfo (dr)
Lord John Russell. Life of William, Lord Russell (bio)
Sir Walter Scott. The Bride of Lammermoor (n)
　　　　　　　　　　. Ivanhoe (n)
　　　　　　　　　　. A Legend of Montrose (n)
　　　　　　　　　　. Provincial Antiquities of Scotland (his)
Percy Bysshe Shelley. The Cenci (dr)
　　　　　　　　　　　. The Cloud (po)
　　　　　　　　　　　. The Masque of Anarchy (po)
　　　　　　　　　　　. Ode to the West Wind (po)
　　　　　　　　　　　. Peter Bell the Third (po, s)
　　　　　　　　　　　. To a Skylark (po)
Richard Whately. Historic Doubts Relative to Napoleon Buonaparte (s)
Helen Maria Williams. Letters on the Events in France Since the Res-
　　　　　　　　　　　　toration in 1815 (e)
William Wordsworth. Peter Bell (po)
　　　　　　　　　　. The Waggoner (po)

                                1820

BIRTHS
　Dion Boucicault
　Nee Bronte
　James Halliwell-Phillipps
　Jean Ingelow
　Henry Mansel
　Herbert Spencer
　James Stirling
　John Tyndall

DEATHS
　Arthur Young

EVENTS
　George IV, King of England, to 1830
　The London Magazine (p, f)

WORKS
　John Clare. Poems Descriptive of Rural Life (pub)
　William Combe. The Second Tour of Dr. Syntax in Search of Consolation
　　　(po)
　John Galt. The Ayrshire Legatees (n)
　William Hazlitt. Dramatic Literature of the Age of Elizabeth (e)
　James Knowles. Virginius (dr)
　Henry Luttrell. Advice to Julia (po)
　Thomas Malthus. Principles of Political Economy (t)
　Charles Maturin. Melmoth the Wanderer (n)
　Sir Walter Scott. The Abbot (n)
　　　　　　　　　　. The Monastery (n)
　Percy Bysshe Shelley. Ode to Liberty (po)
　　　　　　　　　　　. Ode to Naples (po)
　　　　　　　　　　　. Prometheus Unbound (po, dr)
　　　　　　　　　　　. The Sensitive Plant (po)

Robert Southey. The Life of Wesley and the Rise of Methodism (bio)
Joseph Spence. Literary Anecdotes of the Eighteenth Century (pub)

1821

BIRTHS
  Sir Samuel White Baker
  Sir Richard Burton
  Frederick Locker
  George Whyte-Melville

DEATHS
  Elizabeth Inchbald
  John Keats
  Vicesimus Knox

EVENTS
  The Indicator (p,c)
  The Manchester Guardian (p, f)

WORKS
  Joanna Baillie. Metrical Legends (po)
  Thomas Lovell Beddoes. The Improvisatore (po)
  George Gordon, Lord Byron. Cain: A Mystery (po, dr)
  _____. Marino Faliero, Doge of Venice (dr)
  _____. Sardanapalus (dr)
  _____. The Two Foscari (dr)
  John Clare. The Village Minstrel (po)
  William Combe. The Third Tour of Dr. Syntax in Search of a Wife (po)
  Thomas Dibdin. A Bibliographical, Antiquarian, and Picturesque Tour in France and Germany (e)
  Pierce Egan. Life in London; or, the Day and Night Scenes of Jerry Hawthorn (fic)
  John Galt. Annals of the Parish (n)
  William Hazlitt. Table Talk, or Original Essays of Men and Manners, to 1822 (e)
  John Lockhart. Valerius (n)
  James Mill. Elements of Political Economy (e)
  Bryan Procter. Mirandola (dr)
  John Hamilton Reynolds. Garden of Florence and Other Poems (pub)
  Sir Walter Scott. Kenilworth (n)
  _____. The Pirate (n)
  Percy Bysshe Shelley. Adonais. An Elegy on the Death of John Keats (po)
  _____. A Defence of Poetry (e)
  _____. Epipsychidion (po)
  _____. Queen Mab (po, pub)
  Robert Southey. A Vision of Judgment (po)

1822

BIRTHS
  Matthew Arnold
  Frances Power Cobbe
  James Grant
  Thomas Hughes
  Sir Henry Maine

THE NINETEENTH CENTURY   143

DEATHS
  Percy Bysshe Shelley

EVENTS
  The Liberal Magazine (p, f)

WORKS
  Thomas Lovell Beddoes. The Bride's Tragedy (po)
  William Blake. The Ghost of Abel (po)
  George Gordon, Lord Byron. Heaven and Earth (dr)
  _____. The Vision of Judgment (po)
  _____. Werner (dr)
  George Croly. Catiline (dr)
  Allan Cunningham. Traditional Tales of the British and Scottish Pea-
              santry (ed)
  George Darley. The Errors of Ecstacie (po)
  Thomas DeQuincey. Confessions of an English Opium Eater (nar)
  Kenelm Digby. The Broad Stone of Honour (his)
  Maria Edgeworth. Frank (fic)
  John Galt. The Provost (n)
  James Hogg. The Three Perils of Man (e)
  Lady Caroline Lamb. Graham Hamilton (n)
  John Lockhart. Some Passages in the Life of Adam Blair (n)
  Noctes Ambrosianae, to 1835 (nar)
  Thomas Love Peacock. Maid Marian (n)
  Samuel Rogers. Italy, to 1828 (po)
  Sir Walter Scott. The Fortunes of Nigel (n)
  _____. Halidon Hill (dr)
  Percy Bysshe Shelley. Hellas (po, dr)
  Charles Wells. Stories after Nature (fic)
  Richard Whately. The Use and Abuse of Party Feeling in Matters of Re-
              ligion (e)
  William Wordsworth. Memorials of a Tour on the Continent (po)

                                1823

BIRTHS
  Sir John Evans
  Edward Freeman
  Coventry Patmore
  James Rogers
  Alfred Wallace
  Charlotte Yonge

DEATHS
  William Combe
  Ann Radcliffe
  David Ricardo

EVENTS
  The Bannatyne Club (f)
  The Royal Society of Literature (f)

WORKS
  George Gordon, Lord Byron. The Age of Bronze (po)
  _____. The Island (po)

George Canning. Poems (pub)
Thomas DeQuincey. On the Knocking at the Gate in "Macbeth" (e)
Isaac Disraeli. Curiosities of Literature (nar)
John Galt. The Entail (n)
William Hazlitt. Liber Amoris (nar)
Lady Caroline Lamb. Ada Reis, a Tale (n)
Charles Lamb. The Essays of Elia, 1st series (, pub)
Robert Landor. The Count of Arezzi (dr)
John Lockhart. Ancient Spanish Ballads (po)
_____. Reginald Dalton (n)
Thomas Moore. Loves of the Angels (po)
Sir Walter Scott. Macduff's Cross (dr)
_____. Peveril of the Peak (n)
_____. Quentin Durward (n)
_____. St. Ronan's Well (n)
Mary Shelley. Valperga (n)
Robert Southey. History of the Peninsular War, to 1832 (his)

1824

BIRTHS
  Wilkie Collins
  Sydney Dobell
  Julia Kavanagh
  George Macdonald
  Francis Turner Palgrave

DEATHS
  George Gordon, Lord Byron
  Charles Maturin
  Jane Taylor

EVENTS
  The Athenaeum Club (f)
  Pierce Egan's Life in London and Sporting Guide (p, f)
  The Westminster Review (p, f)

WORKS
  George Gordon, Lord Byron. The Deformed Transformed (dr)
  Thomas Campbell. Theodoric (po)
  Thomas Carlyle. Wilhelm Meister's Apprenticeship (trans)
  William Cobbett. History of the Protestant Reformation in England and Ireland (his)
  Thomas Croker. Researches in the South of Ireland (e)
  Thomas Dibdin. Library Companion (ref)
  Susan Ferrier. The Inheritance (n)
  James Hogg. The Confessions of a Justified Sinner (nar)
  Walter Savage Landor. Imaginary Conversations, to 1829 (fic, e)
  John Lockhart. Matthew Wald (n)
  Charles Maturin. The Albigenses (n)
  Mary Mitford. Our Village. Sketches of Rural Life, Character, and Scenery, to 1832 (e)
  James Morier. The Adventures of Hajji Baba of Ispahan (n)
  Lord John Russell. Memoirs of Affairs of Europe, to 1829 (nar, his)
  Sir Walter Scott. Redgauntlet (n)
  Robert Southey. The Book of the Church (e)

THE NINETEENTH CENTURY   145

   Robert Watt. Bibliotheca Britannica, or a General Index to British
              and Foreign Literature (bibl)
   Charles Wells. Joseph and His Brethren: A Dramatic Poem (po)

                                1825

BIRTHS
   Richard Doddridge Blackmore
   John Conington
   Thomas Huxley
   Adelaide Anne Procter
   William Stubbs

WORKS
   Henry Peter Brougham. Observations on the Education of the People (e)
   Thomas Carlyle. Life of Schiller (bio, e)
   Samuel Taylor Coleridge. Aids to Reflection (t)
   Thomas Croker. Fairy Legends and Traditions, to 1828 (e)
   Allan Cunningham. The Songs of Scotland, Ancient and Modern (po, ed)
   Maria Edgeworth. Harry and Lucy (fic)
   William Hazlitt. The Spirit of the Age (e)
   Leigh Hunt. Bacchus in Tuscany (trans)
   James Knowles. William Tell (dr)
   John Stuart Mill. Treatise upon Evidence (ed)
   Thomas Moore. Life of Sheridan (bio)
   Samuel Pepys. Diary (pub)
   James Planche. Success; or, A Hit if you like it (dr)
   John Poole. Paul Pry (dr)
   Sir Walter Scott. The Talisman (n)
   Robert Southey. A Tale of Paraguay (po)
   Charles Waterton. Wanderings in South America (trav)
   Joseph White. Evidences against Catholicism (e)

                                1826

BIRTHS
   Walter Bagehot
   Thomas Alexander Browne
   Richard Hutton
   William Palgrave

DEATHS
   William Gifford
   Lindley Murray
   John Nichols

EVENTS
   St. Peter's Church, Eaton Square, London (blt)
   Zoological Society (f)

WORKS
   Elizabeth Barrett Browning. Essay on Mind; with Other Poems (pub)
   George Darley. Labours of Idleness (fic)
   Benjamin Disraeli. Vivian Grey, to 1827 (n)
   James Duff. History of the Mahrattas (his)
   A Genealogical and Heraldic History of the Peerage and Baronetage of
      the United Kingdom (pub)

William Hazlitt. Notes on a Journey through France and Italy (e)
James Hogg. Queen Hynde (po)
Theodore Hook. Sayings and Doings, to 1829 (n)
Sir Walter Scott. Woodstock (n)
Mary Shelley. The Last Man (n)
Horatio Smith. Brambletye House (n)
Robert Southey. Vindiciae Ecclesiae Anglicanae (t)
Richard Whately. Logic and Rhetoric, to 1828 (e)

1827

BIRTHS
  Patrick Joyce
  George Lawrence

DEATHS
  William Blake
  Helen Maria Williams

EVENTS
  Crockford's Gambling Club, 50 St. James's Street, London (f)

WORKS
  Edward G.E. Bulwer-Lytton. Falkland (n)
  Thomas Carlyle. Wilhelm Meister's Travels (trans)
  John Clare. The Shepherd's Calendar (po)
  George Darley. Sylvia (po)
  Thomas DeQuincey. On Murder As One of the Fine Arts (e)
  Henry Hallam. Constitutional History of England (his)
  John Keble. The Christian Year (po)
  Charles Lamb. On an Infant Dying As Soon As Born (po)
  Thomas Moore. The Epicurean (n)
  Lady Sydney Morgan. The O'Briens and the O'Flahertys (n)
  William Motherwell. Minstrelsy, Ancient and Modern (ed)
  John Poole. 'Twixt the Cup and the Lip (dr)
  Sir Walter Scott. The Highland Widow (n)
  _____. The Life of Napoleon Buonaparte (bio)
  _____. The Surgeon's Daughter (n)
  _____. Tales of a Grandfather, to 1830 (fic)
  _____. The Two Drovers (n)
  Sir Henry Taylor. Isaac Comnenus (po, dr)
  Alfred Tennyson and Frederick Tennyson. Poems, by Two Brothers (pub)

1828

BIRTHS
  George Meredith
  Arthur Munby
  Margaret Oliphant
  Dante Rossetti

DEATHS
  Lady Caroline Lamb
  Dugald Stewart

EVENTS

The Athenaeum (p, f)
The Companion (p, f, c)
London University (f)
The Maitland Club (f)
The Roxburghe (Book) Club (f)
The Spectator (p, f)

WORKS
  Edward G.E. Bulwer-Lytton. Pelham (n)
  Sir Humphry Davy. Salmonia, or Days of Fly-Fishing, by an Angler (dia, e)
  Ebenezer Elliott. Corn Law Rhymes (po)
  Julius Hare and Connop Thirlwall. Roman History (trans)
  James Knowles. The Beggar's Daughter of Bethnal Green (dr)
  Robert Landor. The Impious Feast (po)
  Sir George Lewis. Public Economy of Athens (trans)
  John Lockhart. The Life of Burns (bio)
  David Moir. The Life of Mansie Wauch, Tailor in Dalkeith (n)
  Robert Montgomery. The Omnipresence of the Deity (po)
  Sir William Napier. History of the Peninsular War, to 1840 (his)
  Sir Walter Scott. St. Valentine's Day, or the Fair Maid of Perth (n)
  John Thomas Smith. Nollekens and His Times (bio)
  Patrick Tytler. History of Scotland, from the Reign of Alexander III to the Year 1603, to 1843 (his)
  Joseph White. Night and Death (po)

1829

BIRTHS
  Samuel Gardiner
  Thomas Robertson
  William Rossetti
  Sir James Fitzjames Stephen

EVENTS
  The Gem (p, f)
  The London Magazine (p, c)
  Trafalgar Square, London (op)

WORKS
  Edward G.E. Bulwer-Lytton. Devereaux (n)
  ——————————————————. The Disowned (n)
  William Cobbett. Advice to Young Men (e)
  Thomas Croker. Legends of the Lakes (e)
  George Croly. Salathiel (n)
  Allan Cunningham. Lives of the Most Eminent British Painters, Sculptors, and Architects, to 1833 (bio)
  Gerald Griffin. The Collegians (n)
  Thomas Hood. The Dream of Eugene Aram (po)
  George James. Richelieu (n)
  Douglas Jerrold. Black-ey'd Susan (dr)
  Frederick Marryat. Frank Mildmay (n)
  James Mill. Analysis of the Human Mind (e)
  Thomas Love Peacock. The Misfortunes of Elphin (n)
  John Poole. Lodgings for Single Gentlemen (dr)
  Michael Scott. Tom Cringle's Log, to 1833 (fic)

Sir Walter Scott. Anne of Geierstein, or the Maiden of the Mist (n)
_____. History of Scotland, to 1830 (his)
Robert Southey. All for Love, or A Sinner Well Saved (po)
_____. Sir Thomas More; Colloquies on the Progress and Prospects of Society (e)
Alfred Tennyson. Timbuctoo (po)

1830

BIRTHS
Sebastian Evans
Henry Kingsley
Justin McCarthy
James Payn
Christina Rossetti
Alexander Smith

DEATHS
William Hazlitt

EVENTS
William IV, King of England, to 1837
Fraser's Magazine (p, f)
The Tatler (p, f)

WORKS
Thomas Arnold. The Works of Thucydides, to 1835 (ed)
Jeremy Bentham. Constitutional Code (e)
Edward G.E. Bulwer-Lytton. Paul Clifford (n)
William Cobbett. Rural Rides (trav, e)
William Hazlitt. Conversations of James Northcote (nar)
Theodore Hook. Maxwell (n)
Charles Lamb. Album Verses (po)
Sir Charles Lyell. The Principles of Geology, to 1833 (e)
Sir James Macintosh. Dissertation on the Progress of Ethical Philosophy (e)
_____. History of England, to 1831 (his)
Henry Milman. History of the Jews (his)
Robert Montgomery. Satan (po)
Thomas Moore. Life of Byron (bio)
Sir Walter Scott. Auchindrane, or the Ayrshire Tragedy (dr)
_____. The Doom of Devergoil, a Melo-drama (dr)
Alfred Tennyson. Poems, Chiefly Lyrical (pub)

1831

BIRTHS
Edward R. Bulwer-Lytton
Frederic Harrison
William Hale White ("Mark Rutherford")

DEATHS
Henry Mackenzie
William Roscoe

THE NINETEENTH CENTURY   149

EVENTS
  The British Association for the Advancement of Science (f)
  The Boar's Head Inn (c)
  The Carlton Club (f)
  Exeter Hall (blt)
  The Garrick Club (f)
  London Bridge (des)
  Figaro in London (p, f)
  The New Sporting Magazine (p, f)

WORKS
  John Wilson Croker. Boswell's Life of Johnson (ed)
  _____. Military Events in the French Revolution of 1830
                          (his)
  Kenelm Digby. Mores Catholici (t)
  Benjamin Disraeli. The Young Duke (n)
  Susan Ferrier. Destiny (n)
  Catherine Gore. Mothers and Daughters (n)
  _____. The School for Coquettes (dr)
  George James. Philip Augustus (n)
  Douglas Jerrold. The Bride of Ludgate (dr)
  Thomas Moore. Lord Edward Fitzgerald (bio)
  Thomas Love Peacock. Crotchet Castle (n)
  Sir Walter Scott. Count Robert of Paris (n)
  _____. Castle Dangerous (n)
  Edward Trelawny. Adventures of a Younger Son (n)
  Charles Whitehead. The Solitary (po)

                                1832

BIRTHS
  Charles Dodgson ("Lewis Carroll")
  Shadworth Hodgson
  Sir Leslie Stephen
  Walter Watts-Dunton

DEATHS
  Jeremy Bentham
  George Crabbe
  Sir James Mackintosh
  Sir Walter Scott

EVENTS
  Chambers's Journal (p, f)
  The Gem (p, c)
  The Penny Magazine (p, f)
  Punchinello (p, f)
  The Tatler (p, c)

WORKS
  Sir Archibald Alison. A History of Scottish Criminal Law, to 1833
                            (his)
  John Austin. The Province of Jurisprudence Determined (t)
  Marguerite Power Blessington. A Journal of Conversations with Lord
                                    Byron (nar)
  Edward G.E. Bulwer-Lytton. Eugene Aram (n)

William Carleton. Traits and Stories of the Irish Peasantry (nar, fic)
Thomas DeQuincey. Klosterheim (n)
Benjamin Disraeli. Contarini Fleming (n)
Sir Samuel Ferguson. Forging of the Anchor (po)
John Genest. Some Accounts of the English Stage from the Restoration in 1660 to 1830 (his, ref)
George James. Memoirs of the Great Commanders (nar, his)
Anna Jameson. Shakespeare's Heroines (e)
James Knowles. The Hunchback (dr)
Harriet Martineau. Illustrations of Political Economy, to 1834 (fic)
William Motherwell. Poems, Narrative and Lyrical (pub)
Sir Francis Palgrave. The Rise and Progress of the English Commonwealth (his)
Robert Southey. Essays Moral and Political (pub)
Philip Stanhope. The History of the War of the Succession in Spain (his)
Frances Trollope. Domestic Manners of the Americans (nar)
Martin Tupper. Proverbial Philosophy (po, t)

1833

BIRTHS
Sir George Tomkyns Chesney
John Willis Clark
Richard Dixon
Sir Lewis Morris

DEATHS
Hannah More
John O'Keefe
John Thomas Smith

EVENTS
The Penny Cyclopaedia (p, f)

WORKS
Sir Archibald Alison. The History of Europe during the French Revolution, to 1842 (his)
Elizabeth Barrett Browning. Miscellaneous Poems (pub)
_____. Prometheus Bound (trans)
Robert Browning. Pauline (po)
Edward G.E. Bulwer-Lytton. Godolphin (n)
Thomas Chalmers. The Adaptation of External Nature to the Moral and Intellectual Constitution of Man (t)
Hartley Coleridge. Biographia Borealis, to 1836 (bio)
Benjamin Disraeli. Alroy (n)
_____. Ixion in Heaven (n)
John Kemble. The Poems of Beowulf, to 1837 (ed)
James Knowles. The Wife (dr)
Charles Lamb. The Essays of Elia, 2nd series (e, pub)
Harriet Martineau. Poor Law and Paupers Illustrated (fic)
John Henry Newman. Lead, kindly Light (po)
Amelia Opie. Lays for the Dead (po)
James Planche. High, Low, Jack, and the Game: or, the Card Party (dr)
Frederic Mansel Reynolds. Miserrimus, a Tale (n)
Robert Southey. Lives of the British Admirals, to 1840 (bio)

THE NINETEENTH CENTURY 151

Alfred Tennyson. The Lotos-Eaters (po)
_____. OEnone (po)
Tracts for the Times, to 1841 (e, ed)
William Whewell. Astronomy and Physics in Reference to Natural Philo-
        sophy (e)

                            1834

BIRTHS
    William Carew Hazlitt
    William Morris
    Roden Noel
    Sir John Seeley
    James Thomson

DEATHS
    Samuel Taylor Coleridge
    Charles Lamb
    Thomas Malthus

EVENTS
    The Abbotsford Club (f)
    Leigh Hunt's London Journal (p, f)
    The Lyceum Theatre, London (op)
    St. Stephen's Chapel, Westminster (des)
    Westminster Palace (des)

WORKS
    William Harrison Ainsworth. Rookwood (n)
    Edward G.E. Bulwer-Lytton. The Last Days of Pompeii (n)
    William Carleton. Tales of Ireland (fic)
    Thomas DeQuincey. Autobiographical Sketches, to 1853 (auto, nar)
    Benjamin Disraeli. The Infernal Marriage (n)
    _____. The Rise of Iskander (n)
    Arthur Henry Hallam. Remains in Verse and Prose (pub)
    James Hogg. Domestic Manners and Private Life of Sir Walter Scott (bio)
    Walter Savage Landor. Citation and Examination of William Shakespeare
            Touching Deer-Stealing (fic)
    William Lowndes. The Bibliographer's Manual of English Literature
            (bibl, ref)
    Sir James Mackintosh. History of the Revolution in England in 1688
            (pub)
    Frederick Marryat. Jacob Faithful (n)
    _____. Peter Simple (n)
    Harriet Martineau. Illustrations of Taxation (fic)
    Sir Francis Palgrave. Essay on the Original Authority of the King's
            Council (e)
    James Planche. History of British Costumes (his)
    Michael Scott. The Cruise of the Midge, to 1835 (fic)
    Sir Henry Taylor. Philip van Artevelde (po, dr)
    Charles Whitehead. Jack Ketch (n)

                            1835

BIRTHS
    Samuel Butler

152   CHRONOLOGICAL OUTLINE OF BRITISH LITERATURE

   Edward Caird
   Richard Garnett
   Sir Alfred Lyall
   Walter Skeat
   John Warren

DEATHS
   William Cobbett
   James Hogg
   William Motherwell
   Michael Scott

EVENTS
   Cobbett's Political Register (p, c)
   The Comic Almanack (pub, f)
   Leigh Hunt's London Journal (p, c)
   The Original (p, f, c)

WORKS
   William Beckford. Recollections of an Excursion to the Monasteries of Alobaca and Batalha (trav, nar)
   Robert Browning. Paraclesus (po)
   Edward G.E. Bulwer-Lytton. Rienzi (n)
   John Clare. The Rural Muse (po)
   Benjamin Disraeli. Vindication of the English Constitution (e)
   Leigh Hunt. Captain Sword and Captain Pen (po)
   James Mill. Fragment on Mackintosh (e)
   Mary Mitford. Belford Regis, Sketches of a Country Town (e)
   Thomas Moore. The Fudges in England (po)
   Mary Shelley. Lenore (n)
   Sir Thomas Talfourd. Ion (dr)
   Connop Thirlwall. History of Greece, to 1847 (his)
   Joseph White. Observations on Heresy and Orthodoxy (e)
   William Wordsworth. Yarrow Revisited (po)

1836

BIRTHS
   Sir Walter Besant
   Sir Francis Cowley Burnand
   William S. Gilbert
   Thomas Green

DEATHS
   George Coleman the younger
   William Godwin
   James Mill

WORKS
   Joanna Baillie. Miscellaneous Plays (pub)
   Thomas Carlyle. Sartor Resartus (e)
   Thomas Dibdin. Reminiscences of a Literary Life (nar)
   Charles Dickens. The Posthumous Papers of the Pickwick Club (fic)
   _____. Sketches by Boz, to 1837 (nar, fic)
   _____. The Spirit of Whiggism (e)
   Catherine Gore. Mrs. Armytage (n)

Theodore Hook. Gilbert Gurney (n)
Edward Howard. Rattlin the Reefer (n)
George James. Life of the Black Prince (bio)
Walter Savage Landor. Pericles and Aspasia (fic, e)
Samuel Lover. Rory O'More (n)
Lyra Apostolica (po)
Frederick Marryat. Japhet in Search of a Father (fic)
_____. Mr. Midshipman Easy (n)
_____. The Pacha of Many Tales (n)
Nassau Senior. An Outline of the Science of Political Economy (e)
Philip Stanhope. The History of England, from the Peace of Utrecht to
           the Peace of Versailles, to 1863 (his)
Sir Henry Taylor. The Statesman (s)
Charles Whitehead. The Cavalier (dr)
Thomas Wright. Early English Poetry, 4 vols (ed)
William Yarrell. History of British Fishes (his)

                    1837

BIRTHS
  Alfred Ainger
  Oscar Browning
  John Green
  Sir James Murray
  Ann Ritchie
  Algernon Swinburne

DEATHS
  Sir Samuel Egerton Brydges

EVENTS
  Victoria, Queen of England, to 1901
  Bentley's Miscellany (p, f)
  The Chartists (f)

WORKS
  Robert Browning. Strafford (dr)
  Edward G.E. Bulwer-Lytton. Ernest Maltravers (n)
  Thomas Carlyle. A History of the French Revolution (his)
  Sara Coleridge. Phantasmion (fic)
  Eliza Cook. The Old Arm Chair (po)
  Charles Dickens. Oliver Twist, to 1838 (n)
  Benjamin Disraeli. Henrietta Temple (n)
  _____. Venetia (n)
  Henry Hallam. Introduction to the Literature of Europe during the Fif-
           teenth, Sixteenth, and Seventeenth Centuries, to 1839
           (his, e)
  Theodore Hook. Jack Brag (n)
  James Knowles. The Love Chase (dr)
  Letitia Landon. Ethel Churchill (n)
  Walter Savage Landor. The Pentameron (fic, e)
  Joseph LeFanu. Shamus O'Brien (po)
  Charles Lever. Harry Lorrequer (fic)
  John Lockhart. The Life of Scott, to 1838 (bio)
  Frederick Marryat. Snarleyyow (n)
  Harriet Martineau. Society in America (e)

Mary Mitford. Country Stories (fic)
Sir Francis Palgrave. Truth and Fictions of the Middle Ages: the Merchant and the Friar (his)
Sir Isaac Pitman. Stenographic Sound-Hand (ref)
William Thackeray. The Yellowplush Correspondence (fic)
Frances Trollope. The Vicar of Wrexhill (n)
William Whewell. History of the Inductive Sciences (e)
Sir John Wilkinson. Manners and Customs of the Ancient Egyptians, to 1841 (his)

1838

BIRTHS
James Bryce
William H.E. Lecky
John Morley
William Reade
Henry Sidgwick
George Otto Trevelyan

DEATHS
Thomas Morton

EVENTS
The Camden Society (f)
The National Gallery (op)
The Royal Exchange (des)
The Stirling Club (f)

WORKS
Thomas Arnold. A History of Rome, to 1842 (his)
Elizabeth Barrett Browning. The Seraphim and Other Poems (pub)
Edward G.E. Bulwer-Lytton. The Lady of Lyons (dr)
_____. Richelieu (dr)
Thomas Dibdin. Bibliographical, Antiquarian, and Picturesque Tour in the Northern Counties of England (trav)
Charles Dickens. Nicholas Nickleby, to 1839 (n)
James Ferrier. Introduction to the Philosophy of Consciousness, to 1839 (e)
William Gladstone. The State in Its Relations with the Church (e)
Theodore Hook. Gurney Married (n)
Edward Lane. Thousand and One Nights (trans)
Sir Charles Lyell. The Elements of Geology (e)
Harriet Martineau. Retrospect of Western Travel (e)
John Maurice. The Kingdom of Christ (e)
Thomas Smith. The Diary of a Huntsman (nar)
Robert Smith Surtees. Jorrock's Jaunts and Jollities (fic)
William Thackeray. Some Passages in the Life of Major Gahogan, to 1839 (fic)
William Thoms. The Book of the Court (ed)
Frances Trollope. The Widow Barnaby (n)
Samuel Warren. Passages from the Diary of a Late Physician (fic)
Isaac Williams. The Cathedral (po)
Thomas Wright. Queen Elizabeth and Her Times (his)

THE NINETEENTH CENTURY   155

                                    1839

BIRTHS
  William DeMorgan
  Mary Louise de la Ramee ("Ouida")
  Herman Merivale
  Walter Pater
  Spencer Walpole

DEATHS
  John Galt

EVENTS
  The Cambridge Camden Society (f)
  The Doves Press (f)
  Railway Time Tables (pub)

WORKS
  William Harrison Ainsworth. Jack Sheppard (n)
  Philip James Bailey. Festus, 1st ed (po)
  Henry Peter Brougham. Historical Sketches of Statesmen in the Time of
                    George III, to 1843 (bio)
  William Carleton. Fardorougha, the Miser (n)
  Thomas Carlyle. Chartism (e)
  Thomas Croker. Popular Songs of Ireland (ed)
  Charles Darwin. Journal of Researches into the Geology and Natural
                    History of the Various Countries Visited by H.M.S.
                    Beagle (e, nar, trav)
  Michael Faraday. Experimental Researches in Electricity, to 1855 (e)
  John Frere. Frogs (trans, po)
  John Kemble. Codex Diplomaticus Aevi Saxonici, to 1848 (his)
  Walter Savage Landor. Andrea of Hungary (po)
  _____. Fra Rupert (po)
  _____. Giovanna of Naples (po)
  Samuel Lover. Songs and Ballads (po)
  William Lowndes. The British Librarian (bibl)
  Frederick Marryat. Diary in America (nar)
  _____. The Phantom Ship (n)
  Harriet Martineau. Deerbrook (n)
  Sir James Ross. A Voyage in the Southern and Antarctic Regions, to
                    1847 (trav)
  Catherine Sinclair. Holiday House (fic)
  William Thackeray. Catherine, to 1840 (fic)
  Patrick Tytler. England under the Reign of Edward VI and Mary (his)
  Samuel Warren. Ten Thousand a Year (n)

                                    1840

BIRTHS
  Wilfrid Scawen Blunt
  Rhoda Broughton
  Ingram Bywater
  Henry Austin Dobson
  Thomas Hardy
  John Symonds
  Edward Whymper

DEATHS
   Frances Burney
   Gerald Griffin

EVENTS
   Bentley's Miscellany (p, f)
   The London Library (op)
   The Percy Society (f)

WORKS
   William Harrison Ainsworth. The Tower of London (n)
   Robert Browning. Sordello (po)
   Edward G.E. Bulwer-Lytton. Money (dr)
   Henry Cockton. Valentine Vox the Ventriloquist (n)
   John Frere. Acharnians (trans, po)
   _____. Birds (trans, po)
   _____. Knights (trans, po)
   Julius Hare. The Victory of Faith (e)
   Leigh Hunt. A Legend of Florence (dr)
   Charles Lever. Charles O'Malley (fic)
   Frederick Marryat. Poor Jack (n)
   Henry Milman. History of Christianity from the Birth of Christ (his)
   Agnes Strickland and Elizabeth Strickland. Lives of the Queens of England, to 1848 (bio)
   William Thackeray. The Paris Sketch-Book, by Mr. Titmarsh (n)
   _____. A Shabby Genteel Story (fic)
   William Whewell. Philosophy of the Inductive Sciences (e)
   Thomas Wright. The Vision and the Creed of Piers Plowman (ed)

                               1841

BIRTHS
   William Black
   Robert Buchanan
   Juliana Ewing
   Sir Henry Stanley

DEATHS
   Theodore Hook
   Joseph White

EVENTS
   Punch, or the London Charivari (p, f)
   Royal Botanic Gardens, Kew, Richmond (op)

WORKS
   Sarah Flower Adams. Viva Perpetua (po)
   William Harrison Ainsworth. Guy Fawkes (n)
   _____. Old St. Paul's (n)
   Henry George Bohn. Guinea Catalogue of Old Books (bibl)
   George Borrow. The Zincali, or an Account of the Gypsies in Spain (trav)
   Dion Boucicault. London Assurance (dr)
   Bradshaw's Monthly Railway Guide (pub)
   Robert Browning. Pippa Passes (dr, po)
   Thomas Carlyle. On Heroes, Hero-Worship, and the Heroic in History (e)

THE NINETEENTH CENTURY 157

  Charles Dickens. Barnaby Rudge (n)
  _____. The Old Curiosity Shop (n)
  Isaac Disraeli. Amenities of Literature (nar)
  Mountstuart Elphinstone. The History of India (his)
  Catherine Gore. Cecil, or the Adventures of a Coxcomb (n)
  Thomas Hood. Miss Kilmansegg and Her Precious Leg, to 1843 (po)
  Frederick Marryat. Masterman Ready (n)
  Harriet Martineau. The Hour and the Man (n)
  _____. The Playfellow (fic)
  Hugh Miller. The Old Red Sandstone (e)
  Augustus Pugin. The True Principles of Pointed or Christian Architec-
          ture (t)
  William Thackeray. The Great Hoggarty Diamond (n)
  Richard Trench. Notes on the Parables of Our Lord (e)

                                1842

BIRTHS
  William John Courthope
  Henry Traill

DEATHS
  Thomas Arnold
  Allan Cunningham

EVENTS
  Ainsworth's Magazine (p, f)
  Bentley's Miscellany (p, c)
  The Copyright Act
  The Nation (p, f)
  Pentonville Prison, Caledonian Road, Islington (blt)

WORKS
  William Harrison Ainsworth. The Miser's Daughter (n)
  Robert Browning. Dramatic Lyrics (po)
  Edward G.E. Bulwer-Lytton. Zanoni (n)
  Thomas Campbell. The Pilgrim of Glencoe (po)
  Charles Darwin. Structure and Distribution of Coral Reefs (e)
  Aubrey De Vere. The Waldenses and Other Poems (pub)
  Charles Dickens. American Notes (nar)
  James Ferrier. Berkeley and Idealism (e)
  John Frere. Theognis Restitutus (trans, po)
  Gerald Griffin. Gisippus (dr)
  Samuel Lover. Handy Andy (n)
  Thomas Babington Macaulay. Lays of Ancient Rome (po)
  John Westland Marston. The Patrician's Daughter (dr)
  John Henry Newman. Essay on Miracles (e)
  James Planche. Regal and Ecclesiastical Antiquities of England (ed)
  William Ruff. Ruff's Guide to the Turf (ref)
  Sir William Smith. Dictionary of Greek and Roman Antiquities (ref)
  Sir Henry Taylor. Edwin the Fair (po, dr)
  Alfred Tennyson. Locksley Hall (po)
  _____. Morte d'Arthur (po)
  _____. Ulysses (po)
  William Thackeray. The Fitz-Boodle Papers, to 1843 (n)
  Charles Whitehead. Richard Savage (n)

William Wordsworth. Poems Chiefly of Early and Late Years (pub)
Thomas Wright. Biographia Literaria of the Anglo-Saxon Period (bio)

1843

BIRTHS
 Mandell Creighton
 Sir Charles Dilke
 Charles Doughty
 Edward Dowden
 Henry James
 Frederic Myers

DEATHS
 William Lowndes
 Robert Southey

EVENTS
 William Wordsworth, Poet Laureate of England, to 1850
 The Economist (p, f)
 The Molly Maguires (f)

WORKS
 William Harrison Ainsworth. Windsor Castle (n)
 George Borrow. The Bible in Spain (trav)
 Edward G.E. Bulwer-Lytton. The Last of the Barons (n)
 Thomas Carlyle. Past and Present (e)
 Charles Dickens. A Christmas Carol (fic)
 _____. Martin Chizzlewit, to 1844 (n)
 Catherine Gore. The Banker's Wife (n)
 Thomas Hood. A Song of the Shirt (po)
 Richard Horne. Orion (po)
 Charles Lever. Jack Hinton the Guardsman (fic)
 Thomas Babington Macaulay. Essays (pub)
 John Stuart Mill. System of Logic (e)
 Augustus Pugin. Apology for the Revival of Christian Architecture in England (e)
 John Ruskin. Modern Painters, to 1860 (t)
 Thomas Smith. The Life of a Fox, Written by Himself (fic)
 Robert Smith Surtees. Handley Cross (n)
 William Thackeray. Bluebeard's Ghost (n)
 _____. The Irish Sketch-book (n)
 William Yarrell. The History of British Birds (his)

1844

BIRTHS
 Robert Bridges
 Gerard Manley Hopkins
 Andrew Lang
 Arthur O'Shaughnessy
 William Clark Russell
 William Wallace

DEATHS
 William Beckford

THE NINETEENTH CENTURY   159

     Thomas Campbell
     Henry Francis Cary

EVENTS
     The Penny Cyclopaedia (p, c)
     The Royal Exchange (blt)

WORKS
     William Barnes. Poems of Rural Life, 1st series (pub)
     Elizabeth Barrett Browning. Poems (pub)
     Robert Chambers. Vestiges of Creation (t)
     Richard William Church. St. Wulfstan (bio)
     Mary Cowden-Clarke. Complete Concordance to Shakespeare, to 1845 (ref)
     Charles Darwin. Geological Observations on Volcanic Islands (e, trav)
     Thomas DeQuincey. The Logic of Political Economy (e)
     Charles Dickens. The Chimes (fic)
     Benjamin Disraeli. Coningsby (n)
     Emily Eden. Portraits of the People and Princes of India (trav, bio)
     George Finlay. History of Greece, to 1861 (his)
     Catherine Gore. Lords and Commons (dr)
     _____. Quid pro Quo (dr)
     Leigh Hunt. Imagination and Fancy (e)
     Frances Kemble. Poems (pub)
     Alexander William Kinglake. Eothen (trav)
     Charles Lever. Arthur O'Leary (fic)
     _____. Tom Burke of Ours (fic)
     Frederick Marryat. The Settlers in Canada (n)
     Sir William Smith. Dictionary of Greek and Roman Biography and Mytho-
                           logy, to 1849 (ref)
     Arthur Stanley. Life of Dr. Arnold (bio)
     William Thackeray. The Luck of Barry Lyndon (n)
     William Thoms. Reynard the Fox (ed)
     Martin Tupper. The Crock of Gold (po)
     William Ward. The Ideal of a Christian Church (t)
     Thomas Wright. Anecdota Literaria (bio, nar)

                                    1845

BIRTHS
     William Clifford
     Sir Sidney Colvin
     Emily Lawless
     Sir Frederick Pollock
     George Saintsbury
     Henry Sweet

DEATHS
     Thomas Hood

EVENTS
     The Monthly Review (p, c)
     The Penny Magazine (p, c)

WORKS
     Thomas Arnold. The History of the Later Roman Commonwealth (his, pub)
     Philip James Bailey. Festus, 2nd ed (po)

Robert Browning. Dramatic Romances and Lyrics (po)
Thomas Carlyle. Oliver Cromwell's Letters and Speeches (ed)
Charles Dickens. The Cricket on the Hearth (fic)
Benjamin Disraeli. Sybil (n)
Richard Ford. Handbook for Travellers in Spain (trav)
James Grant. The Romance of War (n)
Douglas Jerrold. Mrs. Caudle's Curtain Lectures (fic)
Geraldine Jewsbury. Zoe (n)
Charles Lever. The O'Donoghue (fic)
George Lewes. Biographical History of Philosophy, to 1846 (bio, his)
Sir Charles Lyell. Travels in North America (trav)
Theodore Martin and William Aytoun. Bon Gaultier Ballads (po)
John Mitchel. Life of Aodh O'Neill, Earl of Tyrone (bio)
John Henry Newman. Essay on the Development of Christian Doctrine (e)
John Thomas Smith. A Book for a Rainy Day, or Recollections of the Events of the Years 1766-1833 (pub)
Robert Smith Surtees. Hillingdon Hall (n)
Tom Taylor. To Parents and Guardians (dr)
William Thackeray. Jeames's Diary (fic)
───────────────. Legend of the Rhine (n)
William Whewell. Elements of Morality (e)

1846

BIRTHS
Francis Herbert Bradley
Francis Gasquet
William Robertson Smith

DEATHS
George Darley
John Frere

EVENTS
The Daily News (p, f)

WORKS
Anne Bronte, Charlotte Bronte, and Emily Bronte. Poems by Currer, Ellis, and Acton Bell (pub)
Robert Browning. Bells and Pomegranates (po)
───────────────. A Soul's Tragedy (po)
Edward G.E. Bulwer-Lytton. The New Timon (po)
John Hill Burton. Life of David Hume (bio)
George Croly. Marston (fic)
Charles Darwin. Geological Observations on South America (e, trav)
Charles Dickens. The Battle of Life (fic)
───────────────. Pictures from Italy (nar)
George Eliot. Life of Jesus (trans)
Ebenezer Elliott. Collected Verse (pub)
Richard Ford. Gatherings from Spain (nar)
Mary Anne Green. Letters of Royal Ladies of Great Britain (ed)
George Grote. History of Greece, to 1856 (his)
Julius Hare. The Mission of the Comforter (e)
Benjamin Haydon. Lectures on Painting and Design (e)
Richard Horne. Ballad Romances (po)
Leigh Hunt. Stories from Italian Poets (fic)

THE NINETEENTH CENTURY   161

    _____. Wit and Humour (e)
  John Keble. Lyra Innocentium (po)
  Robert Landor. The Fawn of Sertorius (fic)
  Walter Savage Landor. The Hellenics (po)
  Edward Lear. The Book of Nonsense (fic, po)
  Thomas Moore. History of Ireland (his)
  Carolina Nairne. Lays from Strathearn (po, pub)
  Augustin Pugin. Contrasts: or, A Parallel between the Noble Edifices
              of the Middle Ages, and Corresponding Buildings of
              the Present Day (his, t)
  William Thackeray. Notes of a Journey from Cornhill to Grand Cairo (fic)
  William Torrens. Industrial History of Free Nations (his)
  Richard Trench. Notes on the Miracles of Our Lord (e)
  Rowland Warburton. Hunting Songs and Ballads (po)
  Sir Daniel Wilson. Memorials of Edinburgh in the Olden Time, to 1848
             (his)

                        1847

BIRTHS
  Alice Meynell
  Archibald Primrose, Earl of Rosebury

DEATHS
  Thomas Dibdin

EVENTS
  Bohn's Antiquarian Library (f)

WORKS
  Sir John Barrow. Autobiographical Memoir (pub)
  Anne Bronte. Agnes Grey (n)
  Charlotte Bronte. Jane Eyre (n)
  John Payne Collier. The Roxburghe Ballads (ed)
  Charles Dickens. The Haunted Man (fic)
  Benjamin Disraeli. Tancred (n)
  Sir Arthur Helps. Friends in Council, to 1859 (e)
  Samuel Hole. Hints to Freshmen (e)
  Leigh Hunt. Men, Women, and Books (e)
  Charles Lever. The Knight of Gwynne (fic)
  John Maurice. Moral and Metaphysical Philosophy (t)
  _____. The Religions of the World (e)
  Hugh Miller. Footprints of the Creator (e)
  John Morton. Box and Cox (dr)
  _____. Done on Both Sides (dr)
  John Mason Neale. History of the Holy Eastern Church, to 1850 (his)
  Robert Smith Surtees. Hawbuck Grange (n)
  Sir Henry Taylor. The Eve of Conquest (po)
  Alfred Tennyson. The Princess (po)
  William Thackeray. Mr. Punch's Prize Novelists (s)
  _____. The Snobs of England (s)
  _____. Vanity Fair, to 1848 (n)
  Anthony Trollope. The Macdermots of Ballycloran (n)

1848

BIRTHS
  Arthur James Balfour
  John Churton Collins

DEATHS
  Sarah Flower Adams
  Sir John Barrow
  Emily Bronte
  Isaac Disraeli
  Frederick Marryat

EVENTS
  The Chartists (c)
  The Fleet Prison (des)

WORKS
  William Harrison Ainsworth. The Lancashire Witches (n)
  Dion Boucicault. The Corsican Brothers (dr)
  Anne Bronte. The Tenant of Wildfell Hall (n)
  Emily Bronte. Wuthering Heights (n)
  Edward G.E. Bulwer-Lytton. Harold (n)
  Arthur Hugh Clough. The Bothie of Tober-na-Vuolich (po)
  Charles Dickens. Dombey and Son (n)
  John Forster. The Life and Adventures of Oliver Goldsmith (bio)
  Elizabeth Gaskell. Mary Barton (n)
  James Grant. Adventures of an Aide-de-Camp (n)
  James Halliwell-Phillipps. Life of Shakespeare (bio)
  Sir Arthur Helps. Conquerors of the New World (his)
  Geraldine Jewsbury. The Half-Sisters (n)
  Charles Kingsley. The Saints' Tragedy (po)
  _____. Yeast (n)
  Robert Landor. The Fountain of Arethusa (fic)
  John Stuart Mill. Principles of Political Economy (e)
  John Henry Newman. Loss and Gain (n)
  William Thackeray. Pendennis (n)
  Anthony Trollope. The Kellys and the O'Kellys (n)

1849

BIRTHS
  Sir Edmund Gosse
  William Ernest Henley

DEATHS
  Thomas Lovell Beddoes
  Anne Bronte
  Hartley Coleridge
  Maria Edgeworth
  Pierce Egan
  Ebenezer Elliott
  James Morier
  Horatio Smith
  Patrick Tytler

THE NINETEENTH CENTURY 163

EVENTS
  Eliza Cook's Journal (p, f)
  The Nation (p, c)
  Notes and Queries (p, f)

WORKS
  Matthew Arnold. The Strayed Reveller and Other Poems (pub)
  Charlotte Bronte. Shirley (n)
  Edward G. E. Bulwer-Lytton. The Caxtons (n)
  _____. King Arthur (po)
  Robert Curzon. Visit to the Monasteries of the Levant (trav)
  Thomas DeQuincey. The English Mail Coach (e)
  Charles Dickens. David Copperfield, to 1850 (n)
  Mary Anne Green. Lives of Princesses of Great Britain, to 1855 (bio)
  John Kemble. The Saxons in England (his)
  Charles Lever. Con Cregan (n)
  Sir George Lewis. On the Influence of Authority in Matters of Opinion (e)
  Sir Charles Lyell. Second Visit to North America (trav)
  Thomas Babington Macaulay. History of England, vols I-II (his)
  Henry Mansel. Artis Logicae Rudimenta (e)
  John Westland Marston. Strathmore (dr)
  Harriet Martineau. History of the Thirty Years' Peace, 1815-1845 (his)
  Margaret Oliphant. Passages in the Life of Mrs. Maitland (fic)
  Robert Owen. Revolution in Mind and Practice (e)
  John Ruskin. Seven Lamps of Architecture (t)
  Sir James Stephen. Essays in Ecclesiastical Biography (e)
  William Thackeray. The Ballad of Bouillabaisse (po)
  George Ticknor. History of Spanish Literature (his)
  Richard Trench. Sacred Latin Poetry, Chiefly Lyrical (pub)
  Who's Who (bio, pub)

1850

BIRTHS
  Augustine Birrell
  Frederic Maitland
  Philip Marston
  Robert Louis Stevenson

DEATHS
  Jane Porter
  William Wordsworth

EVENTS
  Alfred, Loed Tennyson, Poet Laureate of England, to 1892
  Household Words (p, f)
  The Germ (p, f, c)
  The Leader (p, f)

WORKS
  Philip James Bailey. The Angel World (po)
  Thomas Lovell Beddoes. Death's Jest-Book; or, The Fool's Tragedy (dr, pub)
  Elizabeth Barrett Browning. Sonnets from the Portuguese (po)
  Robert Browning. Christmas Eve and Easter Day (po)

Thomas Carlyle. Latter-Day Pamphlets (e)
Wilkie Collins. Antonina, or the Fall of Rome (n)
Sidney Dobell. The Roman (po)
Edward Freeman and G.W. Cox. Poems, Legendary and Historical (ed)
Elizabeth Gaskell. The Moorland Cottage (n)
Richard Horne. The Poor Artist (po)
Leigh Hunt. Autobiography (pub)
Charles Kingsley. Alton Locke, Tailor and Poet (n)
Charles Lever. Roland Cashel (n)
Henry Mansel. Phrontisterion (s)
John Westland Marston. Marie de Meranie (dr)
Charles Merivale. History of the Romans under the Empire, to 1864 (his)
Thomas Mayne Reid. The Rifle Rangers (n)
Dante Rossetti. The Blessed Damozel (po)
Francis Smedley. Frank Fairleigh (n)
Agnes Strickland and Elizabeth Strickland. Lives of the Queens of Scotland and English Princesses, to 1859 (bio)
Alfred Tennyson. In Memoriam A.H.H. (po, pub)
William Thackeray. The Kicklebury's on the Rhine (n)
_____. Rebecca and Rowena (n)

1851

BIRTHS
Henry Drummond
Sir Arthur Evans
Henry Jones
Sir Oliver Lodge
Mary Ward

DEATHS
Joanna Baillie
John Lingard
Mary Shelley
Mary Martha Sherwood

EVENTS
The Great Exhibition, Crystal Palace, Hyde Park, London (op)
Victoria and Albert Museum (blt)

WORKS
George Borrow. Lavengro, the Scholar--the Gypsy--the Priest (n)
Thomas Carlyle. The Life of John Sterling (bio)
Hartley Coleridge. Poems (pub)
Edward Fitzgerald. Euphranor (nar)
Elizabeth Gaskell. Cranford, to 1853 (n)
William Gladstone. Letters to the Earl of Aberdeen (e)
Geraldine Jewsbury. Marian Withers (n)
Julia Kavanagh. Natalie (n)
Henry Mansel. Prolegomena Logica (e)
George Meredith. Poems (pub)
John Henry Newman. Lectures on the Present Position of the Roman Catholics (e)
Sir Francis Palgrave. The History of Normandy and England, to 1864 (his)
Thomas Mayne Reid. The Scalp-Hunters (n)

THE NINETEENTH CENTURY   165

      John Ruskin. Stones of Venice, to 1853 (t)
      Herbert Spencer. Social Statics (e)
      Richard Trench. The Study of Words (e)
      Sir Daniel Wilson. The Archaeology and Prehistoric Annals of Scotland
                              (his)

                                 1852

BIRTHS
   Robert Adamson
   Robert Cunninghame-Graham
   Lady Augusta Gregory
   George Moore

DEATHS
   Thomas Moore
   Augustus Pugin

WORKS
   Sir Archibald Alison. Europe. From the Fall of the First to the Aces-
                            sion of the Third Napoleon, to 1859 (his)
   Matthew Arnold. Empedocles and Other Poems (pub)
   Henry Thomas Cockburn. Life of Lord Jeffrey (bio)
   Charles Dickens. Bleak House, to 1853 (n)
   _____. A Child's History of England, to 1854 (his)
   Benjamin Disraeli. Lord George Bentick: A Political Biography (bio)
   Edward Fitzgerald. Polonius (aphorisms)
   Abraham Haywood. The Art of Dining (e)
   Charles Lever. Maurice Tiernay (n)
   Mary Mitford. Recollections of a Literary Life (auto)
   Arthur Munby. Benoni (po)
   John Henry Newman. The Scope and Nature of University Education (e)
   Charles Reade. Masks and Faces (dr)
   Francis Smedley. Lewis Arundel (n)
   Sir James Stephen. Lectures on the History of France (his)
   William Thackeray. Esmond (n)
   William Whewell. The History of Moral Philosophy in England (his, e)

                                 1853

BIRTHS
   Sir Thomas Henry Hall Caine
   Charles Gore

DEATHS
   Amelia Opie

EVENTS
   Ainsworth's Magazine (p, c)

WORKS
   Matthew Arnold. Balder Dead (po)
   _____. Poems (pub)
   Sir Samuel White Baker. Rifle and Hound in Ceylon (trav)
   Edward G.E. Bulwer-Lytton. My Novel (n)

John Hill Burton. A History of Scotland (his)
Thomas DeQuincey. The Works of Thomas DeQuincey, the "Collective Edi-
          tion," to 1860 (pub)
Edward Fitzgerald. Six Dramas of Calderon (trans)
Elizabeth Gaskell. Ruth (n)
James Halliwell-Phillipps. Curiosities of Modern Shakespearean Criti-
          cism (e)
_____. Shakespearean Forgeries at Bridgewater House
          (bibl, e)
Charles Kingsley. Hypatia (n)
Walter Savage Landor. Imaginary Conversations of Greeks and Romans
          (fic, e)
Charles Lever. The Dodd Family Abroad, to 1854 (n)
Harriet Martineau. Philosophie Positive (trans)
John Maurice. Theological Essays (pub)
Charles Merivale. The Fall of the Roman Republic (his)
John Mason Neale. Theodora Phranza, to 1854 (n)
James Payn. Poems (pub)
Charles Reade. Christie Johnstone (n)
_____. It's Never Too Late To Mend (n)
_____. Peg Woffington (n)
John Ruskin. On Architecture and Painting (e)
Lord John Russell. Memoirs of Thomas Moore, to 1856 (ed)
Alexander Smith. A Life Drama (po)
Robert Smith Surtees. Mr. Sponge's Sporting Tour (n)
William Thackeray. The English Humourists of the Eighteenth Century
          (e, pub)
_____. The Newcomes, to 1855 (n)
Alfred Wallace. Travels on the Amazon and Rio Negro (trav)
William Whewell. Plurality of Worlds (t)
George Whyte-Melville. Digby Grand (n)
Charlotte Yonge. The Heir of Redclyffe (n)

                    1854

BIRTHS
   Sir James George Frazer
   John Round
   Oscar Wilde

DEATHS
   Henry Thomas Cockburn
   Thomas Croker
   Susan Ferrier
   John Lockhart
   John Wilson

EVENTS
   Eliza Cook's Journal (p, c)
   London Working Men's College (f)

WORKS
   John Colenso. Ten Weeks in Natal (nar)
   Wilkie Collins. Hide and Seek (n)
   Robert Curzon. Account of the Most Celebrated Libraries of Italy (his,
             trav)

THE NINETEENTH CENTURY   167

　　　　　　　　　. Armenia (trav, his)
Charles Dickens. Hard Times (n)
Sydney Dobell. Balder (po)
George Eliot. Essence of Christianity (trans)
James Ferrier. The Institutes of Metaphysics (e)
Sir Thomas Erskine May. The Rules, Orders, and Proceedings of the
　　　　　　　　　House of Commons (ref)
Hugh Miller. My Schools and Schoolmasters (auto)
Henry Milman. The History of Latin Christianity, to 1855 (his
Mary Mitford. Atherton (n)
Coventry Patmore. The Betrothel (po)
Charles Reade. The Courier of Lyons (dr)
Arthur Stanley. Memorials of Canterbury (his)
Alfred Tennyson. The Charge of the Light Brigade (po)
　　　　　　　　　. Ode on the Death of Wellington (po)
Frederick Tennyson. Days and Hours (po)
Nicholas Wiseman. Fabiola, or the Church of the Catacombs (n)
Charlotte Yonge. Heartsease (n)
　　　　　　　　　　. The Little Duke (n)

                                1855

BIRTHS
　William Ker
　Mary Mackay ("Marie Corelli")
　Sir Arthur Wing Pinero
　William Sharp ("Fiona Macleod")
　Stanley Weyman

DEATHS
　Charlotte Bronte
　Julius Hare
　Mary Mitford
　Robert Montgomery
　Samuel Rogers

EVENTS
　The Daily Telegraph (p, f)
　The Saturday Review (p, f)

WORKS
　Matthew Arnold. Poems, Second Series (pub)
　Philip James Bailey. The Mystic (po)
　Alexander Bain. The Senses and the Intellect (t)
　Robert Browning. Men and Women (po)
　Sir Richard Burton. Personal Narrative of a Pilgrimage to Al Modinah
　　　　　　　　　and Mecca, to 1856 (trav)
　Caroline Archer Clive. Paul Ferroll (n)
　Francis Cobbe. The Theory of Intuitive Morals, to 1857 (e)
　Charles Dickens. Little Dorrit, to 1857 (n)
　Sydney Dobell and Alexander Smith. Sonnets on the War (po)
　Elizabeth Gaskell. North and South (n)
　Sir George Grey. Polynesian Mythology (e)
　Julius Hare. Miscellaneous Pamphlets on Church Questions (e)
　Sir Arthur Helps. The Spanish Conquest in America, to 1861 (his)
　Charles Kingsley. Glaucus; or, the Wonders of the Shore (e)

_____. Westward Ho! (n)
George Lewis. Enquiry into the Credibility of Ancient Roman History (e)
George Lewes. Life of Geothe (bio)
Thomas Babington Macaulay. History of England, vols III-IV (his)
George Macdonald. Within and Without (po)
Francis Smedley. Harry Coverdale's Courtship (n)
Herbert Spencer. Principles of Psychology (e)
Tom Taylor. Still Waters Run Deep (dr)
Alfred Tennyson. Maude (po)
Anthony Trollope. The Warden (n)
Charlotte Yonge. The Lances of Lynwood (n)

1856

BIRTHS
 Alfred Godley
 Thomas Anstey Guthrie
 H. Rider Haggard
 Richard Haldane
 Frank Harris
 George Bernard Shaw

DEATHS
 Hugh Miller
 William Yarrell

EVENTS
 National Portrait Gallery London (op)
 The Oxford and Cambridge Magazine (p, f, c)

WORKS
 Henry Thomas Cockburn. Memorials of His Times (nar, his)
 Sydney Dobell. England in Time of War (po)
 Alexander Fraser. Essays in Philosophy (e)
 Edward Freeman. History and Conquests of the Saracens (his)
 James Froude. History of England from the Fall of Wolsey to the Defeat of the Spanish Armada, to 1870 (his)
 Charles Kingsley. The Heroes (fic)
 George Meredith. The Shaving of Shagpot: an Arabian Entertainment (fic)
 John Mitchel. Jail Journal, or Five Years in British Prisons (nar)
 John Henry Newman. Callista (n)
 Coventry Patmore. The Espousals (po)
 Edward Pusey. Doctrine of the Real Presence (e)
 Arthur Stanley. Sinai and Palestine (his)
 Charlotte Yonge. The Daisy Chain (n)

1857

BIRTHS
 Ada Ellen Bayly ("Edna Lyall")
 Joseph Conrad
 John Davidson
 George Gissing

DEATHS
  John Wilson Croker
  Douglas Jerrold
  John Kemble

EVENTS
  Crockford's Clerical Directory (ref, f)

WORKS
  George Borrow. The Romany Rye (n)
  Charlotte Bronte. The Professor (n, pub)
  Elizabeth Barrett Browning. Aurora Leigh (po)
  Edward R. Bulwer-Lytton. Wanderer (po)
  Chronicles and Memorials of Great Britain and Ireland, from the Invasion of the Romans to the Reign of Henry VIII, to 1914 (his, pub)
  Wilkie Collins. The Dead Secret (n)
  John Wilson Croker. Essays on the Early Period of the French Revolution (his, e)
  George Eliot. Amos Barton (fic)
  _____. Janet's Repentance (fic)
  _____. Mr. Gilfil's Love-Story (fic)
  Elizabeth Gaskell. The Life of Charlotte Bronte (bio)
  Mary Ann Green. Life and Letters of Henrietta Maria (bio)
  Thomas Hughes. Tom Brown's Schooldays (n)
  John Kemble. State Papers, 1688-1714 (ed)
  Charles Kingsley. Two Years Ago (n)
  George Lawrence. Guy Livingstone (n)
  David Livingstone. Missionary Travels in South Africa (trav)
  Frederick Locker. London Lyrics (po)
  John Westland Marston. A Life's Ransom (dr)
  George Meredith. Farina, a Legend of Cologne (fic)
  Hugh Miller. The Testimony of the Rocks (e, pub)
  Dinah Mulock. John Halifax, Gentleman (n)
  Charles Reade. The Course of True Love Never Did Run Smooth (n)
  John Ruskin. The Political Economy of Art (e)
  Samuel Smiles. Life of George Stephenson (bio)
  Alexander Smith. City Poems (pub)
  William Stubbs. Registrum Sacrum Anglicanum (his)
  William Thackeray. Christmas Books (fic, pub)
  _____. The Virginians, to 1859 (n)
  Anthony Trollope. Barchester Towers (n)
  Charlotte Yonge. Dynevor Terrace (n)

1858

BIRTHS
  Edith Nesbit
  Hastings Rashdall
  Edith Somerville
  Sir William Watson

DEATHS
  Richard Ford
  Robert Owen

EVENTS
  The Society of Doctors' Commons (c)

WORKS
  Matthew Arnold. Merope, a Tragedy (po)
  Philip James Bailey. The Age (s)
  John Brown. Horae Subsecivae, I (e)
  Edward G.E. Bulwer-Lytton. What Will He Do With It? (n)
  Thomas Carlyle. The History of Frederick the Great, to 1865 (bio)
  William Johnson Cory. Ionica (po)
  William Farrar. Eric, or Little by Little (n)
  John Forster. Historical and Biographical Essays (e)
  Elizabeth Gaskell. My Lady Ludlow (n)
  William Gladstone. Studies on Homer and the Homeric Age (e)
  Abraham Hayward. Essays (e)
  Julia Kavanagh. Adele (n)
  George Lewes. Seaside Studies (e)
  George Macdonald. Phantasies: A Faerie Romance (fic, po)
  Henry Mansel. The Limits of Religious Thought (e)
  William Morris. Defence of Guenevere, and Other Poems (pub)
  Adelaide Anne Procter. Legends and Lyrics, to 1861 (po)
  George Rawlinson. The History of Herodotus, to 1860 (trans)
  Charles Reade. The Autobiography of a Thief (n)
  _____. Jack of All Trades (n)
  Robert Smith Surtees. Ask Mamma (n)
  Tom Taylor. Our American Cousin (dr)
  Edward Trelawny. Records of Shelley, Byron, and the Author (bio, nar)
  Anthony Trollope. Doctor Thorne (n)
  _____. The Three Clerks (n)

1859

BIRTHS
  Sir Arthur Conan Doyle
  Havelock Ellis
  A.E. Housman
  Sir Sidney Lee
  James Stephen
  Francis Thompson

DEATHS
  Thomas DeQuincey
  Mountstuart Elphinstone
  Henry Hallam
  Leigh Hunt
  Sir James Stephen
  Thomas Babington Macaulay
  Lady Sydney Morgan

EVENTS
  All the Year Round (p, f)
  The Cornhill Magazine (p, f)
  Household Words (p, c)
  Macmillan's Magazine (p, f)
  Vauxhall Gardens, London (c)

WORKS
  Alexander Bain. The Emotions and the Will (t)
  William Barnes. Poems of Rural Life, 2nd series (pub)
  Dion Boucicault. The Colleen Bawn (dr)
  Edward G.E. Bulwer-Lytton. The Haunted and the Haunters (fic)
  Chambers's Encyclopaedia, to 1868 (ref, pub)
  Charles Darwin. On the Origin of Species by Means of Natural Selection
              (e)
  Sir George Dasent. Popular Tales from the Norse (trans)
  Charles Dickens. A Tale of Two Cities (n)
  Emily Eden. The Semi-Detached House (n)
  George Eliot. Adam Bede (n)
  Edward Fitzgerald. The Rubaiyat of Omar Khayyam (po, trans)
  Elizabeth Gaskell. Lois the Witch (n)
  Samuel Hole. A Little Tour in Ireland (trav)
  Richard Horne. Australian Facts and Prospects (nar)
  Thomas Hughes. The Scouring of the White Horse (n)
  Geraldine Jewsbury. Right or Wrong (n)
  Charles Kingsley. Andromeda (po)
  Henry Kingsley. Geoffrey Hamlyn (n)
  George Lawrence. Sword and Gown (n)
  George Lewes. Physiology of Common Life (e)
  David Masson. Life of Milton, to 1880 (bio)
  George Meredith. The Ordeal of Richard Feverel (n)
  John Stuart Mill. Dissertations and Discussions, 2 vols (e)
  _____. On Liberty (e)
  _____. Thoughts on Parliamentary Reform (e)
  John Henry Newman. Lectures on Universities (e)
  Charles Reade. Love Me Little, Love Me Long (n)
  John Ruskin. Two Paths (e)
  Lord John Russell. Life and Times of Charles James Fox, to 1860 (bio,
              his)
  Nassau Senior. Journals--Kept in Turkey and Greece (nar)
  Samuel Smiles. Self-Help (e)
  Alfred Tennyson. Idylls of the King, to 1885 (po)
  Rowland Warburton. Hunting Songs and Miscellaneous Verses (pub)

                         1860

BIRTHS
  Sir James Matthew Barrie
  Douglas Hyde
  William Inge
  Frederick Rolfe

DEATHS
  George Croly
  George James

WORKS
  Charlotte Bronte. Emma (fic, pub)
  Elizabeth Barrett Browning. Poems before Congress (po)
  Edward R. Bulwer-Lytton. Lucile (po)
  Wilkie Collins. The Woman in White (n)
  Charles Dickens. Great Expectations, to 1861 (n)
  Emily Eden. The Semi-Detached Couple (n)

George Eliot. The Mill on the Floss (n)
Essays and Reviews (e, ed)
Sir John Evans. Flint Implements of the Drift (his)
John Forster. The Arrest of the Five Members (e)
_____. The Debates on the Grand Remonstrance (e)
James Halliwell-Phillipps. Dictionary of Old English Plays (ref)
Benjamin Jowett. The Interpretation of Scripture (e)
William E.H. Lecky. The Religious Tendencies of the Age (e)
Henry Mansel. Metaphysics (e)
George Meredith. Evan Harrington (n)
Coventry Patmore. Faithful For Ever (po)
Mark Pattison. Tendencies of Religious Thought in England, 1688 to 1750 (e, his)
Sir William Smith. Dictionary of the Bible, to 1863 (ref)
Herbert Spencer. Programme of a System of Synthetic Philosophy (e)
Robert Smith Surtees. Plain or Ringlets (n)
Alfred Tennyson. Tithonus (po, pub)
William Thackeray. The Four Georges (e, pub)
_____. Lovel the Widower (n)
John Tyndall. The Glaciers of the Alps (e)
George Whyte-Melville. Holmby House (n)

1861

BIRTHS
Mary Elizabeth Coleridge
Oliver Elton
Maurice Hewlett
Sir Walter Raleigh
George Tyrrell
Alfred North Whitehead

DEATHS
Elizabeth Barrett Browning
Arthur Hugh Clough
Catherine Gore
Sir Francis Palgrave

EVENTS
The Bannatyne Club (c)
The Metropolitan Tabernacle, Newington, London (blt)

WORKS
Matthew Arnold. On Translating Homer (e)
_____. The Popular Education of France (e)
John Brown. Horae Subsecivae, II (e)
John Colenso. Commentary on the Epistle to the Romans (t)
Sir George Dasent. The Story of Burnt Njal (trans)
George Eliot. Silas Marner (n)
Thomas Hughes. Tom Brown at Oxford (n)
Hymns Ancient and Modern (po, pub)
Thomas Babington Macaulay. History of England, vol V (his, pub)
Sir Henry Maine. Ancient Law (e)
Sir Thomas Erskine May. The Constitutional History of England Since the Accession of George III, to 1863 (his)
Henry Mayhew. London Labour and the London Poor, 4 vols, to 1862 (e)

John Stuart Mill. Representative Government (e)
_____. Utilitarianism (e)
Francis Turner Palgrave. The Golden Treasury of Songs and Lyrics, 1st series (ed)
Thomas Love Peacock. Gryll Grange (n)
Charles Reade. The Cloister and the Hearth (n)
Dante Rossetti. The Early Italian Poets (ed, trans)
Samuel Smiles. Lives of the Engineers, to 1862 (bio)
Herbert Spencer. Education: Intellectual, Moral, and Physical (e)
Philip Stanhope. The Life of William Pitt, to 1862 (bio)
Arthur Stanley. Lectures on the History of the Eastern Church (his)
Algernon Swinburne. The Queen Mother. Rosamond. Two Plays (dr)
William Thackeray. The Adventures of Philip, to 1862 (n)
Anthony Trollope. Framley Parsonage (n)
George Whyte-Melville. Tilbury Nogo (n)
Ellen Wood. East Lynne (n)

1862

BIRTHS
  David Hogarth
  Montague James
  Sir Henry Newbolt
  Hugh Stowell Scott ("Henry Merriman")

DEATHS
  James Knowles
  Charles Whitehead

EVENTS
  The Leander Club (f)
  The Morning Chronicle, London (p, c)

WORKS
  George Borrow. Wild Wales (n)
  Mary Elizabeth Braddon. Lady Audley's Secret (n)
  Elizabeth Barrett Browning. Last Poems (pub)
  Edward G.E. Bulwer-Lytton. A Strange Story (fic)
  John Hill Burton. The Book-hunter (e)
  Charles Stuart Calverley. Verses and Translations (po)
  Robert Chambers. Book of Days, to 1864 (ref)
  Arthur Hugh Clough. Amours de Voyage (po)
  _____. Mari Magno (fic)
  John Colenso. A Critical Examination of the Pentateuch (t)
  Wilkie Collins. My Miscellanies (n)
  _____. No Name (n)
  Charles Darwin. The Fertilisation of Orchids (e)
  George Eliot. Romola, to 1863 (n)
  Richard Garnett. Relics of Shelley (nar, ed)
  Frederic Harrison. The Meaning of History (e)
  Henry Kingsley. Ravenshoe (n)
  William E.H. Lecky. Leaders of Public Opinion in Ireland (e)
  George Lewes. Studies of Animal Life (e)
  Sir George Lewis. The Astronomy of the Ancients (e)
  George Meredith. Modern Love (po)
  Coventry Patmore. The Victories of Love (po)

Adelaide Anne Procter. A Chaplet of Verses (po)
Christina Rossetti. Goblin Market and Other Poems (po)
John Ruskin. Unto This Last (e, pub)
Herbert Spencer. First Principles (e)
Sir James Fitzjames Stephen. Essays, by a Barrister (pub)
_____. Horae Sabbaticae (e)
Sir Henry Taylor. St. Clement's Eve (po, dr)
_____. A Sicilian Summer (po, dr)
Anthony Trollope. Orley Farm (n)
John Tyndall. Mountaineering (e)
Ellen Wood. The Channings (n)
Thomas Wright. History of Domestic Manners and Sentiments in England during the Middle Ages (his)

1863

BIRTHS
Sir Charles Eliot
Sir Anthony Hope Hawkins ("Anthony Hope")
William Jacobs
William Locke
Arthur Machen
Sir Arthur Quiller-Couch

DEATHS
Sir George Lewis
William Thackeray
Frances Trollope
Richard Whately

WORKS
John Austin. Lectures on Jurisprudence (e)
William Barnes. Poems of Rural Life, 3rd series (pub)
Edward Freeman. The History of Federal Government (his)
Samuel Gardiner. History of England from the Accession of James I to the Disgrace of Chief Justice Coke (his)
Elizabeth Gaskell. Sylvia's Lovers, to 1864 (n)
Thomas Huxley. Man's Place in Nature (e)
Jean Ingelow. Divided (po)
_____. The High Tide on the Coast of Lincolnshire, 1571 (po)
Alexander William Kinglake. The War in the Crimea, to 1887 (his, nar)
Charles Kingsley. The Water Babies (n)
Henry Kingsley. Austin Elliott (n)
William E.H. Lecky. The Declining Sense of the Miraculous (e)
Joseph LeFanu. The House by the Churchyard (fic)
Charles Lever. A Day's Ride (n)
Sir Charles Lyell. The Antiquity of Man (e)
George Macdonald. David Elginbrod (n)
Margaret Oliphant. Chronicles of Carlingford, to 1876 (n)
Charles Reade. Hard Cash (n)
William Reade. Savage Africa (e, trav)
Nassau Senior. Biographical Sketches (bio)
Alexander Smith. Dreamthorp (e)
John Speke. Journal of the Discovery of the Source of the Nile (nar)
Arthur Stanley. Lectures on the History of the Jewish Church, to 1876 (his, e)

THE NINETEENTH CENTURY 175

Sir James Fitzjames Stephen. A General View of the Criminal Law in
England, to 1890 (e)
George Otto Trevelyan. The Dawk Bungalow (dr)
John Tyndall. Heat Considered As a Mode of Motion (e)
George Whyte-Melville. The Gladiators (n)

1864

BIRTHS
  Barry Pain
  Israel Zangwill

DEATHS
  John Clare
  James Ferrier
  Walter Savage Landor
  Adelaide Anne Procter
  Nassau Senior
  Francis Smedley
  Robert Smith Surtees

EVENTS
  Early English Text Society (f)

WORKS
  Richard Doddridge Blackmore. Clara Vaughan (n)
  Dion Boucicault. Arrah-na-Pogue (dr)
  Robert Browning. Dramatis Personae (po)
  James Bryce. The Holy Roman Empire (his)
  John Hill Burton. The Scot Abroad (trav, e)
  Frances Power Cobbe. Broken Lights (e)
  Charles Darwin. The Movement and Habits of Climbing Plants (e)
  Charles Dickins. Our Mutual Friend, to 1865 (n)
  Sir John Evans. The Coins of Ancient Britons (his)
  John Forster. Life of Sir John Eliot (bio)
  Elizabeth Gaskell. Wives and Daughters, to 1866 (n)
  Charles Kingsley. The Roman and the Teuton (e)
  Joseph LeFanu. Uncle Silas (n)
  Charles Lever. Cornelius O'Dowd (n)
  George Meredith. Emilia in England (n)
  Charles Merivale. Conversion of the Roman Empire (his)
  Hugh Munro. The Works of Lucretius (ed, trans)
  John Henry Newman. Apologia pro Vita Sua (e)
  James Payn. Lost Sir Massingberd (n)
  Thomas Robertson. David Garrick (dr)
  Nassau Senior. Essays on Fiction (pub)
  Walter Skeat. Lancelot of the Laik (ed)
  Herbert Spencer. The Classification of the Sciences (e)
  _____. Principles of Biology (e)
  William Stubbs. Chronicles and Memorials of Richard I, to 1865 (his,
ed)
  Alfred Tennyson. Enoch Arden (po)
  William Thackeray. Denis Duval (n, pub)
  George Otto Trevelyan. Letters of a Competition Wallah (nar)
  Anthony Trollope. The Small House at Allington (n)
  John Wisden and Company. A Cricketer's Almanack (ref, pub)

1865

BIRTHS
　Laurence Housman
　Rudyard Kipling
　Arthur Symons
　William Butler Yeats

DEATHS
　Elizabeth Gaskell

EVENTS
　The Abbotsford Club (c)
　The Christian Mission (f)
　The Contemporary Review (p, f)
　The Fortnightly Review (p, f)
　The Pall-Mall Gazette (p, f)

WORKS
　Matthew Arnold. Essays in Criticism (e)
　Lewis Carroll. Alice's Adventures in Wonderland (fic)
　John Payne Collier. Notes on Rare English Books (ref, bibl)
　George Grote. Plato and Other Companions of Socrates (e)
　Shadworth Hodgson. Time and Space: A Metaphysical Essay (e)
　Charles Kingsley. Hereward the Wake (n)
　Henry Kingsley. The Hillyars and the Burtons (n)
　William E.H. Lecky. History of Rationalism (e)
　Charles Lever. Luttrell of Arran (n)
　David Livingstone. The Zambesi and Its Tributaries (trav)
　George Macdonald. Alec Forbes (n)
　Theodore Martin. Faust, Part I (trans)
　George Meredith. Rhoda Fleming (n)
　John Stuart Mill. Auguste Comte and Positivism (e)
　_____. Examination of Sir William Hamilton's Philosophy (e)
　Arthur Munby. Verses New and Old (pub)
　William Palgrave. Narrative of a Year's Journey through Central and
　　　　　　　　　　Eastern Arabia (trav)
　Thomas Robertson. Society (dr)
　William Rossetti. Inferno (trans, po)
　John Ruskin. Sesame and Lilies (e)
　Sir John Seeley. Ecce Homo (bio)
　Alexander Smith. A Summer in Skye (e)
　James Stirling. Analysis of Sir William Hamilton's Philosophy (e)
　_____. The Secret of Hegel (trans, e)
　Agnes Strickland. How Will It End? (n)
　Robert Smith Surtees. Mr. Facey Romford's Hounds (n, pub)
　Algernon Swinburne. Atalanta in Calydon (po, dr)
　_____. Chastelard (dr)
　George Otto Trevelyan. Cawnpore (his, nar)
　Anthony Trollope. The Belton Estate (n)
　John Tyndale. On Radiation (e)
　Charlotte Yonge. The Prince and the Page (n)

1866

BIRTHS
  Sir Edmund Chambers
  Richard LeGallienne
  John McTaggart
  Gworge Murray
  Beatrix Potter
  H.G. Wells

DEATHS
  Jane Carlyle
  John Keble
  John Mason Neale
  Thomas Love Peacock
  Ann Taylor
  William Whewell

EVENTS
  The Leader (p,c)
  The London Library, St. James's Square (f)

WORKS
  Richard Doddridge Blackmore. Cradock Nowell (n)
  Robert Buchanan. London Poems (pub)
  Sir Francis Cowley Burnand. Black-eyed Susan (dr)
  Wilkie Collins. Armadale (n)
  John Cornington. The Aeneid (trans)
  Emily Eden. Up the Country (trav)
  George Eliot. Felix Holt (n)
  James Ferrier. Lectures on Greek Philosophy and Other Philosophical
          Remains (e)
  William S. Gilbert. Dulcamara (dr)
  Henry Kingsley. Leighton Court (n)
  John Westland Marston. The Favourite of Fortune (dr)
  George Meredith. Vittoria (n)
  Charles Merivale. Conversion of the Northern Nations (his)
  John Henry Newman. The Dream of Gerontius (po)
  Charles Reade. Griffith Gaunt (n)
  Thomas Mayne Reid. The Headless Horseman (n)
  Thomas Robertson. Ours (dr)
  James Rogers. History of Agriculture and Prices in England from 1259
          to 1793, to 1887 (his)
  Christina Rossetti. The Prince's Progress (po)
  John Ruskin. The Crown of Wild Olive (e)
  _____. The Ethics of the Dust (e)
  Walter Skeat. Piers Plowman (ed)
  Robert Louis Stevenson. The Pentland Rising of 1666 (his, e)
  Hesba Stretton. Jessica's First Prayer (n)
  Algernon Swinburne. Poems and Ballads (pub)
  John Warren. Philoctetes (dr)
  Charlotte Yonge. The Dove in the Eagle's Nest (n)

1867

BIRTHS
  Arnold Bennett
  Mrs. P.M.T. Craigie ("John Oliver Hobbes")
  Ernest Dowson
  John Galsworthy
  Lionel Johnson
  Charles Montague
  George William Russell ("AE")

DEATHS
  Sir Archibald Alison
  Alexander Smith

WORKS
  Matthew Arnold. New Poems (pub)
  _____. The Study of Celtic Literature (e)
  Walter Bagehot. The English Constitution (t)
  Philip James Bailey. The Universal Hymn (po)
  Rhoda Broughton. Cometh up As a Flower (n)
  _____. Not Wisely But Too Well (n)
  Sir Francis Cowley Burnand. Cox and Box (dr)
  George Eliot. How Lisa Loved the King (po)
  Edward Freeman. History of the Norman Conquest, to 1879 (his)
  James Froude. Short Studies on Great Subjects (e)
  William Carew Hazlitt. Handbook to the Popular, Political, and Dramatic Literature of Great Britain. . .to the Restoration (ref)
  Henry Huth. Ancient Ballads and Broadsides (ed)
  Jean Ingelow. A Story of Doom (po)
  Henry Kingsley. Silcote of Silcotes (n)
  Henry Liddon. The Divinity of Our Lord and Saviour Jesus Christ (ser)
  Frederick Locker. Lyra Elegantiarum (po)
  John Stuart Mill. Inaugural Address (sp)
  John Morley. Edmund Burke; an Historical Study (bio, his)
  William Morris. Life and Death of Jason (po)
  Frederic Myers. St. Paul (po)
  Ouida. Under Two Flags (n)
  Anne Ritchie. The Village on the Cliff (n)
  Thomas Robertson. Caste (dr)
  William Rossetti. Fine Art, Chiefly Contemporary (e, pub)
  John Ruskin. Time and Tide, by Weare and Tyne (e)
  Algernon Swinburne. A Song of Italy (po)
  Anthony Trollope. The Claverings (n)
  _____. The Last Chronicle of Barset (n)
  John Tyndall. On Sound (e)
  Victoria, Queen of England. Leaves from a Journal of Our Life in the Highlands, 1848-1861 (nar)

1868

BIRTHS
  George Calderon
  George Norman Douglas
  Robert Scott

THE NINETEENTH CENTURY   179

    DEATHS
      Henry Peter Brougham
      Samuel Lover
      Henry Milman

    EVENTS
      The Chaucer Society (f)
      Kottabos (p, f)
      The Royal Historical Society (f)

    WORKS
      William Harrison Ainsworth. The South Sea Bubble (n)
      Matthew Arnold. Schools and Universities on the Continent (e)
      Alexander Bain. Mental and Moral Science (t)
      Robert Browning. The Ring and the Book, to 1869 (po)
      Edward Caird. Philosophy of Kant (t)
      Wilkie Collins. The Moonstone (n)
      John Conington. The Iliad (trans)
      Charles Darwin. Variation of Animals and Plants under Domestication
          (e)
      Sir Charles Dilke. Greater Britain (trav)
      George Eliot. The Spanish Gypsy (po)
      Sir Arthur Helps. Realmah (n)
      Thomas Huxley. The Physical Basis of Life (e)
      Henry Milman. Annals of St. Paul's Cathedral (his, pub)
      William Morris. Earthly Paradise, to 1870 (po)
      John Henry Newman. Verses on Various Occasions (po)
      Thomas Robertson. Play (dr)
      Nassau Senior. Journals--Relating to Ireland (nar, pub)
      Arthur Stanley. Memorials of Westminster Abbey (his)
      Alfred Tennyson. Lucretius (po)
      John Warren. Orsetes (dr)
      Whitaker's Almanack (ref, pub)

                                    1869

    BIRTHS
      Laurence Binyon

    DEATHS
      William Carleton
      John Conington
      Emily Eden
      Robert Landor

    EVENTS
      The Academy (p, f)
      Girton College (f)
      The Harleian Society (f)
      The Historical Manuscripts Commission (f)
      Hudson's Bay Company (c)
      The Metaphysical Society (f)
      The Morning Herald, London (p, c)
      Nature (p, f)

WORKS
  Matthew Arnold. Culture and Anarchy (e)
  Richard Doddridge Blackmore. Lorna Doone (n)
  Arthur Hugh Clough. Dipsychus (po)
  Charles Dodgson. Phantasmagoria and Other Poems (pub)
  George Eliot. Agatha (po)
  John Forster. Walter Savage Landor (bio)
  William S. Gilbert. Bab Ballads (po)
  William Gladstone. Juventus Mundi (e)
  Samuel Hole. Book about Roses (e)
  Patrick Joyce. Irish Names of Places (ref)
  John Keble. Miscellaneous Poems (pub)
  William E.H. Lecky. History of European Morals from Augustus to Char-
           lemagne (his)
  John Westland Marston. Life for Life (dr)
  John Stuart Mill. The Subjugation of Women (e)
  John Mitchel. History of Ireland (his)
  Ouida. Tricotrin (n)
  Charles Reade. Foul Play (n)
  Thomas Robertson. School (dr)
  Alfred Tennyson. The Holy Grail (po)
  George Otto Trevelyan. Horace at the University of Athens (s)
  _____. The Ladies in Parliament (s)
  Anthony Trollope. Phineas Finn (n)
  John Tyndall. On Light (e)
  Alfred Wallace. Malay Archipelago (trav)

                        1870

BIRTHS
  Hilaire Belloc
  Lord Alfred Douglas
  Hector Munro ("Saki")
  Ethel Richardson ("Henry Handel Richardson")

DEATHS
  Charles Dickens

EVENTS
  All the Year Round (p, c)
  Keble College, Oxford (f)

WORKS
  Matthew Arnold. St. Paul and Protestantism (e)
  Alexander Bain. Logic (t)
  Brewer's Dictionary of Phrase and Fable (ref, pub)
  Edward G.E. Bulwer-Lytton. King Arthur, rev ed (po)
  Richard William Church. St. Anselm (bio)
  Wilkie Collins. Man and Wife (n)
  Eliza Cook. Poems (pub)
  Charles Dickens. Edwin Drood (n)
  Benjamin Disraeli. Lothair (n)
  George Eliot. Armgart (po)
  _____. The Legend of Jubal (po)
  William S. Gilbert. The Palace of Truth (po)
  Shadworth Hodgson. The Theory of Practice (e)

Henry Huth. Inedited Poetical Miscellanies (1584-1700) (bibl)
Thomas Huxley. Lay Sermons, Addresses, and Reviews (e)
Edward Lear. Nonsense Songs, Stories, and Botany (po, fic)
George Meredith. The Adventures of Harry Richmond (n)
John Henry Newman. The Grammar of Assent (t)
Arthur O'Shaughnessy. An Epic of Women (po)
Ouida. Puck (n)
Henry Pullen. The Fight in Dame Europa's School (fic)
Charles Reade. Put Yourself in His Place (n)
Thomas Robertson. M.P. (dr)
Dante Rossetti. Poems by D.G. Rossetti (pub)
Walter Skeat. The Bruce (ed)
Herbert Spencer. Principles of Psychology, to 1872 (e)
Philip Stanhope. The History of England, Comprising the Reign of Anne until the Peace of Utrecht (his)
Arthur Stanley. Essays, Chiefly on Questions of Church and State (e)
William Stubbs. Select Charters and Other Illustrations of English Constitutional History (ed)
George Whyte-Melville. Contraband (n)
Charlotte Yonge. The Caged Lion (n)

1871

BIRTHS
William Davies
Ralph Hodgson
John Millington Synge

DEATHS
Robert Chambers
George Grote
Henry Mansel
Thomas Robertson

WORKS
Jane Austen. Lady Susan (fic, pub)
_____. The Watsons (fic, pub)
William Black. A Daughter of Heth (n)
Henry Peter Brougham. The Life and Times of Lord Brougham (bio)
Robert Browning. Balaustion's Adventure (po)
_____. Prince Hohenstiel-Schwangau (po)
Edward G.E. Bulwer-Lytton. The Coming Race (n)
Sir George Tomkyns Chesney. The Battle of Dorking (fic)
William John Courthope. The Poetical Works of Alexander Pope, to 1889 (ed)
Charles Darwin. The Descent of Man (e)
George Eliot. Middlemarch, to 1872 (n)
William S. Gilbert. Pygmalion and Galatea (po, dr)
Thomas Hardy. Desperate Remedies (n)
Sir Arthur Helps. Brevia (e)
Richard Hutton. Essays, Theological and Literary (e)
Charles Kingsley. At Last (trav)
Sir Henry Maine. Village Communities (e)
Philip Marston. Song-tide, and Other Poems (pub)
John Morley. Critical Miscellanies, 1st series (e)
Sir Lewis Morris. Songs of Two Worlds (po)

Ouida. Folle Farine (n)
Charles Reade. A Terrible Temptation (n)
John Ruskin. Fors Clavigera, to 1884 (e)
Nassau Senior. Journals Kept in France and Italy (nar, pub)
Henry Sidgwick. Ethics of Conformity and Subscription (e)
Walter Skeat. Anglo-Saxon Gospels, to 1887 (ed)
Samuel Smiles. Character (e)
Sir Leslie Stephen. The Playground of Europe (nar, trav)
William Stubbs and A.W. Haddan. The Councils and Ecclesiastical Documents of Great Britain, to 1878 (ed)
Algernon Swinburne. Songs before Sunrise (po)
Alfred Tennyson. The Last Tournament (po)
Edward Whymper. Scrambles in the Alps (nar)
George Whyte-Melville. Sarchedon (n)

1872

BIRTHS
Sir Max Beerbohm
John Cowper Powys
Dorothy Richardson
Bertrand Russell

DEATHS
Charles Lever
John Maurice
John Poole

WORKS
Alexander Bain. Mind and Body (t)
Sir Samuel White Baker. The Nile Tributaries of Abyssinia (trav)
William Black. The Strange Adventures of Phaeton (fic)
Richard Doddridge Blackmore. The Maid of Sker (n)
Robert Browning. Fifine at the Fair (po)
Samuel Butler. Erewhon (fic)
Frances Power Cobbe. Darwinism in Morals (t)
Wilkie Collins. Poor Miss Finch (n)
Charles Darwin. The Expression of the Emotions in Man and Animals (e)
Charles Didgson. Through the Looking-Glass (fic)
Alfred Domett. Ranolf and Amohia, a South Sea Day Dream (po)
Emily Eden. Letters from India (nar, pub)
Sir John Evans. The Ancient Stone Implements, Weapons, and Ornaments of Great Britain (his)
Sir Samuel Ferguson. Congal (po)
John Forster. Charles Dickens, to 1874 (bio)
James Froude. The English in Ireland in the Eighteenth Century, to 1874 (his)
George Grote. Aristotle (e, pub)
Thomas Hardy. Under the Greenwood Tree (n)
Samuel Hole. The Six of Spades (e)
Andrew Lang. Ballads and Lyrics of Old France (po)
Joseph LeFanu. In a Glass Darkly (fic)
Charles Lever. Lord Kilgobbin (n)
John Morley. Voltaire (bio)
William Morris. Love is enough (po)
Arthur O'Shaughnessy. Lays of France (po)

Ouida. A Dog in Flanders (fic)
William Palgrave. Hermann Agha (n)
Charles Reade. The Wandering Heir (n)
William Reade. The Martyrdom of Man (e)
Christina Rossetti. Sing-Song (po)
John Ruskin. Munera Pulveris (e, pub)
Nassau Senior. Correspondence and Conversations of A. de Tocqueville (pub)
Arthur Stanley. Lectures on the Church of Scotland (e, his)
Sir Henry Stanley. How I Found Livingstone (nar, trav)
Alfred Tennyson. Gareth and Lynette (po)
John Tyndall. Contributions to Molecular Physics (e)
George Whyte-Melville. Satanella (n)

1873

BIRTHS
  Walter De La Mare
  Ford Madox Ford
  George Edward Moore
  Henry Tomlinson

DEATHS
  Edward G.E. Bulwer-Lytton
  Robert Curzon
  Joseph LeFanu
  David Livingstone
  John Stuart Mill

EVENTS
  The English Dialect Society (f)

WORKS
  Matthew Arnold. Literature and Dogma (e)
  Walter Bagehot. Lombard Street (e)
  William Black. A Princess of Thule (n)
  Robert Bridges. Shorter Poems, various eds to 1893 (pub)
  Thomas Edward Brown. Betsy Lee, a Foc's'le Yarn (po)
  Robert Browning. Red Cotton Nightcap Country (po)
  Edward G.E. Bulwer-Lytton. Kenelm Chillingly (n)
  _____. The Parisians (n)
  Wilkie Collins. The New Magdalen (n)
  Henry Austin Dobson. Vignettes in Rhyme (po)
  Juliana Ewing. A Flat Iron for a Farthing (fic)
  _____. Lob-lie-by-the-Fire (fic)
  _____. The Miller's Thumb (fic)
  William S. Gilbert. More Bab Ballads (po)
  _____ and Arthur a'Beckett. The Happy Land (dr)
  James Grant. British Battles on Land and Sea (his)
  Thomas Hardy. A Pair of Blue Eyes (n)
  Abraham Hayward. Essays (pub)
  Thomas Hughes. Memoir of a Brother (bio)
  Thomas Huxley. Critiques and Addresses (e)
  Charles Kingsley. Prose Idylls (pub)
  George Lewes. Problems of a Life and Mind, to 1879 (e)
  John Stuart Mill. Autobiography (pub)

John Morley. Rousseau (bio)
_____. The Struggle for National Education (e)
Sir James Murray. Dialect of the Southern Counties of Scotland (e)
John Henry Newman. The Idea of a University Defined (e)
Walter Pater. Studies in the History of the Renaissance (e)
William Reade. The African Sketch-book (nar, trav)
Anne Ritchie. Old Kensington (n)
Herbert Spencer. The Study of Sociology (e)
Sir Leslie Stephen. Essays on Free Thinking and Plain Speaking (e)
Sir James Fitzjames Stephen. Liberty, Equality, Fraternity (e)
John Symonds. Studies of the Greek Poets (e)
Anthony Trollope. The Eustace Diamonds (n)
John Tyndall. Lectures on Light (pub)

1874

BIRTHS
Maurice Baring
G.K. Chesterton
Winston Churchill
W. Somerset Maugham

DEATHS
Sydney Dobell
Agnes Strickland

EVENTS
The Cavendish Laboratory, Cambridge (f)

WORKS
Sir Samuel White Baker. Ismailia (trav)
Robert Buchanan. Master Spirits (po)
Marcus Andrew Clarke. For the Term of His Natural Life (n)
Sir Charles Dilke. The Fall of Prince Florestan of Monaco (s)
George Eliot. Daniel Deronda, to 1876 (n)
Samuel Gardiner. The Thirty Years' War (his)
William Gladstone. The Vatican Decrees in Their Bearing on Civil Allegiance (e)
John Green. A Short History of the English People (his)
Thomas Hardy. Far from the Madding Crowd (n)
Abraham Hayward. Essays (pub)
Henry Huth. Prefaces, Dedications, and Epistles (1540-1701) (bibl)
David Livingstone. Last Journals in Central Africa, 1865 to His Death (nar, pub)
John Morley. On Compromise (e)
Arthur O'Shaughnessy. Music and Moonlight (po)
Roden Noel. Livingstone in Africa (po)
Ouida. Two Little Wooden Shoes (n)
Charles Reade. A Hero and a Martyr (n)
_____. A Woman Hater (n)
Henry Sidgwick. Methods of Ethics (e)
Sir Leslie Stephen. Hours in a Library, to 1879 (e, pub)
William Stubbs. The Constitutional History of England and Its Origin and Development, to 1878 (his)
Henry Sweet. History of English Sounds, to 1888 (e, his)
Algernon Swinburne. Bothwell, a Tragedy (dr)

THE NINETEENTH CENTURY   185

   John Symonds. Sketches in Italy and Greece (nar)
   James Thomson. The City of Dreadful Night (po)
   Anthony Trollope. Phineas Redux (n)
   William Wallace. The Logic of Hegel (trans)
   Ellen Wood. Johnny Ludlow, to 1890 (n)

                              1875

BIRTHS
   John Buchan
   Sir Walter Greg
   Theodore Powys
   Forrest Reid
   Edgar Wallace

DEATHS
   Sir Arthur Helps
   Charles Kingsley
   Sir Charles Lyell
   John Mitchel
   William Reade
   Philip Stanhope
   Connop Thirwall

EVENTS
   The Tabard Inn, Southwark (des)

WORKS
   Matthew Arnold. God and the Bible (e)
   Richard Doddridge Blackmore. Alice Lorraine (n)
   Dion Boucicault. The Shaughraun (dr)
   Robert Browning. Aristophanes' Apology (po)
   _____. The Inn Album (po)
   Thomas Carlyle. The Early Kings of Norway (his)
   Charles Darwin. Insectivorous Plants (e)
   Sydney Dobell. Poetical Works (pub)
   Edward Dowden. Shakespeare, His Mind and Art (e)
   William Gladstone. Vaticanism (e)
   Sir Edmund Gosse. Ethical Conditions of Early Scandinavian Peoples (e)
   Frederick Harrison. Order and Progress (e)
   Henry Huth. Fugitive Tracts (1493-1700) (bibl)
   Henry James. Roderick Hudson (n)
   Justin McCarthy. Dear Lady Disdain (n)
   Sir Henry Maine. Early History of Institutions (his)
   Henry Manning. The Vatican Decrees (e)
   Philip Marston. All in All (po)
   Theodore Martin. Biography of a Prince Consort, to 1880 (bio)
   George Meredith. Beauchamp's Career (n)
   Alice Meynell. Preludes (po)
   William Morris. Aeneids of Virgil (po, trans)
   _____. Three Northern Love Songs (po)
   James Rogers. A Complete Collection of the Protests of the Lords (his)
   William Clark Russell. John Holdsworth, Chief Mate (n)
   Samuel Smiles. Thrift (e)
   Algernon Swinburne. Essays and Studies (pub)
   John Symonds. History of the Renaissance in Italy, to 1886 (his)

Alfred Tennyson. Queen Mary (dr)
George Whyte-Melville. Katerfelto (n)

1876

BIRTHS
George Macaulay Trevelyan

DEATHS
John Forster
Henry Kingsley
George Lawrence
Harriet Martineau

EVENTS
The Beef-Steak Club (f)
The Grosvenor Gallery, Bond Street, London (op)
The Mind (p, f)
Newnham College for Women, Cambridge (f)

WORKS
Walter Bagehot. Physics and Politics (e)
Francis Herbert Bradley. Ethical Studies (e)
Robert Bridges. The Growth of Love (po)
Robert Buchanan. The Shadow of the Sword (n)
Sir George Tomkyns Chesney. The Dilemma (n)
Mandell Creighton. The Age of Elizabeth (his)
_____. Simon de Montfort (bio)
_____. The Tudors and the Reformation (his)
Charles Darwin. Cross and Self-Fertilisation (e)
Charles Dodgson. The Hunting of the Snark (po)
John Forster. The Life of Swift (bio)
William Gladstone. Bulgarian Horrors and the Question of the East (e)
_____. Homeric Synchronism (e)
John Green. Studies from England and Italy (e)
George Grote. Fragments on Ethical Subjects (e, pub)
William Carew Hazlitt. Bibliographical Collections and Notes, to 1889 (bibl, e)
Sir Richard Jebb. The Attic Orators, from Aniphon to Isaeus, to 1880 (e)
Sir Lewis Morris. Epic of Hades, to 1877 (po)
William Morris. Sigurd the Volsung (po)
Sir Frederick Pollock. The Principles of Contract (e)
Herbert Spencer. Principles of Sociology, to 1896 (e)
Sir Leslie Stephen. Agnostic's Apology (e)
_____. History of English Thought in the Eighteenth Century (e, his)
William Stubbs. The Early Plantagenets (his)
Henry Sweet. Anglo-Saxon Reader (ed)
Algernon Swinburn. Erectheus (dr, po)
Alfred Tennyson. Harold (dr)
George Otto Trevelyan. The Life and Letters of Lord Macaulay (bio)
Anthony Trollope. The Prime Minister (n)
Alfred Wallace. Geographical Distribution of Animals (e)

1877

BIRTHS
  Harley Granville-Barker

DEATHS
  Walter Bagehot
  Julia Kavanagh
  Samuel Warren
  Thomas Wright

EVENTS
  Cremorne Gardens, Chelsea (c)
  The Kyrle Society (f)
  The Nineteenth Century (p, f)
  Society for the Protection of Ancient Buildings (f)

WORKS
  Richard Doddridge Blackmore. Cripps the Carrier (n)
  Robert Browning. The Agamemnon (trans)
  Samuel Butler. Life and Habit (e)
  Ingram Bywater. The Fragments of Heraclitus (ed)
  Richard William Church. The Beginnings of the Middle Ages (his)
  Richard Dixon. History of the Church of England from the Abolition of Roman Jurisdiction, to 1900 (his)
  Henry Austin Dobson. Proverbs in Porcelain (po)
  Alfred Domett. Flotsam and Jetsam (po)
  Edward Dowden. A Shakespeare Primer (ref)
  Richard Garnett. John Milton (bio)
  _____. Thomas Carlyle (bio)
  William Gladstone. Lessons in Massacre (e)
  John Green. The History of the English People, to 1880 (his)
  Henry James. The American (n)
  William Mallock. The New Republic (s)
  George Meredith. The Idea of Comedy and the Uses of the Comic Spirit (e)
  John Morley. Critical Miscellanies, 2nd series (e)
  Coventry Patmore. The Unknown Eros (po)
  William Clark Russell. The Wreck of the Grosvenor (n)
  Anna Sewell. Black Beauty (fic)
  Sir Charles Wyville Thomson. The Voyage of the Challenger (trav)
  Anthony Trollope. The American Senator (n)

1878

BIRTHS
  Alfred Coppard
  Edward Dunsany
  John Masefield
  Philip Edward Thomas

DEATHS
  Henry Huth
  George Lewes
  Lord John Russell
  George Whyte-Melville

EVENTS
   The Salvation Army (f)

WORKS
   The Ballad Society. The Bagford Ballads (ed, pub)
   Richard William Church. Dante, De Monarchia (trans)
   John Churton Collins. The Works of Cyril Tourneur (ed)
   Charles Cowden-Clarke and Mary Cowden-Clarke. Recollections of Writers (nar, bio)
   Sir George Grove. Dictionary of Music and Musicians, 4 vols, to 1889 (ref)
   Thomas Hardy. The Return of the Native (n)
   Shadworth Hodgson. The Philosophy of Reflection (e)
   Henry James. The Europeans (n)
   _____. French Poets and Novelists (e)
   William E.H. Lecky. History of England in the Eighteenth Century, to 1890 (his)
   Justin McCarthy. Miss Misanthrope (n)
   Theodore Martin. Heine's Poems (trans)
   John Morley. Diderot and the Encyclopaedists (e)
   Hugh Monro. Criticisms and Elucidations of Catullus (e)
   Coventry Patmore. Amelia (po)
   James Payn. By Proxy (n)
   William Rossetti. Lives of Famous Poets (bio)
   Sir John Seeley. The Life and Times of Stein, or Germany and Prussia in the Napoleonic Age (his)
   Nassau Senior. Conversations with M. Thiers, M. Guizot, and Other Distinguished Persons during the Second Empire (pub)
   Sir Henry Stanley. Through the Dark Continent (trav)
   Sir Leslie Stephen. Johnson (bio)
   Robert Louis Stevenson. Inland Voyage (trav)
   Algernon Swinburne. Poems and Ballads (pub)
   John Symonds. Many Moods (po)
   Anthony Trollope. Is He Popenjoy? (n)
   Spencer Walpole. History of England from 1815 to 1856, to 1890 (his)
   George Whyte-Melville. Roy's Wife (n)
   Ellen Wood. Pomeroy Abbey (n)

1879

BIRTHS
   E.M. Forster
   Percy Lubbock

DEATHS
   William Clifford
   Charles Wells

WORKS
   Robert Adamson. On the Philosophy of Kant (t)
   Sir Edwin Arnold. The Light of Asia, or the Great Renunciation (po)
   Walter Bagehot. Literary Studies (e, pub)
   Arthur James Balfour. A Defence of Philosophic Doubt (t)
   William Black. Macleod of Dare (fic)
   Robert Browning. Dramatic Idyls, 1st series (po)
   Samuel Butler. Evolution Old and New (e)

_____. God the Known and God the Unknown (e)
Richard William Church. Spenser (bio)
William Clifford. Lectures and Essays (pub)
_____. Seeing and Thinking (t)
Wilkie Collins. Little Novels (fic)
_____. A Rogue's Life (n)
Henry Austin Dobson. William Hogarth (bio)
Charles Dodgson. Euclid and His Modern Rivals (t)
George Eliot. Impressions of Theophrastus (s)
Edward Fitzgerald. Readings from Crabbe (ed)
William Gladstone. Gleanings of Past Years, 7 vols (e)
Sir Edmund Gosse. Northern Studies (e)
Henry James. Daisy Miller (n)
_____. Hawthorne (e)
Henry Jones. A Clerical Error (dr)
Andrew Lang and S.H. Butcher. The Odyssey (trans)
Charlton T. Lewis and Charles Short. Latin-English Dictionary (ref)
Frederick Locker. Patchwork (po, e)
Justin McCarthy. History of Our Own Times, to 1907 (his)
James Martineau. Ideal Substitutes for God (e)
George Meredith. The Egoist (n)
_____. The Tale of Chloe (n)
John Morley. Burke (bio)
Sir Lewis Morris. Gwen, a Dream in Monologue (po)
Charles Reade. Drink (dr)
Walter Skeat. Etymological Dictionary, to 1910 (ref)
Herbert Spencer. Principles of Ethics, to 1893 (e)
Robert Louis Stevenson. Travels with a Donkey in the Cevennes (trav)
Alfred Tennyson. The Falcon (dr)
George Whyte-Melville. Black But Comely (n, pub)
Charlotte Yonge. History of France (his)

1880

BIRTHS
 Alfred Noyes
 Sean O'Casey
 Giles Lytton Strachey

DEATHS
 Kenelm Digby
 Mary Ann Evans ("George Eliot")
 Geraldine Jewsbury
 James Planche
 Tom Taylor

EVENTS
 The Examiner (p, c)
 The Pall Mall Gazette (p, c)
 The St. James's Gazette (p, f)

WORKS
 Walter Bagehot. Economic Studies (e, pub)
 Wilfrid Scawen Blunt. The Love Songs of Proteus (po)
 Robert Browning. Dramatic Idyls, 2nd series (po)
 Samuel Butler. Unconscious Memory (e)

John Caird. An Introduction to the Philosophy of Religion (t)
Charles Darwin. The Power of Movement in Plants (e)
Benjamin Disraeli. Endymion (n)
Sir Charles Duffy. Young Ireland, 1840-1850, to 1883 (his)
Sir Samuel Ferguson. Conary (po)
_____. Deirdre (po)
George Gissing. Workers in the Dawn (n)
James Grant. Old and New Edinburgh (his, trav)
Henry James. Washington Square (n)
Andrew Lang. Ballades in Blue China, to 1881 (po)
George Meredith. The Tragic Comedians (n)
Arthur Munby. Dorothy (po)
Margaret Oliphant. A Beleaguered City (n)
Ouida. Moths (n)
Samuel Smiles. Duty (e)
Sir Leslie Stephen. Pope (bio)
Robert Louis Stevenson and William E. Henley. Deacon Brodie (dr)
Algernon Swinburne. Songs of the Springtides (po)
_____. Studies in Song (po)
John Symonds. New and Old (po)
Alfred Tennyson. The Revenge (po)
_____. Rizpah (po)
George Otto Trevelyan. The Early History of Charles James Fox (bio, his)
Anthony Trollope. The Duke's Children (n)
John Warren. Guide to Bookplates (ref)

1881

BIRTHS
Lascelles Abercrombie
Clive Bell
Constance Holme
William Houghton
Dame Rose Macaulay
Leopold Myers
Mary Webb

DEATHS
George Borrow
John Hill Burton
Thomas Carlyle
Benjamin Disraeli
Arthur O'Shaughnessy
Arthur Stanley
Edward Trelawny

EVENTS
The Metaphysical Society (c)

WORKS
Richard Doddridge Blackmore. Christowell (n)
Thomas Edward Brown. Foc's'le Yarns (po)
Robert Buchanan. God and the Man (n)
Sir Francis Cowley Burnand. The Colonel (dr)
Samuel Butler. Alps and Sanctuaries of Piedmont and the Ticino (trav)

Thomas Carlyle. Reminiscences (nar)
Frances Power Cobbe. The Duties of Women (e)
John Churton Collins. The Poems of Lord Herbert of Cherbury (ed)
Wilkie Collins. The Black Robe (n)
Sir Sidney Colvin. Walter Savage Landor (bio, e)
Charles Darwin. Formation of Vegetable Mould through the Action of Worms (e)
Sir John Evans. The Ancient Bronze Implements, Weapons, and Ornaments of Great Britain and Ireland (his)
Edward Freeman. Historical Geography of Europe, to 1882 (his, e)
John Green. The Making of England (his)
James Halliwell-Phillipps. Outlines of the Life of Shakespeare (bio, ref)
Thomas Hardy. A Loadicean (n)
Henry James. The Portrait of a Lady (n)
Patrick Joyce. Grammar of Irish (ref)
Andrew Lang. The Library (bibl)
John Morley. The Life of Richard Cobden (bio)
Frederic Myers. Wordsworth (bio, e)
Roden Noel. A Little Child's Monument (po)
Ouida. A Village Commune (n)
Francis Turner Palgrave. The Visions of England (po)
Sir Arthur Wing Pinero. The Money Spinner (dr)
Christina Rossetti. A Pageant and Other Poems (pub)
Dante Rossetti. Ballads and Sonnets (pub)
Mark Rutherford. The Autobiography of Mark Rutherford (n)
Joseph Shorthouse. John Inglesant (n)
Walter Skeat. Aelfric. Lives of the Saints, to 1900 (ed)
William Robertson Smith. The Old Testament in the Jewish Church (e)
Robert Louis Stevenson. Virginibus Puerisque (pub)
James Stirling. A Text Book of Kant (e)
Algernon Swinburne. Mary Stuart (dr)
Alfred Tennyson. The Cup (dr)
James Thomson. Vane's Story and Other Poems (pub)
Anthony Trollope. Aeyala's Angel (n)
—————————. Dr. Wortle's School (n)
John Tyndall. Floating Matter in the Air (e)
Oscar Wilde. Poems (pub)

1882

BIRTHS
  John Drinkwater
  Eric Gill
  James Joyce
  Virginia Woolf

DEATHS
  William Harrison Ainsworth
  Charles Darwin
  Thomas Green
  Edward Pusey
  Dante Rossetti
  James Thomson
  Anthony Trollope

EVENTS
  Fraser's Magazine (p, c)
  The Scottish Text Society (f)

WORKS
  Alfred Ainger. The Life of Charles Lamb (bio)
  Alexander Bain. James Mill. A Biography (bio)
  _____. John Stuart Mill. A Criticism, with Personal Recollections (e, bio)
  Sir Walter Besant. The Revolt of Man (s)
  John Brown. Horae Subsecivae, III (e)
  Robert Buchanan. Ballads of Life, Love, and Humour (po)
  Mandell Creighton. History of the Papacy during the Reformation, to 1894 (his)
  Dictionary of National Biography, to 1950 (ref)
  Edward Freeman. The Reign of William Rufus and the Accession of Henry I (his)
  Sir Edmund Gosse. Life of Thomas Gray (bio)
  Thomas Anstey Guthrie. Vice Versa (n)
  Thomas Hardy. Two on a Tower (n)
  Henry Jones. The Silver King (dr)
  Frances Kemble. Records of Later Life (auto)
  Andrew Lang. Helen of Troy (po)
  Sir Alfred Lyall. Asiatic Studies, 1st series (e)
  Edith Lyall. Donovan (n)
  James Martineau. A Study of Spinoza (e)
  Herman Merivale. Faucit of Balliol (n)
  Margaret Oliphant. A Little Pilgrim of the Unseen (n)
  Ouida. Stories for Children (fic)
  _____. In Maremma (n)
  James Payn. Some Private Views (e)
  Sir Frederic Pollock. Essays in Jurisprudence and Ethics (e)
  William Clark Russell. My Watch Below (pub)
  George Saintsbury. A Short History of French Literature (his)
  William Robertson Smith. The Prophets of Israel (his)
  Sir Leslie Stephen. Science of Ethics (e)
  _____. Swift (bio)
  Robert Louis Stevenson. Familiar Studies of Men and Books (e)
  _____. The New Arabian Nights (fic)
  Algernon Swinburne. Athens, an Ode (po)
  _____. Tristram of Lyonesse (po)
  John Symonds. Animi Figura (po)
  Alfred Tennyson. The Promise of May (dr)
  James Thomson. Insomnia (po)
  Henry Traill. Recaptured Poems (po)

1883

BIRTHS
  John Maynard Keynes
  Sir Compton Mackenzie

DEATHS
  John Colenso
  John Payne Collier
  Edward Fitzgerald

THE NINETEENTH CENTURY   193

  John Green
  Thomas Mayne Reid

EVENTS
  The National Review (p, f)
  The Primrose League (f)

WORKS
  Alfred Ainger. The Works of Charles Lamb, to 1888 (ed)
  Francis Herbert Bradley. Principles of Logic (t)
  Robert Browning. Jocoseria (po)
  Edward Caird. Hegel (e)
  Jane Carlyle. Letters (pub)
  Francis James Child. English and Scottish Popular Ballads, to 1898 (ed)
  Richard Dixon. Mano. . .the Adventures of a Norman Knight (po)
  Henry Austin Dobson. Old World Idylls (po)
  Charles Dodgson. Rhyme? and Reason? (po)
  Henry Drummond. Natural Law in the Spiritual World (e)
  Sir Arthur Evans. Antiquarian Researches in Illyricum, to 1885 (trav,
                    his, e)
  Samuel Gardiner. History of England from the Accession of James I to
                    the Outbreak of the Civil War, 1603-1642, to 1884
                    (his)
  John Green. The Conquest of England (his)
  Thomas Green. Prolegomena to Ethics (e, pub)
  Thomas Anstey Guthrie. The Giant's Robe (n)
  Andrew Lang, W. Leaf, and E. Myers. The Iliad (trans)
  Sir Henry Maine. Dissertation on Early Law and Custom (e)
  Philip Marston. Wind Voices (po)
  Theodore Martin. Life of Lord Lyndhurst (bio)
  George Meredith. Poems and Lyrics of the Joy of Earth (po)
  Herman Merivale. The White Pilgrim (po, dr)
  George Moore. A Modern Lover (n)
  Sir Lewis Morris. Songs Unsung (po)
  Frederic Myers. Essays Classical and Modern (pub)
  William Clark Russell. Round the Galley Fire (pub)
  Sir John Seeley. Expansion of England in the Eighteenth Century (his)
  Henry Sidgwick. Principles of Political Economy (e)
  Sir James Fitzjames Stephen. History of the Criminal Law (his)
  Robert Louis Stevenson. The Silverado Squatters (fic)
  _____. Treasure Island (n)
  Victoria, Queen of England. More Leaves (nar)

                              1884

BIRTHS
  James Flecker
  Llewelyn Powys
  Hugh Walpole
  Sir Arnold Wilson

DEATHS
  Abraham Hayward
  Richard Horne
  Mark Pattison
  Charles Reade

EVENTS
  The Fabian Society (f)
  The New Monthly Magazine (p, c)
  Pusey House, Oxford (op)

WORKS
  Sir Walter Besant. Dorothy Forster (n)
  Robert Bridges. Prometheus, the Firegiver (po)
  Robert Browning. Ferishtah's Fancies (po)
  Robert Buchanan. Alone in London (dr)
  Samuel Butler. A Psalm of Montreal (s)
  Richard William Church. Bacon (bio)
  William John Courthope. Addison (bio, e)
  Juliana Ewing. Jackanapes (fic)
  George Gissing. The Unclassed (n)
  Henry Jones. Saints and Sinners (dr)
  Andrew Lang. Custom and Myth (e)
  _____. Rhymes a la Mode (po)
  Edna Lyall. We Two (n)
  Herman Merivale. Binko's Blues (fic)
  _____. Florien (dr)
  Hugh Munro. Translations into Latin and Greek Verse (po, trans)
  Sir James Murray. The Oxford English Dictionary (ref, ed)
  James Payn. Some Literary Recollections (e)
  James Rogers. Six Centuries of Work and Wages (his)
  Herbert Spencer. The Man Versus the State (e)
  Alfred Tennyson. Becket (dr)
  James Thomson. Satires and Profanities (e, pub)
  Henry Traill. The New Lucian (s)
  Mary Ward. Miss Bretherton (n)

                    1885

BIRTHS
  D. H. Lawrence
  Ezra Pound
  Andrew Young

DEATHS
  Juliana Ewing
  William Thoms

EVENTS
  Revised Text, Old Testament (pub)
  The Selborne Society (f)

WORKS
  Edward R. Bulwer-Lytton. Glenaveril (po)
  Sir Richard Burton. The Arabian Nights, to 1888 (trans)
  Sir Thomas H.H. Caine. The Shadow of a Crime (n)
  Albert Venn Dicey. Introduction to the Study of the Law of the Constitution (t)
  Henry Austin Dobson. At the Sign of the Lyre (po)
  Sir Edmund Gosse. From Shakespeare to Pope (e)
  Thomas Green. Collected Works, to 1888 (pub)
  Thomas Anstey Guthrie. The Tinted Venus (n)

Sir Sidney Lee. Stratford-on-Avon, from the Earliest Times to the
             Death of Shakespeare (his)
Edward Lefroy. Echoes from Theocritus, and Other Sonnets (po)
Edna Lyall. In the Golden Days (n)
Sir Henry Maine. Popular Government (e)
James Martineau. Types of Ethical Theory (e)
George Meredith. Diana of the Crossways (n)
George Moore. A Mummer's Wife (n)
William Morris. The Pilgrims of Hope (po)
Roden Noel. Songs of the Heights and Deeps (po)
Walter Pater. Marius the Epicurean (fic)
James Payn. The Luck of the Darrells (n)
Sir Arthur Wing Pinero. The Magistrate (dr)
John Ruskin. Praeterita, to 1889 (auto)
Mark Rutherford. Mark Rutherford's Deliverance (n)
Henry Sidgwick. The Scope and Method of Economic Science (e)
Robert Louis Stevenson. A Child's Garden of Verses (po)
_____. Prince Otto (fic)
William Stubbs. Historia Novella (ed)
Algernon Swinburne. Marino Faliero (dr)
Alfred Tennyson. Balin and Balan (po)
_____. Tiresias (po)
Mary Ward. Journal in-time (trans)
Walter Watts-Dunton. Poetry (e)

                          1886

BIRTHS
  Ronald Firbank
  Percy Wyndham Lewis
  Lennox Robinson
  Siegfried Sassoon
  Charles Williams

DEATHS
  William Barnes
  Sir Samuel Ferguson
  Sir Thomas Erskine May
  Sir Henry Taylor
  Richard Trench

WORKS
  Rhoda Broughton. Doctor Cupid (n)
  Frances Eliza Hodgeson Burnett. Little Lord Fauntleroy (n, dr)
  John Willis Clark and Robert Willis. Architectural History of the Col-
              leges of Cambridge (his)
  Marie Corelli. A Romance of Two Worlds (n)
  Henry Austin Dobson. Sir Richard Steele (bio)
  Edward Dowden. The Life of Shelley (bio, e)
  Edward Freeman. Chief Periods of European History (his)
  _____. Methods of Historical Study (e)
  James Froude. Oceana, or England and Her Colonies (e)
  Samuel Gardiner. The History of the Great Civil War, to 1891 (his)
  George Gissing. Demos (n)
  Thomas Anstey Guthrie. A Fallen Idol (n)
  H. Rider Haggard. King Solomon's Mines (n)

Thomas Hardy. The Mayor of Casterbridge (n)
Frederick Harrison. The Choice of Books (e)
Thomas Huxley. Science and Morals (e)
Henry James. The Bostonians (n)
―――――. The Princess Casamassima (n)
Rudyard Kipling. Departmental Ditties (po)
Andrew Lang. Letters to Dead Authors (e)
―――――. The Mark of Cain (n)
Emily Lawless. Hurrish (n)
Theodore Martin. Faust, Part II (trans)
Herman Merivale. The Butler (dr)
Sir Lewis Morris. Gycia, a Tragedy (po)
Coventry Patmore. Collected Poetical Works (pub)
Sir Arthur Wing Pinero. The Schoolmistress (dr)
George Bernard Shaw. Cashel Byron's Profession (n)
Henry Sidgwick. Outlines of the History of Ethics (e)
Robert Louis Stevenson. Kidnapped (n)
―――――. The Strange Case of Dr. Jekyll and Mr. Hyde (n)
Algernon Swinburne. Miscellanies (pub)
Arthur Symons. An Introduction to the Study of Browning (e)
Alfred Tennyson. Locksley Hall, Sixty Years After (po)
William Butler Yeats. Mosada (po)

1887

BIRTHS
  Rupert Brooke
  Sir Julian Huxley
  Edwin Muir
  Dame Edith Sitwell

DEATHS
  Alfred Domett
  James Grant
  Philip Marston
  Henry Mayhew
  Ellen Wood

EVENTS
  The Selden Society (f)

WORKS
  Richard Doddridge Blackmore. Springhaven (n)
  Robert Browning. Parleyings with Certain People (po)
  Samuel Butler. Luck or Cunning (e)
  Sir Thomas H.H. Caine. The Deemster (n)
  Sir Sidney Colvin. John Keats (bio, e)
  ―――――. Letters of Keats (ed)
  Aubrey DeVere. Critical Essays (pub)
  Sir Arthur Conan Doyle. A Study in Scarlet (fic)
  Mountstuart Elphinstone. The Rise of the British Power in the East (his, pub)
  Sir Samuel Ferguson. Ogham Inscriptions in Ireland, Wales, and Scotland (his, trav)
  Sir James George Frazer. Totemism (t)
  Alfred Godley. The Histories of Tacitus (ed)

H. Rider Haggard. Allan Quatermain (n)
_____. She (n)
Richard Haldane. Life of Adam Smith (bio)
Richard Hutton. Essays on Some Modern Guides of English Thought (e)
Andrew Lang. Books and Bookmen (bibl)
_____. Myth, Ritual, and Religion, 1st ed (e)
Frederick Maitland. Bracton's Note-Book (ed)
_____. The Constitutional History of England (e, his)
Philip Marston. For a Song's Sake (fic, pub)
_____. Garden Secrets (po, pub)
George Meredith. Ballads and Poems of Tragic Life (po)
William Morris. The Odyssey (po, trans)
Walter Pater. Imaginary Portraits (fic)
Sir Arthur Wing Pinero. Dandy Dick (dr)
Sir Frederick Pollock. The Law of Torts (e)
Bernard Quaritch. A General Catalogue of Old Books and MSS., to 1889 (bibl)
William Rossetti. Life of Keats (bio)
Mark Rutherford. The Revolution in Tanner's Lane (n)
George Saintsbury. Elizabethan Literature (his)
Samuel Smiles. Life and Labour (e)
Herbert Spencer. Factors of Organic Evolution (e)
Robert Louis Stevenson. Memories and Portraits (bio)
_____. The Merry Men (fic)
_____. Underwoods (po)
Algernon Swinburne. Locrine (dr)

1888

BIRTHS
　Kathleen Mansfield Beauchamp ("Katherine Mansfield")
　Joyce Cary
　Osborne Henry Mavor ("James Bridie")
　T.S. Eliot
　Ronald Knox
　T.E. Lawrence

DEATHS
　Matthew Arnold
　Edward Lear
　Sir Henry Maine
　William Palgrave

EVENTS
　Kottabos (p, c)

WORKS
　Matthew Arnold. Essays in Criticism (e)
　Arthur James Balfour. The Religion of Humanity (t)
　Sir Walter Besant. For Faith and Freedom (n)
　Thomas Alexander Browne. Robbery under Arms (n)
　James Bryce. The American Commonwealth (e)
　Mandell Creighton. Cardinal Wolsey (bio)
　Henry Austin Dobson. Oliver Goldsmith (bio)
　Charles Doughty. Travels in Arabia Deserta (trav, nar)
　James Froude. The English in the West Indies (e)

Richard Garnett. Emerson (bio)
_____. The Twilight of the Gods (po)
Francis Gasquet. Henry VIII and the English Monasteries, to 1889 (his)
George Gissing. A Life's Morning (n)
Sir Edmund Gosse. Life of Congreve (bio)
Thomas Hardy. The Trumpet-Major (n)
Frederic Harrison. Oliver Cromwell (bio)
William Ernest Henley. Book of Verses (po)
Henry James. Partial Portraits (e)
_____. The Reverberator (n)
Rudyard Kipling. Soldiers Three (fic)
Andrew Lang. Perrault's Popular Tales (ed, e)
James Martineau. A Study of Religion (e)
George Meredith. A Reading of Earth (po)
Herman Merivale. The Don (dr)
Henry Meriman. Young Mistley (n)
George Moore. Confessions of a Young Man (auto)
William Morris. The Dream of John Ball (po, fic)
Margaret Oliphant. Makers of Florence (his, bio)
Sir Arthur Wing Pinero. Sweet Lavender (dr)
William Sharp. Romantic Ballads and Poems of Phantasy (pub)
Robert Louis Stevenson. The Black Arrow (n)
John Symonds. Autobiography of Benvenuto Cellini (trans)
Mary Ward. Robert Elsmere (n)
Charlotte Yonge. Life of Hannah More (bio)

1889

BIRTHS
  Enid Bagnold
  Elizabeth Bowen
  Robin Collingwood
  Philip Guedalla
  John Middleton Murry
  Arnold Toynbee
  Walter Turner
  Arthur Waley

DEATHS
  Robert Browning
  Wilkie Collins
  Eliza Cook
  James Halliwell-Phillipps
  Gerard Manley Hopkins
  Martin Tupper

EVENTS
  The Granta (p, f)
  The Library (p, f)
  The White Hart Inn, Southwark (c)

WORKS
  Philip James Bailey. Festus, 3rd ed (po)
  Robert Browning. Asolando (po)
  Robert Buchanan. A Man's Shadow (dr)
  Edward Caird. The Critical Philosophy of Immanuel Kant (t)

John Davidson. Scaramouch in Noxos (dr)
Charles Dodgson. Sylvie and Bruno (po)
Sir Arthur Conan Doyle. Micah Clarke (n)
The Fabian Essays (e, ed)
George Gissing. The Nether World (n)
Thomas Anstey Guthrie. The Pariah (n)
Henry Jones. The Middleman (dr)
Sir Alfred Lyall. Verses Written in India (po)
_____. Warren Hastings (bio)
William Morris. The House of the Wolfings (n)
Margaret Oliphant. Makers of Venice (his, bio)
Walter Pater. Appreciations (e)
Coventry Patmore. Principle in Art (e)
Mark Pattison. Essays (pub)
William Sharp. The Children of Tomorrow (n)
Robert Louis Stevenson. The Master of Ballantrae (n)
_____ and Lloyd Osbourne. The Wrong Box (n)
Algernon Swinburne. Poems and Ballads (pub)
Alfred Tennyson. Crossing the Bar (po)
_____. Demeter (po)
Alfred Wallace. Darwinism (e)
Spencer Walpole. Life of Lord Russell (bio)
William Butler Yeats. The Wanderings of Oisin (po)

1890

BIRTHS
  Agatha Christie
  Isaac Rosenberg

DEATHS
  Dion Boucicault
  Sir Richard Burton
  Richard William Church
  John Westland Marston
  John Henry Newman
  James Rogers

EVENTS
  The Kelmscott Press, Hammersmith (f)
  The Review of Reviews (p, f)

WORKS
  Thomas Alexander Browne. A Colonial Reformer (n)
  _____. The Miner's Right (n)
  _____. Squatter's Dream (n)
  Sir Thomas H.H. Caine. The Bondman (n)
  Philip Dormer Stanhope, fourth Earl of Chesterfield. Letters to his
                godson (pub)
  John Davidson. Perfervid (n)
  Sir Charles Dilke. Problems of Greater Britain (e, trav)
  Henry Austin Dobson. Four Frenchwomen: Corday, Roland, de Lamballe,
                de Genlis (e)
  _____. Horace Walpole (bio)
  Sir Charles Duffy. Life of Thomas Davies (bio)
  Havelock Ellis. The New Spirit (e)
  Sir James George Frazer. The Golden Bough, to 1915 (t, e, ref)

Samuel Gardiner. The Student's History of England, to 1891 (his)
George Gissing. The Emancipated (n)
Alfred Godley. The Histories of Tacitus (ed)
Thomas Anstey Guthrie. Voces Populi (fic)
Henry James. The Tragic Muse (n)
Rudyard Kipling. The Light That Failed (n)
James Martineau. The Seat of Authority in Religion (e)
Sir Lewis Morris. A Vision of Saints (po)
William Morris. The Roots of the Mountains (n)
―――――――. The Story of the Glittering Plain (n)
Margaret Oliphant. Kirsteen (fic)
Edith Somerville. Some Experiences of an Irish R.M. (fic)
Frederick Tennyson. The Isles of Greece (po)
Henry Traill. Saturday Songs (po)
William Wallace. Life of Arthur Schopenhauer (bio, pub)

1891

DEATHS
Edward R. Bulwer-Lytton
Alexander William Kinglake
John Morton
Rowland Warburton

EVENTS
Romanes Lectures, Oxford (f)

WORKS
Maurice Baring. Pastels and Other Rhymes (po)
Sir James Matthew Barrie. The Little Minister (dr)
Robert Bridges. Eden (po)
Sir Thomas H.H. Caine. The Scapegoat (n)
Richard William Church. The Oxford Movement (e, his)
Sir Arthur Conan Doyle. The Adventures of Sherlock Holmes (fic)
―――――――. The White Company (n)
William Freeman. History of Sicily to 300 B.C., to 1894 (his)
George Gissing. New Grub Street (n)
Thomas Anstey Guthrie. Tourmalin's Time Cheques (fic)
H. Rider Haggard and Andrew Lang. The World's Desire (fic)
Thomas Hardy. A Group of Noble Dames (fic)
―――――――. Tess of the D'Urbervilles (n)
William Ernest Henley. Lyra Heroica (po, ed)
Henry Jones. The Crusaders (dr)
―――――――. The Dancing Girl (dr)
Philip Marston. A Last Harvest (po, pub)
George Meredith. One of Our Conquerors (n)
John Morley. Studies in Literature (e)
William Morris. News from Nowhere (fic)
―――――――. Poems by the Way (po)
Sir Arthur Wing Pinero. Lady Bountiful (dr)
Archibald Primrose, Earl of Rosebury. Pitt (bio)
William Sharp. Sospiri di Roma (n)
George Bernard Shaw. The Quintessence of Ibsenism (e)
Henry Sidgwick. Elements of Politics (e)
James Stephen. Lapsus Calami (po, pub)
―――――――. Quo Musa Tendis (po, pub)

Oscar Wilde. Intentions (dia)
_____. The Picture of Dorian Gray (n)

                          1892

BIRTHS
  Richard Aldington
  Ivy Compton-Burnett
  Christopher Murray Grieve ("Hugh Macdiarmid")
  John B. S. Haldane
  Sir Osbert Sitwell
  John Tolkien
  Dame Rebecca West

DEATHS
  Edward Freeman
  James Stephen
  Alfred Tennyson
  Sir Daniel Wilson

EVENTS
  Alfred Austin, Poet Laureate of England, to 1913
  The Bibliographical Society (f)
  The Idler (p, f)
  Rowton House, Vauxhall (f)

WORKS
  Edward R. Bulwer-Lytton. King Poppy (po, pub)
  _____. Marah (po, pub)
  George Curzon. Persia and the Persian Question (e)
  Henry Austin Dobson. Eighteenth-Century Vignettes, 1st series (e)
  Sir Charles Duffy. Conversations with Thomas Carlyle (dia, nar)
  George Gissing. Born in Exile (n)
  Alfred Godley. Verses to Order (po)
  Thomas Anstey Guthrie. The Talking Horse (n)
  William Ernest Henley. The Song of the Sword (po)
  John Oliver Hobbes. The Ambassador (dr)
  _____. The Sinner's Comedy (n)
  Samuel Hole. Memories (auto, nar)
  Thomas Huxley. Essays upon Some Controverted Questions (e)
  Rudyard Kipling. Barrack-Room Ballads (po)
  Andrew Lang. Grass of Parnassus (po)
  Emily Lawless. Grania (n)
  Henry Merriman. The Slave of the Lamp (n)
  Sir Arthur Wing Pinero. The Cabinet Minister (dr)
  John Round. Geoffrey de Mandeville: A Study of Anarchy (his)
  John Ruskin. The Poetry of Architecture (e, pub)
  George Bernard Shaw and William Archer. Widowers' Houses (dr)
  Robert Louis Stevenson. Across the Plains (trav)
  _____ and William Ernest Henley. Beau Austin (dr)
  _____ and Lloyd Osbourne. The Wrecker (n)
  Henry Sweet. A New English Grammar, to 1898 (ref)
  Algernon Swinburne. The Sisters (dr)
  Alfred Tennyson. The Death of OEnone, and Other Poems (po)
  _____. The Foresters (po)
  Henry Traill. Number Twenty, Fables and Fantasies (fic)

Mary Ward. The History of David Grieve (n)
Sir William Watson. Lachrymae Musarum (po)
_____. Lyric Love (po)
Edward Whymper. Travels among the Great Andes of the Equator (trav)
Oscar Wilde. Lady Windermere's Fan (dr)
William Butler Yeats. The Countess Cathleen (dr)
Israel Zangwill. Children of the Ghetto (n)

1893

BIRTHS
  Wilfred Owen
  Sir Herbert Read
  I.A. Richards
  Dorothy Sayers

DEATHS
  Sir Samuel White Baker
  Benjamin Jowett
  Frances Kemble
  Charles Merivale
  Sir William Smith
  John Symonds
  John Tyndale

WORKS
  Arthur James Balfour. Essays and Addresses (e)
  Frances Herbert Bradley. Appearance and Reality (e)
  Robert Bridges. Milton's Prosody (e)
  Edward Caird. The Evolution of Religion (t)
  Mary Elizabeth Coleridge. The Seven Sleepers of Epheseus (n)
  Marie Corelli. Barabbas (n)
  John Davidson. Fleet Street Eclogues (po)
  George Gissing. The Odd Women (n)
  Thomas Anstey Guthrie. The Man from Blankley's (n)
  _____. Mr. Punch's Pocket Ibsen (fic)
  William Ernest Henley. London Voluntaries (po)
  Fenton J.A. Hort. The Way, the Truth, the Life (e)
  Thomas Huxley. Ethics and Evolution (e)
  Andrew Lang. Homer and the Epic (e)
  Sir Alfred Lyall. The Rise and Expansion of the British Dominion in India (e)
  Alice Meynell. Poems (pub)
  _____. The Rhythm of Life (e)
  Walter Pater. Plato and Platonism (e)
  Coventry Patmore. Religio Poetiae (e)
  Sir Arthur Wing Pinero. The Second Mrs. Tanqueray (dr)
  Mark Rutherford. Catharine Furze (n)
  Robert Louis Stevenson. Catriona (n)
  _____. Island Nights Entertainments (fic)
  Francis Thompson. Hound of Heaven (po)
  William Torrens. Twenty Years in Parliament (auto)
  Henry Traill. Social England, 6 vols, to 1897 (his, ed)
  John Warren. Poems Dramatic and Lyrical, to 1895 (pub)
  Sir William Watson. The Eloping Angels (po)
  Stanley Weyman. A Gentleman of France (n)

Oscar Wilde. Salome (dr)
_____. A Woman of No Importance (dr)
Israel Zangwill. Ghetto Tragedies (fic)
_____. Merely Mary Ann (n)

1894

BIRTHS
  Aldous Huxley
  Charles Morgan
  J.B. Priestley

DEATHS
  James Froude
  Roden Noel
  Walter Pater
  Christina Rossetti
  William Robertson Smith
  Sir James Fitzjames Stephen
  Robert Louis Stevenson
  William Torrens

EVENTS
  The Yellow Book (p, f)

WORKS
  AE. Homeward (po)
  Sir James Matthew Barrie. The Professor's Love Story (dr)
  Laurence Binyon. Lyric Poems (po)
  Robert Bridges. Eros and Psyche (po)
  Robert Buchanan. The Charlatan (dr)
  Sir Thomas H.H. Caine. The Manxman (n)
  Sir Sidney Colvin. The Works of Robert Louis Stevenson, to 1897 (ed)
  John Davidson. Ballads and Songs (po)
  Henry Austin Dobson. Eighteenth-Century Vignettes, 2nd series (e)
  Sir Arthur Conan Doyle. Memoirs of Sherlock Holmes (fic)
  Henry Drummond. Ascent of Man (e)
  Havelock Ellis. Man and Woman (e)
  James Froude. The Life and Letters of Erasmus (e)
  Samuel Gardiner. History of the Commonwealth and Protectorate, to 1901 (his)
  Thomas Hardy. Life's Little Ironies (fic)
  Samuel Hole. More Memories (auto, nar)
  Anthony Hope. The Dolly Dialogues (fic)
  _____. The Prisoner of Zenda (n)
  Richard Hutton. Criticisms on Contemporary Thought and Thinkers (e)
  Thomas Huxley. Collected Essays (pub)
  Douglas Hyde. Love Songs of Connacht (po)
  Henry Jones. The Case of Rebellious Susan (dr)
  _____. The Masqueraders (dr)
  Rudyard Kipling. The Jungle Book (fic)
  Andrew Lang. Ban and Arriere Ban (po)
  Fiona Macleod. Pharais (fic)
  George Meredith. Lord Ormont and His Aminta (n)
  Henry Merriman. With Edged Tools (n)
  George Moore. Esther Waters (n)

William Morris. The Wood beyond the World (fic)
James Payn. Gleams of Memory (auto)
Sir Arthur Wing Pinero. The Weaker Sex (dr)
Walter Skeat. The Works of Geoffrey Chaucer, 7 vols, to 1897 (ed)
Robert Louis Stevenson and Lloyd Osbourne. The Ebb-Tide (n)
Algernon Swinburne. Astrophel (po)
William Wallace. Hegel's Philosophy of Mind (e)
Mary Ward. Marcella (n)
Sir William Watson. Odes and Other Poems (pub)
William Butler Yeats. The Land of Hearts Desire (dr)

1895

BIRTHS
William Gerhardi
Robert Graves
Leslie Hartley
David Jones
F.R. Leavis
Jean Rhys

DEATHS
Sir George Tomkyns Chesney
Mary Anne Green
Thomas Huxley
Frederick Locker
Hugh Munro
Sir John Seeley
John Warren

EVENTS
The Ashendene Press (f)

WORKS
Grant Allen. The Woman Who Did (n)
Arthur James Balfour. The Foundations of Belief (t)
Robert Bridges. John Keats (e)
Robert Buchanan. The Strange Adventures of Miss Brown (dr)
Joseph Conrad. Almayer's Folly (n)
Marie Corelli. Sorrows of Satan (n)
William John Courthope. The History of English Poetry, to 1910 (e)
Sir Arthur Evans. Through Bosnia (trav)
Alexander Fraser. The Philosophy of Theism, to 1896 (e)
James Froude. English Seamen in the Sixteenth Century (his)
Frederic Harrison. Victorian Literature (e)
Lionel Johnson. Poems (po)
Henry Jones. The Triumph of the Phillistines (dr)
Fiona Macleod. The Mountain Lovers (fic)
_____. The Sin Eater (fic)
Frederic Maitland. Bracton and Azo (his)
_____ and Sir Frederick Pollock. History of English Law before the Time of Edward I,(his)
George Meredith. The Amazing Marriage (n)
George Moore. Celibates (n)
William Morris. Child Christopher (fic)
Walter Pater. Greek Studies (pub)
Sir Arthur Wing Pinero. The Amazons (dr)

THE NINETEENTH CENTURY 205

_____. The Notorious Mrs. Ebbsmith (dr)
Hastings Rashdall. The Universities of Europe in the Middle Ages (his)
John Round. Feudal England: Historical Studies in the Eleventh and
    Twelfth Centuries (his)
Sir John Seeley. The Growth of British Policy (his)
William Sharp. The Gypsy Christ (n)
Francis Thompson. Sister Songs (po)
Sir William Watson. The Father of the Forest (po)
H.G. Wells. The Time Machine (n)
_____. The Wonderful Visit (n)
Oscar Wilde. An Ideal Husband (dr)
_____. The Importance of Being Earnest (dr)
William Butler Yeats. Poems (pub)
Israel Zangwill. The Master (n)

1896

BIRTHS
  Edmund Blunden
  Austin Clarke
  Margaret Kennedy
  Robert Sherriff

DEATHS
  Sir George Dasent
  Thomas Hughes
  William Morris
  Coventry Patmore

EVENTS
  The Vale Press (f)

WORKS
  Sir James Matthew Barrie. Margaret Ogilvy (bio)
  Sir Max Beerbohm. The Works of Max Beerbohm (pub)
  Joseph Conrad. An Outcast of the Islands (n)
  Marie Corelli. The Mighty Atom (n)
  Mandell Creighton. Queen Elizabeth (bio)
  John Davidson. A Second Series of Fleet Street Eclogues (po)
  Henry Austin Dobson. Eighteenth-Century Vignettes, 3rd series (e)
  Ernest Dowson. Verses (po)
  Sir Arthur Conan Doyle. The Exploits of General Gerard (fic)
  _____. Rodney Stone (n)
  Sir Arthur Evans. Pre-Phoenician Script (his, e)
  James Froude. The Council of Trent (his)
  Alfred Godley. Echoes from the Oxford Magazine (po)
  Thomas Hardy. Jude the Obscure (n)
  Frederic Harrison. Introduction to Comte's Positive Philosophy (e)
  David Hogarth. A Wandering Scholar in the Levant (nar, trav)
  A.E. Housman. A Shropshire Lad (po)
  William Jacobs. Many Cargoes (fic)
  Lionel Johnson. The Art of Thomas Hardy (e)
  Henry Jones. Michael and His Lost Angel (dr)
  _____. The Renascence of the English Drama (e)
  Rudyard Kipling. The Seven Seas (po)
  William E.H. Lecky. Democracy and Liberty (e)

John McTaggart. Studies in the Hegelian Dialectic (e)
George Meredith. Collected Works, to 1911 (pub)
Henry Merriman. The Sowers (n)
Alice Meynell. The Children (e)
_____. The Colour of Life (e)
William Morris. The Well at the World's End (fic)
Francis Turner Palgrave. The Golden Treasury of Songs and Lyrics, 2nd
  series (ed)
Walter Pater. Gaston de Latour (fic, pub)
John Cowper Powys. Odes (po)
Christina Rossetti. New Poems (pub)
Mark Rutherford. Clara Hopgood (n)
George Saintsbury. Nineteenth-Century Literature (e)
William Sharp. Wives in Exile (n)
Flora Annie Steel. On the Face of the Waters (n)
Sir Leslie Stephen. Social Rights and Duties (e)
Robert Louis Stevenson. Weir of Hermiston (n, pub)
Algernon Swinburne. A Tale of Balen (po)
Mary Ward. Sir George Tressady (n)
Sir William Watson. The Year of Shame (po)
H.G. Wells. The Island of Dr. Moreau (n)

                              1897

BIRTHS
  Lettice Cooper
  Liam O'Flaherty
  Sacheverell Sitwell
  Cecil Woodham-Smith

DEATHS
  Henry Drummond
  Richard Hutton
  Jean Ingelow
  Margaret Oliphant
  Francis Turner Palgrave
  William Wallace

EVENTS
  Literature (p, f)
  Tate Gallery, London (op)
  The Yellow Book (p, c)

WORKS
  Sir Max Beerbohm. The Happy Hypocrites (fic)
  James Bryce. Impressions of South Africa
  Sir Thomas H.H. Caine. The Christian (n)
  John Willis Clark. Barnwell Priory (his, e)
  Mary Elizabeth Coleridge. The King with Two Faces (n)
  Joseph Conrad. The Nigger of the Narcissus (n)
  John Davidson. New Ballads (po)
  Aubrey DeVere. Recollections (nar)
  Havelock Ellis. Studies in the Psychology of Sex, to 1910 (e)
  Richard Garnett. A History of Italian Literature (his)
  Thomas Hardy. The Well-Beloved (n)
  Frederic Harrison. William the Silent (bio)
  William Carew Hazlitt. Confessions of a Collector (nar, e)

William Ernest Henley and Robert Louis Stevenson. Admiral Guinea (dr, pub)
William Jacobs. The Skipper's Wooing (fic)
Henry James. The Spoils of Poynton (n)
_____. What Maisie Knew (n)
Lionel Johnson. Ireland (po)
Henry Jones. The Liars (dr)
William Ker. Epic and Romance (e)
Andrew Lang. Pickle the Spy (his)
Didgson Madden. The Diary of William Silence; a Study of Shakespeare and Elizabethan Sport (e)
Frederic Maitland. Domesday Book and Beyond (e)
W. Somerset Maugham. Liza of Lambeth (n)
Henry Merriman. In Kedar's Tents (n)
William Morris. The Water of the Wondrous Isles (fic, pub)
Sir Henry Newbolt. Admirals All and Other Verses (po)
Margaret Oliphant. Annals of a Publishing House: William Blackwood and His Sons (his)
George Saintsbury. Periods of European Literature, to 1907 (ed)
Robert Louis Stevenson. St. Ives (n, pub)
Bram Stoker. Dracula (fic)
Francis Thompson. New Poems (po)
George Tyrrell. Nova et Vetera (t)
Walter Watts-Dunton. The Coming of Love (po)
H.G. Wells. The Invisible Man (n)
William Butler Yeats. The Adoration of the Magi (fic)
_____. The Secret Rose (fic)
_____. Tables of Law (fic)

1898

BIRTHS
C.S. Lewis
Alec Waugh

DEATHS
William Black
Charles Dodgson ("Lewis Carroll")
William Gladstone
James Payn
Frederick Tennyson

WORKS
Robert Bridges. Poetical Works (pub)
Winston Churchill. The Story of the Malakand Field Force (his)
Joseph Conrad. Tales of Unrest (fic)
Robert Cunningham-Graham. Mogreb-el-Acksa (fic)
Sir Charles Duffy. My Life in Two Hemispheres (auto)
Havelock Ellis. Affirmations (e)
Sir Arthur Evans. Further Discoveries of Cretan and Aegean Script (his)
Sebastian Evans. The High History of the Holy Grael, to 1903, 1910 (trans)
_____. In Quest of the Holy Grail (e)
Sir James George Frazer. Description of Greece (trans)
Richard Garnett. Edward Gibbon Wakefield (bio)
George Gissing. Human Odds and Ends (fic)

_____. The Town Traveller (n)
Alfred Godley. The Odes of Horace (trans)
Charles Gore. Epistle of the Ephesians (t)
Thomas Hardy. Wessex Poems (po)
George Henty. Dr. Thorndyke's Secret (n)
Maurice Hewlett. The Forest Lovers (n)
Shadworth Hodgson. The Metaphysic of Experience (e)
Anthony Hope. Rupert of Hentzau (n)
Henry James. In the Cage (n)
_____. The Turn of the Screw (fic)
Andrew Lang. The Companions of Pickle (his)
_____. The Making of Religion (e)
Sir Sidney Lee. Life of William Shakespeare (bio)
Frederic Maitland. Roman Canon Law in the Church of England (e, his)
_____. Township and Borough (e)
George Meredith. Odes in Contribution to the Song of French History (po)
Alice Meynell. The Spirit of Peace (e)
George Moore. Evelyn Innes (n)
William Morris. The Story of the Sundering Flood (fic, pub)
Sir Arthur Wing Pinero. The Princess and the Butterfly (dr)
_____. Trelawny of the Wells (dr)
Frederick Rolfe. Stories Toto Told Me (fic)
Elizabeth Mary, Countess Russell. Elizabeth and Her German Garden (n)
George Saintsbury. Short History of English Literature (his)
George Bernard Shaw. Arms and the Man (dr)
_____. Candida (dr)
_____. The Man of Destiny (dr)
_____. Mrs. Warren's Profession (dr)
_____. The Perfect Wagnerite (e)
_____. The Philanderer (dr)
_____. You Never Can Tell (dr)
Sir Leslie Stephen. Studies of a Biographer, to 1902 (e)
George Tyrrell. Hard Sayings (e)
Alfred Wallace. The Wonderful Century (e)
William Wallace. Lectures on Natural Theology and Ethics (e, pub)
Mary Ward. Helbeck of Bannisdale (n)
Walter Watts-Dunton. Aylwin (n)
H.G. Wells. The War of the Worlds (n)
Oscar Wilde. Ballad of Reading Gaol (po)

1899

BIRTHS
Noel Coward

WORKS
AE. Literary Ideals in Ireland (e)
Sir Max Beerbohm. More (e)
Robert Bridges. Chants for the Psalter (ed)
Winston Churchill. The River War (his)
Sir Sidney Colvin. Letters of Robert Louis Stevenson, to 1911 (ed)
John Davidson. The Last Ballad (po)
Lord Alfred Douglas. The City of the Sorel (po)
Oliver Elton The Augustan Ages (e)
Sir John Fortesque. The History of the British Army, to 1929 (his)

George Gissing. The Crown of Life (n)
Alfred Godley. Lyra Frivola (po)
Charles Gore. Epistle to the Romans (t)
Sir Edmund Gosse. Life and Letters of John Donne (bio, nar, ed)
William Ernest Henley. Hawthorn and Lavender (po)
John Oliver Hobbes. A Repentance (dr)
Richard Hutton. Aspects of Religious and Scientific Thought (e, pub)
Douglas Hyde. Literary History of Ireland (his)
Henry James. The Awkward Age (n)
Rudyard Kipling. The Ballad of East and West (po)
_____. Stalky and Co. (fic)
_____. The White Man's Burden (po)
Andrew Lang. Homeric Hymns (trans)
_____. Myth, Ritual, and Religion, 2nd ed (e)
William E.H. Lecky. Democracy and Liberty, rev ed (e)
_____. The Map of Life (e)
Sir Alfred Lyall. Asiatic Studies, 2nd series (e)
Edith Nesbit. The Treasure Seekers (fic)
Margaret Oliphant. Autobiography (pub)
James Payn. The Backwater of Life (e, pub)
Sir Arthur Wing Pinero. The Gay Lord Quex (dr)
John Cowper Powys. Poems (pub)
Archibald Primrose, Earl of Rosebury. Robert Peel (bio)
Algernon Swinburne. Rosamund, Queen of the Lombards (dr)
Arthur Symons. The Symbolist Movement in Literature (e)
George Tyrrell. External Religion (e)
H.G. Wells. When the Sleeper Wakes (n)
William Butler Yeats. The Wind among the Reeds (po)
Israel Zangwill. Dreamers of the Ghetto (n)

7 The Twentieth Century

1900

BIRTHS
  Basil Bunting
  Geoffrey Household
  Richard Hughes
  Sean O'Faolain
  Victor Pritchett
  Gilbert Ryle

DEATHS
  Richard Doddridge Blackmore
  Richard Dixon
  Ernest Dowson
  James Martineau
  John Ruskin
  Henry Sidgwick
  Henry Traill
  Oscar Wilde

WORKS
  Winston Churchill. Ian Hamilton's March (his, nar)
  _____. London to Ladysmith via Pretoria (nar)
  Joseph Conrad. Lord Jim (n)
  Marie Corelli. The Master Christian (n)
  Robert Cunninghame-Graham. Thirteen Stories (fic)
  Sir Arthur Conan Doyle. The Great Boer War (e)
  _____. Story of Waterloo (dr)
  Sir Charles Firth. Oliver Cromwell (bio, his)
  Sir James George Frazer. Pausanias and Other Greek Sketches (his, bio)
  Thomas Anstey Guthrie. The Brass Bottle (fic)
  Frank Harris. Mr. and Mrs. Daventry (dr)
  Frederic Harrison. Byzantine History in the Early Middle Ages (his)
  Maurice Hewlett. The Life and Death of Richard Yea-and-Nay (n)
  John Oliver Hobbes. Robert Orange (n)

William Jacobs. A Master of Craft (fic)
Andrew Lang. The History of Scotland from the Roman Occupation to the Suppression of the Last Jacobite Rising, to 1907 (his)
_____. Prince Charles Edward (his, bio)
Fiona Macleod. The House of Usna (dr)
_____. The Immortal Hour (dr)
John Morley. Oliver Cromwell (bio)
Barry Pain. Eliza (n)
Sir Arthur Quiller-Couch. The Oxford Book of English Verse (ed)
Sir Walter Raleigh. Milton (bio)
Archibald Primrose, Earl of Rosebury. Cromwell (bio)
_____. Napoleon--the Last Phase (his)
George Saintsbury. A History of Criticism, to 1904 (his)
Sir Leslie Stephen. The English Utilitarians (his)
Henry Sweet. The History of Language (his)
H.G. Wells. Love and Mr. Lewisham (n)
William Butler Yeats. The Shadowy Waters (po)

1901

BIRTHS
Roy Campbell
James Hanley

DEATHS
Sir Walter Besant
Robert Buchanan
Mandell Creighton
Frederic Myers
William Stubbs
Charlotte Yonge

EVENTS
Edward VII, King of England, to 1910

WORKS
Sir James Matthew Barrie. Quality Street (dr)
George Douglas Brown. The House with the Green Shutters (n)
James Bryce. Studies in History and Jurisprudence (e)
Samuel Butler. Erewhon Revisited (fic)
Sir Thomas H.H. Caine. The Eternal City (n)
John Willis Clark. The Care of Books (his)
John Churton Collins. Ephemera Critica (e)
Sir Charles Eliot. Turkey in Europe (his)
Sir Arthur Evans. The Myccenaean Tree and Pillar Cult (his)
Ford Madox Ford and Joseph Conrad. The Inheritors (n)
George Gissing. By the Ionian Sea (nar)
_____. Our Friend the Charlatan (n)
Harley Granville-Barker. The Marrying of Ann Leete (dr)
John Oliver Hobbes. The Serious Wooing (n)
Samuel Hole. Then and Now (e, nar)
Henry James. The Sacred Fount (n)
Rudyard Kipling. Kim (n)
Andrew Lang. The Mystery of Mary Stuart (his)
John McTaggart. Studies in Hegelian Cosmology (e)
Frederic Maitland. English Law and the Renaissance (e)

George Meredith. A Reading of Life (po)
Alice Meynell. Later Poems (pub)
George Moore. Sister Teresa (n)
Arthur Munby. Poems, Chiefly Lyrical and Elegiac (po)
Edith Nesbit. The Wouldbegoods (fic)
Sir Arthur Wing Pinero. Iris (dr)
Frederick Rolfe. Chronicles of the House of Borgia (fic)
John Round. Studies in Peerage and Family History (his)
George Bernard Shaw. Caesar and Cleopatra (dr)
_____. Captain Brassbound's Conversion (dr)
_____. The Devil's Disciple (dr)
George Tyrrell. The Faith of the Millions, to 1902 (e)
H.G. Wells. The First Men in the Moon (n)
Stanley Weyman. Count Hannibal (n)
World's Classics (pub)

1902

BIRTHS
  Michael Roberts
  Florence Margaret Smith ("Stevie Smith")

DEATHS
  Philip James Bailey
  Samuel Butler
  Aubrey DeVere
  Samuel Gardiner
  Lionel Johnson

EVENTS
  Times Literary Supplement, London (p, f)

WORKS
  Maurice Baring. The Black Prince (po)
  James Matthew Barrie. The Admirable Crichton (dr)
  Hilaire Belloc. The Path to Rome (trav)
  Arnold Bennett. Anna of the Five Towns (n)
  Augustine Birrell. William Hazlitt (e, bio)
  Joseph Conrad. Heart of Darkness (n)
  _____. Typhoon (fic)
  _____. Youth (fic)
  Marie Corelli. Temporal Power (n)
  Robert Cunninghame-Graham. Success (fic)
  Walter De La Mare. Songs of Childhood (po)
  Henry Austin Dobson. Samuel Richardson (bio)
  Sir Arthur Conan Doyle. The Hound of the Baskervilles (n)
  Ford Madox Ford. Rossetti (e)
  Alfred Godley. Second Strings (po)
  Thomas Hardy. Poems of the Past and the Present (po)
  Frederic Harrison. Ruskin (bio, e)
  Henry James. The Wings of a Dove (n)
  Rudyard Kipling. Just So Stories for Little Children (fic)
  Andrew Lang. The Disentanglers (n)
  _____. James VI and the Gowrie Conspiracy (his)
  Emily Lawless. With the Wild Geese (po)
  Sir Sidney Lee. Life of Queen Victoria (bio)

Sir Alfred Lyall. Alfred, Lord Tennyson (bio)
Arthur Machen. Hieroglyphics (fic)
Henry Merriman. Barlasch of the Guard (n)
Barry Pain. The One Before (n)
Beatrix Potter. The Tale of Peter Rabbit (fic)
Sir Leslie Stephen. George Eliot (bio)
Philip Edward Thomas. Horae Solitariae (e)
George Tyrrell. Oil and Wine (e)
H.G. Wells. The Sea Lady (n)
William Butler Yeats. Cathleen ni Houlihan (dr)
─────────────────. Where There Is Nothing (dr)

1903

BIRTHS
  Eric Blair ("George Orwell")
  Cyril Connolly
  Frank Darling
  Rhys Davies
  Walter Greenwood
  Charles Ewart Milne
  Michael Francis O'Donovan ("Frank O'Connor")
  Alfred Leslie Rowse
  Evelyn Waugh

DEATHS
  Alexander Bain
  Ada Ellen Bayly ("Edna Lyall")
  Edward Caird
  Sir Charles Duffy
  George Gissing
  William Ernest Henley
  William E.H. Lecky
  Herbert Spencer
  Hugh Stowell Scott ("Henry Merriman")

WORKS
  Robert Adamson. The Development of Modern Philosophy (t)
  AE. The Divine Vision (po)
  Alfred Ainger. The Life of George Crabbe (bio)
  Sir James Matthew Barrie. Little Mary (dr)
  James Bryce. Studies in Contemporary Biography (bio, e)
  Samuel Butler. The Way of All Flesh (n, pub)
  Sir Edmund Chambers. The Medieval Stage (e)
  Gilbert Keith Chesterton. Robert Browning (e)
  Erskine Childers. The Riddle of the Sands (n)
  Robert Cunninghame-Graham. Hernando de Soto (fic)
  Henry Austin Dobson. Fanny Burney (bio)
  Ford Madox Ford and Joseph Conrad. Romance (n)
  George Gissing. The Private Papers of Henry Ryecroft (n)
  Richard Haldane. Pathway to Reality (e)
  Thomas Hardy. The Dynasts, Part I (po, dr)
  William Ernest Henley. In Hospital (po)
  Henry James. The Ambassadors (n)
  Patrick Joyce. A Social History of Ireland (his)
  Frederic Maitland. Year Books of Edward III, to 1905 (ed, trans)

John Masefield. Ballads (po)
George Moore. Untilled Fields (fic)
George Edward Moore. Principia Ethica (e)
John Morley. Life of Gladstone (bio)
Beatrix Potter. The Tailor of Gloucester (fic)
Sir Walter Raleigh. Wordsworth (bio)
Bertrand Russell. The Principles of Mathematics (t)
George Bernard Shaw. Man and Superman (dr)
John Millington Synge. The Shadow of the Glen (dr)
George Tyrrell. Lex Orandi (e)
Alfred Wallace. Man's Place in the Universe (e)
H.G. Wells. Mankind in the Making (e)
William Butler Yeats. The Hourglass (dr)
_____. Ideas of Good and Evil (e)
_____. In the Seven Woods (po)

1904

BIRTHS
  George Buchanan
  Cecil Day-Lewis
  Graham Greene
  Christopher Isherwood

DEATHS
  Alfred Ainger
  Frances Power Cobbe
  Samuel Hole
  Samuel Smiles
  Sir Henry Stanley
  Sir Leslie Stephen

EVENTS
  Abbey Theatre, Dublin (op)

WORKS
  AE. Controversy in Ireland (e)
  Sir James Matthew Barrie. Peter Pan (dr)
  Sir Max Beerbohm. The Poet's Corner (e)
  Andrew Cecil Bradley. Shakespearean Tragedy (e)
  Henry Bradley. The Making of English (e)
  Sir Thomas H.H. Caine. The Prodigal Son (n)
  Gilbert Keith Chesterton. The Napoleon of Notting Hill (fic)
  John Churton Collins. Studies in Shakespeare (e)
  Joseph Conrad. Nostromo (n)
  Walter De La Mare. Henry Brocken (n)
  Alexander Fraser. Biographia Philosophica (auto, e)
  John Galsworthy. The Island Pharisees (n)
  Richard Garnett. Coleridge (bio)
  George Gissing. Veranilda (n, pub)
  Sir Edmund Gosse. Life of Jeremy Taylor (bio)
  Lady Augusta Gregory. Spreading the News (dr)
  Maurice Hewlett. The Queen's Quair (n)
  David Hogarth. The Penetration of Arabia (e)
  William Hudson. Green Mansions (n)
  Henry James. The Golden Bowl (n)

THE TWENTIETH CENTURY   215

   William Ker. The Dark Ages (e)
   Sir Sidney Lee. Great Englishmen of the 16th Century (bio)
   Hector Munro. Reginald (fic)
   Edith Nesbit. The Phoenix and the Carpet (fic)
   Sir Henry Newbolt. Songs of the Sea (po)
   Sir Frederick Pollock. The Expansion of the Common Law (e)
   Frederick Rolfe. Hadrian the Seventh (fic)
   Sir Leslie Stephen. English Literature and Society in the Eighteenth
                       Century (his, e)
   _____. Hobbes (bio)
   Algernon Swinburne. A Channel Passage (po)
   John Millington Synge. Riders to the Sea (dr)
   Spencer Walpole. The History of Twenty-Five Years (1856-1880), to 1908
                    (his)
   H.G. Wells. The Food of the Gods (n)
   William Butler Yeats. The King's Threshold (dr)
   _____. On Baile's Strand (dr)
   _____. Stories of Red Hanrahan (fic)

                                 1905

BIRTHS
   Leonard Clark
   Geoffrey Grigson
   Arthur Koestler
   Anthony Powell
   C.P. Snow
   Rex Warner
   George Emlyn Williams
   Henry Vincent Yorke ("Henry Green")

DEATHS
   George Macdonald
   William Sharp ("Fiona Macleod")

WORKS
   Alfred Ainger. Lectures and Essays (e)
   Sir James Matthew Barrie. Alice Sit-by-the-Fire (dr)
   Mrs. Montagu Barstow. The Scarlet Pimpernel (n)
   Augustine Birrell. Andrew Marvell (e, bio)
   Robert Bridges. Demeter (po)
   Rhoda Broughton. A Waif's Progress (n)
   John Churton Collins. Studies in Poetry and Criticism (e)
   _____. The Works of Robert Greene (ed)
   _____. Voltaire, Montesquieu, and Rousseau in England
                                (e)
   Edward Dunsany. The Gods of Pegana (fic)
   Ford Madox Ford. The Benefactor (n)
   E.M. Forster. Where Angels Fear To Tread (n)
   George Gissing. Will Warburton (n, pub)
   Sir Edmund Gosse. Life of Sir Thomas Browne (bio)
   Harley Granville-Barker. The Voysey Inheritance (dr)
   Lady Augusta Gregory. In White Cockade (dr)
   H. Rider Haggard. Ayesha, or the Return of She (n)
   Frederick Harrison. Chatham (bio, e)
   William Ker. Essays on Medieval Literature (e)

Andrew Lang. John Knox and the Reformation (his)
_____. New Collected Rhymes (po)
William Locke. Morals of Marcus Ordeyne (fic)
Sir Alfred Lyall. Lord Dufferin (bio)
John Masefield. A Mainsail Haul (po)
Sir Lewis Morris. The New Rambler (e)
Frederick Rolfe. Don Tarquinio (fic)
Robert Scott. The Voyage of the Discovery (nar, trav)
John Millington Synge. The Well of the Saints (dr)
Francis Thompson. Health and Holiness (e)
Edgar Wallace. The Four Just Men (n)
Mary Ward. The Marriage of William Ashe (n)
H.G. Wells. Kipps (n)
_____. A Modern Utopia (n)
Oscar Wilde. De Profundis (auto, pub)

1906

BIRTHS
  Samuel Beckett
  John Betjeman
  Ronald Bottrall
  William Empson
  Vernon Watkins
  Terence White

DEATHS
  Mrs. P.M.T. Craigie ("John Oliver Hobbes")
  Richard Garnett
  Frederic Maitland
  Herman Merivale

EVENTS
  The English Association (f)
  The Malone Society (f)

WORKS
  Hillaire Belloc. Hills to the Sea (po)
  Winston Churchill. Lord Randolph Churchill, to 1907 (bio)
  Joseph Conrad. The Mirror of the Sea (auto)
  William DeMorgan. Joseph Vance (n)
  Charles Doughty. The Dawn in Britain (po)
  Edward Dunsany. Time and the Gods (fic)
  H.W. Fowler and F.G. Fowler. The King's English (ref)
  John Galsworthy. The Man of Property (n)
  Francis Gasquet. Parish Life in Medieval England (his)
  George Gissing. The House of Cobwebs (fic, pub)
  Lady Augusta Gregory and Douglas Hyde. The Rising of the Moon (dr)
  Thomas Anstey Guthrie. Salted Almonds (n)
  Thomas Hardy. The Dynasts, Part II (po, dr)
  Rudyard Kipling. Puck of Pook's Hill (fic)
  Andrew Lang. Homer and His Age (his)
  Sir Sidney Lee. Shakespeare and the Modern Stage (e)
  William Locke. The Beloved Vagabond (fic)
  John McTaggart. Some Dogmas of Religion (e)
  Arthur Machen. The House of Souls (fic)

THE TWENTIETH CENTURY   217

   Henry Downes Miles. Pugilistica (his)
   George Moore. Memoirs of My Dead Life (auto)
   Sir Arthur Wing Pinero. His House in Order (dr)
   George Saintsbury. A History of English Prosody, to 1910 (his)
   Siegfried Sassoon. Poems (pub)
   Edith Somerville. Some Irish Yesterdays (fic)
   George Tyrrell. Letter to a Professor of Anthropology (e)
   _____. Lex Credendi (e)
   Sir William Watson. Collected Poems (pub)
   H.G. Wells. Faults of the Fabians (e)
   _____. Socialism and the Family (e)
   Stanley Weyman. Chippinge (n)
   William Butler Yeats. Poems, 1899-1905 (pub)
   _____. The Poetical Works, 2 vols, to 1907 (pub)

                              1907

BIRTHS
   Wystan Hugh Auden
   Richard Henry Michael Clayton ("William Haggard")
   Christopher Fry
   Daphne du Maurier
   Rumer Godden
   Ray Coryton Hutchinson
   John Lehmann
   Louis Macneice
   Christopher St. John Sprigg ("Christopher Caudwell")

DEATHS
   Mary Elizabeth Coleridge
   Sir Lewis Morris
   Francis Thompson
   Spencer Walpole

EVENTS
   The Gem (p, f)
   Macmillan's Magazine (p, c)

WORKS
   Sir Max Beerbohm. A Book of Caricatures (e)
   Arnold Bennett. The Grim Smile of the Five Towns (fic)
   Andrew Clark. The Shirburne Ballads (ed, pub)
   Mary Elizabeth Coleridge. Poems Old and New (po)
   Joseph Conrad. The Secret Agent (n)
   William DeMorgan. Alice-for-Short (n)
   Sir Charles Eliot. Letters from the Far East (e)
   James Flecker. The Bridge of Fire (po)
   Ford Madox Ford. An English Girl (n)
   _____. The Pre-Raphaelite Brotherhood (e)
   _____. The Spirit of the People: Analysis of the English
                       Mind (e)
   E.M. Forster. The Longest Journey (n)
   John Galsworthy. The Country House (n)
   Sir Edmund Gosse. Father and Sons (auto)
   Frederic Harrison. The Philosophy of Common Sense (e)
   James Joyce. Chamber Music (po)

George Murray. The Rise of the Greek Epic (e)
Edith Nesbit. The Enchanted Castle (fic)
Sir Walter Raleigh. Shakespeare (bio)
Hastings Rashdall. The Theory of Good and Evil (e)
George Bernard Shaw. Major Barbara (dr)
John Millington Synge. The Aran Islands (e)
⎯⎯⎯⎯⎯⎯⎯⎯⎯⎯⎯⎯⎯⎯⎯. The Playboy of the Western World (dr)
⎯⎯⎯⎯⎯⎯⎯⎯⎯⎯⎯⎯⎯⎯⎯. The Tinker's Wedding (dr)
George Macaulay Trevelyan. Garibaldi's Defence of the Roman Republic (his)
George Tyrrell. Through Scylla and Charybdis (e)
William Butler Yeats. Deidre (dr)
⎯⎯⎯⎯⎯⎯⎯⎯⎯⎯⎯⎯⎯⎯⎯. Discoveries (e)
Israel Zangwill. Ghetto Comedies (fic)

1908

BIRTHS
  Kathleen Raine

DEATHS
  Robert Adamson
  John Churton Collins
  Marie Louise de la Ramee ("Ouida")
  Sir John Evans

EVENTS
  The English Review (p, f)
  The Magnet (p, f)

WORKS
  Lascelles Abercrombie. Interludes and Poems (po)
  Algernon Blackwood. John Silence (n)
  Sir James Matthew Barrie. What Every Woman Knows (dr)
  Hillaire Belloc. Mr. Clutterbuck's Election (n)
  Arnold Bennett. Buried Alive (n)
  ⎯⎯⎯⎯⎯⎯⎯⎯⎯⎯⎯⎯. The Old Wives' Tale (n)
  Sir Thomas H.H. Caine. My Story (bio, nar)
  Joyce Cary. Verse (po)
  Gilbert Keith Chesterton. The Man Who Was Thursday (fic)
  ⎯⎯⎯⎯⎯⎯⎯⎯⎯⎯⎯⎯. Thackeray (e)
  Winston Churchill. My African Journey (nar)
  William Davies. The Autobiography of a Super-Tramp (auto)
  William DeMorgan. Somehow Good (n)
  Charles Doughty. Adam Cast Forth (dr, po)
  Edward Dunsany. The Sword of Welleran (fic)
  Havelock Ellis. The Soul of Spain (e)
  Ford Madox Ford. Mr. Apollo (n)
  E.M. Forster. A Room with a View (n)
  Charles Gore. The Old Theology and the New Religion (e)
  Edmund Gosse. Life of Ibsen (bio)
  Thomas Hardy. The Dynasts, Part III (po, dr)
  Maurice Hewlett. Halfway House (fic)
  William Houghton. The Dear Departed (dr)
  Jerome Jerome. The Passing of the Third Floor Back (dr)
  Henry Jones. Dolly Reforming Herself (dr)

THE TWENTIETH CENTURY   219

Andrew Lang. The Maid of France (bio)
William E.H. Lecky. Historical and Political Essays (pub)
Edith Nesbit. The Railway Children (fic)
Alfred Noyes. Brake (po)
Sir Arthur Wing Pinero. The Thunderbolt (dr)
Ezra Pound. A lume spento (po)
Henry Handel Richardson. Maurice Guest (n)
Anne Ritchie. The Blackstick Papers (e)
Lennox Robinson. The Clancy Name (dr)
Edith Somerville. Further Experiences of an Irish R.M. (fic)
Henry Sweet. The Sounds of English: An Introduction (e, ref)
Algernon Swinburne. The Duke of Gandia (dr)
George Tyrrell. Medievalism (e)
H.G. Wells. New Worlds for Old (e)
William Butler Yeats. The Golden Helmet (dr)
_____ and Lady Augusta Gregory. The Unicorn from the Stars (dr)
_____ and Lionel Johnson. Poetry and Ireland (e)

                            1909

BIRTHS
  Eric Ambler
  George Bruce
  Malcolm Lowry
  John Pudney
  James Reeves
  Stephen Spender

DEATHS
  John Davidson
  Sebastian Evans
  Sir Theodore Martin
  George Meredith
  James Stirling
  Algernon Swinburne
  John Millington Synge
  George Tyrrell

EVENTS
  The Academy (p, c)

WORKS
  Arthur James Balfour. Questionings on Criticism and Beauty (e)
  Sir Max Beerbohm. Yet Again (e)
  Arnold Bennett. Cupid and Commonsense (dr)
  Ingram Bywater. The Poetics of Aristotle (ed)
  Sir Thomas H.H. Caine. The White Prophet (n)
  George Calderon. The Fountain (dr)
  Gilbert Keith Chesterton. The Ball and Cross (fic)
  Winston Churchill. Liberalism and the Social Problem (e)
  William Davies. Beggars (auto)
  William DeMorgan. It Can Never Happen Again (n)
  Charles Doughty. The Cliffs (po)
  Lord Alfred Douglas. Sonnets (po)
  Edward Dunsany. The Glittering Gate (dr)

John Galsworthy. Fraternity (n)
—————————. Joy (dr)
—————————. The Silver Box (dr)
—————————. Strife (dr)
Thomas Hardy. Time's Laughingstocks (po)
Frank Harris. The Man Shakespeare (bio)
Maurice Hewlett. The Open Country (fic)
William Houghton. Independent Means (dr)
Andrew Lang. Life of Sir George Mackenzie (bio)
Sir Oliver Lodge. The Survival of Man (e)
John Masefield. The Tragedy of Nan (dr)
George Meredith. Last Poems (pub)
Arthur Munby. Relicta (po)
Sir Arthur Wing Pinero. Mid-Channel (dr)
Ezra Pound. Canzoni (po)
Philip Edward Thomas. Richard Jefferies (e)
Francis Thompson. Essay on Shelley (e)
George Macaulay Trevelyan. Garibaldi and the Thousand (his)
George Otto Trevelyan. The American Revolution (his)
George Tyrrell. Christianity at the Crossroads (e)
H.G. Wells. Ann Veronica (n)
—————————. Tono-Bungay (n)

                              1910

BIRTHS
  Alfred Jules Ayer
  Basil Dowling
  Harry Summerfield Hoff ("William Cooper")
  Norman MacCaig
  Nicholas Monsarrat

DEATHS
  John Willis Clark
  Arthur Munby

EVENTS
  George V, King of England, to 1936
  The Mariner's Mirror (p, f)
  The Round Table (p, f)

WORKS
  Maurice Baring. Diminutive Dramas (dr)
  Sir James Matthew Barrie. The Twelve-Pound Look (dr)
  Arnold Bennett. Clayhanger (n)
  Gilbert Keith Chesterton. George Bernard Shaw (e)
  —————————————————————. William Blake (e)
  Mary Elizabeth Coleridge. Gathered Leaves (po)
  Walter De La Mare. The Return (n)
  ————————————————. The Three Mulla-mulgars (fic)
  William DeMorgan. An Affair of Dishonour (n)
  Edward Dunsany. A Dreamer's Tales (fic)
  Encyclopaedia Britannica, 11th ed, to 1911 (ref, pub)
  E.M. Forster. Howards End (n)
  John Galsworthy. Justice (dr)
  Harley Granville-Barker. The Madras House (dr)

THE TWENTIETH CENTURY   221

Frank Harris. Shakespeare and His Love (dr)
Maurice Hewlett. Rest Harrow (fic)
David Hogarth. Accidents of an Antiquary's Life (nar)
William Houghton. The Master of the House (dr)
_____. The Younger Generation (dr)
Rudyard Kipling. Rewards and Fairies (fic)
Andrew Lang. The World of Homer (his)
Sir Sidney Lee. The French Renaissance in England (e)
John McTaggart. Commentary on Hegel's Logic (e)
John Masefield. Ballads (po)
_____. Martin Hyde, the Duke's Messenger (n)
George Meredith. Celt and Saxon (fic, pub)
_____. The Sentimentalists (dr, pub)
Alice Meynell. Ceres' Runaway (e)
Hector Munro. Reginald in Russia (fic)
Edith Nesbit. The Magic City (fic)
Sir Henry Newbolt. Songs of the Fleet (po)
Ezra Pound. The Spirit of Romance (e)
Sir Arthur Quiller-Couch. The Oxford Book of Ballads (ed)
Sir Walter Raleigh. Six Essays on Johnson (e)
Henry Handel Richardson. The Getting of Wisdom (n)
William Rossetti. Dante and His Convito (e)
John Round. Peerage and Pedigree (his)
Bertrand Russell and Alfred North Whitehead. Principia Mathematica (t)
George Bernard Shaw. Misalliance (dr)
John Millington Synge. Deirdre of the Sorrows (po, dr, pub)
_____. Works (pub)
Philip Edward Thomas. The Feminine Influence on the Poets (e)
_____. Rest and Unrest (e)
Hugh Walpole. Maradick at Forty (n)
H.G. Wells. The History of Mr. Polly (n)
_____. The Sleeper Wakes (n)
William Butler Yeats. The Green Hamlet (po)
Andrew Young. Songs of Night (po)

                                  1911

BIRTHS
   Maurice Edelman
   William Golding
   Rayner Heppenstall
   Terence Rattigan

DEATHS
   Sir Charles Dilke
   William S. Gilbert
   Sir Alfred Lyall
   William Clark Russell
   Edward Whymper

WORKS
   AE. The Renewal of Youth (e)
   Sir Max Beerbohm. Zuleika Dobson (n)
   Hillaire Belloc. The French Revolution (his)
   Arnold Bennett. Hilda Lessways (n)
   Rupert Brooke. Poems (pub)

George Calderon. The Little Stone House (dr)
Gilbert Keith Chesterton. Charles Dickens (e)
Ivy Compton-Burnett. Delores (n)
Joseph Conrad. Under Western Eyes (n)
William DeMorgan. A Likely Story (n)
George Norman Douglas. Siren Land (trav)
James Flecker. Forty-two Poems (po)
Ford Madox Ford. The Critical Attitude (e)
E.M. Forster. The Celestial Omnibus (fic)
H.W. Fowler and F.G. Fowler. The Concise Oxford Dictionary (ref)
John Galsworthy. The Patrician (n)
Sir Edmund Gosse. Collected Poems (pub)
_____. Two Visits to Denmark (trav)
Lady Augusta Gregory. The Full Moon (dr)
Frank Harris. The Women of Shakespeare (bio, e)
William Houghton. Fancy-Free (dr)
Henry James. The Outcry (n)
D.H. Lawrence. The White Peacock (n)
Sir Sidney Lee. The Principles of Biography (e)
Katherine Mansfield. In a German Prison (fic)
George Moore. Ave (auto)
Hector Munro. The Chronicles of Clovis (fic)
Barry Pain. Eliza Getting On (n)
Forrest Reid. The Brackwells (n)
George Bernard Shaw. The Doctor's Dilemma (dr)
George Macaulay Trevelyan. Garibaldi and the Making of Italy (his)
Hugh Walpole. Mr. Perrin and Mr. Traill (n)
Mary Ward. The Case of Richard Meynell (n)
H.G. Wells. The Country of the Blind (fic)
_____. The New Machiavelli (n)
William Butler Yeats. Synge and the Ireland of His Time (e)

1912

BIRTHS
  Paul Dehn
  Lawrence Durrell
  Roy Fuller
  Salvator Aubrey Clarence Menen
  William Sansom
  Sydney Tremayne
  Laurence Whistler

DEATHS
  Shadworth Hodgson
  Andrew Lang
  Justin McCarthy
  Robert Scott
  Walter Skeat
  Henry Sweet

EVENTS
  The Poetry Review (p, f)

WORKS
  Lascelles Abercrombie. Emblems of Love (po)

THE TWENTIETH CENTURY   223

_____. Deborah (po)
_____. Thomas Hardy. A Critical Study (e)
Maurice Baring. The Grey Stocking (dr)
Sir Max Beerbohm. A Christmas Garland (e, s)
Hillaire Belloc. The Green Overcoat (n)
_____. The Servile State (e)
Arnold Bennett. The Matador of the Five Towns (fic)
_____. Milestones (dr)
Robert Bridges. Poetical Works (pub)
Oscar Browning. A History of the Modern World, 1815-1910 (his)
James Bryce. South America. Observations and Impressions (trav, e)
George Calderon. Revolt (dr)
Joseph Conrad. 'Twixt Land and Sea (fic)
William Davies. The True Traveller (nar)
Walter De La Mare. The Listeners (po)
Charles Doughty. The Clouds (po)
George Norman Douglas. Fountains in the Sand (e)
Sir Arthur Conan Doyle. The Lost World (n)
John Drinkwater. William Morris (e)
Edward Dunsany. The Book of Wonder (fic)
Havelock Ellis. The Task of Social Hygiene (e)
Oliver Elton. Survey of English Literature, 1780-1830 (his)
Sir George James Frazer. The Letters of William Cowper (ed)
John Galsworthy. The Eldest Son (dr)
Alfred Godley. The Casual Ward (po)
Lady Augusta Gregory. Irish Folk History Plays (dr)
Frederic Harrison. Among My Books (e)
_____. The Positive Evolution of Religion (e)
William Houghton. Hindle Wakes (dr)
Lionel Johnson. Postliminium (e, pub)
James Joyce. Gas from a Burner (po)
Andrew Lang. The History of English Literature (e, his)
_____. Shakespeare, Bacon and the Great Unknown (e)
D.H. Lawrence. The Trespasser (n)
Sir Compton Mackenzie. Carnival (n)
John Masefield. The Widow in the Bye Street (po)
George Moore. Salve (auto)
Hector Munro. The Unbearable Bassington (n)
Barry Pain. Exit Eliza (n)
Sir Arthur Wing Pinero. The Widow of Wasdale Head (dr)
Sir Frederick Pollock. Spinoza, His Life and Philosophy (bio, e)
Ezra Pound. Ripostes (po)
Sir Arthur Quiller-Couch. The Oxford Book of Victorian Verse (ed)
Isaac Rosenberg. Night and Day (po)
Siegfried Sassoon. An Ode for Music (po)
James Stephens. The Crock of Gold (fic)
Giles Lytton Strachey. Landmarks in French Literature (e)
Henry Tomlinson. The Sea and the Jungle (n)
George Otto Trevelyan. George III and Charles Fox, 2 vols, to 1914
                       (his)
Hugh Walpole. The Cathedral (n)
_____. Prelude to Adventure (n)
Sir William Watson. The Heralds of Dawn (po)
H.G. Wells. The Great State (e)
William Butler Yeats. The Cutting of an Agate (e)

1913

BIRTHS
  George Granville Barker
  Hammond Innes
  Edward Lowbury
  Ronald Thomas
  Angus Wilson

DEATHS
  Edward Dowden
  William Carew Hazlitt
  William Houghton
  Emily Lawless
  Frederick Rolfe
  Alfred Wallace
  William Hale White ("Mark Rutherford")

EVENTS
  Robert Bridges, Poet Laureate of England, to 1930
  The New Statesman (p, f)
  The Society for Pure English (f)

WORKS
  AE. Collected Poems (pub)
  Oscar Browning. A General History of the World (his)
  John Buchan. Montrose (bio)
  Sir Thomas H.H. Caine. The Woman Thou Gavest Me (n)
  Gilbert Keith Chesterton. The Victorian Age in Literature (e)
  Joseph Conrad. Chance (n)
  Walter De La Mare. The Old Man (po)
  _____. Peacock Pie (po)
  John Drinkwater. Swinburne (e)
  James Flecker. The Golden Journey to Samarkand (po)
  Ford Madox Ford. Henry James (e)
  _____. The Young Lovell (n)
  John Galsworthy. The Fugitive (dr)
  Thomas Hardy. A Changed Man (fic)
  Ralph Hodgson. The Bull (po)
  _____. Eve (po)
  _____. A Song of Honour (po)
  Henry James. A Small Boy and Others (auto)
  Henry Jones. Foundations of a National Drama (e)
  Ronald Knox. Some Loose Stones (e)
  D.H. Lawrence. Love Poems (po)
  _____. Sons and Lovers (n)
  Richard LeGallienne. The Lonely Dancer (po)
  Sir Compton Mackenzie. Sinister Street, vol I (n)
  George Murray. Euripides and His Age (e)
  Alfred Noyes. Tales of the Mermaid Tavern (po)
  Barry Pain. Eliza's Son (n)
  Sir Arthur Wing Pinero. Playgoers (dr)
  Anne Ritchie. From the Porch (e)
  Robert Scott. Scott's Last Expedition (nar, trav, pub)
  Philip Edward Thomas. The Country (e)
  _____. Walter Pater (e)

THE TWENTIETH CENTURY 225

George Macaulay Trevelyan. The Life of John Bright (bio)
Hugh Walpole. Fortitude (n)
H.G. Wells. The Passionate Friends (n)

1914

BIRTHS
Patric Dickinson
Colin MacInnes
John Masters
Norman Nicholson
Charles Hubert Sisson
Dylan Thomas

DEATHS
Ingram Bywater
Alexander Fraser
Patrick Joyce
Walter Watts-Dunton

EVENTS
The Egoist (p, f)
The Gentleman's Magazine (p, c)

WORKS
Lascelles Abercrombie. The Epic (e)
Clive Bell. Art (t)
Laurence Binyon. For the Fallen (po)
Wilfred Scawen Blunt. Complete Poems (pub)
Francis Herbert Bradley. Essay on Truth and Reality (e)
Robert Bridges. October, and Other Poems (po)
Gilbert Keith Chesterton. The Flying Inn (fic)
Robert Cunninghame-Graham. Scottish Stories (fic)
William DeMorgan. When Ghost Meets Ghost (n)
Edward Dunsany. Five Plays (dr)
Ford Madox Ford. Collected Poems (pub)
Philip Guedalla. The Partition of Europe, 1715-1815 (his)
Thomas Hardy. Satires of Circumstance (po)
Constance Holme. The Lonely Plough (n)
William Jacobs. Night Watches (fic)
Henry James. Notes of a Son and Brother (auto)
_____. Notes on Novelists (e)
Henry Jones. The Theatre of Ideas, a Burlesque Allegory (s)
James Joyce. Dubliners (fic)
D.H. Lawrence. The Prussian Officer (fic)
Sir Compton Mackenzie. Sinister Street, vol II (n)
George Moore. Vale (auto)
John Morley. Politics and History (e)
Hector Munro. Beasts and Superbeasts (fic)
George Bernard Shaw. Androcles and the Lion (dr)
George Tyrrell. Essays on Faith and Immortality (e, pub)
H.G. Wells. An Englishman Looks at the World (e)
William Butler Yeats. Responsibilities (po, dr)

1915

BIRTHS
  Patrick Anderson
  Francis Berry
  Monica Dickens
  Alun Lewis
  Emanuel Litvinoff
  Gilbert Phelps
  Sydney Goodsir Smith

DEATHS
  Rupert Brooke
  Thomas Alexander Browne
  George Calderon
  James Flecker
  Sir James Murray

EVENTS
  St. Dunstan's Hospital, Regent's Park, London (f)

WORKS
  Arthur James Balfour. Theism and Humanism (e)
  Arnold Bennett. These Twain (n)
  John Buchan. The Thirty-Nine Steps (n)
  Joseph Conrad. Victory (n)
  _____. Within the Tides (fic)
  George Norman Douglas. Old Cambria (trav)
  Ronald Firbank. Vainglory (n)
  James Flecker. The Old Ships (po)
  Ford Madox Ford. The Good Soldier (n)
  D.H. Lawrence. The Rainbow (n)
  Sir Sidney Lee. Shakespeare and the Italian Renaissance (e)
  Sir Alfred Lyall. Studies in Literature and History (e, pub)
  Arthur Machen. The Great Return (fic)
  Sir Compton Mackenzie. Guy and Pauline (n)
  John Masefield. The Faithful (dr)
  W. Somerset Maugham. Of Human Bondage (n)
  John Cowper Powys. Visions and Revisions (e)
  _____. Wood and Stone (n)
  Dorothy Richardson. Pointed Roofs (n)
  Isaac Rosenberg. Youth (po)
  Siegfried Sassoon. Discoveries (po)
  Dame Edith Sitwell. The Mother (po)
  Arnold Toynbee. Nationality and the War (e)
  Virginia Woolf. The Voyage Out (n)
  William Butler Yeats. Reveries over Childhood and Youth (auto)

1916

BIRTHS
  Thomas Blackburn
  Jack Clemo
  David Gascoyne

THE TWENTIETH CENTURY 227

DEATHS
  Henry James
  Hector Munro ("Saki")

EVENTS
  British Humanities Index, to present (ref, bibl)

WORKS
  Laurence Binyon. The Anvil and Other Poems (po)
  Robert Bridges. The Spirit of Man (po, e)
  John Buchan. Greenmantle (n)
  Joseph Conrad. A Personal Record (auto)
  Charles Doughty. The Titans (po)
  George Norman Douglas. London Street Games (e)
  Ronald Firbank. Inclinations (n)
  Charles Gore. The Religion of the Church (e)
  Robert Graves. Over the Brazier (po)
  Maurice Hewlett. Song of the Plow (po)
  James Joyce. A Portrait of the Artist As a Young Man (n)
  D.H. Lawrence. Twi-light in Italy (trav)
  Sir Oliver Lodge. Raymond, or Life and Death (e)
  George Moore. The Brook Kerith (n)
  Ezra Pound. Gaudier-Brzeska: A Memoir (nar)
  _____. Lustra (po)
  John Cowper Powys. Rodmoor (n)
  _____. Suspended Judgments (e)
  _____. Wolf's Bane: Rhymes (po)
  Sir Arthur Quiller-Couch. On the Art of Writing (e)
  Dorothy Richardson. Backwater (n)
  George Bernard Shaw. Pygmalion (dr)
  Hugh Walpole. The Dark Forest (n)
  _____. Joseph Conrad (e)
  H.G. Wells. Mr. Britling Sees It Through (n)
  _____. What Is Coming (e)

1917

BIRTHS
  Anthony Burgess
  Charles Causley
  Robert Conquest

DEATHS
  Sir Francis Cowley Burnand
  William John Courthope
  William DeMorgan
  Philip Edward Thomas

WORKS
  Sir James Matthew Barrie. Dear Brutus (dr)
  Oscar Browning. A Short History of Italy (his)
  Austin Clarke. The Vengeance of Fionn (po)
  Sir Sidney Colvin. John Keats, His Life and Poetry (bio, e)
  Joseph Conrad. The Shadow-Line (n)
  Marie Corelli. The Young Diana (n)
  George Norman Douglas. South Wind (n)

Edward Dunsany. Plays of Gods and Men (dr)
T.S. Eliot. Ezra Pound, His Metric and Poetry (e)
_____. Prufrock and Other Observations (po)
Ronald Firbank. Caprice (n)
Sir Edmund Gosse. Life of A.C. Swinburne (bio)
Robert Graves. Fairies and Fusiliers (po)
Henry James. The Ivory Tower (n, pub)
_____. The Middle Years (auto, pub)
_____. The Sense of Past (n, pub)
D.H. Lawrence. Look! We Have Come Through (po)
John Masefield. Lollingdon Downs (po)
John Morley. Recollections (auto)
Ezra Pound. Homage to Sextus Propertius (po)
John Cowper Powys. Mandragon (po)
Dorothy Richardson. Honeycomb (n)
Henry Handel Richardson. Australia Felix (n)
George Bernard Shaw. Heartbreak House (dr)
Philip Edward Thomas. A Literary Pilgrim in England (e)
_____. Poems (pub)
Alec Waugh. The Loom of Youth (n)
Mary Webb. Gone to Earth (n)
Virginia Woolf and Leonard Woolf. Two Stories (fic)
William Butler Yeats. The Wild Swans at Coole (po, dr)

1918

BIRTHS
 Martin Bell
 Michael Bullock
 John Heath-Stubbs
 Tom Scott
 Muriel Spark
 Edward Henry Willis ("Ted Willis")

DEATHS
 Wilfred Owen
 Isaac Rosenberg

WORKS
 AE. The Candle of Vision (e)
 Rupert Brooke. Collected Poems (pub)
 John Drinkwater. Abraham Lincoln (dr)
 John Galsworthy. Indian Summer of a Forsyte (fic)
 Francis Gasquet. Religio Religiosi (e)
 Eric Gill. Sculpture: An Essay on Stonecutting, with a Preface about God (e)
 Frank Harris. Oscar Wilde (bio)
 Gerard Manley Hopkins. Poems (pub)
 James Joyce. Exiles (dr)
 Ronald Knox. A Spiritual Aeneid (auto)
 Percy Wyndham Lewis. Tarr (n)
 Katherine Mansfield. Je ne parle pas francais (fic)
 _____. Prelude (fic)
 Alice Meynell. A Father of Women (po)
 Edwin Muir. Enigmas and Guesses (e)
 Ezra Pound. Poems, eds to 1921 (pub)

Sir Arthur Quiller-Couch. Studies in Literature (e)
Lennox Robinson. The Lost Leader (dr)
Giles Lytton Strachey. Eminent Victorians (bio)
Philip Edward Thomas. Last Poems (pub)
Henry Tomlinson. Old Junk (n)
Walter Turner. The Dark Fire (po)
Hugh Walpole. The Green Mirror (n)
Alec Waugh. Resentment Poems (po)
Dame Rebecca West. The Return of the Soldier (n)
William Butler Yeats. Per Amica Silentia Lunae (e)

1919

BIRTHS
Arthur David Beaty
Emyr Humphreys
Doris Lessing
Stanley Middleton
Iris Murdock
Norman Simpson

DEATHS
Anne Ritchie
William Rossetti

EVENTS
The Egoist (p, c)

WORKS
Sir Max Beerbohm. Seven Men (fic)
John Buchan. Mr. Standfast (n)
Joseph Conrad. The Arrow of Gold (n)
T.S. Eliot. Poems (pub)
Ronald Firbank. Valmouth (n)
Thomas Hardy. Collected Poems (pub)
Constance Holme. The Splendid Fairing (n)
William Inge. Outspoken Essays, 1st series (e)
John Maynard Keynes. The Economic Consequences of the Peace (e)
Rudyard Kipling. Rudyard Kipling's Verse (po, pub)
D.H. Lawrence. Bay (po)
Percy Wyndham Lewis. The Caliph's Design (e)
W. Somerset Maugham. The Moon and Sixpence (n)
Ezra Pound. Quia pauper amavi (po)
Hastings Rashdall. The Idea of Atonement in Christian Theology (e)
Sir Herbert Read. Naked Warriors (po)
Dorothy Richardson. Interim (n)
_____. Tunnel (n)
Siegfried Sassoon. The War Poems (po, pub)
George Bernard Shaw. Great Catherine (dr)
Hugh Walpole. Jeremy (n)
Virginia Woolf. Kew Gardens (fic)
_____. Night and Day (n)
William Butler Yeats. Two Plays for Dancers (dr)

1920

BIRTHS
  Bob Cobbing
  Alex Comfort
  D.J. Enright
  John Clive Hall
  John Holloway
  Alexander Scott
  John Stuart Williams
  David Wright

DEATHS
  Rhoda Broughton
  Mary Ward

EVENTS
  The Library (p, c)

WORKS
  Enid Bagnold. The Happy Foreigner (n)
  Arthur James Balfour. Essays Speculative and Political (e)
  Sir James Matthew Barrie. Mary Rose (dr)
  William John Courthope. The Country Town and Other Poems (po)
  Charles Doughty. Mansoul, or the Riddle of the World (po)
  George Norman Douglas. They Went (n)
  T.S. Eliot. The Sacred Wood (e)
  Oliver Elton. Survey of English Literature, 1830-1880 (e, his)
  James Flecker. Collected Prose (e)
  John Galsworthy. Awakening (fic)
  _____. In Chancery (n)
  _____. The Skin Game (dr)
  Charles Gore. Epistle of St. John (t)
  Philip Guedalla. Supers and Supermen (his, bio)
  Maurice Hewlett. In a Green Shade (e)
  Aldous Huxley. Limbo (fic)
  D.H. Lawrence. The Lost Girl (n)
  _____. Touch and Go (dr)
  _____. Women in Love (n)
  Dame Rose Macaulay. Potterism (n)
  Katherine Mansfield. Bliss (fic)
  John Masefield. Enslaved (po)
  Sir Henry Newbolt. Naval History of the War, 1914-1918 (his)
  Wilfred Owen. Poems (pub)
  Ezra Pound. Hugh Selwyn Mauberley (po)
  Sir Arthur Quiller-Couch. On the Art of Reading (e)
  Lennox Robinson. The White-headed Boy (dr)
  George Saintsbury. Notes on a Cellar Book (e)
  Philip Edward Thomas. Collected Poems (pub)
  Hugh Walpole. The Captives (n)
  H.G. Wells. The Outline of History (his)
  William Butler Yeats. Michael Robartes and the Dancer (po)

1921

BIRTHS
  George MacKay Brown
  Theodore Wilson Harris

THE TWENTIETH CENTURY 231

Robert Morgan
Johnny Speight

DEATHS
Henry Austin Dobson

EVENTS
Association of Poets, Playwrights, Editors, Essayists, and Novelists (f)
The Nation and Athenaeum (p, f)

WORKS
George Calderon. Cromwell: Mall o'Monks (po, dr)
Austin Clarke. The Fires of Baal (po)
_____. The Sword of the West (po)
Sir Sidney Colvin. Memoirs and Notes of Persons and Places (nar)
Joseph Conrad. Notes on Life and Letters (e)
Alfred Coppard. Adam and Eve and Pinch Me (fic)
Marie Corelli. The Secret Power (n)
Walter De La Mare. Memoirs of a Midget (n)
_____. The Veil (po)
George Norman Douglas. Alone (trav)
John Drinkwater. Oliver Cromwell (dr)
_____. Mary Stuart (dr)
Sir Charles Eliot. Hinduism and Buddhism (e)
John Galsworthy. To Let (n)
Richard Haldane. Reign of Relativity (e)
Maurice Hewlett. Wiltshire Essays (e)
Constance Holme. The Trumpet in the Dust (n)
Aldous Huxley. Crome Yellow (n)
D.H. Lawrence. Sea and Sardinia (trav)
_____. Psychoanalysis and the Unconscious (e)
Percy Lubbock. The Craft of Fiction (e)
John McTaggart. The Nature of Existence, vol I (t)
W. Somerset Maugham. The Circle (dr)
Alice Meynell. The Second Person Singular (e)
Dorothy Richardson. Deadlock (n)
Bertrand Russell. The Analysis of Mind (e)
George Bernard Shaw. Back to Methuselah (dr)
Giles Lytton Strachey. Queen Victoria (bio)
Henry Tomlinson. London River (n)
Arthur Waley. The No Plays of Japan (ed)
William Butler Yeats. Four Plays for Dancers (dr)

1922

BIRTHS
Kingsley Amis
Brendon Behan
John Braine
Donald Davie
Sidney Keyes
Philip Larkin
Alan Ross
Vernon Scannell

DEATHS
  Wilfrid Scawen Blunt
  James Bryce
  Alice Meynell
  Sir Walter Raleigh

EVENTS
  The British Broadcasting Company (f)
  The Criterion (p, f)

WORKS
  Lascelles Abercrombie. Theory of Art (e)
  AE. The Interpreters (e)
  Sir Max Beerbohm. Rossetti and His Circle (e)
  James Bryce. Modern Democracies (e)
  Alfred Coppard. Clorinda Walks in Heaven (fic)
  Walter De La Mare. Down-adown-derry (po)
  T.S. Eliot. The Waste Land (po)
  Sir Arthur Evans. The Palace of Minos at Knossos, to 1935 (his)
  James Flecker. Hassan (dr)
  E.M. Forster. Alexandria: A History and a Guide (his, trav)
  John Galsworthy. A Family Man (dr)
  _____. The Forsyte Saga (fic)
  _____. Loyalties (dr)
  Francis Gasquet. Monastic Life in the Middle Ages (his)
  William Gerhardi. Futility: A Novel on Russian Themes (n)
  Lady Augusta Gregory. Three Wonder Plays (dr)
  Philip Guedalla. The Second Empire (his)
  Richard Haldane. Philosophy of Humanism (e)
  Thomas Hardy. Late Lyrics and Earlier (po)
  Maurice Hewlett. Extemporary Essays (e)
  A.E. Housman. Last Poems (po)
  Richard Hughes. Gipsy Night (po)
  _____. The Sisters' Tragedy (dr)
  Aldous Huxley. Mortal Coils (fic)
  William Inge. Outspoken Essays, 2nd series (e)
  James Joyce. Ulysses (n)
  D.H. Lawrence. Aaron's Rod (n)
  _____. England, My England (fic)
  _____. Fantasia of the Unconscious (e)
  Katherine Mansfield. The Garden Party (fic)
  John Masefield. The Dream (po)
  _____. Melloney Hotspur (dr)
  W. Somerset Maugham. East of Suez (dr)
  Charles Montague. Disenchantment (nar)
  George Edward Moore. Philosophical Studies (e)
  John Middleton Murry. Countries of the Mind (e)
  _____. The Problem of Style (e)
  Leopold Myers. The Orissers (n)
  Alfred Noyes. The Torchbearers, to 1937 (po)
  John Cowper Powys. Samphire (po)
  Sir Walter Raleigh. War in the Air (e)
  George Saintsbury. A Scrap Book (e)
  Dame Edith Sitwell. Facade (po)
  Giles Lytton Strachey. Books and Characters (e)
  Philip Edward Thomas. Cloud Castle (e, pub)

John Tolkien. A Middle English Vocabulary (ref)
Walter Turner. The Man Who Ate the Popomak (dr)
H.G. Wells. The Secret Places of the Heart (n)
Dame Rebecca West. The Judge (n)
Virginia Woolf. Jacob's Room (n)
William Butler Yeats. Later Poems (pub)
_____. The Player Queen (dr)

1923

BIRTHS
  Dannie Abse
  David Holbrook
  James Kirkup

DEATHS
  Kathleen Mansfield Beauchamp ("Katherine Mansfield")
  Oscar Browning
  Frederic Harrison
  Maurice Hewlett
  William Ker
  John Morley

EVENTS
  The Adelphi (p, f)
  The English Place-Name Society (f)

WORKS
  Arthur James Balfour. Theism and Thought (e)
  Arnold Bennett. Riceyman Steps (n)
  Laurence Binyon. Arthur (dr)
  Elizabeth Bowen. Encounters (fic)
  John Buchan. Midwinter (n)
  Sir Edward Chambers. The Elizabethan Stage (e)
  Winston Churchill. The World Crisis, to 1929 (e)
  Joseph Conrad. The Rover (n)
  Walter De La Mare. The Riddle (n)
  George Norman Douglas. Capri (trav)
  John Drinkwater. Robert E. Lee (dr)
  Edward Dunsany. Plays of Near and Far (dr)
  Ronald Firbank. The Flower beneath the Foot (n)
  William Gerhardi. Anton Chekov (e, bio)
  Harley Granville-Barker. The Secret Life (dr)
  Philip Guedalla. Masters and Men (his)
  Aldous Huxley. Antic Hay (n)
  _____. On the Margin (e)
  Sir Julian Huxley. Essays of a Biologist (e)
  Andrew Lang. Collected Poems (pub)
  D.H. Lawrence. Birds, Beasts, and Flowers (po)
  _____. Kangaroo (n)
  _____. The Ladybird (fic)
  _____. Studies in Classic American Literature (e)
  Percy Lubbock. Roman Pictures (e)
  Dame Rose Macaulay. Told by an Idiot (n)
  Arthur Machen. Things Near and Far (fic)
  Katherine Mansfield. The Dove's Nest (fic)

_____. Poems (pub)
Alice Meynell. Last Poems (pub)
John Cowper Powys. Psychoanalysis and Morality (e)
Theodore Powys. Black Byrony (n)
_____. The Left Leg (fic)
Sir Walter Raleigh. Some Authors (e, pub)
I.A. Richards and C.K. Ogden. The Meaning of Meaning (e)
Dorothy Richardson. Revolving Lights (n)
H.G. Wells. Men Like Gods (n)

1924

BIRTHS
Patricia Beer
John Bowen
David Campton

DEATHS
Francis Herbert Bradley
Joseph Conrad
Mary Mackay ("Marie Corelli")
Edith Nesbit
Hastings Rashdall

EVENTS
Transatlantic Review (p, f)

WORKS
Enid Bagnold. Serena Blandish; or, The Difficulty of Getting Married (n)
Sir Max Beerbohm. Around Theatres (e)
Arnold Bennett. London Life (dr)
Roy Campbell. The Flaming Terrapin (po)
Lord Alfred Douglas. In Excelsis (po)
Ronald Firbank. Sorrow in Sunlight (n)
Ford Madox Ford. Joseph Conrad, a Personal Remembrance (nar, bio)
_____. Some Do Not (n)
_____ and Joseph Conrad. The Nature of Crime (n)
E.M. Forster. A Passage to India (n)
H.W. Fowler. The Pocket Oxford Dictionary (ref)
John Galsworthy. The White Monkey (n)
Lady Augusta Gregory. The Story Brought by Brigit (dr)
John B.S. Haldane. Daedalus, or, Science and the Future (e)
Maurice Hewlett. Last Essays (e, pub)
Laurence Housman. Trimblerigg (n)
Thomas Ernest Hulme. Speculations: Essays on Humanism and the Philosophy of Art (e, pub)
Montague James. The Apocryphal New Testament (trans, ed)
Margaret Kennedy. The Constant Nymph (n)
Dame Rose Macaulay. Orphan Island (n)
Arthur Machen. The Shining Pyramid (fic)
Katherine Mansfield. Something Childish (fic, pub)
John Masefield. Sard Harker (n)
George Moore. Ulick and Soracha (n)
Edwin Muir. Latitudes (e)
John Middleton Murry. To the Unknown God (e)

Ezra Pound. Antheil and the Treatise on Harmony (e)
Theodore Powys. Mark Only (n)
Lennox Robinson. Crabbed Youth and Age (dr)
_____. The Round Table (dr)
George Bernard Shaw. St. Joan (dr)
Dame Edith Sitwell. The Sleeping Beauty (po)
Sir Osbert Sitwell. Triple Fugue (fic)
Hugh Walpole. The Old Ladies (n)
Mary Webb. Precious Bane (n)
Virginia Woolf. Mr. Bennett and Mrs. Brown (e)
Percival Christopher Wren. Beau Geste (n)
William Butler Yeats. The Cat and the Moon and Certain Poems (pub)

1925

BIRTHS
  Brian Aldiss
  Nina Bawden
  William Hamilton Canaway
  Laurence Collinson
  Lawrence Lerner
  John Wain

DEATHS
  Alfred Godley
  H. Rider Haggard
  John McTaggart

EVENTS
  Review of English Studies (p, f)

WORKS
  Maurice Baring. Collected Poems (pub)
  Robert Bridges. New Verse (po)
  Austin Clarke. The Cattledrive in Connaught (po)
  Ivy Compton-Burnett. Pastors and Masters (n)
  Joseph Conrad. Suspence (n)
  _____. Tales of Hearsay (fic)
  Lettice Cooper. The Lighted Room (n)
  Alfred Coppard. Fishmonger's Fiddle (fic)
  William Davies. Later Days (auto)
  Cecil Day-Lewis. Beechen Vigil (po)
  Walter De La Mare. Never More Sailor (po)
  James Flecker. Don Juan (dr)
  Ford Madox Ford. No More Parades (n)
  Robert Graves. Contemporary Techniques of Poetry: A Political Analogy
               (e)
  _____. Poetic Unreason and Other Studies (e)
  Sir Walter Greg. English Literary Autographs, 1550-1650, to 1932 (ref)
  Thomas Hardy. Human Shows (po)
  Aldous Huxley. Those Barren Leaves (n)
  D.H. Lawrence. Reflections on the Death of a Porcupine (e)
  _____. St. Mawr (fic)
  Sir Sidney Lee. Life of King Edward VII, to 1927 (bio)
  Sir Oliver Lodge. Ether and Reality (e)
  _____. Relativity (e)

Hugh Macdiarmid. Sangschaw (po)
W. Somerset Maugham. The Letter (dr)
Edwin Muir. First Poems (po)
John Middleton Murry. Keats and Shakespeare (e)
Leopold Myers. The Clio (n)
Sean O'Casey. Juno and the Peacock (dr)
_____. The Shadow of a Gunman (dr)
Liam O'Flaherty. The Informer (n)
John Cowper Powys. Ducdame (n)
Theodore Powys. Mockery Gap (n)
J.B. Priestley. The English Comic Characters (e)
Sir Arthur Quiller-Couch. The Oxford Book of English Prose (ed)
Sir Herbert Read. In Retreat (nar)
I.A. Richards. Principles of Literary Criticism (e)
Dorothy Richardson. Trap (n)
Henry Handel Richardson. The Way Home (n)
Lennox Robinson. The Golden Treasury of Irish Verse (ed)
Dame Edith Sitwell. Poetry and Criticism (e)
Arthur Waley. The Tale of Genji, 6 vols, to 1933 (n, trans)
Hugh Walpole. The English Novel (e)
Alfred North Whitehead. Science and the Modern World (e)
Virginia Woolf. The Common Reader (e)
_____. Mrs. Dalloway (n)
William Butler Yeats. The Bounty of Sweden (e)
_____. A Vision (e)

1926

BIRTHS
 John Fowles
 John Hale
 Sir Thomas Willes Chitty ("Thomas Hinde")
 Elizabeth Jennings
 Christopher Logue
 Christopher Middleton
 Peter Shaffer
DEATHS
 Charles Doughty
 Ronald Firbank
 Sir Sidney Lee
 Israel Zangwill
WORKS
 AE. Collected Poems (pub)
 Hilaire Belloc. A Companion to Mr. Wells's Outline of History (his)
 John Buchan. Dancing Floor (n)
 Agatha Christie. The Murder of Roger Ackroyd (n)
 Joseph Conrad. Last Essays (pub)
 William Davies. The Adventures of Johnny Walker, Tramp (nar)
 Sir Arthur Conan Doyle. The History of Spiritualism (e)
 Ronald Firbank. Concerning the Eccentricities of Cardinal Pirelli (n)
 Ford Madox Ford. A Man Could Stand Up (n)
 _____. A Mirror to France (e)
 H.W. Fowler. A Dictionary of Modern English Usage, 1st ed (ref)
 John Galsworthy. Escape (dr)
 _____. The Silver Spoon (n)
 Alfred Godley. Reliquiae A.D. Godley (po, pub)

Henry Green. Blindness (n)
Philip Guedalla. Palmerston (bio)
Richard Hughes. Confessio Juvenis (po)
_____. A Moment of Time (fic)
Aldous Huxley. Jesting Pilate (e)
James Joyce. Pomes Penyeach (po)
D.H. Lawrence. David (dr)
_____. Glad Ghosts (fic)
_____. The Plumed Serpent (n)
T.E. Lawrence. Seven Pillars of Wisdom (nar)
Richard LeGallienne. The Romantic Nineties (nar)
Percy Wyndham Lewis. The Art of Being Ruled (e)
Hugh Macdiarmid. Contemporary Scottish Studies (e)
_____. A Drunk Man Looks at the Thistle (po)
Edwin Muir. Chorus of the Newly Dead (po)
_____. Transition (e)
John Middleton Murry. The Life of Jesus (bio, e)
Sean O'Casey. The Plough and the Stars (dr)
Liam O'Flaherty. Darkness (dr)
_____. Mr. Gilhooly (dr)
_____. Spring Sowing (fic)
Theodore Powys. The Bride (fic)
_____. Feed My Swine (fic)
_____. Innocent Birds (n)
_____. The Rival Pastors (fic)
_____. A Strong Girl (fic)
Sir Herbert Read. Collected Poems, 1913-1925 (pub)
Lennox Robinson. The White Blackbird (dr)
Siegfried Sassoon. Satirical Poems (pub)
Sir Osbert Sitwell. Before the Bombardment (n)
George Macaulay Trevelyan. History of England (his)
H.G. Wells. The World of William Clissold (n)
Alfred North Whitehead. Religion in the Making (e)

1927

BIRTHS
 Edwin Brock
 Molly Holden
 Ann Jellicoe
 Peter Richard Nichols
 Simon Raven
 Charles Tomlinson

DEATHS
 Sir Sidney Colvin
 David Hogarth
 Mary Webb

EVENTS
 The British Broadcasting Corporation (f)

WORKS
 Arthur James Balfour. Opinions and Arguments (e)
 Arnold Bennett. Mr. Prohack (dr)
 Walter De La Mare. Alone (po)

Austin Clarke. The Son of Learning (dr)
Lettice Cooper. The Old Fox (n)
Rhys Davies. Aaron (fic)
_____. The Song of Songs (fic)
_____. The Withered Root (n)
George Norman Douglas. Birds and Beasts of the Greek Anthology (e)
_____. In the Beginning (n)
Ford Madox Ford. New York Essays (e)
E.M. Forster. Aspects of the Novel (e)
John Galsworthy. Passers By (fic)
_____. A Silent Wooing (fic)
Eric Gill. Art and Love (e)
Robert Graves. Poems (pub)
_____ and Laura Riding. A Survey of Modernist Poetry (e)
Sir Walter Greg. The Calculus of Variants (e)
John B.S. Haldane. Possible Worlds (e)
_____ and Julian Huxley. Animal Biology (e)
Rudyard Kipling. Rudyard Kipling's Verse (po)
Ronald Knox. The Belief of Catholics (e)
D.H. Lawrence. Mornings in Mexico (trav)
Percy Wyndham Lewis. The Lion and the Fox: The Role of the Hero in Shakespeare (e)
_____. Time and Western Man (e)
John McTaggart. The Nature of Existence, vol II (t, pub)
Hugh Macdiarmid. Albyn, or Scotland and the Future (e)
Sir Compton Mackenzie. Vestal Fire (n)
John Masefield. The Midnight Folk (n)
Charles Montague. Right Off the Map (n)
Theodore Powys. Mr. Weston's Good Wine (n)
J.B. Priestley. The English Novel (e)
Dorothy Richardson. Oberland (n)
Dame Edith Sitwell. Rustic Elegies (po)
Henry Tomlinson. Gallions Reach (n)
Edgar Wallace. The Squeaker (dr)
_____. The Terror (dr)
H.G. Wells. Democracy under Revision (e)
Alfred North Whitehead. Symbolism (e)
Virginia Woolf. To the Lighthouse (n)
William Butler Yeats. October Blast (po)

1928

BIRTHS
   William Trevor Cox ("William Trevor")
   John Brendan Keane
   Thomas Kinsella
   Frank Marcus
   David Mercer
   Basil Payne
   Alan Sillitoe
   Ian Crichton Smith

DEATHS
   Sir Edmund Gosse
   Richard Haldane
   Thomas Hardy

THE TWENTIETH CENTURY   239

Charles Montague
Barry Pain
John Round
George Otto Trevelyan
Stanley Weyman

WORKS
  AE. Midsummer Eve (po)
  Sir Max Beerbohm. The Dreadful Dragon of Hay Hill (fic)
  Clive Bell. Civilization (e)
  Edmund Blunden. Undertones of War (e)
  Lettice Cooper. Good Venture (n)
  Alfred Coppard. Collected Poems (pub)
  T.S. Eliot. For Lancelot Andrewes (e)
  Oliver Elton. Survey of English Literature, 1730-1780 (e, his)
  E.M. Forster. The Eternal Moment (fic)
  John Galsworthy. Swan Song (n)
  Eric Gill. Christianity and Art (e)
  Sir Walter Greg. Principles of Emendation in Shakespeare (e)
  John B.S. Haldane. Science and Ethics (e)
  Thomas Hardy. Winter Words (po)
  David Hogarth. The Life of C.M. Doughty (bio)
  Laurence Housman. The Duke of Flamborough (n)
  Aldous Huxley. Point Counter Point (n)
  Christopher Isherwood. All the Conspirators (n)
  James Joyce. Anna Livia Plurabelle (fic)
  _____. Haveth Children Everywhere (fic)
  Ronald Knox. Essays in Satire (e)
  D.H. Lawrence. Lady Chatterley's Lover (n)
  _____. Rawdon's Roof (fic)
  _____. Selected Poems (pub)
  _____. The Woman Who Rode Away (n)
  Percy Wyndham Lewis. The Childermass (n)
  _____. Tarr, rev ed (n)
  Sir Compton Mackenzie. The Extraordinary Women (n)
  Edwin Muir. The Structure of the Novel (e)
  Sean O'Casey. The Silver Tassie (dr)
  Llewelyn Powys. The Pathetic Fallacy (e)
  Theodore Powys. The Dewpond (fic)
  Sir Herbert Read. English Prose Style (e)
  The Revised Book of Common Prayer (pub)
  Lennox Robinson. The Far-Off Hills (dr)
  Siegfried Sassoon. Memoirs of a Fox-hunting Man (n)
  George Bernard Shaw. The Intelligent Woman's Guide to Socialism and
                         Capitalism (e)
  Stephen Spender. Nine Experiments: Being Poems Written at the Age of
                     Eighteen (po)
  Giles Lytton Strachey. Elizabeth and Essex: A Tragic History (his)
  Arthur Waley. The Pillow-Book of Sei Shonagon (ed)
  Hugh Walpole. Anthony Trollope (e)
  _____. Wintersmoon (n)
  Evelyn Waugh. Decline and Fall (n)
  _____. Rossetti: His Life and Works (bio, e)
  Sir Arnold Wilson. The Persian Gulf (trav, e)
  Virginia Woolf. Orlando (n)
  William Butler Yeats. The Tower (po)

1929

BIRTHS
  Alfred Alvarez
  Anne Beresford
  Brigid Brophy
  Len Deighton
  Gillian Freeman
  Thom Gunn
  Henry Livings
  John Montague
  John Osborne
  Cecil P. Taylor

DEATHS
  Francis Gasquet
  Henry Jones
  Archibald Primrose, Earl of Rosebery

EVENTS
  The Edinburgh Review (p, c)
  Encyclopaedia Britannica, 14th ed (ref, pub)

WORKS
  Richard Aldington. Death of a Hero (n)
  Clive Bell. Proust (e)
  Elizabeth Bowen. Joining Charles (fic)
  _____. The Last September (n)
  Austin Clarke. Pilgrimage (po)
  Robert Bridges. The Testament of Beauty (po)
  Ivy Compton-Burnett. Brothers and Sisters (n)
  Lettice Cooper. Likewise the Lion (n)
  Rhys Davies. A Bed of Feathers (fic)
  George Norman Douglas. The Angel of Manfredonia (n)
  _____. Footnotes on East and West (e)
  William Empson. Letter IV (po)
  Ford Madox Ford. The English Novel (e)
  Sir James George Frazer. Fasti of Ovid (trans)
  John Galsworthy. Exiled (dr)
  _____. A Modern Comedy (fic)
  Robert Graves. Good-bye to All That (auto, e)
  Henry Green. Living (n)
  Graham Greene. The Man Within (n)
  Richard Hughes. A High Wind in Jamaica (n)
  Sir Julian Huxley, H.G. Wells, and G.P. Wells. The Science of Life (e)
  James Joyce. Tales Told of Shem and Shaun (fic)
  D.H. Lawrence. Pansies (po)
  _____. Pornography and Obscenity (e)
  Percy Wyndham Lewis. Paleface: The Philosophy of the Melting Pot (e)
  Percy Lubbock. Shades of Eton (e)
  Sir Compton Mackenzie. Gallipoli Memories (auto, nar)
  Louis Macneice. Blind Fireworks (po)
  John Masefield. Easter (dr)
  Charles Morgan. Portrait in a Mirror (n)
  Leopold Myers. The Near and the Far (n)
  Liam O'Flaherty. The Mountain Tavern (fic)

John Cowper Powys. The Meaning of Culture (e)
_____. Wolf Salent (n)
J.B. Priestley. The Good Companions (n)
Victor Prichett. Clare Drummer (n)
Sir Arthur Quiller-Couch. Collected Poems (pub)
I.A. Richards. Practical Criticism (e)
Henry Handel Richardson. Ultima Thule (n)
Lennox Robinson. The Little Anthology of Irish Verse (ed)
Robert Sherriff. Journey's End (dr)
Alec Waugh. Portrait of a Celibate (n)
_____. Three Score and Ten (n)
Dame Rebecca West. Harriet Hume (n)
Laurence Whistler. Children of Hertha (po)
Alfred North Whitehead. Process and Reality (e)
Virginia Woolf. A Room of One's Own (e)
William Butler Yeats. A Packet for Ezra Pound (e)
_____. St. Patrick's Breastplate (e)
_____. The Winding Stair (po)

1930

BIRTHS
  John Arden
  Tony Connor
  Elaine Feinstein
  Ted Hughes
  Harold Pinter
  Jon Silkin
  Anthony Thwaite
  Derek Walcott

DEATHS
  Arthur James Balfour
  Robert Bridges
  Sir Arthur Conan Doyle
  D.H. Lawrence
  William Locke

EVENTS
  John Masefield, Poet Laureate of England, to 1967

WORKS
  Lascelles Abercrombie. Collected Poems (pub)
  Arnold Bennett. Imperial Palace (n)
  James Bridie. The Anatomist (dr)
  _____. Tobias and the Angel (dr)
  Roy Campbell. Adamastor (po)
  Sir Edmund Chambers. William Shakespeare (e, bio)
  Winston Churchill. My Early Life (auto)
  Lettice Cooper. The Ship of Truth (n)
  Noel Coward. Private Lives (dr)
  Robert Cunninghame-Graham. The Horses of the Conquest (fic)
  Rhys Davies. Rings on Her Fingers (n)
  _____. The Stars, the World, and the Women (fic)
  _____. Tale (fic)
  Walter De La Mare. The Hostage (n)

_____. Poems for Children (po)
John Drinkwater. Samuel Pepys (bio)
T.S. Eliot. Ash Wednesday (po)
William Empson. Seven Types of Ambiguity (e)
John Galsworthy. On Forsyte Change (fic)
Thomas Hardy. Collected Poems (pub)
R.C. Hutchinson. Thou Hast a Devil: A Fable (n)
Gerard Manley Hopkins. Poems (pub)
Aldous Huxley. Brief Candles (fic)
_____. Vulgarity in Literature (e)
Sir James Jeans. The Mysterious Universe (e)
Margaret Kennedy. The Fool of the Family (n)
Rudyard Kipling. The Complete Stalky and Co. (fic)
D.H. Lawrence. Apocalypse (fic)
_____. Love among the Haystacks (fic)
_____. Nettles (po)
_____. The Virgin and the Gypsy (n)
F.R. Leavis. Mass Civilization and Minority Culture (e)
Percy Wyndham Lewis. Apes of God (n)
_____. Satire and Fiction (e)
Sir Oliver Lodge. The Reality of a Spiritual World (e)
Hugh Macdiarmid. Scotland in 1980 (e)
W. Somerset Maugham. Cakes and Ale (n)
George Moore. Aphrodite in Aulis (n)
Llewelyn Powys. Apples Be Ripe (n)
Theodore Powys. Kindness in a Corner (n)
_____. Uncle Dottery (fic)
J.B. Priestley. Angel Pavement (n)
Sir Herbert Read. Ambush (nar)
Siegfried Sassoon. Memoirs of an Infantry Officer (n)
George Bernard Shaw. The Apple Cart (dr)
Robert Sherriff. Badger's Green (dr)
Dame Edith Sitwell. Alexander Pope (e, bio)
_____. Collected Poems (pub)
Stephen Spender. Twenty Poems (pub)
Henry Tomlinson. All Our Yesterdays (n)
George Macaulay Trevelyan. England under Queen Anne, 3 vols (his)
Hugh Walpole. Rogue Herries (n)
Evelyn Waugh. Vile Bodies (n)
H.G. Wells. The Autobiography of Mr. Parkham (n)
Charles Williams. War in Heaven (n)

1931

BIRTHS
Alan Brownjohn
Anthony Conran
David John Moore Cornwell ("John Le Carre")
Brian Glanville
Patrick Joseph Kavanagh

DEATHS
Arnold Bennett
Sir Thomas Henry Hall Caine
Sir Charles Eliot
Frank Harris

THE TWENTIETH CENTURY   243

EVENTS
  The New Statesman (p, f)

WORKS
  AE. Vale (po)
  Richard Aldington. The Colonel's Daughter (n)
  Ronald Bottrall. The Loosening (po)
  British Institute of Industrial Art. The Art of Lettering and Its Use
              in Divers Crafts and Trades (t)
  John Buchan. The Blanket of the Dark (n)
  Ivy Compton-Burnett. Men and Wives (n)
  Lettice Cooper. Private Enterprise (n)
  Noel Coward. Cavalcade (dr)
  Rhys Davies. Afron (fic)
  _____. A Pig in a Poke (fic)
  _____. A Woman (fic)
  Cecil Day-Lewis. From Feathers to Iron (po)
  Daphne Du Maurier. The Loving Spirit (n)
  John Galsworthy. Maid in Waiting (n)
  William Gerhardi. Memoirs of a Polygot (e, nar)
  Sir Walter Greg. Dramatic Documents from the Elizabethan Playhouses
              (ref)
  Philip Guedalla. The Duke (bio: Duke of Wellington)
  Richard Hughes. The Spider's Place (fic)
  Aldous Huxley. Music at Night (e)
  Montague James. Ghost Stories of an Antiquary (fic)
  D.H. Lawrence. The Man Who Died (n, pub)
  Sir Compton Mackenzie. First Athenian Memories (auto)
  _____. Our Street (n)
  Hugh Macdiarmid. Warning Democracy (e)
  John Middleton Murry. Son of Woman, the Story of D.H. Lawrence (bio, e)
  Leopold Myers. Prince Jali (n)
  Frank O'Connor. Guests of the Nation (fic)
  Liam O'Flaherty. The Puritan (n)
  Wilfred Owen. Collected Poems (pub)
  Ezra Pound. How To Read (e)
  Anthony Powell. Afternoon Men (n)
  John Cowper Powys. Dorothy M. Richardson (e, bio)
  Theodore Powys. The Only Penitent (fic)
  _____. Unclay (n)
  Forrest Reid. Uncle Stephen (n)
  Dorothy Richardson. Dawn's Left Hand (n)
  Siegfried Sassoon. To the Red Rose (po)
  Robert Sherriff. A Fortnight in September (n)
  Giles Lytton Strachey. Portraits in Miniature (bio)
  Walter Turner. Pursuit of Psyche (po)
  Hugh Walpole. Judith Paris (n)
  H.G. Wells. The Work, Wealth, and Happiness of Mankind (e)
  Virginia Woolf. The Waves (n)

                              1932

BIRTHS
  Geoffrey Hill
  Philip Hobsbaum
  George MacBeth

Peter Redgrove
Arnold Wesker

DEATHS
Charles Gore
Lady Augusta Gregory
Giles Lytton Strachey
Edgar Wallace

EVENTS
Scrutiny (p, f)

WORKS
Richard Aldington. All Men Are Enemies (n)
Patrick Anderson. On This Side Nothing (po)
James Bridie. Jonah and the Whale (dr)
John Buchan. Gap in the Curtain (n)
_____. Julius Caesar (bio)
_____. Sir Walter Scott (bio)
Roy Campbell. Pomegranates (po)
Joyce Cary. Aissa Saved (n)
Gilbert Keith Chesterton. Chaucer (e)
Austin Clarke. The Bright Temptations: A Romance (n)
_____. The Flame (dr)
Rhys Davies. Count Your Blessings (n)
_____. The Red Hills (n)
_____. Daisy Matthews (fic)
Daphne Du Maurier. I'll Never Be Young Again (n)
T.S. Eliot. Selected Essays, 1917-1932 (pub)
_____. Sweeney Agonistes (dr)
John Galsworthy. Flowering Wilderness (n)
David Gascoyne. Roman Balcony (po)
Robert Graves. No Decency Left (n)
Graham Greene. Stamboul Train (n)
John B.S. Haldane. The Inequality of Man (e)
Leslie Hartley. The Killing Bottle (fic)
R.C. Hutchinson. The Answering Glory (n)
Aldous Huxley. Brave New World (n)
_____. Texts and Pretexts (e)
Sir Julian Huxley. The Captive Shrew and Other Poems (po)
Ronald Knox. Broadcast Minds (e)
D.H. Lawrence. Etruscan Places (trav)
_____. Last Poems (pub)
F.R. Leavis. New Bearings in English Poetry (e)
Percy Wyndham Lewis. The Enemy of the Stars (e)
_____. Snooty Baronet (n)
_____. The Wild Body (e)
Hugh Macdiarmid. Scots Unbound (po)
_____. Tarras (po)
Charles Morgan. The Fountain (n)
Frank O'Connor. The Saint and Mary Kate (fic)
_____. The Wild Bird's Nest (po, trans)
Sean O'Faolain. Midsummer Night Madness (fic)
Liam O'Flaherty. The Wild Swan (fic)
John Cowper Powys. A Glastonbury Romance (n)
Theodore Powys. The Two Thieves (fic)

THE TWENTIETH CENTURY   245

   J.B. Priestley. Dangerous Corner (dr)
   Sir Herbert Read. Form in Modern Poetry (e)
   Michael Roberts. New Signatures: Poems by Several Hands (po, ed)
   C.P. Snow. Death under Sail (n)
   Alec Waugh. Tropic Seed (n)
   Evelyn Waugh. Black Mischief (n)
   Laurence Whistler. Armed October (po)
   _____. Proletaria, en avant! A Poem of Socialism (po)
   Virginia Woolf. The Common Reader, 2nd series (e)
   _____. A Letter to a Young Poet (e)
   William Butler Yeats. Poems in Words for Music, Perhaps (po)

                                1933

BIRTHS
   John Antrobus
   Maureen Duffy
   Michael Frayn
   Duncan Glen
   Brian Stanley Johnson
   John Peter Scupham
   David Storey
   Edward Anthony Whitehead
   Charles Wood

DEATHS
   Augustine Birrell
   John Galsworthy
   Sir Anthony Hope Hawkins ("Anthony Hope")
   George Moore
   George Saintsbury

WORKS
   George Granville Barker. Thirty Preliminary Poems (po)
   Francis Berry. Gospel of Fire (po)
   John Betjeman. Ghastly Good Taste (po)
   _____. Mount Zion (po)
   James Bridie. A Sleeping Clergyman (dr)
   Joyce Cary. An American Visitor (n)
   Gilbert Keith Chesterton. Collected Poems (pub)
   Winston Churchill. Marlborough. His Life and Times, to 1938 (bio, his)
   Robin Collingwood. Essay on Philosophical Method (e)
   Ivy Compton-Burnett. More Women Than Men (n)
   Lettice Cooper. Hark to a Rover (n)
   Noel Coward. Design for Living (dr)
   Rhys Davies. Love Provoked (fic)
   Cecil Day-Lewis. The Magnetic Mountain (po)
   George Norman Douglas. Looking Back (auto)
   Daphne Du Maurier. The Progress of Julius (n)
   Sir Arthur Eddington. The Expanding Universe (e)
   T.S. Eliot. The Use of Poetry and the Use of Criticism (e)
   John Galsworthy. Over the River (n)
   Walter Greenwood. Love on the Dole (n)
   A.E. Housman. The Name and Nature of Poetry (e)
   R.C. Hutchinson. The Unforgotten Prisoner (n)
   Rudyard Kipling. All the Mowgli Stories (fic)

_____. Rudyard Kipling's Verse (po)
D.H. Lawrence. The Lovely Lady (fic, pub)
C.S. Lewis. The Pilgrim's Progress (e)
Malcolm Lowry. Ultramarine (n)
John Masefield. The Bird of Dawning (n)
_____. End and Beginning (po)
Harold Monro. Collected Poems (pub)
Hector Munro. The Novels and Plays of Saki (pub)
George Murray. Aristophanes: A Study (e)
John Middleton Murry. The Life of Katherine Mansfield (bio, e)
_____. William Blake (bio, e)
Sean O'Casey. Within the Gates (dr)
Sean O'Faolain. A Nest of Simple Folk (n)
George Orwell. Down and Out in Paris and London (nar)
Anthony Powell. From a View to a Death (n)
John Cowper Powys. A Philosophy of Solitude (e)
J.B. Priestley. Laburnum Grove (dr)
John Pudney. Spring Encounter (po)
Sir Herbert Read. The End of a War (po)
_____. The Innocent Eye (auto)
Siegfried Sassoon. Satirical Poems (po, pub)
Dame Edith Sitwell. Five Variations on a Theme (po)
C.P. Snow. New Lives for Old (n)
Alec Waugh. Wheels within Wheels (n)
Hugh Walpole. The Fortress (n)
H.G. Wells. The Shape of Things To Come (e)
Terence White. Farewell Victoria (n)
Alfred North Whitehead. Adventures of Ideas (e)

1934

BIRTHS
  Fleur Adcock
  Beryl Bainbridge
  Edward Bond
  Tom Gallacher
  David Gill
  John McGahern

DEATHS
  Thomas Anstey Guthrie
  Sir Arthur Wing Pinero

WORKS
  AE. The House of the Vale (po)
  Ronald Bottrall. Festivals of Fire (po)
  John Buchan. Oliver Cromwell (bio)
  George Buchanan. Dance Night (dr)
  Cecil Day-Lewis. A Hope for Poetry (e)
  T.S. Eliot. After Strange Gods (e)
  _____. Elizabethan Essays (e)
  _____. The Rock (dr)
  E.M. Forster. G.L. Dickinson (e)
  John Galsworthy. Collected Poems (pub)
  _____. End of the Chapter (fic)
  William Gerhardi. Resurrection (n)

Winston Graham. The House with the Stained-Glass Windows (n)
Robert Graves. Claudius the God (n)
_____. I, Claudius (n)
Graham Greene. It's a Battlefield (n)
Walter Greenwood. His Worship the Mayor (n)
Aldous Huxley. Beyond the Mexique Bay (fic)
James Joyce. The Mime of Mick, Nick, and the Maggies (fic)
D.H. Lawrence. A Collier's Friday Night (dr, pub)
_____. A Modern Lover (fic, pub)
_____. The Tales (fic, pub)
Percy Wyndham Lewis. Men without Art (e)
Edward Lowbury. Fire: A Symphonic Ode (po)
Dame Rose Macaulay. Going Abroad (e)
Hugh Macdiarmid. At the Sign of the Thistle (e)
_____. Selected Poems (pub)
_____. Stony Limits (po)
W. Somerset Maugham. Collected Works, 20 vols, to 1950 (pub)
Nicholas Monsarrat. Think of Tomorrow (n)
Edwin Muir. Variations on a Time Theme (po)
Liam O'Flaherty. Shame the Devil (auto)
George Orwell. Burmese Days (n)
Ezra Pound. ABC of Reading (e)
_____. Make It New (e)
John Cowper Powys. Autobiography (auto)
Sir Herbert Read. Art and Industry (e)
Frederick Rolfe. Desire and Pursuit of the Whole (pub)
Siegfried Sassoon. Vigils (po)
Dorothy Sayers. The Nine Tailors (fic)
George Bernard Shaw. Too True To Be Good (dr)
Dame Edith Sitwell. Aspects of Modern Poetry (e)
C.P. Snow. The Search (n)
Stephen Spender. Vienna (po)
Dylan Thomas. Eighteen Poems (po, pub)
Arnold Toynbee. A Study of History, 10 vols, to 1954 (his)
Alec Waugh. The Balliols (n)
Evelyn Waugh. A Handful of Dust (n)
Laurence Whistler. Four Walls (po)
Virginia Woolf. Walter Sickert: A Conversation (e, nar)
William Butler Yeats. The King of the Great Clocktower (po)
_____. Letters to the New Island (e)
_____. Wheels and Butterflies (e)

1935

BIRTHS
  David Lodge
  Jon Stallworthy
  Donald Michael Thomas

DEATHS
  T.E. Lawrence
  George William Russell ("AE")
  Sir William Watson

WORKS
  Wystan Hugh Auden and Christopher Isherwood. The Dog beneath the Skin
            (dr)

Enid Bagnold. National Velvet (n)
George Granville Barker. Poems (pub)
Elizabeth Bowen. The House in Paris (n)
Ivy Compton-Burnett. A House and Its Head (n)
Cyril Connolly. The Rock Pool (n)
Lettice Cooper. We Have Come to a Country (n)
Alfred Coppard. Cherry Ripe (po)
Rhys Davies. Honey and Bread (n)
_____. One of Norah's Early Days (fic)
Cecil Day-Lewis. Revolution in Writing (e)
Lord Alfred Douglas. Lyrics (po)
Lawrence Durrell. Panic Spring (n)
_____. Pied Piper of Lovers (n)
T.S. Eliot. Murder in the Cathedral (dr)
William Empson. Poems (pub)
_____. Some Versions of Pastoral (e)
Graham Greene. England Made Me (n)
R.C. Hutchinson. One Light Burning: A Romantic Story (n)
Christopher Isherwood. Mr. Norris Changes Trains (n)
Ronald Knox. Barchester Pilgrimage (e)
Louis Macneice. Poems (pub)
John Masefield. The Box of Delights (n)
_____. Collected Works, 10 vols, to 1938 (pub)
Nicholas Monsarrat. At First Sight (n)
Edwin Muir. Journeys and Places (po)
Leopold Myers. The Root and the Flower (n)
Sean O'Casey. Five Irish Plays (dr)
Sean O'Faolain. There's a Birdie in the Cage (fic)
George Orwell. A Clergyman's Daughter (n)
Ezra Pound. Jefferson and/or Mussolini (e)
John Cowper Powys. The Art of Happiness (e)
_____. Jobber Skald (n)
Llewelyn Powys. Dorset Essays (e)
John Pudney. Open the Sky (po)
Sir Herbert Read. The Green Child (n)
_____. Poems, 1914-1934 (pub)
Dorothy Richardson. Clear Horizon (n)
Stephen Spender. The Destructive Element (e)
Walter Turner. Blow for Balloons (n)

1936

BIRTHS
 Jim Burns
 Barry Cole
 Stewart Conn
 Nell Dunn
 Brendan Kennelly
 James David Rudkin
 Auberon Waugh

DEATHS
 Gilbert Keith Chesterton
 Robert Cunninghame-Graham
 Montague James
 Rudyard Kipling

THE TWENTIETH CENTURY 249

EVENTS
    Edward VIII, King of England
    George VI, King of England, to 1952
    New Writing (p, f)

WORKS
    Eric Ambler. The Dark Frontier (n)
    Wystan Hugh Auden. Look, Stranger (po)
    Alfred Jules Ayer. Language, Truth, and Logic (e)
    Francis Berry. Snake in the Moon (po)
    George Buchanan. A London Story (n)
    Joyce Cary. The African Witch (n)
    Charles Causley. Runaway (dr)
    Austin Clarke. The Singing Men at Cashel (n)
    Robin Collingwood and J.N.L. Myres. Roman Britain and the English Settlements (his)
    Lettice Cooper. The New House (n)
    Rhys Davies. The Things Men Do (fic)
    Walter De La Mare. The Nap (n)
    Daphne Du Maurier. Jamaica Inn (n)
    T.S. Eliot. Essays Ancient and Modern (e)
    Ford Madox Ford. Collected Poems (pub)
    E.M. Forster. Abinger Harvest (e)
    Sir James George Frazer. Aftermath, a Supplement to the Golden Bough (t, e, ref)
    Roy Fuller. Full Measure (n)
    David Gascoyne. Man's Life Is This Meat (po)
    William Gerhardi. Of Mortal Love (n)
    Rumer Godden. Chinese Puzzle (n)
    Graham Greene. A Gun for Sale (n)
    _____. Journey without Maps (trav, e)
    Walter Greenwood. Standing Room Only (n)
    A.E. Housman. More Poems (pub)
    R.C. Hutchinson. Shining Scabbard (n)
    Aldous Huxley. Eyeless in Gaza (n)
    James Joyce. Collected Poems (pub)
    John Maynard Keynes. A General Theory of Employment, Interest, and Money (e)
    D.H. Lawrence. Phoenix (e, pub)
    F.R. Leavis. Tradition and Development in English Poetry (e)
    C.S. Lewis. The Allegory of Love (e)
    Percy Wyndham Lewis. Left Wings over Europe (e)
    Nicholas Monsarrat. The Visitor (dr)
    Charles Morgan. Sparkenbroke (n)
    Edwin Muir. Scott and Scotland: The Predicament of the Scottish Writer (e)
    Leopold Myers. Strange Glory (n)
    Sean O'Faolain. Bird Alone (n)
    _____. A Born Genius (fic)
    George Orwell. Keep the Aspidistra Flying (n)
    James Reeves. The Natural Need (po)
    Forrest Reid. The Retreat (n)
    Michael Roberts. The Faber Book of Modern Verse (ed)
    Sacheverell Sitwell. A Life of Liszt (e, bio)
    Stevie Smith. Novel on Yellow Paper (n)
    Philip Edward Thomas. Collected Poems (pub)

Walter Turner. Songs and Incantations (po)
Alec Waugh. Jill Somerset (n)
Dame Rebecca West. The Thinking Reed (n)
Laurence Whistler. The Emperor Heart (po)
Charles Williams. Thomas Cranmer (po, dr)
William Butler Yeats. Modern Poetry (e)

1937

BIRTHS
  Keith Bosley
  John Fuller
  Roger McGough
  Tom Stoppard

DEATHS
  Sir James Matthew Barrie
  John Drinkwater
  Sir Frederick Pollock
  Christopher St. John Sprigg ("Christopher Caudwell")

EVENTS
  The Morning Post, London (p, c)
WORKS
  Eric Ambler. Uncommon Danger (n)
  Wystan Hugh Auden and Christopher Isherwood. The Ascent of Fo (dr)
  John Betjeman. Continual Dew (po)
  James Bridie. Susannah and the Elders (dr)
  Agatha Christie. Death on the Nile (n)
  Charles Causley. The Conquering Hero (dr)
  Alex Comfort. The Silver River (n)
  Rhys Davies. A Time To Laugh (n)
  Walter De La Mare. This Year, Next Year (po)
  Edward Dunsany. Plays for Earth and Air (dr)
  Walter Greenwood. The Cleft Stick (n)
  Reyner Heppenstall. Sebastian (po)
  Geoffrey Household. The Third Hour (n)
  Aldous Huxley. Ends and Means (e)
  Hammond Innes. Air Disaster (n)
  _____. Doppleganger (n)
  Christopher Isherwood. Sally Bowles (n)
  David Jones. In Parenthesis (nar, po)
  James Joyce. Storiello As She Is Syung (fic)
  Percy Wyndham Lewis. Blasting and Bombarding (e, auto)
  _____. The Revenge for Love (n)
  Sir Compton Mackenzie. The Four Winds of Love, to 1945 (n)
  Louis Macneice and Wystan Hugh Auden. Letters from Iceland (trav, e)
  John Masefield. The Country Scene (po)
  Nicholas Monsarrat. The Whipping Boy (n)
  Frank O'Connor. In the Train (dr)
  _____. The Invincibles (dr)
  Sean O'Faolain. A Purse of Coppers (fic)
  _____. She Had To Do Something (dr)
  Liam O'Flaherty. Famine (n)
  George Orwell. The Road to Wigan Pier (e)
  Llewelyn Powys. Somerset Essays: A Pagan's Pilgrimage (e)

John Cowper Powys. Morwyn, or the Vengeance of God (n)
Victor Pritchett. Dead Man Leading (n)
Alfred Leslie Rowse. Sir Richard Grenville of the Revenge (bio)
Siegfried Sassoon. The Complete Memoirs of George Sherston (n)
Sacheverell Sitwell. La Vie Parisienne (e)
Stephen Spender. Forward from Liberalism (e)
John Tolkien. The Hobbit (n)
_____. Beowulf: The Monsters and the Critics (e)
Rex Warner. Poems (po)
Charles Williams. Descent into Hell (n)
Virginia Woolf. The Years (n)
William Butler Yeats. Essays, 1931-1936 (pub)
_____. A Vision, rev version (e)

1938

BIRTHS
  Peter Dale
  Roger Howard

DEATHS
  Lascelles Abercrombie
  Sir Henry Newbolt

WORKS
  Eric Ambler. Cause for Alarm (n)
  _____. Epitaph for a Spy (n)
  Wystan Hugh Auden and Christopher Isherwood. On the Frontier (dr)
  Enid Bagnold. The Squire (dr)
  Samuel Beckett. Murphy (n)
  Francis Berry. The Iron Christ (po)
  Elizabeth Bowen. The Death of the Heart (n)
  George Buchanan. Entanglement (n)
  Michael Bullock. Transmutations (po)
  Christopher Caudwell. Studies in a Dying Culture (e, pub)
  Charles Causley. Benedict (dr)
  Austin Clarke. Night and Morning (po)
  Robin Collingwood. The Principles of Art (e)
  Cyril Connolly. Enemies of Promise (e)
  Lettice Cooper. National Provincial (n)
  Frank Darling. Wild Country (trav)
  Rhys Davies. Jubilee Blues (n)
  Daphne Du Maurier. Rebecca (n)
  William Empson. English Pastoral Poetry (e)
  Ford Madox Ford. Mightier Than the Sword (nar, auto)
  David Gascoyne. Holderlin's Madness (po)
  Rumer Godden. The Lady and the Union (n)
  Robert Graves. Count Belisarius (n)
  Graham Greene. Brighton Rock (n)
  Walter Greenwood. Only Mugs Work (n)
  _____. The Secret Kingdom (n)
  John B.S. Haldane. The Marxist Philosophy and the Sciences (e)
  Geoffrey Household. The Salvation of Pisco Gabar (fic)
  Richard Hughes. In Hazard (n)
  R.C. Hutchinson. Last Train South (dr)
  _____. Testament (n)

Aldous Huxley. The Giaconda Smile (fic)
Hammond Innes. Sabotage Broadcast (n)
Christopher Isherwood. Lions and Shadows (auto)
C.S. Lewis. Out of the Silent Planet (fic)
Hugh Macdiarmid. Direadh (po)
Louis Macneice. The Earth Compels (po)
_____. I Crossed the Minch (trav)
_____. Modern Poetry (e)
John Masefield. Plays, 2 vols (dr)
Charles Ewart Milne. Forty North, Fifty West (po)
Frank O'Connor. Moses' Rock (dr)
George Orwell. Homage to Catalonia (nar)
Ezra Pound. Guide to Kulchur (e)
John Cowper Powys. The Enjoyment of Literature (e)
_____. Maiden Castle (n)
J.B. Priestley. When We Are Married (dr)
John Pudney. Jacobson's Ladder (n)
Dorothy Richardson. Dimple Hill (n)
Stevie Smith. Over the Frontier (n)
Stephen Spender. Trial of a Judge (po)
Arthur Waley. The Analects of Confucius (ed)
Evelyn Waugh. Scoop (n)
Dame Rebecca West. The Strange Necessity (e)
Laurence Whistler. Sir John Vanbrugh (bio)
Charles Williams. Taliessin through Logres (po)
Emlyn Williams. The Corn Is Green (dr)
Virginia Woolf. Three Guineas (e)
William Butler Yeats. The Herne's Egg (dr)
_____. New Poems (po)

1939

BIRTHS
 Alan Ayckbourn
 Gavin Bantock
 Melvyn Bragg
 Margaret Drabble
 Michael Longley

DEATHS
 Havelock Ellis
 Ford Madox Ford
 A.E. Housman
 Llewelyn Powys
 William Butler Yeats

EVENTS
 The Criterion (p, c)
 The Gem (p, c)
 Horizon (p, f)

WORKS
 Eric Ambler. The Mask of Dimitrios (n)
 George Granville Barker. Elegy on Spain (po)
 Ronald Bottrall. The Turning Path (po)
 Roy Campbell. Flowering Rifle (po)

Joyce Cary. Mister Johnson (n)
_____. Power in Men (e)
Christopher Caudwell. Illusion and Reality (e, pub)
_____. Poems (pub)
Ivy Compton-Burnett. A Family and Its Fortune (n)
Frank Darling. A Naturalist on Rona (trav)
Cecil Day-Lewis. Child of Misfortune (po)
Walter De La Mare. Animal Stories (fic)
_____. Behold This Dreamer (ed)
T.S. Eliot. The Family Reunion (dr)
_____. The Idea of a Christian Society (e)
_____. Old Possum's Book of Practical Cats (po)
E.M. Forster. Reading As Usual (e)
Rumer Godden. Black Narcissus (n)
Henry Green. Party Going (n)
Walter Greenwood. How the Other Man Lives (n)
Geoffrey Grigson. Several Observations (po)
Reyner Heppenstall. The Blaze of Noon (n)
Geoffrey Household. Rogue Male (n)
A.E. Housman. Collected Poems (pub)
Aldous Huxley. After Many a Summer (n)
Hammond Innes. All Roads Lead to Friday (n)
Christopher Isherwood. Goodbye to Berlin (n)
_____. Journey to a War (e)
James Joyce. Finnegans Wake (n)
Arthur Koestler. The Gladiators (n)
Ronald Knox. Let Dons Delight (e)
D.H. Lawrence. Poems, 2 vols (pub)
Percy Wyndham Lewis. The Jews, Are They Human? (e)
Louis Macneice. Autumn Journal (po)
Nicholas Monsarrat. This Is the Schoolroom (n)
Edwin Muir. The Present Age, from 1914 (e)
Sean O'Casey. I Knock at the Door (auto)
George Orwell. Coming up for Air (n)
Llewelyn Powys. Love and Death (n)
J.B. Priestley. Let the People Sing (n)
Sir Arthur Quiller-Couch. The Oxford Book of English Verse (ed)
Henry Handel Richardson. Young Cosima (n)
George Bernard Shaw. In Good King Charles's Golden Days (dr)
Stephen Spender. The New Realism (e)
_____. Poems for Spain (po)
_____. The Still Centre (po)
Dylan Thomas. The Map of Love (po)
Hugh Walpole. The Sea Tower (n)
H.G. Wells. The Fate of Homo Sapiens (e)
_____. The Holy Terror (n)
Charles Williams. The Descent of the Dove (e)
William Butler Yeats. Last Poems (pub)

1940

BIRTHS
Michael Dennis Browne
Donald Campbell

DEATHS
  John Buchan
  William Davies
  Eric Gill
  Sir Oliver Lodge
  Sir Arnold Wilson

EVENTS
  The Magnet (p, c)
  New Writing (p, c)

WORKS
  Eric Ambler. Journey into Fear (n)
  Alfred Jules Ayer. The Foundations of Empirical Knowledge (e)
  George Granville Barker. Lament and Triumph (po)
  Hilaire Belloc. Cautionary Verse (po)
  John Betjeman. Old Lights for New Channels (po)
  George Buchanan. The Soldier and the Girl (n)
  Joyce Cary. Charley Is My Darling (n)
  Rhys Davies. Under the Rose (n)
  Monica Dickens. Mariana (n)
  Daphne Du Maurier. Rebecca (dr)
  T.S. Eliot. East Coker (po)
  William Empson. The Gathering Storm (po)
  Roy Fuller. Poems (pub)
  William Gerhardi. The Romanoffs (bio, his)
  Rumer Godden. Gypsy, Gypsy (n)
  Robert Graves. Selected Poems, pub)
  _____ and Alan Hodge. The Long Weekend: Social History of Great Britain, 1918-1939 (his)
  Henry Green. Pack My Bag (auto)
  Graham Greene. The Power and the Glory (n)
  John B.S. Haldane. Science in Peace and War (e)
  Reyner Heppenstall. Blind Men's Flowers Are Green (po)
  Richard Hughes. Don't Blame Me (fic)
  R.C. Hutchinson. The Fire and the Wood: A Love Story (n)
  Hammond Innes. The Trojan Horse (n)
  _____. Wreckers Must Breathe (n)
  Arthur Koestler. Darkness at Noon (n)
  C.S. Lewis. The Problem of Pain (e)
  Louis Macneice. The Last Ditch (po)
  John Masefield. Basilissa (n)
  Charles Ewart Milne. Letter from Ireland (po)
  Charles Morgan. A Voyage (n)
  Edwin Muir. The Story and the Fable (auto)
  George Murray. Aeschylus, the Creator of Tragedy (e)
  Leopold Myers. The Pool of Vishnu (n)
  Sean O'Casey. Purple Dust (dr)
  _____. The Star Turns Red (dr)
  Frank O'Connor. Dutch Interior (n)
  Sean O'Faolain. Come Back to Erin (n)
  George Orwell. Inside the Whale (e)
  John Cowper Powys. Owen Glendower (n)
  Sir Herbert Read. Annals of Innocence and Experience (auto)
  Bertrand Russell. An Inquiry into the Meaning and Truth (e)
  Dame Edith Sitwell. Poems New and Old (pub)

THE TWENTIETH CENTURY 255

Sacheverell Sitwell. Sacred and Profane Love (e)
C.P. Snow. Strangers and Brothers (n)
Dylan Thomas. Portrait of the Artist As a Young Dog (fic)
H.G. Wells. The Rights of Man (e)
Laurence Whistler. In Time of Suspense (po)
William Butler Yeats. If I Were Four-and-Twenty (e, pub)

1941

BIRTHS
  David Black
  Derek Mahon
  John Mole

DEATHS
  Sir Arthur Evans
  Sir James George Frazer
  James Joyce
  Hugh Walpole
  Virginia Woolf

WORKS
  Wystan Hugh Auden. New Year Letter (po)
  George Granville Barker. Sacred and Secular Elegies (po)
  Elizabeth Bowen. Look At All Those Roses (fic)
  Joyce Cary. The Case for African Freedom (e)
  _____. Herself Surprised (n)
  _____. House of Children (n)
  Austin Clarke. Black Fast (dr)
  _____. Sister Eucharia (dr)
  Alex Comfort. France and Other Poems (po)
  _____. No Such Liberty (n)
  Ivy Compton-Burnett. Parents and Children (n)
  Noel Coward. Blithe Spirit (dr)
  Rhys Davies. Tomorrow to Fresh Woods (n)
  Basil Dowling. A Day's Journey (po)
  Daphne Du Maurier. Come Wind, Come Weather (fic)
  _____. Frenchman's Creek (n)
  T.S. Eliot. Burnt Norton (po)
  _____. The Dry Salvages (po)
  Philip Guedalla. Mr. Churchill (bio)
  Aldous Huxley. Grey Eminence (e)
  Hammond Innes. Attack Alarm (n)
  Emanuel Litvinoff. Conscripts: A Symphonic Declaration (po)
  Louis Macneice. Plant and Phantom (po)
  _____. The Poetry of W.B. Yeats (e)
  Charles Ewart Milne. Listen Mangan (po)
  Charles Morgan. The Empty Room (n)
  George Orwell. The Lion and the Unicorn: Socialism and the English
        Genius (e)
  Michael Roberts. The Recovery of the West (e)
  Alan Ross. Summer Thunder (po)
  Sydney Goodsir Smith. Skail Wind (po)
  Vernon Watkins. Ballad of the Mari Lwyd (po)
  Alec Waugh. No Truce with Time (n)
  Sir Arnold Wilson. South West Persia (trav, e, pub)

Virginia Woolf. Between the Acts (n)

1942

BIRTHS
Howard Brenton
Douglas Dunn
Hugo Williams

WORKS
Enid Bagnold. Lottie Dundass (dr)
Joyce Cary. To Be a Pilgrim (n)
Austin Clarke. The Kiss (dr)
Alex Comfort. The Almond Tree: A Legend (n)
_____. Into Egypt (dr)
_____. A Wreath for the Living (po)
Rhys Davies. A Finger in Every Pie (fic)
T.S. Eliot. Little Gidding (po)
E.M. Forster. Virginia Woolf (e)
Roy Fuller. The Middle of a War (po)
Rumer Godden. Breakfast with the Nikolides (n)
Graham Greene. British Dramatists (e)
John Heath-Stubbs. Wounded Thammuz (po)
Sir Julian Huxley. Evolution, the Modern Synthesis (e)
Sidney Keyes. The Iron Laurel (po)
Alun Lewis. Raider's Dawn (po)
C.S. Lewis. The Screwtape Letters (fic)
Emanuel Litvinoff. The Untried Soldier (po)
John Masefield. Land Workers (po)
Sean O'Casey. Pictures in the Hallway (auto)
_____. Red Roses for Me (dr)
Victor Pritchett. In My Good Books (e)
John Pudney. Dispersal Point and Other Air Poems (po)
Alfred Leslie Rowse. Poems of a Decade (po)
Siegfried Sassoon. The Weald of Youth (auto)
Dorothy Sayers. The Man Born To Be King (dr)
Stephen Spender. Ruins and Visions (po)
Arthur Waley. Monkey (n,trans)
Evelyn Waugh. Put Out More Flags (n)
_____. Work Suspended (fic)
Dame Rebecca West. Black Lamb and Grey Falcon (his, e)
Laurence Whistler. Ode to the Sun (po)
Virginia Woolf. Death of the Moth (e, pub)

1943

BIRTHS
Alan Bold

DEATHS
Laurence Binyon
Robin Collingwood
William Jacobs
Sidney Keyes
Beatrix Potter

THE TWENTIETH CENTURY   257

WORKS
   Sir Max Beerbohm. Lytton Strachey (bio, e)
   Francis Berry. Fall of a Tower (po)
   James Bridie. Mr. Bolfry (dr)
   Joyce Cary. The Process of Real Freedom (n)
   Austin Clarke. The Plot Is Ready (dr)
   Alex Comfort. Cities of the Plain (dr)
   Cecil Day-Lewis. Word over All (po)
   Monica Dickens. The Fancy (n)
   Daphne Du Maurier. Hungry Hill (n)
   Lawrence Durrell. A Private Country (po)
   T.S. Eliot. Four Quartets (po)
   David Gascoyne. Poems, 1937-1942 (pub)
   Robert Graves. Selected Poems (pub)
   Henry Green. Caught (n)
   Graham Greene. The Ministry of Fear (n)
   Geoffrey Grigson. Under the Cliff (po)
   John Heath-Stubbs. Beauty and the Beast (po)
   Reyner Heppenstall. Saturnine (n)
   Sidney Keyes. The Cruel Solstice (po)
   Arthur Koestler. Arrival and Departure (n)
   Norman MacCaig. Far Cry (po)
   Hugh Macdiarmid. Cornish Heroic Song for Valda (po)
   _____. Lucky Poet (auto)
   Nicholas Monsarrat. H.M. Corvette (n)
   _____. East Coast Corvette (n)
   Edwin Muir. The Narrow Place (po)
   John Pudney. Beyond the Disregard (po)
   _____. South of Forty (po)
   Kathleen Raine. Stone and Flower: Poems, 1935-1943 (po)
   Sir Herbert Read. Education through Art (e)
   Siegfried Sassoon. Selected Poems (pub)
   Dame Edith Sitwell. A Poet's Notebook (e)
   Sydney Goodsir Smith. The Wanderer and Other Poems (po)
   Dylan Thomas. New Poems (pub)
   Charles Williams. The Figure of Beatrice (e)

                            1944

BIRTHS
   Martin Booth

DEATHS
   Philip Guedalla
   Alun Lewis
   Leopold Myers
   Sir Arthur Quiller-Couch

WORKS
   George Granville Barker. Eros in Dogma (po)
   John Betjeman. Bats in Old Belfries (po)
   George Bruce. Sea Talk (po)
   Joyce Cary. The Horse's Mouth (n)
   Leonard Clark. Passage to the Pole (po)
   Alex Comfort. Elegies (po)
   _____. The Powerhouse (n)

Cyril Connolly. The Unquiet Grave (e)
Rhys Davies. The Black Venus (n)
Patric Dickinson. The Seven Days of Jericho (po)
Basil Dowling. Signs and Wonders (po)
Daphne Du Maurier. The Years Between (dr)
Roy Fuller. A Lost Season (po)
Rumer Godden. Rungli-Rungliot (n)
Robert Graves. Homer's Daughter (fic)
Leslie Hartley. The Shrimp and the Anemone (n)
Louis Macneice. Christopher Columbus (dr)
_____. Springboard: Poems, 1941-1944 (po)
W. Somerset Maugham. The Razor's Edge (n)
Christopher Middleton. Poems (po)
Charles Ewart Milne. Jubilo (po)
Nicholas Monsarrat. Corvette Command (n)
Norman Nicholson. Five Rivers (po)
Frank O'Connor. Crab Apple Jelly (fic)
John Pudney. Almanack of Hope (po)
_____. Flight above Cloud (po)
_____. Ten Summers (po)
Forrest Reid. Young Tom (n)
Alfred Leslie Rowse. Poems Chiefly Cornish (po)
William Sansom. Fireman Flower (fic)
Dame Edith Sitwell. Green Song (po)
George Macaulay Trevelyan. English Social History (his)
Charles Williams. All Hallow's Eve (n)
_____. Region of the Summer Stars (po)
Laurence Whistler. Who Live in Unity (po)

1945

BIRTHS
  Steve Gooch

DEATHS
  Maurice Baring
  Lord Alfred Douglas
  Oliver Elton
  Arthur Symons
  Charles Williams

WORKS
  Patrick Anderson. A Tent for April (po)
  Wystan Hugh Auden. For the Time Being (po)
  Ronald Bottrall. Farewell and Welcome (po)
  Elizabeth Bowen. The Demon Lover (fic)
  Joyce Cary. Marching Soldier (po)
  Leonard Clark. Rhandanim (po)
  Alex Comfort. The Song of Lazarus (po)
  Cyril Connolly. The Condemned Playground: Essays, 1927-1944 (e, pub)
  Rhys Davies. Selected Stories (fic)
  Walter De La Mare. The Burning-Glass (po)
  Monica Dickens. Thursday Afternoons (n)
  T.S. Eliot. What Is a Classic? (e)
  Henry Green. Loving (n)
  Rumer Godden. Fugue in Time (n)

Winston Graham. Ross Poldark: A Novel of Cornwall, 1783-1787 (n)
R.C. Hutchinson. Interim (n)
Aldous Huxley. The Perennial Philosophy (e)
Christopher Isherwood. Prater Violet (n)
Ronald Knox. God and the Atom (e)
_____. The New Testament (trans)
Arthur Koestler. Twilight Bar: An Escapade (dr)
Philip Larkin. The North Ship (po)
Alun Lewis. Ha! Ha! Amongst the Trumpets (po, pub)
Katherine Mansfield. Collected Stories (pub)
Christopher Middleton. Nocturne in Eden (po)
Nicholas Monsarrat. Leave Cancelled (n)
Norman Nicholson. The Old Man of the Mountains (dr)
Sean O'Casey. Drums under the Window (auto)
Frank O'Connor. Towards an Appreciation of Literature (e)
George Orwell. Animal Farm: A Fairy Story (n, s)
J.B. Priestley. An Inspector Calls (dr)
Alfred Leslie Rowse. West Country Stories (fic)
Siegfried Sassoon. Siegfried's Journey, 1916-1920 (auto)
Rex Warner. Poems and Contradictions (po)
Vernon Watkins. The Lamp and the Veil (po)
Evelyn Waugh. Brideshead Revisited (n)

1946

BIRTHS
Howard Barker

DEATHS
Harley Granville-Barker
John Maynard Keynes
Ethel Richardson ("Henry Handel Richardson")
Walter Turner
H.G. Wells

WORKS
Patrick Anderson. The White Centre (po)
Frances Bellerby. Plash Mill (po)
Edmund Blunden. Shelley, a Life Story (bio)
Roy Campbell. Talking Bronco (po)
Joyce Cary. The Moon-Light (n)
Winston Churchill. War Speeches, 1940-1945 (sp)
Austin Clarke. The Second Kiss (dr)
Robin Collingwood. The Idea of History (e)
Alex Comfort. The Signal to Engage (po)
Rhys Davies. The Trip to London (fic)
Monica Dickens. The Happy Prisoner (n)
Patric Dickinson. Theseus and the Minotaur (dr)
George Norman Douglas. Late Harvest (auto)
Daphne Du Maurier. The King's General (n)
Lawrence Durrell. Cities, Plains, and People (po)
Christopher Fry. A Phoenix Too Frequent (dr)
Roy Fuller. Savage Gold (n)
Rumer Godden. The River (n)
Winston Graham. Demelza: A Novel of Cornwall, 1788-1790 (n)
Robert Graves. King Jesus (n)

Henry Green. Back (n)
Geoffrey Grigson. The Isles of Scilly (po)
Leslie Hartley. Eustace and Hilda (n)
_____. The Sixth Heaven (n)
Hammond Innes. Dead and Alive (n)
Sidney Keyes. Collected Poems (pub)
Arthur Koestler. Thieves in the Night: Chronicle of an Experiment (n)
Philip Larkin. Jill (n)
Edward Lowbury. Crossing the Line (po)
Norman MacCaig. The Inward Eye (po)
Nicholas Monsarrat. H.M. Frigate (n)
Edwin Muir. The Scots and Their Country (e)
_____. The Voyage (po)
George Murray. Greek Studies (e)
Norman Nicholson. The Fire of the Lord (n)
Frank O'Connor. Selected Stories (fic)
George Orwell. Collected Essays (e)
Theodore Powys. Bottle's Path (fic)
Victor Pritchett. The Living Novel (e)
John Pudney. Selected Poems (po)
Kathleen Raine. Living in Time (po)
Sir Herbert Read. Poems (pub)
Alfred Leslie Rowse. Poems of Deliverance (po)
William Sansom. Three (fic)
Sydney Goodsir Smith. The Deevil's Waltz (po)
Stephen Spender. Poetry Since 1939 (e)
Dylan Thomas. Deaths and Entrances (po)
Ronald Thomas. The Stones of the Field (po)
Sydney Tremayne. For Whom There Is No Spring (po)
Evelyn Waugh. When the Going Was Good (nar)

1947

DEATHS
 Richard LeGallienne
 Arthur Machen
 Forest Reid
 Alfred North Whitehead

WORKS
 Kingsley Amis. Bright November (po)
 George Granville Barker. Love Poems (po)
 Francis Berry. Murdock (po)
 James Bridie. Dr. Angelus (dr)
 Joyce Cary. The Drunken Sailor (po)
 Alex Comfort. Letters from an Outpost (fic)
 Lettice Cooper. Black Bethlehem (n)
 Alfred Coppard. The Dark-Eyed Lady (fic)
 Rhys Davies. The Dark Daughters (n)
 Cecil Day-Lewis. The Colloquial Element in English Poetry (e)
 _____. The Poetic Image (e)
 William Gerhardi. Collected Works (pub)
 John Heath-Stubbs. The Divided Ways (po)
 Reyner Heppenstall. Poems, 1933-1945 (po)
 Emyr Humphreys. The Little Kingdom (n)
 Hammond Innes. The Killer Mine (n)

_____. The Lonely Skier (n)
James Kirkup. The Drowned Sailor (po)
Philip Larkin. A Girl in Winter (n)
Malcolm Lowry. Under the Volcano (n)
Percy Lubbock. Portrait of Edith Wharton (bio)
Hugh Macdiarmid. A Kist of Whistles (po)
Sir Compton Mackenzie. Whisky Galore (n)
Louis Macneice. The Dark Tower (dr)
Charles Ewart Milne. Boding Day (po)
Nicholas Monsarrat. Depends What You Mean by Love (n)
Charles Morgan. The Judge's Story (n)
Norman Nicholson. The Green Shore (n)
Frank O'Connor. The Art of the Theatre (e)
_____. The Common Chord (fic)
Sean O'Faolain. Teresa and Other Stories (fic)
George Orwell. The English People (e)
John Cowper Powys. Obstinate Cymric: Essays, 1935-1947 (pub)
John Pudney. Low Life Verses (po)
_____. Selected Poems (po)
Alan Ross. The Derelict Day: Poems in Germany (po)
Sydney Goodsir Smith. Selected Poems (po)
C.P. Snow. The Light and the Dark (n)
Stephen Spender. Poems of Dedication (po)
Virginia Woolf. The Moment (e, pub)

1948

BIRTHS
 David Edgar

DEATHS
 Michael Roberts

EVENTS
 The Adelphi (p, c)
WORKS
 Dannie Abse. Fire in Heaven (dr)
 Wystan Hugh Auden. The Age of Anxiety (po)
 _____. The Dyer's Hand, rev 1962 (e)
 Arthur David Beaty. The Takeoff (n)
 Charles Causley. How Pleasant To Know Mrs. Lear (dr)
 Agatha Christie. Witness for the Prosecution (fic)
 Winston Churchill. The Second World War, to 1954 (his)
 Leonard Clark. The Mirror (po)
 Jack Clemo. Wilding Graft (n)
 Alex Comfort. On This Side Nothing (n)
 Cecil Day-Lewis. Collected Poems, 1929-1936 (pub)
 _____. Poems, 1943-1947 (pub)
 Monica Dickens. Joy and Josephine (n)
 Patric Dickinson. Stone in the Midst (dr)
 Lawrence Durrell. On Seeming to Presume (po)
 T.S. Eliot. Notes towards a Definition of Culture (e)
 E.M. Forster. Collected Short Stories (pub)
 _____. The Development of English Prose between 1918 and 1939 (e)
 Roy Fuller. With My Little Eye (n)

Rumer Godden. A Candle for St. Jude (n)
Robert Graves. The White Goddess (e)
Henry Green. Concluding (n)
Graham Greene. The Heart of the Matter (n)
Gerard Manley Hopkins. Poems (pub)
Geoffrey Household. Arabesque (n)
Aldous Huxley. Ape and Essence (e)
Hammond Innes. The Blue Ice (n)
_____. Maddon's Rock (n)
F.R. Leavis. The Great Tradition: George Eliot, James, and Conrad (e)
Alun Lewis. In the Green Tree (po, pub)
Emanuel Litvinoff. A Crown for Cain (po)
Louis Macneice. Holes in the Sky: Poems, 1944-1947 (pub)
Aubrey Menen. The Prevalence of Witches (n)
Nicholas Monsarrat. My Brother Denys (n)
Norman Nicholson. Rock Face (po)
Liam O'Flaherty. Two Lovely Beasts (fic)
Ezra Pound. Cantos 1-84 (po)
John Pudney. Commemorations (po)
_____. Estuary: A Romance (n)
_____. Shuffley Wanderers (n)
Terence Rattigan. The Browning Version (dr)
Bertrand Russell. Human Knowledge: Its Scope and Limits (e)
William Sansom. The Equilibriad (fic)
_____. Something Terrible, Something Lovely (fic)
_____. South: Aspects and Images from Corsica, Italy, and Southern France (fic)
Vernon Scannell. Graves and Resurrections: Poems (po)
Alexander Scott. Prometheus 48 (dr)
Robert Sherriff. Miss Mabel (dr)
Dame Edith Sitwell. A Notebook on William Shakespeare (e
Sacheverell Sitwell. Selected Poems (pub)
Sydney Goodsir Smith. Under the Eildon Tree (po)
Arnold Toynbee. Civilization on Trial (e)
Sydney Tremayne. Time and the Wind (po)
Vernon Watkins. The Lady with the Unicorn (po)
_____. Selected Poems (pub)
Evelyn Waugh. The Loved One (n)
Charles Williams. Seed of Adam (po, dr, pub)

1949

DEATHS
  Douglas Hyde
  Edith Somerville

WORKS
  Dannie Abse. After Every Green Thing (po)
  Frances Bellerby. The Brightening Cloud (po)
  Ronald Bottrall. The Palisades of Fear (po)
  Elizabeth Bowen. The Heat of the Day (n)
  James Bridie. Daphne Laureola (dr)
  Roy Campbell. Collected Poems (pub)
  Joyce Cary. A Fearful Joy (n)
  Cyril Connolly. Enemies of Promise, rev (e)
  Rhys Davies. Boy with a Trumpet (pub)

THE TWENTIETH CENTURY 263

Paul Dehn. The Day's Alarm (po)
Monica Dickens. Flowers on the Grass (n)
Basil Dowling. Canterbury (po)
Daphne Du Maurier. The Parasites (n)
T.S. Eliot. The Cocktail Party (dr)
Christopher Fry. The Lady's Not for Burning (dr)
Roy Fuller. Epitaphs and Occasions (po)
Robert Graves. The Common Asphodel (e)
John Heath-Stubbs. The Charity of the Stars (po)
Emyr Humphreys. The Voice of a Stranger (n)
R.C. Hutchinson. Elephant and Castle: A Reconstruction (n)
_____. Recollection of a Journey (n)
Sir Julian Huxley. Soviet Genetics and World Science (e)
Hammond Innes. The White South (n)
John Maynard Keynes. My Early Beliefs (e, pub)
Ronald Knox. The Old Testament, 2 vols (trans)
Louis Macneice. Collected Poems, 1925-1948 (pub)
W. Somerset Maugham. A Writer's Notebook (trav, nar)
Aubrey Menen. The Stumbling Stone (n)
Charles Morgan. The River Line (n)
Edwin Muir. Essays on Literature and Society (e)
_____. The Labyrinth (po)
Norman Nicholson. Prophesy to the Wind (dr)
Sean O'Casey. Cock-a-doodle-dandy (dr)
_____. Inishfallen, Fare Thee Well (auto)
George Orwell. Nineteen Eighty-four (n)
Kathleen Raine. The Pythoness and Other Poems (po)
James Reeves. The Imprisoned Sea (po)
Isaac Rosenberg. Collected Poems (pub)
Gilbert Ryle. The Concept of Mind (e)
William Sansom. The Body (n)
Dorothy Sayers. Inferno (trans)
Alexander Scott. The Latest in Elegies (po)
Stevie Smith. The Holiday (n)
C.P. Snow. Time of Hope (n)
Stephen Spender. The Edge of Being (po)
Dame Rebecca West. The Meaning of Treason (e)
Laurence Whistler. The World's Room: The Collected Poems of Laurence Whistler (po)
Angus Wilson. The Wrong Set (fic)
David Wright. Poems (po)

1950

DEATHS
  Eric Blair ("George Orwell")
  George Bernard Shaw

EVENTS
  Horizon (p,c)

WORKS
  Dannie Abse. Hands around the Wall (dr)
  Richard Aldington. Portrait of a Genius, But (auto)
  George Granville Barker. The Dead Seagull (dr)
  _____. News of the World (po)

_____. The True Confessions of George Barker, Book I (auto, po)
James Bridie. The Queen's Comedy (dr)
George Buchanan. Rose Forbes (n)
Basil Bunting. Poems (pub)
Austin Clarke. The Plot Succeeds (dr)
William Cooper. Scenes from Provincial Life (n)
Daphne Du Maurier. September Tide (dr)
Lawrence Durrell. Sappho (dr, po)
Christopher Fry. Ring around the Moon (trans, dr)
_____. Venus Observed (dr)
David Gascoyne. A Vagrant (po)
Rumer Godden. A Breath of Air (n)
Winston Graham. Jeremy Poldark: A Novel of Cornwall, 1790-1791 (n)
Henry Green. Nothing (n)
Graham Greene. The Third Man (n)
John Heath-Stubbs. The Swarming of the Bees (po)
Geoffrey Household. The High Place (n)
Aldous Huxley. Themes and Variations (e)
Hammond Innes. The Angry Mountain (n)
Ronald Knox. Enthusiasm (e)
D.H. Lawrence. Selected Essays (pub)
Doris Lessing. The Grass Is Singing (n)
Dame Rose Macaulay. The World My Wilderness (n)
Colin MacInnes. To the Victors the Spoils (n)
Aubrey Menen. The Backward Bride: A Sicilian Scherzo (n)
Charles Ewart Milne. Diamond Cut Diamond (po)
Alfred Noyes. Collected Poems (pub)
George Orwell. Shooting an Elephant (e)
Ezra Pound. Patria Mia (pub)
John Pudney. The Accomplice (n)
William Sansom. The Passionate North (fic)
Siegfried Sassoon. Common Chords (po)
Robert Sherriff. Home at Seven (dr)
Jon Silkin. The Portrait (po)
Dame Edith Sitwell. Facade, enl ed (po)
_____. Poor Men's Music (po)
John Tolkien. Farmer Giles of Ham (n)
Evelyn Waugh. Helena (n)
Angus Wilson. Such Darling Dodos (fic)
Cecil Woodham-Smith. Florence Nightingale (bio)
William Butler Yeats. The Collected Poems (pub)
Andrew Young. Collected Poems (pub)

1951

DEATHS
  Osborne Henry Mavor ("James Bridie")
WORKS
  Eric Ambler. Judgment on Deltchev (n)
  Wystan Hugh Auden. The Enchafed Flood (e)
  Enid Bagnold. The Loved and Envied (n)
  Samuel Beckett. Malone Dies (n)
  _____. Molloy (n)
  Thomas Blackburn. The Outer Darkness (po)
  Roy Campbell. Light on a Dark Horse (auto)
  Charles Causley. Farewell, Aggie Weston (po)

_____. Hands To Dance (fic)
Jack Clemo. The Clay Verge (po)
Alex Comfort. And All But He Departed (po)
Ivy Compton-Burnett. Darkness and Day (n)
William Cooper. High Life (dr)
_____. Scenes from Metropolitan Life (n)
Rhys Davies. Marianne (n)
Cecil Day-Lewis. The Poet's Task (e)
Walter De La Mare. Winged Chariot
Daphne Du Maurier. My Cousin Rachel (n)
Maurice Edelman. A Trial of Love (n)
T.S. Eliot. Selected Essays (pub)
William Empson. The Structure of Complex Words (e)
E.M. Forster. Two Cheers for Democracy (e)
Christopher Fry. A Sleep of Prisoners (dr)
Robert Graves. The Golden Ass (trans)
_____. Hercules My Shipmate (n)
Graham Greene. The End of the Affair (n)
_____. The Lost Childhood (e)
John Clive Hall. The Summer Dance (po)
Geoffrey Household. A Rough Shoot (n)
_____. A Time to Kill (n)
Emyr Humphreys. A Change of Heart (n)
Hammond Innes. Air Bridge (n)
Christopher Isherwood. Vedanta for Modern Man (e)
David Jones. The Anathemata (po)
James Kirkup. The Submerged Village (po)
_____. The Creation (po)
Arthur Koestler. The Age of Longing (n)
Philip Larkin. Poems (pub)
John Lehmann. The Age of the Dragon (po)
_____. The Whispering Gallery (auto)
Doris Lessing. This Was the Old Chief's Country (fic)
John Masters. Nightrunners of Bengal (n)
W. Somerset Maugham. Complete Short Stories, 3 vols (pub)
Charles Ewart Milne. Elegy for a Lost Submarine (po)
Nicholas Monsarrat. The Cruel Sea (n)
Sean O'Casey. Collected Plays, to 1952, 4 vols (pub)
Frank O'Connor. Traveller's Samples (fic)
Ezra Pound. Guide to Kulchur, rev ed (e)
Anthony Powell. A Question of Upbringing (n)
John Cowper Powys. Porius: A Romance of the Dark Ages (n)
Victor Pritchett. Mr. Beluncle (n)
William Sansom. The Face of Innocence (n)
John Pudney. Hero of a Summer's Day (n)
Alfred Leslie Rowse. The England of Elizabeth (his)
Sydney Goodsir Smith. The Aipple and the Hazel (po)
C.P. Snow. The Masters (n)
Stephen Spender. World within World (auto)
Arnold Toynbee. War and Civilization (e)
Sydney Tremayne. The Hardest Freedom (po)
Arthur Waley. The Poetry and Career of Li Po, A.D. 701-762 (e, bio)
Terence White. The Goshawk (nar)
William Butler Yeats and George Moore. Diarmuid and Grania (dr, pub)

1952

DEATHS
George Norman Douglas

EVENTS
Elizabeth II, Queen of England

WORKS
Dannie Abse. Walking under Water (po)
Alfred Alvarez. The End of It (po)
Enid Bagnold. Gertie (dr)
Samuel Beckett. Waiting for Godot (dr)
Francis Berry. The Galloping Centaur (po)
George Buchanan. A Place to Live (n)
Joyce Cary. Prisoner of Grace (n)
Austin Clarke. The Sun Dances at Easter (n)
Laurence Collinson. Poet's Dozen (po)
Alex Comfort. A Giant's Strength (n)
William Cooper. The Struggle of Albert Woods (n)
Paul Dehn. Romantic Landscape (po)
Patric Dickinson. The Sailing Race (po)
Daphne Du Maurier. The Apple Tree (fic, n)
Lawrence Durrell. A Key to Modern Poetry (e)
T.S. Eliot. The Complete Poems and Plays, 1909-1950 (pub)
Brian Glanville. The Reluctant Dictator (n)
Henry Green. Doting (n)
Thomas Hinde. Mr. Nicholas (n)
Geoffrey Household. Tales of Adventurers (fic)
Emyr Humphreys. Hear and For ive
R.C. Hutchinson. The Stepmother (n)
Hammond Innes. Campbell's Kingdom (n)
Christopher Isherwood. The World in the Evening (n)
Augustus John. Chiaroscuro (auto)
Thomas Kinsella. The Starlit Eye (po)
_____. Three Legendary Sonnets (po)
James Kirkup. A Correct Compassion (po)
F.R. Leavis. The Common Pursuit (e)
Doris Lessing. Martha Quest (n)
Percy Wyndham Lewis. The Writer and the Absolute (e)
Louis Macneice. Ten Burnt Offerings (po)
John Masters. The Deceivers (n)
Aubrey Menen. The Duke of Gallodoro (n)
Charles Morgan. The River Line (dr)
Edwin Muir. Collected Poems, 1921-1951 (pub)
Anthony Powell. A Buyer's Market (n)
John Cowper Powys. The Inmates (n)
John Pudney. The Net (n)
Kathleen Raine. Selected Poems (po)
_____. The Year One (po)
Terence Rattigan. The Deep Blue Sea (dr)
James Reeves. The Password (po)
William Sansom. A Touch of the Sun (fic)
Alexander Scott. Untrue Thomas (dr)
Sydney Goodsir Smith. So Late in the Night: Fifty Lyrics, 1944-1948 (po)

Stephen Spender. Shelley (e)
Dylan Thomas. Collected Poems, 1934-1952 (pub)
Ronald Thomas. An Acre of Land (po)
Evelyn Waugh. Men at Arms (n)
Cecil Woodham-Smith. The Reason Why (his)
Angus Wilson. Emile Zola (e)
_____. Hemlock and After (n)
David Wright. Moral Stories (po)
William Butler Yeats. The Collected Plays (pub)

1953

BIRTHS
Stephen Poliakoff

DEATHS
Hilaire Belloc
Theodore Powys
Dylan Thomas

EVENTS
Scrutiny (p, c)

WORKS
Eric Ambler. The Schirmer Inheritance (n)
Kingsley Amis. A Frame of Mind (po)
Patrick Anderson. The Colour As Naked (po)
Nina Bawden. Who Calls the Tune (n)
Samuel Beckett. The Unameable (n)
Brigid Brophy. The Crown Princess and Other Stories (fic)
_____. Hackenfeller's Ape (n)
Joyce Cary. Except the Lord (n)
Charles Causley. Survivor's Leave (po)
Leonard Clark. English Morning (po)
Austin Clarke. The Moment Next to Nothing (dr)
Cyril Connolly. Ideas and Places (e)
Lettice Cooper. Fenny (n)
William Cooper. The Ever-Interesting Topic (n)
Cecil Day-Lewis. An Italian Visit (po)
_____. The Lyrical Poetry of Thomas Hardy (e)
Monica Dickens. No More Meadows (n)
Lawrence Durrell. Reflections on a Marine Venus (nar, trav)
Maurice Edelman. Who Goes Home (n)
T.S. Eliot. The Three Voices of Poetry (e)
D.J. Enright. The Laughing Hyena (po)
E.M. Forster. The Hill of Devi (e)
Roy Fuller. The Second Curtain (n)
Winston Graham. Warleggan: A Novel of Cornwall, 1792-1793 (n)
Graham Greene. The Living Room (dr)
Geoffrey Grigson. Legenda Suecana (po)
Leslie Hartley. The Go-Between (n)
Reyner Heppenstall. The Lesser Infortune (n)
John Holloway. The Victorian Stage (e)
John Masters. The Lotus and the Wind (n)
Charles Ewart Milne. Galion (po)
_____. Life Arboreal (po)
Nicholas Monsarrat. The Story of Esther Costello (n)

George Edward Moore. Some Main Problems of Philosophy (e)
Iris Murdoch. Sartre (e)
Norman Nicholson. A Match for the Devil (dr)
George Orwell. England, Your England (pub)
Gilbert Phelps. The Dry Stone (n)
Ezra Pound. The Spirit of Romance, rev ed (e)
John Pudney. A Ring for Luck (n)
_____. Sixpenny Songs (po)
Terence Rattigan. Collected Plays, 3 vols, to 1964 (dr)
Sir Herbert Read. Collected Poems (pub)
_____. The True Voice of Feeling (e)
Vernon Scannell. The Fight (n)
_____. The Wound and the Scar (n)
Tom Scott. Seeven Poems o Maister Francis Villon (po, trans)
Charles Hubert Sisson. An Asiatic Romance (n)
Dame Edith Sitwell. Gardeners and Astronomers (po)
Sydney Goodsir Smith. Cokkils (po)
Stephen Spender. The Creative Element (e)
Dylan Thomas. In Country Sleep (po)
Ronald Thomas. The Minister (po)
Anthony Thwaite. Poems (po)
Arnold Toynbee. The World and the West (e)
John Wain. Hurry on Down (n)
Evelyn Waugh. Love among the Ruins (n)

1954

DEATHS
Sir Edmund Chambers
Rev. William Inge

EVENTS
The London Magazine (p, f)

WORKS
Dannie Abse. Ash on a Young Man's Sleeve (n)
Kingsley Amis. Lucky Jim (n)
_____. Poems (pub)
Nina Bawden. The Odd Flamingo (n)
Arthur David Beaty. The Heart of the Storm (n)
John Betjeman. A Few Late Chrysanthemums (po)
Thomas Blackburn. The Holy Stone (po)
Ronald Bottrall. Adam Unparadised (po)
George Mackay Brown. The Storm (po)
Alan Brownjohn. Travellers Alone (po)
Rhys Davies. The Painted King (n)
Cecil Day-Lewis. Collected Poems (pub)
Daphne Du Maurier. Mary Anne (n)
Maurice Edelman. A Dream of Treason (n)
T.S. Eliot. The Confidential Clerk (dr)
Christopher Fry. The Dark Is Light Enough (dr)
Roy Fuller. Counterparts (po)
_____. Fantasy and Fugue (n)
Brian Glanville. Henry Sows the Wind (n)
William Golding. Lord of the Flies (n)
Thom Gunn. Fighting Terms (po)

_____. Poems (pub)
John B.S. Haldane. The Biochemistry of Genetics (e)
John Heath-Stubbs. A Charm against the Toothache (po)
Aldous Huxley. The Doors of Perception (e)
Hammond Innes. The Strange Land (n)
James Kirkup. The Spring Journey (po)
Philip Larkin. Poems (pub)
Doris Lessing. A Proper Marriage (n)
C.S. Lewis. English Literature in the Sixteenth Century (e)
Percy Wyndham Lewis. The Demon of Progress in the Arts (e)
George MacBeth. A Form of Words (po)
Louis Macneice. Autumn Sequal (po)
_____. The Other Wing (po)
John Masefield. A Mainsail Haul, rev ed (po)
John Masters. Bhowani Junction (n)
Aubrey Menen. Rama Retold (n)
Edwin Muir. An Autobiography (auto)
_____. Prometheus (po)
Iris Murdoch. Under the Net (n)
John Middleton Murry. Swift (bio, e)
Norman Nicholson. The Pot Geranium (po)
Sean O'Casey. Sunset and Evening Star (auto)
Ezra Pound. The Literary Essays (e, pub)
John Cowper Powys. Atlantis (n)
Terence Rattigan. Separate Tables (dr)
Alan Ross. Something of the Sea: Poems, 1942-1952 (po)
Gilbert Ryle. Dilemmas (e)
William Sansom. A Bed of Roses (n)
_____. Lord Love Us (fic)
Alexander Scott. Mouth Music (po)
_____. Right Royal (dr)
_____. Shetland Yard (dr)
Jon Silkin. The Peaceable Kingdom (po)
_____. The Two Freedoms (po)
C.P. Snow. The New Men (n)
Dylan Thomas. A Child's Christmas in Wales (nar, pub)
_____. Quite Early One Morning (nar, pub)
_____. Under Milk Wood (po, dr, pub)
John Tolkien. The Fellowship of the Ring (n)
Vernon Watkins. The Death Bell (po)
Terence White. The Book of Beasts (trans)
David Wright. Moral Stories (po)

1955

DEATHS
Constance Holme

WORKS
Richard Aldington. Lawrence of Arabia (bio)
Brian Aldiss. The Brightfount Diaries (n)
Kingsley Amis. That Uncertain Feeling (n)
Wystan Hugh Auden. The Shield of Achilles (po)
Enid Bagnold. The Chalk Garden (dr)
Nina Bawden. Change Here for Babylon (n)
Elizabeth Bowen. A World of Love (n)

Basil Bunting. The Spoils (po)
Joyce Cary. Not Honour More (n)
Austin Clarke. Ancient Lights (po)
Ivy Compton-Burnett. Mother and Son (n)
Robert Conquest. A World of Difference (n)
Rhys Davies. Collected Stories (fic, pub)
Walter De La Mare. A Beginning (fic)
Monica Dickens. The Winds of Heaven (n)
Patric Dickinson. The Scale of Things (po)
Lawrence Durrell. Private Drafts (po)
_____. The Tree of Idleness (po)
William Empson. Collected Poems (pub)
D.J. Enright. Academic Year (n)
Gillian Freeman. The Liberty Man (n)
Christopher Fry. The Lark (trans, dr)
_____. Tiger at the Gates (trans, dr)
Rumer Godden. An Episode of Sparrows (n)
William Golding. The Inheritors (n)
Robert Graves. The Greek Myths, 2 vols (e)
Leslie Hartley. A Perfect Woman (n)
Geoffrey Household. Fellow Passenger (n)
Emyr Humphreys. A Man's Estate (n)
Elizabeth Jennings. A Way of Looking (po)
Ronald Knox. A Retreat for Lay People (e)
Philip Larkin. The Less Deceived (po)
D.H. Lawrence. Complete Short Stories, 3 vols (pub)
_____. Selected Literary Criticism (e, pub)
F.R. Leavis. D.H. Lawrence, Novelist (e)
Percy Wyndham Lewis. Childermass, rev ed (n)
_____. Malign Fiesta (n)
_____. Monstre Gai (n)
_____. Self-Condemned (n)
Edward Lowbury. Metamorphoses (po)
Norman MacCaig. Riding Lights (po)
Hugh Macdiarmid. In Memoriam James Joyce (e)
John Masters. Coromandel (n)
Nicholas Monsarrat. Castle Garac (n)
Sean O'Casey. The Bishop's Bonfire (dr)
Gilbert Phelps. A Man in His Prime (n)
Anthony Powell. The Acceptance World (n)
John Cowper Powys. Visions and Revisions, rev ed (e)
Dorothy Sayers. Purgatorio (trans)
Alexander Scott. Tam O'Shanter's Tryst (dr)
Robert Sherriff. The Long Sunset (dr)
Charles Hubert Sisson. Versions and Perversions of Heine (po)
Sacheverell Sitwell. Selected Works (e, dr, po)
Ian Crichton Smith. The Long River (po)
Sydney Goodsir Smith. Omens (po)
_____. Orpheus and Euridice (po)
Stephen Spender. Collected Poems, 1928-1953 (pub)
_____. The Making of a Poem (e)
Dylan Thomas. Adventures in the Skin Trade (fic, pub)
Ronald Thomas. Song at the Year's Turning: Poems, 1942-1954 (pub)
John Tolkien. The Two Towers (n)
Sydney Tremayne. The Rock and the Bird (po)
John Wain. Living in the Present (n)

THE TWENTIETH CENTURY   271

   Evelyn Waugh. Officers and Gentlemen (n)

                                1956

DEATHS
   Sir Max Beerbohm
   Walter De La Mare
   Arthur Waley

WORKS
   Dannie Abse. Some Corner of an English Field (n)
   Eric Ambler. The Night Comes (n)
   Kingsley Amis. A Case of Samples (po)
   Wystan Hugh Auden. Making, Knowing, and Judging (e)
   Alfred Jules Ayer. The Problem of Knowledge (e)
   Nina Bawden. The Solitary Child (n)
   Arthur David Beaty. The Proving Flight (n)
   Brendan Behan. The Quare Fellow (dr)
   John Betjeman. The English Towns in the Last Hundred Years (e)
   Thomas Blackburn. In the Fire (po)
   Brigid Brophy. The King of a Rainy Country (n)
   Anthony Burgess. Time before a Tiger (n)
   Winston Churchill. A History of the English-Speaking Peoples, to 1958
              (his)
   William Cooper. Disquiet and Peace (n)
   Monica Dickens. The Angel in the Corner (n)
   T.S. Eliot. Essays on Elizabethan Drama (e)
   D.J. Enright. Bread Rather Than Blossoms (po)
   E.M. Forster. Marianne Thornton (e)
   Gilliam Freeman. Fall of Innocence (n)
   David Gascoyne. Night Thoughts (po)
   Brian Glanville. Along the Arno (n)
   William Golding. Pincher Martin (n)
   Graham Greene. The Quiet American (n)
   John Holloway. The Minute (po)
   Aldous Huxley. Adonis and the Alphabet (e)
   _____. Heaven and Hell (e)
   Hammond Innes. The Mary Deare (n)
   Thomas Kinsella. The Death of a Queen (po)
   _____. Poems (po)
   Percy Wyndham Lewis. The Red Priest (n)
   Dame Rose Macaulay. The Towers of Trebizond (n)
   Aubrey Menen. The Abode of Love (n)
   Nicholas Monsarrat. The Tribe That Lost Its Head (n)
   Edwin Muir. One Foot in Eden (po)
   Iris Murdoch. The Flight from the Enchanter (n)
   Liam O'Flaherty. The Stories of Liam O'Flaherty (fic)
   Ezra Pound. Rock Drill (po)
   John Cooper Powys. The Brazen Head (n)
   _____. Lucifer (po)
   Victor Pritchett. Collected Stories (fic, pub)
   _____. The Sailor, the Sense of Humour, and Other Stories
              (fic)
   Kathleen Raine. Collected Poems (po)
   William Sansom. A Contest of Ladies (fic)
   _____. The Loving Eye (n)

Tom Scott. An Ode til New Jerusalem (po)
C.P. Snow. Homecomings (n)
John Tolkien. The Return of the Ring (n)
John Wain. A Word Carved on a Sill (po)
Alec Waugh. Island in the Sun (n)
Dorothy Wellesley, Duchess of Wellington. Early Light (po, pub)
Laurence Whistler. The View from the Window (po)
Angus Wilson. Anglo-Saxon Attitudes (n)
_____. The Mulberry Bush (dr)

1957

DEATHS
  Roy Campbell
  Joyce Cary
  Alfred Coppard
  Edward Dunsany
  Ronald Knox
  Percy Wyndham Lewis
  Malcolm Lowry
  George Murray
  John Middleton Murry
  Dorothy Richardson
  Dorothy Sayers

WORKS
  Dannie Abse. Tenants of the House (po)
  Brian Aldis. Space, Time and Nathaniel (fic)
  George Granville Barker. Collected Poems, 1930-1935 (pub)
  Nina Bawden. Devil by the Sea (n)
  Samuel Beckett. All That Fall (dr)
  _____. Endgame and Act without Words (dr)
  John Braine. Room at the Top (n)
  Christine Brooke-Rose. The Language of Love (n)
  Charles Causley. Union Street (po)
  Austin Clarke. Too Great a Vine (po)
  Laurence Collinson. The Moods of Love (po)
  Lettice Cooper. Three Lives (n)
  Donald Davie. Articulate Energy (e)
  _____. Purity of Diction in English Verse (e)
  Rhys Davies. The Perishable Quality (n)
  Cecil Day-Lewis. Pegasus (po)
  Daphne Du Maurier. The Scapegoat (n)
  Lawrence Durrell. Bitter Lemons (nar)
  _____. Justine (n)
  Maurice Edelman. The Happy Ones (n)
  T.S. Eliot. On Poetry and Poets (e)
  _____. Poems Written in Early Youth (po, pub)
  Roy Fuller. Brutus's Orchard (po)
  Rumer Godden. Mooltiki:Stories and Poems from India (fic, po)
  Robert Graves. Selected Poems (pub)
  Graham Greene. The Potting Shed (dr)
  Thom Gunn. The Sense of Movement (po)
  Leslie Hartley. The Hireling (n)
  Thomas Hinde. Happy As Larry (n)
  Ted Hughes. The Hawk in the Rain (po)

Emyr Humphreys. The Italian Wife (n)
R.C. Hutchinson. March the Ninth (n)
Sir Julian Huxley. Towards a New Humanism (e)
James Kirkup. The Descent into the Cave (po)
Ronald Knox. Bridegroom and Bride (e)
_____. On Translation (e)
D.H. Lawrence. Complete Poems, 3 vols (pub)
Norman MacCaig. The Sinai Sort: Poems (po)
Hugh Macdiarmid. The Battle Continues (po)
_____. Three Hymns to Lenin (po)
Louis Macneice. Visitations (po)
John Masters. Far, Far the Mountain Peak (n)
Iris Murdoch. The Sandcastle (n)
Frank O'Connor. Domestic Relations (fic)
_____. The Mirror in the Roadway: Study of the Modern Novel (e)
Sean O'Faolain. The Finest Stories of Sean O'Faolain (fic)
John Osborne. The Entertainer (dr)
_____. Look Back in Anger (dr)
Anthony Powell. At Lady Molly's (n)
John Pudney. Collected Poems (po)
_____. Trespass in the Sun (n)
James Reeves. A Health to John Patch: A Ballad Operatta (dr)
William Sansom. Among the Dahlias (fic)
Vernon Scannell. A Mortal Pitch (po)
Alexander Scott. The Last Time I Saw Paris (dr)
Alan Sillitoe. Without Beer or Bread (po)
Dame Edith Sitwell. The Collected Poems (pub)
Muriel Spark. The Comforters (n)
Anthony Thwaite. Home Truths (po)
John Wain. Preliminary Essays (e, pub)
Evelyn Waugh. The Ordeal of Gilbert Pinfold (n)
Dame Rebecca West. The Fountain Overflows (n)
Angus Wilson. A Bit Off the Map (e)
William Butler Yeats. Complete Poems, Variorum (pub)

1958

DEATHS
  Dame Rose Macaulay
  George Edward Moore
  Charles Morgan
  Alfred Noyes
  Lennox Robinson
  Henry Tomlinson

WORKS
  Brian Aldiss. Non-Stop (n)
  Kingsley Amis. I Like It Here (n)
  Samuel Beckett. Krapp's Last Tape (dr)
  _____. Watt (n)
  Brendan Behan. Borstal Boy (auto)
  _____. The Hostage (dr)
  Frances Bellerby. The Stone Angel and the Stone Man (po)
  John Betjeman. Collected Poems (pub)
  Thomas Blackburn. The Next Word (po)

Christine Brook-Rose. The Sycamore Tree (n)
George Buchanan. Bodily Responses (po)
Anthony Burgess. The Enemy in the Blanket (n)
William Hamilton Canaway. The Ring-Givers (n)
Joyce Cary. Art and Reality (e)
Charles Causley. The Ballad of Charlotte Dymond (pO)
William Cooper. Prince Genji (dr)
_____. Young People (n)
Rhys Davies. The Darling of Her Heart (fic)
Monica Dickens. Man Overboard (n)
Lawrence Durrell. Balthazar (n)
_____. Mountolive (n)
Christipher Fry. Duel of Angels (trans, dr)
Brian Glanville. The Bankrupts (n)
Rumer Godden. The Greengage Summer (n)
William Golding. The Brass Butterfly (n)
Graham Greene. Our Man in Havana (n)
John Heath-Stubbs. The Triumph of the Muse (po)
Geoffrey Household. The Brides of Solomon (fic)
Aldous Huxley. Brave New World Revisited (e)
Hammond Innes. The Land God Gave to Cain (n)
Thomas Kinsella. Another September (po)
Stanley Middleton. A Short Answer (n)
Charles Ewart Milne. Once More to Tourney (po)
John Montague. Forms of Exile (po)
Iris Murdoch. The Bell (n)
Sean O'Casey. Mirror in My House (auto)
John Osborne and Anthony Creighton. Epitaph for George Dillon (dr)
Gilbert Phelps. The Centenarians: A Fable (n)
Terence Rattigan. Variations on a Theme (dr)
James Reeves. The Talking Skull (po)
I.A. Richards. Goodbye Earth (po)
Lennox Robinson and Donagh MacDonagh. The Oxford Book of Irish Verse (ed)
Alan Ross. To Whom It May Concern: Poems, 1952-1957 (po)
William Sansom. The Cautious Heart (n)
Alexander Scott. Truth To Tell (dr)
Peter Shaffer. Five Finger Exercise (dr)
Jon Silkin. The Two Freedoms (po)
Alan Sillitoe. Saturday Night and Sunday Morning (n)
C.P. Snow. The Conscience of the Rich (n)
Muriel Spark. The Go-Away Bird (fic)
_____. Robinson (n)
Jon Stallworthy. The Earthly Paradise (po)
Ronald Thomas. Poetry for Supper (po)
Charles Tomlinson. Seeing Is Believing (po)
John Wain. The Contenders (n)
Rex Warner. The Young Caesar (n)
Dame Rebecca West. The Court and the Castle (e)
Terence White. The Once and Future King (fic)
Angus Wilson. The Middle Age of Mrs. Eliot (n)
David Wright. Monologue of a Deaf Man (po)
Andrew Young. Out of the World and Back (po)

THE TWENTIETH CENTURY

1959

DEATHS
  Sir Walter Greg
  Laurence Housman
  Edwin Muir

WORKS
  Brian Aldiss. The Canopy of Time (fic)
  _____. No Time Like Tomorrow (fic)
  _____. Vanguard from Alpha (n)
  Eric Ambler. Passage of Arms (n)
  John Arden. Serjeant Musgrave's Dance (dr)
  Arthur David Beaty. Cone of Silence (n)
  Samuel Beckett. Embers (dr)
  Patricia Beers. Loss of the Magyar and Other Poems (po)
  John Braine. The Vodi (n)
  Edwin Brock. An Attempt at Exorcism (po)
  George Mackay Brown. Loaves and Fishes (po)
  Roy Campbell. Collected Poems (pub)
  William Hamilton Canaway. The Seal (n)
  Joyce Cary. The Captive and the Free (n)
  Ivy Compton-Burnett. A Heritage and Its History (n)
  Peter Dale. Nerve (po)
  Daphne Du Maurier. The Breaking Point (fic)
  _____. Early Stories (fic, pub)
  Lawrence Durrell. Art and Outrage (e)
  Maurice Edelman. A Call on Kuprin (n)
  T.S. Eliot. The Cultivation of Christmas Trees (po)
  _____. The Elder Statesman (dr)
  Gillian Freeman. Jack Would Be a Gentleman (n)
  Roy Fuller. The Ruined Boys (n)
  Brian Glanville. After Rome, Africa (n)
  William Golding. Free Fall (n)
  Robert Graves. The Anger of Achilles (trans)
  Graham Greene. The Complaisant Lover (dr)
  William Haggard. Venetian Blind (n)
  Emyr Humphreys. A Toy Epic (n)
  David Jones. Epoch and Artist (e)
  James Joyce. The Critical Writings of James Joyce (e, pub)
  Patrick Joseph Kavanagh. One and One (po)
  John B. Keane. Sive (dr)
  James Kirkup. The Prodigal Son: Poems, 1956-1959 (po)
  Laurence Lerner. Domestic Interior (po)
  _____. The Englishmen (n)
  Doris Lessing. A Ripple from the Storm (n)
  Emanuel Litvinoff. The Lost Europeans (n)
  Hugh Macdiarmid. Burns Today and Tomorrow (e)
  John Masters. Fandango Rock (n)
  Aubrey Menen. The Fig Tree (n)
  Nicholas Monsarrat. The Ship That Died of Shame (fic)
  Norman Nicholson. Birth by Drowning (dr)
  Frank O'Connor. Kings, Lords, and Commons (po, trans)
  John Pudney. The Trampoline (po)
  Simon Raven. Brother Cain (n)
  _____. The Feathers of Death (n)

Alfred Leslie Rowse. Poems Partly American (po)
Alan Sillitoe. The Loneliness of the Long-Distance Runner (fic)
Sydney Goodsir Smith. Figs and Thistles (po)
C.P. Snow. The Affair (n)
Muriel Spark. Momento Mori (n)
John Wain. A Travelling Woman (n)
Vernon Watkins. Cypress and Acacia (po)
Evelyn Waugh. The Life of Ronald Knox (bio)
Arnold Wesker. Chicken Soup with Barley (dr)
_____. Roots (dr)

1960

WORKS
Dannie Abse. House of Cowards (dr)
Brian Aldiss. Bow Down to Nul (n)
_____. Galaxies Like Grains of Sand (fic)
Kingsley Amis. New Maps of Hell (e)
_____. Take a Girl Like You (n)
Wystan Hugh Auden. Homage to Clio (po)
Enid Bagnold. The Last Joke (dr)
Nina Bawden. Just Like a Lady (n)
Arthur David Beaty. Call Me Captain (n)
John Betjeman. Summoned by Bells: An Autobiography in Verse (po)
David Black. Rocklestrakes (po)
Edwin Brock. A Family Affair: Two Sonnet Sequences (po)
George Buchanan. A Trip to the Castle (dr)
Anthony Burgess. The Doctor Is Sick (n)
Roy Campbell. Collected Poems (pub)
Joyce Cary. Spring Song (fic)
Austin Clarke. The Horse-Eaters (po)
Anthony Conrans. Formal Poems (po)
Lettice Cooper. A Certain Compass (n)
Rhys Davies. Girl Waiting in the Shade (n)
Cecil Day-Lewis. The Buried Day (auto)
Patric Dickinson. The World I See (po)
Daphne Du Maurier. The Treasury of Du Maurier Short Stories (fic)
Lawrence Durrell. Clea (n)
_____. Collected Poems (pub)
D.J. Enright. Heaven Knows Where (n)
_____. Insufficient Poppy (n)
_____. Some Men Are Brothers (po)
Wilson Harris. Palace of the Peacock (n)
Leslie Hartley. Facial Justice (n)
John Holloway. The Chartered Mirror (e)
_____. The Fugue (po)
Geoffrey Household. Watcher in the Shadows (n)
Ted Hughes. Lupercal (po)
Hammond Innes. The Doomed Oasis (n)
John B. Keane. Sharon's Grave (dr)
Thomas Kinsella. Moralities (po)
John LeCarre. Call for the Dead (n)
John Lehmann. I Am My Brother (auto)
Doris Lessing. The Habit of Loving (fic)
C.S. Lewis. The Four Loves (pub)
David Lodge. The Picturegoers (n)

Norman MacCaig. A Common Grace (po)
John Masters. The Venus of Konpara (n)
Stanley Middleton. Harris's Requiem (n)
Nicholas Monsarrat. The Nylon Pirates (n)
John Montague. The Old People (po)
Edwin Muir. Collected Poems, 1921-1958 (pub)
Sean O'Casey. The Drums of Father Ned (dr)
Frank O'Connor. Shakespeare's Progress (e)
Gilbert Phelps. The Love before the First (n)
Harold Pinter. The Birthday Party (dr)
_____. The Caretaker (dr)
_____. The Dumb Waiter (dr)
Anthony Powell. Casanovia's Chinese Restaurant (n)
John Cowper Powys. All or Nothing (n)
J.B. Priestley. Literature and Western Man (e)
Kathleen Raine. Christmas 1960 (po)
Simon Raven. Doctors Wear Scarlet (n)
Peter Redgrove. The Collector (po)
James Reeves. Collected Poems: 1929-1959 (po)
I.A. Richards. The Screens (po)
Siegfried Sassoon. The Path to Peace (po)
Vernon Scannell. The Big Chance (n)
_____. The Masks of Love (po)
Alan Sillitoe. The General (n)
_____. The Rats (po)
Norman Simpson. One Way Pendulum (dr)
Ian Crichton Smith. Deer on the High Hills (po)
Sydney Goodsir Smith. The Wallace: A Triumph (dr)
_____. The Vision of the Prodigal Son (po)
Muriel Spark. The Bachelors (n)
_____. The Ballad of Peckham Rye (n)
John Wain. Nuncle (fic)
Rex Warner. Imperial Caesar (n)
Arnold Wesker. I'm Talking about Jerusalem (dr)
William Butler Yeats. The Senate Speeches (sp, pub)

1961

EVENTS
Bradshaw's Monthly Railway Guide (c)

WORKS
Dannie Abse. The Eccentric (dr)
Brian Aldiss. Equator (n)
_____. The Male Response (n)
_____. The Primal Urge (n)
Nina Bawden. In Honour Bound (n)
Samuel Beckett. Happy Days (dr)
Francis Berry. Morant Bay (po)
Thomas Blackburn. A Smell of Burning (po)
Christine Brooke-Rose. The Dear Deceit (n)
_____. The Middlemen: A Satire (n)
Alan Brownjohn. The Railings (po)
George Buchanan. Conversation with Strangers (po)
_____. Tresper Revolution (dr)
Michael Bullock. Sunday Is a Day of Incest (po)

Anthony Burgess. The Worm and the Ring (n)
William Hamilton Canaway. Horse on Fire (dr)
───────────. Sammy Going South (n)
Charles Causley. Johnny Alleluia (po)
Jack Clemo. The Map of Clay (po)
Alex Comfort. Come Out To Play (n)
Stewart Conn. Break-Down (dr)
Anthony Conrans. Metamorphoses (po)
William Cooper. Scenes from Married Life (n)
Paul Dehm. Quake, Quake, Quake (po)
Monica Dickens. The Heart of London (n)
Maurice Edelman. The Ministers (n)
William Empson. Milton's God (e)
Gillian Freeman. The Leather Boys (n)
Christopher Fry. Curtmantle (dr)
John Fuller. Fairground Music (po)
Roy Fuller. The Father's Comedy (n)
Brian Glanville. A Bad Streak (fic)
Rumer Godden. China Court: The Hours of a Country House (n)
Winston Graham. Marnie (n)
Graham Greene. A Burnt-out Case (n)
Thom Gunn. My Sad Captains (po)
Wilson Harris. The Far Journey of Oudin (n)
Leslie Hartley. Two for the River and Other Stories (fic)
Thomas Hinde. For the Good of the Company (n)
David Holbrook. Imaginings (po)
John Holloway. The Story of the Night: Studies in Shakespeare's Major Tragedies (e)
Richard Hughes. The Fox in the Attic (n)
Ted Hughes. Meet My Folks! (fic)
R.C. Hutchinson. Image of My Father (n)
Elizabeth Jennings. Every Changing Hope (e)
───────────. Poetry Today (e)
───────────. Song for a Birth or a Death (po)
Thomas Kinsella. Poems and Translations (po)
Edward Lowbury. Time for Sale (po)
Louis Macneice. Solstices (po)
Stanley Middleton. A Serious Woman (n)
John Mole. A Feather for Memory (n)
Nicholas Monsarrat. The White Rajah (n)
John Montague. Poisoned Lands (po)
Iris Murdoch. A Severed Head (n)
Sean O'Faolain. I Remember! I Remember! (fic)
John Osborne. Luther (dr)
───────────. A Subject for Scandal and Concern (dr)
Harold Pinter. A Slight Ache and Other Plays (dr)
J.B. Priestley. Saturn over Water (n)
───────────. The Thirty-First of June (n)
Victor Pritchett. When My Girl Comes Home (fic)
John Pudney. Thin Air (n)
Peter Redgrove. The Nature of Cold Weather (po)
William Sansom. The Last Hours of Sandra Lee (n)
Siegfried Sassoon. Collected Poems, 1908-1956 (pub)
Vernon Scannell. The Face of the Enemy (n)
───────────. The Shadowed Place (n)
Jon Silkin. The Re-ordering of the Stones (po)

Alan Sillitoe. Key to the Door (n)
Charles Hubert Sisson. The London Zoo (po)
Ian Crichton Smith. Thistles and Roses (po)
Muriel Spark. The Prime of Miss Jean Brodie (n)
_____. Voices at Play (fic, dr)
Jon Stallworthy. The Astronomy of Love (po)
Ronald Thomas. Tares (po)
Auberon Waugh. The Foxglove Saga (n)
Evelyn Waugh. Unconditional Surrender (n)
Arnold Wesker. The Kitchen (dr)
Laurence Whistler. Audible Silence (po)
Emlyn Williams. The Collected Plays (pub)
Angus Wilson. The Old Men at the Zoo (n)

1962

DEATHS
Richard Aldington
Ralph Hodgson
George Macaulay Trevelyan

WORKS
Dannie Abse. Gone (dr)
_____. The Joker (dr)
Brian Aldiss. Hothouse (n)
Eric Ambler. The Light of Day (n)
Kingsley Amis. My Enemy's Enemy (n)
George Granville Barker. The View from a Blind I (po)
Arthur David Beaty. Village of Stars (n)
_____. The Wind off the Sea (n)
Brendan Behan. Island, an Irish Sketch Book (trav)
John Braine. Life at the Top (n)
Edwin Brock. The Little White God (n)
Brigid Brophy. Flesh (n)
Anthony Burgess. A Clockwork Orange (n)
William Hamilton Canaway. The Hunter and the Horns (n)
Austin Clarke. Forget-Me-Not (po)
Alex Comfort. Haste to the Wedding (po)
Ivy Compton-Burnett. A God and His Gifts (n)
Tony Connor. With Love Somehow (po)
Robert Conquest. Between Mars and Venus (po)
Lettice Cooper. The Double Heart (n)
Peter Dale. Walk from the House (po)
Len Deighton. The Ipcress File (n)
Maureen Duffy. The Lay Off (dr)
_____. That's How It Was (n)
T.S. Eliot. Collected Plays (dr, pub)
D.J. Enright. Addictions (po)
Roy Fuller. Collected Poems, 1936-1961 (pub)
Brian Glanville. Diamond (n)
Robert Graves. Greek Gods and Heroes (e)
_____. New Poems (po)
_____. Oxford Addresses on Poetry (e)
Thom Gunn. Fighting Terms, rev (po)
William Haggard. The Unquiet Sleep (n)
Wilson Harris. The Whole Armour (n)

John Heath-Stubbs. The Blue Fly in His Head (po)
Reyner Heppenstall. The Connecting Door (n)
_____. The Woodshed (n)
Thomas Hinde. The Cage (n)
_____. A Place Like Home (n)
David Holbrook. Lights in the Sky Country (fic)
John Holloway. The Landfallers (po)
Ted Hughes and Thom Gunn. Selected Poems (pub)
Emyr Humphreys. The Gift (n)
Aldous Huxley. Island (n)
Hammond Innes. Atlantic Fury (n)
Christopher Isherwood. Down There on a Visit (n)
Thomas Kinsella. Downstream (po)
James Kirkup. The Love of Others (n)
D.H. Lawrence. The Symbolic Meaning (e, pub)
John LeCarre. A Murder of Quality (n)
Doris Lessing. The Golden Notebook (n)
David Lodge. Ginger, You're Barmy (n)
Christopher Logue. Patrochleia (po)
Malcolm Lowry. Hear Us, O Lord, from Heaven (n, pub)
George MacBeth. Lecture to the Trainees (po)
Norman MacCaig. A Round of Applause (po)
Hugh Macdiarmid. Collected Poems (pub)
_____. The Ugly Birds without Wings (e)
John Masters. To the Coral Strand (n)
Aubrey Menen. She La: A Satire (n)
Christopher Middleton. Torse 3: Poems, 1949-1961 (po)
Stanley Middleton. The Just Exchange (n)
Charles Ewart Milne. A Garland for the Green (po)
Nicholas Monsarrat. The Time before This (n)
Iris Murdoch. An Unofficial Rose (n)
Basil Payne. Sunlight on a Square (po)
Harold Pinter. Three Plays (dr, pub)
Anthony Powell. The Kindly Ones (n)
J.B. Priestley. The Shapes of Sleep (n)
Simon Raven. Close of Play (n)
Alan Ross. African Negatives (po)
Alfred Leslie Rowse. William Shakespeare (bio)
Vernon Scannell. The Dividing Night (n)
_____. A Sense of Danger (po)
George Bernard Shaw. Complete Plays, with Prefaces (pub)
Stevie Smith. Selected Poems (pub)
David Storey. This Sporting Life (n)
John Millington Synge. Poems (pub)
Sydney Tremayne. The Swans of Berwick (po)
John Wain. Sprightly Running (auto)
_____. Strike the Father Dead (n)
Vernon Watkins. Affinities (po)
Arnold Wesker. Chips with Everything (dr)
Laurence Whistler. For Example: Two Sonnets in Sequence (po)
John Stuart Williams. Last Fall (po)

1963

DEATHS
Aldous Huxley

THE TWENTIETH CENTURY   281

   C.S. Lewis
   Louis Macneice
   John Cowper Powys

WORKS
   Brian Aldiss. The Airs of Earth (fic)
   Kingsley Amis. One Fat Englishman (n)
   John Arden. Ironhand (dr)
   Nina Bawden. Tortoise by Candlelight (n)
   Patricia Beer. The Survivors (po)
   Brendan Behan. Have Another (e)
   _____. Hold Your Hour (e)
   David Black. From the Mountains (po)
   Edwin Brock. With Love from Judas (po)
   Brigid Brophy. The Finishing Touch (n)
   Michael Bullock. World without Beginning, Amen! (po)
   Anthony Burgess. Honey for the Bears (n)
   _____. Inside Mr. Enderby (n)
   William Hamilton Canaway. My Feet upon a Rock (n)
   Austin Clarke. Flight to Africa (po)
   Cyril Connolly. Previous Convictions (e)
   Anthony Conran. Asymptotes (po)
   _____. For the Marraige of Gerald and Linda (po)
   _____. Icons (po)
   _____. The Mountain (po)
   _____. Sequence of the Blue Flower (po)
   _____. A String o Blethers (po)
   William Davies. The Complete Poems (pub)
   Len Deighton. Horse under Water (n)
   Margaret Drabble. A Summer Bird-Cage (n)
   Nell Dunn. Up the Junction (fic)
   Lawrence Durrell. An Irish Faustus (po, dr)
   Maurice Edelman. The Fratricides (n)
   John Fowles. The Collector (n)
   Gillian Freeman. The Campaign (n)
   Roy Fuller. The Perfect Fool (n)
   Brian Glanville. The Director's Wife (fic)
   _____. The Rise of Gerry Logan (n)
   Rumer Godden. The Battle of the Villa Fiorita (n)
   Winston Graham. The Grove of Eagles (n)
   Wilson Harris. The Secret Ladder (n)
   Thomas Hinde. Ninety Double Martinis (n)
   David Holbrook. Against the Cruel Frost (po)
   Geoffrey Household. Thing to Love (n)
   Ted Hughes. The Earth Owl (fic)
   Aldous Huxley. Literature and Science (e)
   Brian Stanley Johnson. Traveling People (n)
   Brendan Kennelly. The Crooked Cross (n)
   _____. Let Fall No Burning Leaf (po)
   James Kirkup. The Refusal To Conform: Last and First Poems (po)
   John LeCarre. The Spy Who Came in from the Cold (n)
   John Lehmann. Collected Poems, 1930-1963 (po)
   Laurence Lerner. The Directions of Memory: Poems, 1958-1962 (po)
   Doris Lessing. A Man and Two Women (fic)
   George MacBeth. The Broken Places (po)
   Hugh Macdiarmid. Poetry Like the Hawthorn (po)

Sir Compton Mackenzie. My Life and Times. Octave 1, 1883-1891 (auto)
——————————. My Life and Times. Octave 2, 1891-1900 (auto)
Louis Macneice. The Burning Perch (po)
John Masefield. Complete Poems (po)
John McGahern. The Barracks (n)
Stanley Middleton. Two's Company (n)
Nicholas Monsarrat. Smith and Jones (n)
Iris Murdoch. The Unicorn (n)
Frank O'Connor. The Little Monasteries (po, trans)
——————————. The Lonely Voice: Study of the Short Story (e)
——————————. My Oedipus Complex (fic)
John Osborne. Plays for England: The Blood of the Bambergs, Under Plain Cover (dr)
Wilfred Owen. Collected Poems (pub)
Gilbert Phelps. The Winter People (n)
Harold Pinter. The Lover (dr); A Night Out (dr)
Victor Pritchett. The Key to My Heart (fic)
John Cowper Powys. Jobber Skald, rev ed (n)
Terence Rattigan. Man and Boy (dr)
Peter Redgrove. At the White Monument (po)
William Sansom. The Stories of William Sansom (fic)
Tom Scott. The Ship (po)
C.P. Snow. Corridors of Power (n)
Muriel Spark. The Girls of Slender Means (n)
——————————. Doctors of Philosophy (fic, dr)
Stephen Spender. The Struggle of the Modern (e)
Jon Stallworthy. Out of Bounds (po)
Ronald Thomas. The Bread of Truth (po)
Anthony Thwaite. An Owl in the Tree (po)
John Wain. Essays on Literature and Ideas (e)
Rex Warner. Pericles the Athenian (n)
Auberon Waugh. Path of Dalliance (n)
Laurence Whistler. Fingal's Cave (po)
Angus Wilson. The Wild Garden, or, Speaking of Writing (e)

1964

DEATHS
Brendan Behan
Clive Bell
John B.S. Haldane
Sean O'Casey
Dame Edith Sitwell
Terence White

WORKS
Fleur Adcock. The Eye of the Hurricane (po)
Brian Aldiss. The Dark Light Years (n)
——————————. Greybeard (n)
——————————. Starswarm (fic)
Eric Ambler. A Kind of Anger (n)
John Arden. The Workhouse Donkey (dr)
Enid Bagnold. The Chinese Prime Minister (dr)
Nina Bawden. Under the Skin (n)
Arthur Beaty. The Siren Song (n)
Brendan Behan. The Scarperer (n)

Thomas Blackburn. A Breathing Space (po)
Elizabeth Bowen. The Little Girls (n)
Christine Brooke-Ross. Out (n)
Brigid Brophy. The Snow Ball (n)
_____. The Waste Disposal (dr)
Stewart Conn. Birds in a Wilderness (dr)
Donald Davie. Events and Wisdoms, 1957-1963 (po)
Cecil Day-Lewis. Requiem for the Living (po)
Len Deighton. Funeral in Berlin (n)
Monica Dickens. Cobbler's Dream (n)
_____. Kate and Emma (n)
Patric Dickinson. This Cold Universe (po)
Margaret Drabble. The Garrick Year (n)
Maureen Duffy. The Single Eye (n)
Maurice Edelman. The Prime Minister's Daughter (n)
T.S. Eliot. Knowledge and Experience in the Philosophy of F.H. Bradley
    (e)
Brian Glanville. Goalkeepers Are Crazy (fic)
William Golding. The Spire (n)
Robert Graves. Collected Stories (fic, pub)
Graham Greene. Carving a Statue (dr)
William Haggard. The Antagonists (n)
Wilson Harris. Heartland (n)
Leslie Hartley. The Brickfield (n)
Thomas Hinde. The Day the Call Came (n)
Philip Hobsbaum. The Place's Fault (po)
Molly Holden. The Bright Cloud (po)
John Holloway. The Colours of Clarity (e)
_____. The Lion Hunt (e)
R.C. Hutchinson. A Child Possessed (n)
Ann Jellicoe. The Knack (dr)
_____. The Spot of My Mad Mother (dr)
Elizabeth Jennings. Recoveries (po)
Brian Stanley Johnson. Albert Angelo (n)
Brendan Kennelly. My Dark Fathers (po)
Philip Larkin. The Whitsun Wedding (po)
Doris Lessing. African Stories (fic)
George MacBeth. The Doomsday Show (dr)
Hugh Macdiarmid. The Terrible Crystal: A Vision of Scotland (po)
Sir Compton Mackenzie. My Life and Times. Octave 3, 1900-1907 (auto)
Louis Macneice. The Administrator (dr, pub)
_____. The Mad Islands (dr, pub)
Frank Marcus. The Formation Dancers (dr)
John Masters. Trial at Monomoy (n)
David Mercer. The Generations (dr)
Stanley Middleton. Him They Compelled (n)
Nicholas Monsarrat. A Fair Day's Work (n)
John Montague. Death of a Chieftain and Other Stories (fic)
Iris Murdoch. The Italian Girl (n)
Frank O'Connor. Collection Two (fic)
Anthony Powell. The Valley of Bones (n)
John Cowper Powys. Selected Poems (pub)
J.B. Priestley. Sir Michael and Sir George (n)
Simon Raven. The Rich Pay Late (n)
James Reeves. The Questioning Tiger (po)
Alfred Leslie Rowse. Christopher Marlowe (bio)

Peter Shaffer. The Royal Hunt of the Sun (dr)
John Silkin. Flower Poems (po)
Norman Simpson. The Hole and Other Plays (dr)
David Storey. Flight into Camden (n)
Ronald Thomas. Words and the Poet (e)
Arthur Waley. The Secret History of the Mongols and Other Pieces (ed)
Angus Wilson. Late Call (n)

1965

DEATHS
Winston Churchill
T.S. Eliot
Percy Lubbock
W. Somerset Maugham

WORKS
Brian Aldiss. Best SF Stories of Brian Aldiss (fic)
_____. Earthworks (n)
John Arden. Armstrong's Last Goodnight (dr)
_____. Left-handed Liberty (dr)
Wystan Hugh Auden. About the House (po)
Gavin Bantock. Christ: A Poem in Twenty-Six Parts (po)
George Granville Barker. The True Confessions of George Barker, Book II (auto, po)
Arthur David Beaty. The Gun Garden (n)
_____. Sword of Honour (n)
Samuel Beckett. Play and Two Short Pieces for Radio: Words and Music; Cascandia (dr)
Alan Bold. Society Inebrious (po)
Elizabeth Bowen. A Day in the Dark (fic)
Melvyn Bragg. For Want of a Nail (n)
George Mackay Brown. The Year of the Whale (po)
George Bruce. To Scotland (dr)
George Buchanan. War Song (dr)
Basil Bunting. Loquitur (po)
William Hamilton Canaway. Crows in a Green Tree (n)
Bob Cobbing. Sound Poems. An ABC in Sound (po)
Cyril Connolly. The Modern Movement, 1880-1920 (e)
Tony Connor. Lodgers (po)
_____. 12 Secret Poems (po)
Anthony Conran. Stelae (po)
Cecil Day-Lewis. The Lyrical Impulse (e)
Paul Dehn. The Fern on the Rock (po)
Margaret Drabble. The Millstone (n)
T.S. Eliot. To Criticize the Critic (e)
D. J. Enright. Figures of Speech (n)
_____. The Old Adam (po)
E.M. Forster. Collected Short Stories (pub)
H.W. Fowler. A Dictionary of Modern English Usage, 2nd ed (ref)
Gillian Freeman. The Leader (n)
Roy Fuller. Buff (po)
_____. My Child, My Sister (n)
David Gascoyne. Collected Poems (pub)
Brian Glanville. The King of Hackney Marshes (fic)
_____. A Second Home (n)

William Golding. The Hot Gates (e)
Robert Graves. Collected Poems (pub)
William Haggard. The Powder Barrel (n)
Wilson Harris. The Eye of the Scarecrow (n)
Thomas Hinde. Games of Chance: The Interviewer and the Investigator (n)
Philip Hobsbaum. Snapshots (po)
John Holloway. Wood and Windfall (po)
Geoffrey Household. Olura (n)
Emyr Humphreys. Outside the House of Baal (n)
Hammond Innes. The Strode Venturer (n)
Elizabeth Jennings. Christianity and Poetry (e)
John B. Keane. The Field (dr)
Brendan Kennelly. Up and At It (po)
James Kirkup. Japan Marine (po)
D.H. Lawrence. Complete Plays (pub)
John LeCarre. The Looking-Glass War (n)
John Lehmann. Christ the Hunter (po)
Doris Lessing. Landlocked (n)
Henry Livings. Eh? (dr)
David Lodge. The British Museum Is Falling Down (n)
Michael Longley. Ten Poems (po)
Edward Lowbury. New Poems (po)
George MacBeth. The Calf (po)
_____. A Doomsday Book: Poems and Poem-Games (po)
_____. Missile Commander (po)
_____. The Twelve Hotels (po)
Norman MacCaig. Measures (po)
Hugh Macdiarmid. The Fire of the Spirit (po)
_____. The Ministry of Water (po)
Sir Compton Mackenzie. My Life and Times. Octave 4, 1907-1915 (auto)
Louis Macneice. The Strings Are False (auto, pub)
_____. Varieties of Parable (e, pub)
Derek Mahon. Twelve Poems (po)
Frank Marcus. The Killing of Sister George (dr)
John Masters. Fourteen Eighteen (n)
Aubrey Menen. A Conspiracy of Women (n)
Christopher Middleton. Nonsequences: Selfpoems (po)
Nicholas Monsarrat. The Pillow Fight (n)
Iris Murdoch. The Red and the Green (n)
Harold Pinter. The Birthday Party, rev (dr)
_____. The Homecoming (dr)
J.B. Priestley. Lost Empires (n)
John Osborne. Inadmissable Evidence (dr)
Kathleen Raine. The Hollow Hill and Other Poems, 1960-1964 (po)
Simon Raven. Friends in Low Places (n)
Alan Ross. North from Sicily: Poems, 1961-1964 (po)
Vernon Scannell. The Big Time (n)
_____. Walking Wounded (po)
Peter Shaffer. Black Comedy (dr)
Alan Sillitoe. The Death of William Posters (n)
_____. A Falling Out of Love (po)
Charles Hubert Sisson. Christopher Homm (n)
_____. Numbers (po)
Ian Crichton Smith. The Law and the Grace (po)
Sydney Goodsir Smith. Kynd Kittock's Land (po)

Muriel Spark. The Mandelbaum Gate (n)
Stephen Spender. Selected Poems (pub)
John Wain. The Living World of Shakespeare (e)
_____. Sprightly Running, rev (auto)
_____. Wildtrack (po)
_____. The Young Visitors (n)
Auberon Waugh. Who Are the Violets Now? (n)
Evelyn Waugh. Sword of Honour (n)
Hugo Williams. Symptoms of Love (po)
David Wright. Adam at Evening (po)

1966

DEATHS
Evelyn Waugh

EVENTS
New Abbey Theatre, Dublin (op)

WORKS
Brian Aldiss. The Saliva Tree (fic)
Wystan Hugh Auden. Collected Shorter Poems, 1927-1957 (pub)
George Granville Barker. Dreams of a Summer Night (po)
Nina Bawden. A Little Love, a Little Learning (n)
Francis Berry. Ghosts of Greenland (po)
John Betjeman. High and Low (po)
David Black. Theory of Diet (po)
Alan Bold. The Voyage (po)
Edward Bond. Saved (dr)
Melvyn Bragg. The Second Inheritance (n)
Christine Brooke-Rose. Such (n)
George Mackay Brown. The Five Voyages of Arnor (po)
Basil Bunting. Briggflatts (po)
David Compton. Little Brother, Little Sister (dr)
William Hamilton Canaway. The Grey Seas of Jutland (n)
Austin Clarke. Mnemosyne Lay in Dust (po)
Bob Cobbing. Eyearun (po)
Anthony Conran. Collected Poems, to 1967 (po)
_____. Guernica (po)
Cecil Day-Lewis. The Room and Other Poems (po)
Len Deighton. The Billion Dollar Brain (n)
Monica Dickens. The Room Upstairs (n)
Maureen Duffy. The Microcosm (n)
_____. The Silk Room (dr)
Elaine Feinstein. In a Green Eye (po)
John Fowles. The Magus (n)
David Gill. Men without Evenings (po)
Brian Glanville. A Roman Marriage (n)
Duncan Glen. Stanes (po)
Robert Graves. Seventeen Poems (po, pub)
Graham Greene. The Comedians (n)
John Clive Hall. The Burning Hare (po)
Leslie Hartley. The Betrayal (n)
Thomas Hinde. The Village (n)
Philip Hobsbaum. In Retreat (po)
David Holbrook. Flesh Wounds (n)

THE TWENTIETH CENTURY 287

John Holloway. Widening Horizons in English Verse (e)
A.E. Housman. Complete Poems (pub)
Christopher Isherwood. Exhumations (e)
Ann Jellicoe. Shelley, or the Idealist (dr)
Elizabeth Jennings. The Mind Has Mountains (po)
Brian Stanley Johnson. Trawl (n)
Geoffrey Household. Sabres on the Sand (fic)
Brendan Kennelly. Collection One: Getting Up Early (po)
Thomas Kinsella. Wormwood (po)
D.H. Lawrence. Phoenix II (e, pub)
Christopher Logue. Logue's ABC (po)
George MacBeth. The Castle (po)
_____. The Humming Bird: A Monodrama (po)
Norman MacCaig. Surroundings (po)
Hugh Macdiarmid. The Company I've Kept (auto)
Louis Macneice. Collected Poems (pub)
Sir Compton Mackenzie. My Life and Times. Octave 5, 1915-1923 (auto)
John McGahern. The Dark (n)
Stanley Middleton. Terms of Reference (n)
Nicholas Monsarrat. Something To Hide (n)
John Montague. All Legendary Obstacles (po)
_____. Patriotic Suite (po)
Iris Murdoch. The Time of the Angels (n)
Norman Nicholson. Selected Poems (po)
Sean O'Faolain. The Heat of the Day (fic)
John Osborne. A Bond Honoured (dr)
_____. A Patriot for Me (dr)
Wilfred Owen. Collected Poems (pub)
Anthony Powell. The Soldier's Art (n)
J.B. Priestley. Salt Is Leaving (n)
Simon Raven. Royal Foundation and Other Plays (dr, pub)
_____. The Sabre Squadron (n)
Peter Redgrove. The Force (po)
_____. The Gold-Trap (po)
Jean Rhys. Wide Sargasso Sea (n)
Alfred Leslie Rowse. The Churchills: The Story of a Family (bio)
_____. Bosworth Field and the Wars of the Roses (his)
William Sansom. Goodbye (n)
_____. The Ulcerated Milkman (fic)
Jon Silkin. Poems New and Selected (po)
Alan Sillitoe. The Ragman's Daughter (dr)
Norman Simpson. The Cresta Run (dr)
Charles Hubert Sisson. Catullus (po)
Stevie Smith. More Selected Poems (pub)
Tom Stoppard. Rosencrantz and Guildenstern Are Dead (dr)
Ronald Thomas. Pieta (po)
Charles Tomlinson. American Scenes (po)
John Wain. Death of the Hind Legs (fic)
H.G. Wells. Experiment in Autobiography, 2 vols (auto, pub)
Arnold Wesker. The Four Seasons (dr)
_____. Their Very Own and Golden City (dr)
David Wright. Poems (po)
William Butler Yeats. Complete Plays, Variorum (pub)

1967

DEATHS

John Masefield
Michael Francis O'Donovan ("Frank O'Connor")
Siegfried Sassoon
Vernon Watkins

WORKS
  Fleur Adcock. Tigers (po)
  Brian Aldiss. An Age (n)
  Eric Ambler. Dirty Story (n)
  Kingsley Amis. The James Bond Dossier (e)
  _____. A Look around the Estate (po)
  John Arden. Soldier, Soldier (dr)
  Enid Bagnold. Call Me Jacky (dr)
  Beryl Bainbridge. A Weekend with Claude (n)
  Nina Bawden. A Woman of My Age (n)
  Patricia Beer. Just Like the Resurrection (po)
  Anne Beresford. Walking without Moving (po)
  David Black. With Decorum (po)
  Alan Bold. To Find the New (po)
  Martin Booth. Paper Pennies (po)
  Brigid Brophy. The Burglar (dr)
  Alan Brownjohn. The Lions' Mouths (po)
  George Bruce. Landscapes and Figures (po)
  Jim Burns. My Sad Story (po)
  William Hamilton Canaway. The Mules of Borgo San Marco (n)
  Agatha Christie. Endless Night (n)
  Leonard Clark. Fields and Territories (po)
  Austin Clarke. Old Fashioned Pilgrimage (po)
  Jack Clemo. Cactus on Carmel (po)
  Bob Cobbing. Kurrirrurriri (po)
  Barry Cole. Blood Ties (po)
  Laurence Collinson. Who Is Wheeling Grandma? (po)
  Stewart Conn. The Chinese Tower (po)
  _____. I Didn't Always Live Here (dr)
  _____. The King (dr)
  _____. Thunder in the Air (po)
  Rhys Davies. The Chosen One and Other Stories (fic)
  Len Deighton. An Expensive Place to Die (n)
  Margaret Drabble. Jerusalem the Golden (n)
  Maureen Duffy. The Paradox Players (n)
  Daphne Du Maurier. The Flight of the Falcon (n)
  Nell Dunn. Poor Cow (n)
  Maurice Edelman. Shark Island (n)
  John Fuller. The Tree That Walked (po)
  Brian Glanville. The Artist Type (n)
  Duncan Glen. Idols: When Alexander Our King Was Dead (po)
  William Golding. The Pyramid (n)
  Walter Greenwood. There Was a Time (auto)
  Geoffrey Grigson. A Skull in Salop (po)
  Thom Gunn. Touch (po)
  William Haggard. The Conspirators (n)
  Wilson Harris. The Waiting Room (n)
  David Holbrook. Object Relations (po)
  Gerard Manley Hopkins. Poems (pub)
  Geoffrey Household. The Courtesy of Death (n)
  Ted Hughes. Wodwo (po)
  Christopher Isherwood. A Meeting by the River (n)

Ann Jellicoe. Some Unconscious Influence in the Theatre (e)
Patrick Joseph Kavanagh. On the Way to the Depot (po)
Brendan Kennelly. The Florentines (n)
_____. Good Souls To Survive (po)
Thomas Kinsella. Nightwalker (po)
Christopher Logue. Pax (po, trans)
George MacBeth. The Colour of Blood (po)
_____. The Screens (po)
Hugh Macdiarmid. A Lap of Honour (po)
John Masters. The Breaking Strain (n)
Roger McGough. Frinck: A Life in the Day of, and Summer with, Monika (po, fic)
David Mercer. Belcher's Luck (dr)
_____. The Parachute (dr)
Charles Ewart Milne. Time Stopped: A Poem Sequence (po)
John Montague. A Chosen Light (po)
_____. Home Again (po)
Robert Morgan. The Night's Vision (po, dr)
Peter Nichols. A Day in the Death of Joe Egg (dr)
Norman Nicholson. No Star on the Way Back (po)
Harold Pinter. The Tea Party and Other Plays (dr)
J.B. Priestley. It's an Old Country (n)
John Pudney. Spill Out: Poems and Ballads (po)
Simon Raven. Fielding Gray (n)
James Reeves. Selected Poems (po)
Alan Ross. Poems, 1942-1967 (po)
Alfred Leslie Rowse. Cornish Stories (fic)
_____. Poems of Cornwall and America (po)
Alan Sillitoe. A Tree on Fire (n)
Charles Hubert Sisson. The Discarnation; or, How the Flesh Became Word and Dwelt among Us (po)
Jon Stallworthy. The Almond Tree (po)
_____. A Day in the City (po)
David Storey. The Restoration of Arnold Middleton (n)
Anthony Thwaite. The Stones of Emptiness: Poems, 1963-1966 (po)
John Tolkien. Smith of Wooton Manner (n)
John Wain. The Smaller Sky (n)
Rex Warner. The Converts (n)
Laurence Whistler. To Celebrate Her Living (po)
John Stuart Williams. Green Rain (po)
Angus Wilson. No Laughing Matter (n)

1968

DEATHS
  Sir Herbert Read

EVENTS
  Cecil Day-Lewis, Poet Laureate of England, to 1972

WORKS
  Dannie Abse. A Small Desperation (po)
  Brian Aldiss. Report on Probability A (n)
  Alfred Alvarez. Lost (po)
  Kingsley Amis. I Want It Now (n)
  John Arden. The True History of Squire Jonathan and His Unfortunate Treasure (dr)

Wystan Hugh Auden. Collected Longer Poems (pub)
_____. Secondary Worlds (e)
Beryl Bainbridge. Another Part of the Wood (n)
Gavin Bantock. Juggernaut (po)
_____. The Last of the Kings: Frederick the Great (dr)
George Granville Barker. The Golden Chains (po)
Nina Bawden. The Grain of Truth (n)
Anne Beresford. The Lair (po)
Edward Bond. Early Morning (dr)
_____. Narrow Road to the Deep North (dr)
Martin Booth. Supplication to the Himalayas (po)
John Braine. The Crying Game (n)
Christine Brooke-Rose. Between (n)
George Mackay Brown. A Calendar of Love (fic)
Anthony Burgess. Enderby Outside (n)
Charles Causley. Ballad of the Bread Man (po)
_____. Underneath the Water (po)
Austin Clarke. The Echo at Coole (po)
_____. A Sermon on Swift (po)
Bob Cobbing. SO: Six Sound Poems (po)
Barry Cole. Moonsearch (po)
_____. A Run across the Island (n)
_____. Ulysses in the Town of Coloured Glass (po)
Stewart Conn. Broche (dr)
_____. Stoats in the Sunlight (po)
Tony Connor. Kon in Springtime (po)
Peter Dale. The Storms (po)
Len Deighton. Only When I Larf (n)
Monica Dickens. The Landlord's Daughter (n)
Basil Dowling. Hatherley: Recollective Lyrics (po)
Maureen Duffy. Lyrics for the Dog Hour (po)
Lawrence Durrell. Collected Poems (pub)
_____. Tunc (n)
D.J. Enright. Unlawful Assembly (po)
John Fuller. The Art of Love (po)
Roy Fuller. New Poems (po)
Rumer Godden. Swans and Turtles (fic)
Robert Graves. Poems (pub)
William Haggard. A Cool Day for Killing (n)
Wilson Harris. Tumatumari (n)
Leslie Hartley. Collected Stories (pub); Poor Clare (n)
_____. The Novelist's Responsibility (e)
John Heath-Stubbs. Satires and Epigrams (po)
Geoffrey Hill. King Log (po)
Thomas Hinde. High (n)
Molly Holden. To Make Me Grieve (po)
James Hanley. It Wasn't Me (dr)
John Holloway. Blake: The Lyric Poetry (e)
Geoffrey Household. Dance of the Dwarfs (n)
Emyr Humphreys. Natives (fic)
Patrick Joseph Kavanagh. A Song and Dance (n)
Brendan Kennelly. Dream of a Black Fox (po)
James Kirkup. Windows: Poems from Japan (po)
Arthur Koestler. Drinkers of Infinity: Essays, 1955-1967 (e)
John Le Carre. A Small Town in Germany (n)
Laurence Lerner. A Free Man (n)

THE TWENTIETH CENTURY   291

Emanuel Litvinoff. The Man Next Door (n)
Henry Livings. Good Grief (dr)
Michael Longley. Secret Marriages (po)
Edward Lowbury. Daylight Astronomy (po)
George MacBeth. The Night of Stones (po)
Norman MacCaig. Rings on a Tree (po)
Hugh Macdiarmid. Early Lyrics (po, pub)
Derek Mahon. Night-Crossing (po)
Stanley Middleton. The Golden Evening (n)
Nicholas Monsarrat. Richer Than All His Tribe (n)
Robert Morgan. Poems and Extracts (po)
Iris Murdoch. The Nice and the Good (n)
George Orwell. Collected Essays, Journalism and Letters, 4 vols (pub)
John Osborne. A Hotel in Amsterdam (dr)
_____. Time Present (dr)
Harold Pinter. Poems (pub)
Ezra Pound. Collected Shorter Poems (pub)
J.B. Priestley. The Image Men (n)
Kathleen Raine. Six Dreams and Other Poems (po)
_____. Ninfa Revisited (po)
Simon Raven. The Case of Father Brendan (dr)
_____. The Judas Boy (n)
Peter Redgrove. The Old White Man (po)
Alexander Scott. Cantripes (po)
Tom Scott. At the Shrine o the Unkent Sodger: A Poem for Recitation
           (po)
Alan Sillitoe. Guzman Go Home (fic)
_____. Love in the Environs of Voronezh (po)
_____. Shaman (po)
Norman Simpson. Some Tall Tinkles (dr)
Charles Hubert Sisson. Metamorphoses (po)
_____. Roman Poems (po)
Ian Crichton Smith. At Helensburgh (po)
_____. Consider the Lilies (n)
Sydney Goodsir Smith. Girl with Violin (po)
C.P. Snow. A Sleep of Reason (n)
Muriel Spark. The Public Image (n)
Donald Michael Thomas. Two Voices (po)
Ronald Thomas. The Mountains (po)
_____. Not That He Brought Flowers (po)
Sydney Tremayne. The Turning Sky (po)
Vernon Watkins. Fidelities (po)
Auberon Waugh. Consider the Lilies (n)
Laurence Whistler. On Llangynidr Bridge (po)

                              1969

DEATHS
  Ivy Compton-Burnett
  Sir Osbert Sitwell

WORKS
  Dannie Abse. Demo (po)
  _____. The Dogs of Pavlov (dr)
  Brian Aldiss. Barefoot in the Head (n)
  _____. A Brian Aldiss Omnibus (fic)

_____. Intangibles, Inc. (fic)
Eric Ambler. The Intercom Conspiracy (n)
Wystan Hugh Auden. City without Walls (po)
Gavin Bantock. A New Thing Breathing (po)
George Granville Barker. At Thurgarton Church (po)
Samuel Beckett. Film (dr)
David Black. The Educators (po)
Alan Bold. A Perpetual Motion Machine (po)
_____. The State of the Nation (po)
Martin Booth. In the Yenan Caves (po)
Keith Bosley. The Possibility of Angels (po)
Melvyn Bragg. Without a City Wall (n)
Howard Brenton. Revenge (dr)
Edwin Brock. Fred's Primer: A Little Girl's Guide to the World around Her (po)
Brigid Brophy. In Transit (n)
George Mackay Brown. A Time to Keep (fic)
Alan Brownjohn. Being a Garoon (po)
_____. A Day by Indirections (po)
_____. Sandgrains on a Tray (po)
_____. Woman Reading Aloud (po)
Michael Bullock. A Savage Darkness (po)
_____. Sixteen Stories As They Happened (fic)
Jim Burns. The Store of Things (po)
Charles Causley. Figure of 8: Narrative Terms (po)
William Hamilton Canaway. A Moral Obligation (n)
Bob Cobbing. Octo: Visual Poems (po)
_____. Whisper Piece (po)
_____. Whississippi (po)
_____. Why Shiva Has Ten Arms (po)
Barry Cole. Joseph Winter's Patronage (n)
Stewart Conn. Fancy Seeing You, Then (dr)
Robert Conquest. Arias from a Love Opera (po)
Anthony Conran. Claim, Claim, Claim (po)
Margaret Drabble. Bird of Paradise (dr)
_____. The Waterfall (n)
Donald Davie. Essex Poems, 1963-1967 (pub)
Maureen Duffy. Rites (dr)
_____. Wounds (n)
Daphne Du Maurier. The House on the Strand (n)
Douglas Dunn. Terry Street (po)
Maurice Edelman. All on a Summer's Night (n)
T.S. Eliot. Complete Poems and Plays (pub)
Gillian Freeman. Pursuit (dr)
John Fowles. The French Lieutenant's Woman (n)
John Fuller. The Labours of Hercules (po)
Brian Glanville. A Betting Man (fic)
_____. The Olympian (n)
Duncan Glen. Kythings (po)
_____. Sunny Summer Sunday Afternoon in the Park? (po)
Rumer Godden. In This House of Brede (n)
Graham Greene. Collected Essays (pub)
_____. Travels with My Aunt (n)
Geoffrey Grigson. Ingestion of Ice-Cream (po)
Leslie Hartley. The Love-Adept (n)
Reyner Heppenstall. The Shearers (n)

Philip Hobsbaum. Come Out Fighting (po)
_____. Some Lovely Glorious Nothing (po)
David Holbrook. Old World, New World (po)
R.C. Hutchinson. Johanna at Daybreak (n)
Brian Stanley Johnson. The Unfortunates (n)
David Jones. The Tribune's Visitation (po)
John B. Keane. Big Maggie (dr)
Brendan Kennelly. Selected Poems (po)
Thomas Kinsella. Tear (po)
James Kirkup. Japan Physical (po)
Laurence Lerner. Selves (po)
Doris Lessing. The Four-Gated City (n)
Henry Livings. Honour and Offer (dr)
Christopher Logue. New Numbers (po)
Michael Longley. No Continuing City: Poems, 1963-1968 (po)
Edward Lowbury. Figures of Eight (po)
George MacBeth. A Death (po)
_____. A War Quartet (po)
_____. Zoo's Who (po)
Norman MacCaig. A Man in My Position (po)
Hugh Macdiarmid. A Clyack Sheaf (po)
_____. Selected Essays (pub)
Colin MacInnes. Visions of London (n, pub)
Roger McGough. Watchwords (po)
Christopher Middleton. Our Flowers and Nice Bones (po)
Stanley Middleton. Wages of Virtue (n)
Robert Morgan. Voices in the Dark (po)
Iris Murdoch. Bruno's Dream (n)
Peter Nichols. The National Health (dr)
Frank O'Connor. Collection Three (fic, pub)
Harold Pinter. Landscape and Silence (dr)
_____. Night (dr)
Ezra Pound. Cantos cx-cxvii (po)
Victor Pritchett. Blind Love (fic)
John Pudney. Spandrels: Poems and Ballads (po)
Kathleen Raine. A Question of Poetry (po)
James Reeves. Subsong (po)
William Sansom. The Vertical Ladder (fic)
Vernon Scannell. Epithets of War: Poems, 1965-1969 (po)
Ian Crichton Smith. The Last Summer (n)
Sydney Goodsir Smith. Fifteen Poems and a Play (po, dr)
Johnny Speight. The Salesman (dr)
John Stallworthy. Positives (po)
_____. Root and Branch (po)
David Storey. In Celebration (dr)
Charles Tomlinson. The Way of a World (po)
John Wain. Letters to Five Artists (po)
Laurence Whistler. Way: Two Affirmations (po)
Hugo Williams. Poems (po)
Angus Wilson. Death Dance: 25 Stories (fic)
David Wright. Nerve Ends (po)

1970

DEATHS
E.M. Forster
Bertrand Russell

Dannie Abse. O. Jones, O. Jones (n)
Brian Aldiss. The Hand-Reared Boy (n)
_____. The Moment of Eclipse (fic)
_____. Neanderthal Planet (fic)
Gavin Bantock. Ankaga (po)
Nina Bawden. The Birds on the Trees (n)
Samuel Beckett. Mercier and Camier (n)
Martin Bell. Letters from Cyprus (po)
Frances Bellerby. The Sheltering Water (po)
Martin Booth. The Borrowed Gull: After Virginia Woolf (po)
Melvyn Bragg. A Place in England (n)
John Braine. Stay with Me Till Morning (n)
Howard Brenton. Christie in Love (dr)
_____. Wesley (dr)
Edwin Brock. A Cold Day at the Zoo (po)
Christine Brooke-Rose. Go When You See the Green Man Walking (fic)
Michael Dennis Browne. The Wife of Winter (po)
Alan Brownjohn. Frateretto Calling (po)
_____. Synopsis (po)
George Buchanan. Annotations (po)
Basil Bunting. Collected Poems (pub)
Leonard Clark. Walking with Trees (po)
Austin Clarke. Orphide (po)
Bob Cobbing. Etcetera: A New Collection of Found and Sound Poems (po)
_____. Kris Kringles Kesmes Korals (po)
_____. Kwatz (po)
_____. Sonic Icons (po)
Barry Cole. The Search for Rita (n)
_____. The Visitors (po)
Stewart Conn. Victims (dr)
Peter Dale. Mortal Fire (po)
Donald Davie. Six Epistles to Eva Hesse (po)
Len Deighton. Bomber (n)
Monica Dickens. The Listeners (n)
Patric Dickinson. More Than Time (po)
Maureen Duffy. Solo, Olde Thyme (dr)
Lawrence Durrell. Nunquam (n)
Elain Feinstein. The Circle (n)
Michael Frayn. The Two of Us (dr)
Gillian Freeman. The Alabaster Egg (n)
Christopher Fry. A Yard of Sun (dr)
John Fuller. Annotations of Giant's Town (po)
_____. The Wreck (po)
Roy Fuller. The Carnal Island (n)
_____. To an Unknown Reader (po)
David Gascoyne. Collected Verse Translations (pub)
_____. Sun at Midnight (po)
David Gill. The Pagoda (po)
Brian Glanville. A Cry of Cricketts (n)
Duncan Glen. Underneath the Bed (po)
Robert Graves. Advice from a Mother (po)
_____. Poems, 1945-1968 (pub)
Wilson Harris. Ascent to Omai (n)
_____. The Sleepers of Roraima (fic)
Leslie Hartley. My Sister's Keeper (n)
John Heath-Stubbs. Artorius (po)

Thomas Hinde. Bird (n)
John Holloway. New Poems (po)
Ted Hughes. Crow (po)
Christopher Isherwood. A Meeting by the River (n)
Ann Jellicoe. The Giveaway (dr)
Elizabeth Jennings. Hurt (po)
──────────. Lucidities (po)
Patrick Joseph Kavanagh. About Time (po)
Brendan Kennelly. A Drinking Cup: Poems for the Irish (po)
James Kirkup. White Shadows, Black Shadows: Poems of Peace and War (po)
Philip Larkin. All What Jazz? A Record Diary, 1961-1966 (e, nar)
──────────. The Explosion (po)
David Lodge. Out of the Shelter (n)
George MacBeth. The Bamboo Nightingale (po)
──────────. The Burning Cone (po)
──────────. The Hiroshima Dream (po)
Norman MacCaig. Midnights (po)
Hugh Macdiarmid. More Collected Poems (pub)
──────────. Selected Poems (pub)
Colin MacInnes. Three Years to Play (n)
Derek Mahon. Beyond Howth Head (po)
──────────. Ecclesiastes (po)
John Masters. The Rock (n)
David Mercer. After Haggerty (dr)
──────────. Flint (dr)
──────────. On the Eve of Publication (dr)
Christopher Middleton. The Fossil Fish: 15 Micropoems (po)
Stanley Middleton. Apple of the Eye (n)
John Mole. The Instruments (po)
John Montague. Tides (po)
Sean O'Faolain. The Talking Trees (fic)
Iris Murdoch. A Fairly Honourable Defeat (n)
John Osborne. The Right Prospectus (dr)
Victor Pritchett. George Meredith and English Comedy (e)
Simon Raven. Places Where They Sing (n)
Peter Redgrove. The Mother, the Daughter and the Sighing Bridge (po)
──────────. The Shirt, the Skull, and the Grape (po)
Vernon Scannell. Mastering the Craft (po)
Peter Shaffer. The Battle of Shrivings (dr)
Alan Sillitoe. A Start in Life (n)
──────────. This Foreign Field (dr)
Ian Crichton Smith. From Bourgeois Land (po)
──────────. Selected Poems (po)
──────────. Survival without Errors (fic)
C.P. Snow. Last Things (n)
Muriel Spark. The Driver's Seat (n)
Jon Stallworthy. A Dinner of Herbs (po)
David Storey. The Contractor (dr)
──────────. Home (dr)
John Wain. A Winter in the Hills (n)
Arnold Wesker. The Friends (dr)
Hugo Williams. Sugar Daddy (po)
John Stuart Williams. Dic Penderyn and Other Poems (po)
Angus Wilson. The World of Charles Dickens (his, biog)
Charles Wood. Colliers Wood (dr)

1971

DEATHS
Florence Margaret Smith ("Stevie Smith")

WORKS
Fleur Adcock. High Tide in the Garden (po)
Brian Aldiss. Omnibus 2 (fic)
_____. A Soldier Erect; or, Further Adventures of the Hand-Reared Boy (n)
Alfred Alvarez. Apparition (po)
Kingsley Amis. Girl '70 (n)
John Arden. The Bagman (dr)
George Granville Barker. Poems of Places and People (po)
Arthur David Beaty. The Temple Tree (n)
Patricia Beer. The Estuary (po)
Francis Berry. The Near Singing Dome (dr)
John Betjeman. A Wembley Lad and the Crem (po)
Thomas Blackburn. The Feast of the Wolf (po)
_____. The Fourth Man (po)
Alan Bold. The Auld Symie (po)
_____. A Century of People (po)
_____. He Will Be Greatly Missed (po)
_____. A Pint of Bitter (po)
Edward Bond. Lear (dr)
Martin Booth. The Crying Embers (po)
_____. A Winnowing of Silence (po)
Melvyn Bragg. The Nerve (n)
George Mackay Brown. Fishermen with Ploughs (po)
_____. Lifeboat (po)
Alan Brownjohn. An Equivalent (po)
_____. Transformation Scene (po)
George Buchanan. Naked Reason (n)
Michael Bullock. Green Beginning Black Ending (fic)
Anthony Burgess. MF (n)
William Hamilton Canaway. A Declaration of Independence (n)
_____. Roll Me Over (dr)
Leonard Clark. All Along Down Along (po)
_____. Every Voice (po)
Austin Clarke. Tiresias (po)
Jack Clemo. The Echoing Tip (po)
Bob Cobbing. Beethoven Today (po)
_____. Five Visual Poems (po)
_____. The Judith Poem (po)
_____. Konkrete Canticle (po)
_____. Poster No. 2 (po)
_____. Spearhead (po)
_____. Three Poems for Voice and Movement (po)
Barry Cole. The Giver (n)
_____. Vanessa in the City (po)
Stewart Conn. The Burning (dr)
Tony Connor. Billy's Wonderful Kettle (dr)
_____. I am Real and So Are You (dr)
_____. In the Happy Valley (po)
Lettice Cooper. Late in the Afternoon (n)
William Cooper. You Want the Right Frame of Reference (n)

Rhys Davies. Nobody Answered the Bell (n)
Len Deighton. Declarations of War (fic)
Basil Dowling. A Little Gallery of Characters (po)
Maureen Duffy. Love Child (n)
_____. The Venus Touch (po)
Daphne Du Maurier. Not after Midnight (fic)
Douglas Dunn. Backwaters (po)
_____. Night (po)
Nell Dunn. The Incurable (n)
Lawrence Durrell. The Red Limbo Lingo (po)
David Edgar. The National Interest (dr)
D.J. Enright. In the Basilica of the Annunciation (po)
_____. The Typewriter Revolution (po)
E.M. Forster. Maurice (n, pub)
Michael Frayn. The Sandboy (dr)
Elaine Feinstein. The Magic Apple Tree (po)
Duncan Glen. Clydesdale (po)
_____. Feres (po)
_____. In Appearances (po)
William Golding. The Scorpion God (fic)
Winston Graham. The Japanese Girl (fic)
Robert Graves. The Green-Sailed Vessel (po)
Graham Greene. A Sort of Life: Autobiography (auto)
Geoffrey Grigson. Discoveries of Bones and Stones (po)
Thom Gunn. Moly (po)
Wilson Harris. The Age of the Rainmakers (fic)
Leslie Hartley. The Harness Room (n)
Geoffrey Hill. Mercian Hymns (po)
Molly Holden. Air and Chill Earth (po)
_____. A Tenancy of Flint (n)
Geoffrey Household. Doom's Caravan (n)
Roger Howard. Slaughter and Other Plays (dr)
Emyr Humphreys. National Winner (n)
R.C. Hutchinson. Origins of Kathleen: A Diversion (pub)
Hammond Innes. Levkas Man (pub)
Brian Stanley Johnson. House Mother Normal (n)
Brendan Kennelly. Bread (po)
James Kirkup. A Berwick Bestiary (po)
_____. The Body Servant: Poems of Exile (po)
_____. Broad Daylight (po)
_____. Transmental Vibrations (po)
John LeCarre. The Naive and Sentimental Lover (n)
John Lehmann. Photograph (po)
Doris Lessing. Briefing for a Descent into Hell (n)
Henry Livings. Pongo Plays, 1-6 (dr)
George MacBeth. Collected Poems, 1958-1970 (po)
_____. The Orlando Poems (po)
Norman MacCaig. Selected Poems (po)
John McGahern. Nightlines (fic)
Roger McGough. After the Merrymaking (po)
Stanley Middleton. Brazen Prison (n)
Robert Morgan. The Master Miners (dr)
Iris Murdoch. An Accidental Man (n)
Peter Nichols. Forget-Me-Not Lane (pub)
John Osborne. Very Like a Whale (dr)
_____. West of Suez (dr)

Basil Payne. Love in the Afternoon (po)
Gilbert Phelps. Tenants of the House (n)
Anthony Powell. Books Do Furnish a Room (n)
John Pudney. The Long Time Growing Up (n)
_____. Take This Orange (po)
Kathleen Raine. The Lost Country (po)
Simon Raven. Sound the Retreat (n)
Peter Redgrove. The Bedside Clock (po)
_____. Love's Journeys: A Selection (po)
Alan Ross. A Calcutta Grandmother (po)
Alfred Leslie Rowse. The Elizabethan Renaissance, to 1972 (his)
William Sansom. Hans Feet in Love (n)
Vernon Scannell. Company of Women (po)
_____. Selected Poems (po)
Alexander Scott. Greek Fire (po)
Jon Silkin. Amana Grass (po)
_____. Killhope Wheel (po)
Alan Sillitoe. Travels in Nihilon (n)
Ian Crichton Smith. My Last Duchess (n)
Muriel Spark. Not to Disturb (n)
Stephen Spender. The Generous Days (po)
Donald Michael Thomas. Logan Stone (po)
John Wain. The Life Guard (fic)
E.A. Whitehead. The Foursome (dr)

1972

DEATHS
  Cecil Day-Lewis
  Leslie Hartley
  Ezra Pound

EVENTS
  John Betjeman, Poet Laureate of England

WORKS
  Dannie Abse. The Courting of Essie Glass (dr)
  Alfred Alvarez. The Legacy (po)
  Eric Ambler. The Green Circle Incident (n)
  _____. The Levanter (n)
  Kingsley Amis. Dear Illusion (fic)
  Beryl Bainbridge. Harriet Said (n)
  Gavin Bantock. Gleeman (po)
  George Granville Barker. III Hallucination Poems (po)
  Nina Bawden. Anna Apparent (n)
  Anne Beresford. The Courtship (po)
  _____. Footsteps in Snow (po)
  _____. Modern Fairy Tale (po)
  David Black. The Old Hag (po)
  Martin Booth. Nature Study (po)
  _____. On the Death of Archbishop Broix (po)
  _____. Pilgrims and Petitions (po)
  _____. Teller (po)
  Keith Bosley. Snake Charm (po)
  Melvyn Bragg. The Hunt (n)
  _____. Josh Lawton (n)

John Braine. The Queen of a Distant Country (n)
Edwin Brock. Invisibility Is the Art of Survival (po)
George Mackay Brown. Greenvoe (n)
Alan Brownjohn. Warrior's Career (po)
George Buchanan. Minute-Book of a City (po)
Michael Bullock. The Island Abode of Bliss (dr)
Anthony Burgess. Joysprick: An Introduction to the Language of James Joyce (e)
Jim Burns. A Single Flower (po)
Donald Campbell. Rhymes 'n Reasons (po)
Leonard Clark. Secret As Toads (po)
──────────. Singing in the Streets (po)
Bob Cobbing. 15 Shakespeare-Kaku (po)
──────────. Songsignals (po)
──────────. Tomatomato (po)
──────────. Trigram (po)
Barry Cole. Doctor Fielder's Common Sense (n)
Stewart Conn. An Ear to the Ground (po)
──────────. A Slight Touch of the Sun (dr)
Tony Connor. A Couple with a Cat (dr)
──────────. The Last of the Feinsteins (dr)
Len Deighton. Close-Up (n)
Basil Dowling. Bedlam: A Mid-Century Satire (po)
Margaret Drabble. The Needle's Eye (n)
Daphne Du Maurier. Rule Britannia (n)
Douglas Dunn. The Happier Life (po)
Lawrence Durrell. On the Suchness of the Old Boy (po)
Maurice Edelman. Disraeli in Love (n)
David Edgar. Rent; or, Caught in the Act (dr)
──────────. State of Emergency (dr)
D.J. Enright. Daughters of Earth (po)
──────────. Foreign Devils (po)
Elaine Feinstein. The Amberstone Exit (n)
──────────. At the Edge (po)
──────────. Matters of Chance (fic)
John Fuller. Boys in a Pie (po)
──────────. Cannibals and Missionaries (po)
Roy Fuller. Song Cycle from a Record Sleeve (po)
Brian Glanville. The Financiers (n)
Duncan Glen. A Journey Past (po)
Robert Graves. Poems: 1970-1972 (po)
Graham Greene. Collected Stories (fic)
James Hanley. Another World (n)
──────────. Leave Us Alone (dr)
Wilson Harris. Black Marsden (n)
Leslie Hartley. The Collections (n)
Thomas Hinde. Generally a Virgin (n)
Philip Hobsbaum. Women and Animals (po)
Molly Holden. White Roses and Wanderer (n)
Geoffrey Household. The Three Sentinels (n)
Ted Hughes. Crow, enl ed (po)
──────────. In the Little Girl's Angel Gaze (po)
Elizabeth Jennings. Relationships (po)
Patrick Joseph Kavanagh. A Happy Man (n)
Brendan Kennelly. Love-Cry (po)
──────────. Salvation (po)

Thomas Kinsella. Finistere (po)
———————. Butcher's Dozen (po)
———————. Notes from the Land of the Dead (po)
———————. A Selected Life (po)
James Kirkup. The Magic Drum (dr)
Arthur Koestler. The Call-Girls: A Tragi-Comedy (n)
Doris Lessing. The Story of a Non-Marrying Man, and Other Stories (fic)
———————. The Temptation of Jack Orkney (fic)
Emanuel Litvinoff. Journey through a Small Planet (fic)
Michael Longley. Lares (po)
George MacBeth. A Farewell (po)
———————. A Litany (po)
———————. Lasus: A Verse Lecture (po)
Derek Mahon. Lives (po)
———————. The Man Who Built His City in Snow (po)
John Masters. The Ravi Lancers (n)
Christopher Middleton. Briefcase History: 9 Poems (po)
Stanley Middleton. Cold Gradations (n)
John Mole. Something about Love (po)
John Montague. The Rough Field (po)
———————. Small Secrets (po)
Robert Morgan. Fragments of a Dream (dr)
Norman Nicholson. A Local Habitation (po)
Peter Nichols. Neither Up nor Down (dr)
John Osborne. The Gift of Friendship (dr)
———————. A Sense of Detachment (dr)
John Pudney. The Little Giant (dr)
Simon Raven. Come Like Shadows (n)
Peter Redgrove. Dr. Faust's Sea-Spiral Spirit (po)
———————. In the Country of the Skin (n)
James Reeves. Poems and Paraphrases (po)
I.A. Richards. Internal Colloquies: Poems and Plays (po, dr)
Alan Ross. Tropical Ice (po)
Alfred Leslie Rowse. Strange Encounter (po)
Alexander Scott. Double Agent (po)
John Peter Scupham. Children Dancing (po)
———————. The Nondescript (po)
———————. The Small Containers (po)
———————. The Snowing Globe (po)
Alan Sillitoe. Raw Material (n)
Sacheverell Sitwell. Agamemnon's Tomb (po)
———————. Rosario d'Arabeschi and Other Poems, 23 vols, to 1974 (po)
———————. To Henry Woodward (po)
———————. Tropicalia (po)
Ian Crichton Smith. Hamlet in Autumn (po)
———————. Love Poems and Elegies (po)
C.P. Snow. The Malcontents (n)
Muriel Spark. The Hothouse by the East River (n)
David Storey. Pasmore (n)
Ronald Thomas. H'm: Poems (po)
Anthony Thwaite. Points (po)
Charles Tomlinson. Written on Water (po)
John Wain. A House for the Truth (e)
———————. The Shape of Feng (po)
Auberon Waugh. A Bed of Flowers; or, As You Like It (n)

Arnold Wesker. The Old Ones (dr)
E.A. Whitehead. Alpha Beta (dr)
Hugo Williams. Cherry Blossom (po)
Ted Willis. Black Beauty (n)
Charles Wood. Veterans; or, Hairs in the Gates of the Hellespont (dr)

1973

DEATHS
Wystan Hugh Auden
Bryan Stanley Johnson
John Tolkien
Henry Vincent Yorke ("Henry Green")

WORKS
Dannie Abse. Funland and Other Poems (po)
Brian Aldiss. The Comic Inferno (fic)
_____. Frankenstein Unbound (n)
Kingsley Amis. The Riverside Villas Murder (n)
Beryl Bainbridge. The Dressmaker (n)
Gavin Bantock. Eirenikon (po)
George Granville Barker. In Memory of David Archer (po)
Samuel Beckett. Eh Joe; Act without Words II; Film (dr)
_____. The North (fic)
Patricia Beer. Spanish Balcony (po)
Alan Bold. A Lunar Event (po)
Edward Bond. Bingo (dr)
_____. The Sea (dr)
Martin Booth. Coronis (po)
Keith Bosley. The Song of Aino (po)
Ronald Bottrall. Day and Night (po)
Edwin Brock. The Portraits and the Poses (po)
Brigid Brophy. The Adventures of God in His Search for the Black Girl
           (n, fic)
George Mackay Brown. Magnus (n)
Michael Bullock. The Black Wings White Dead (po)
Jim Burns. Leben in Preston (po)
William Hamilton Canaway. Harry Doing Good (n)
Austin Clarke. The Impuritans (dr)
_____. The Wooing of Becfola (po)
Bob Cobbing. Alphapitasuite (po)
_____. Circa 73-74 (po)
_____. E colony (po)
_____. In Any Language (po)
Barry Cole. Pathetic Fallacies (po)
Laurence Collinson. Cupid's Crescent (n)
Stewart Conn. The Aquarium (dr)
Tony Connor. Otto's Interview
Lettice Cooper. Tea on Sunday (n)
William Cooper. Love on the Coast (n)
Patric Dickinson. A Wintering Tree (po)
Basil Dowling. The Unreturning Native (po)
Maureen Duffy. I Want to Go to Moscow (n)
_____. A Nightingale in Bloomsbury Square (dr)
Lawrence Durrell. The Black Book (n)
_____. Plant-Magic Man (po)

_____. Vega and Other Poems (po)
D.J. Enright. The Terrible Shears (po)
Elaine Feinstein. The Celebrants (po)
_____. The Glass Alembic (n)
John Fuller. Epistles to Several Persons (po)
_____. Hut Groups (po)
Roy Fuller. Professors and Gods: Last Oxford Lectures on Poetry (e)
_____. Tiny Trees (po)
Brian Glanville. The Thing He Loves (fic)
Winston Graham. The Black Moon: A Novel of Cornwall, 1794-1799 (n)
Robert Graves. Deya (po)
_____. Timeless Meeting (po)
Graham Greene. The Honorary Consul (n)
Geoffrey Grigson. The First Folio (po)
_____. Sad Grave of an Imperial Mongoose (po)
William Haggard. The Old Masters (n)
John Clive Hall. A House of Voices (po)
James Hanley. Darkness (fic)
_____. A Woman in the Sky (n)
Leslie Hartley. The Will and the Way (n)
Molly Holden. Reivers' Weather (n)
Geoffrey Household. The Lives and Times of Bernard Brown (n)
Richard Hughes. The Wooden Shepherdess (n)
Hammond Innes. Golden Soak (n)
Brian Stanley Johnson. Christie Mabry's Own Double-Entry (n)
Brendan Kennelly. The Voices (po)
Thomas Kinsella. The Good Fight (po)
_____. New Poems (po)
_____. Selected Poems, 1956-1968 (po)
_____. Vertical Man (po)
Doris Lessing. The Summer before the Dark (n)
_____. The Sun between Their Feet (fic)
_____. This Was the Old Chief's Country (fic)
Emanuel Litvinoff. A Death Out of Season (n)
_____. Notes for a Survivor (po)
Michael Longley. An Exploded View: Poems, 1968-1972 (po)
Edward Lowbury. Two Confessions (po)
George MacBeth. A Poet's Year (po)
_____. Prayers (po)
_____. Shrapnel (po)
_____. The Vision (po)
Norman MacCaig. The White Bird (po)
Hugh Macdiarmid. Song of the Seraphim (po)
Roger McGough. Gig (po)
_____. Out of Sequence (po)
Stanley Middleton. A Man Made of Smoke (n)
Nicholas Monsarrat. The Kapillan of Malta (n)
John Montague. A Fair House (trans, po)
_____. The Rough Field (dr)
Robert Morgan. On the Banks of the Cynon (po)
Iris Murdoch. The Black Prince (n)
_____. Three Arrows, and the Servants and the Snow: Two Plays (dr, pub)
Liam O'Flaherty. The Wounded Cormorant (fic)
Basil Payne. In Dublin's Quare (dr)
Gilbert Phelps. The Old Believer (n)

Anthony Powell. Temporary Kings (n)
Ezra Pound. Selected Prose, 1909-1965 (pub)
Victor Pritchett. Balzac (bio)
John Pudney. Selected Poems, 1967-1973 (po)
Kathleen Raine. On a Deserted Shore (po)
Alan Ross. The Taj Express: Poems, 1967-1973 (po)
Alfred Leslie Rowse. Shakespeare the Man (bio)
William Sansom. The Marmelade Bird (fic)
Vernon Scannell. The Winter Man (po)
John Peter Scupham. The Gift (po)
Jon Silkin. Air That Pricks Earth (po)
Ian Crichton Smith. The Black and the Red (fic)
Johnny Speight. Till Death Do Us Part (dr)
David Storey. Cromwell (dr)
_____. The Farm (dr)
_____. A Temporary Life (n)
Donald Michael Thomas. The Shaft (po)
Anthony Thwaite. Inscriptions (po)
Sydney Tremayne. Selected and New Poems (po)
William Trevor. The Last Lunch of the Season (fic)
Alec Waugh. The Fatal Gift (n)
Angus Wilson. As If by Magic (n)
Derek Walcott. Another Life (po)

1974

DEATHS
  Edmund Blunden
  Austin Clarke
  David Jones

WORKS
  Fleur Adcock. The Scenic Route (po)
  Brian Aldiss. The Eighty Minute Hour (n)
  Alfred Alvarez. Hers (n)
  Eric Ambler. Doctor Frigo (n)
  Kingsley Amis. Ending Up (n)
  John Antrobus. The Illegal Immigrant (dr)
  Wystan Hugh Auden. Thank You Fog: Last Poems (po)
  Alan Ayckbourn. Absent Friends (dr)
  _____. Confusions (dr)
  Beryl Bainbridge. The Bottle Factory Outing (n)
  Nina Bawden. George Beneath a Paper Moon (n)
  Samuel Beckett. First Love and Other Shorts (fic)
  _____. Not I (dr)
  Frances Bellerby. The First-Known and Other Poems (po)
  John Betjeman. A Nip in the Air (po)
  David Black. The Happy Crow (po)
  Alan Bold. The Hammer and the Thistle (fic)
  Martin Booth. Brevities (po)
  _____. Spawning the Os (po)
  _____. Yogh (po)
  Ronald Bottrall. Poems, 1955-1973 (po)
  John Bowen. Heil Caesar (dr)
  Melvyn Bragg. The Silken Net (n)
  Edwin Brock. I Never Saw It Lit (po)

_____. Paroxisms (po)
George Mackay Brown. Hawkfall (fic)
_____. The Two Fiddlers (fic)
Michael Dennis Browne. The Sun Fetcher (po)
Michael Bullock. Randolph Cranstone and the Pursuing River (fic)
Anthony Burgess. The Clockwork Testament; or, Enderby's End (n)
_____. Napoleon Symphony (n)
William Hamilton Canaway. The Glory of the Sea (n)
Agatha Christie. Akhnaton (dr)
Charles Causley. Six Women (po)
Leonard Clark. The Broad Atlantic (po)
_____. Four Seasons (po)
_____. The Hearing Heart (po)
Bob Cobbing. The Five Vowels (po)
Tony Connor. Crankenheim's Mixed-Up Monster (dr)
_____. The Memoirs of Uncle Harry (po)
_____. Seven Last Poems (po)
Anthony Conran. Poems, 1951-1967 (po)
_____. Spirit Level (po)
Peter Dale. The Seasons of Cankam (po)
Donald Davie. Orpheus (po)
_____. The Shires (po)
Len Deighton. Spy Story (n)
Monica Dickens. Last Year When I Was Young (n)
Margaret Drabble. Arnold Bennett (bio)
Douglas Dunn. Love or Nothing (po)
Nell Dunn. Tear His Head Off His Shoulders (n)
Lawrence Durrell. The Best of Antrobus (fic)
_____. The Revolt of Aphrodite (n)
David Edgar. Dick Deterred (dr)
_____. Blood Sports (dr)
Elaine Feinstein. The Children of the Rose (n)
John Fowles. The Ebony Tower (fic)
John Fuller. Squeaking Crust (po)
Roy Fuller. An Old War (po)
David Gill. Peaches and Apercus (po)
Brian Glanville. The Comic (n)
Duncan Glen. A Cled Score (po)
Robert Graves. At the Gate (po)
Graham Greene. Lord Rochester's Monkey: Being the Life of John Wilmot, Second Earl of Rochester (bio)
Geoffrey Grigson. Angels and Circles (po)
Thom Gunn. Mandrakes (po)
_____. Song Book (po)
_____. To the Air (po)
John Hale. The Love School (n)
Thomas Hinde. Agent (n)
_____. Our Father (n)
Molly Holden. A Speckled Bush (po)
Emyr Humphreys. Flesh and Blood (n)
Hammond Innes. North Star (n)
David Jones. The Sleeping Lord and Other Fragments (po)
Patrick Joseph Kavanagh. Edward Thomas in Heaven (po)
Thomas Kinsella. One (po)
Arthur Koestler. The Heel of Achilles: Essays, 1968-1973 (e)
Philip Larkin. High Windows (po)
John LeCarre. Tinker, Tailor, Soldier, Spy (n)

John Lehmann. The Reader at Night (po)
Laurence Lerner. A.R.T.H.U.R.: The Life and Opinions of a Digital Computer (po)
Doris Lessing. The Memoirs of a Survivor (n)
Edward Lowbury. The Night Watchman (po)
George MacBeth. Elegy for the Gas Dowsers (po)
Norman MacCaig. The World's Room (po)
Hugh Macdiarmid. Complete Poems (po)
John Masters. Thunder at Sunset (n)
Roger McGough. Sporting Relations (po)
Christopher Middleton. Fractions for Another Telemachus (po)
Stanley Middleton. Holiday (n)
John Mole. The Love Horse (po)
John Montague. The Cave of Night (po)
_____. O'Riada's Farewell (po)
Robert Morgan. The Storm (po)
Iris Murdoch. The Sacred and Profane Love Machine (n)
Peter Nichols. Chez Nous (dr)
_____. The Freeway (dr)
Norman Nicholson. Hard of Hearing (po)
John Osborne. Jill and Jack (dr)
Basil Payne. Another Kind of Optimism (po)
Victor Pritchett. The Camberwell Beauty (fic)
John Pudney. Ted (dr)
Simon Raven. Bring Forth the Body (n)
James Reeves. Collected Poems, 1929-1974 (po)
I.A. Richards. Beyond: Springs of the Human Endeavor (e)
David Rudkin. No Title (dr)
William Sansom. A Young Wife's Tale (n)
Jon Silkin. The Principle of Water (po)
Alan Sillitoe. Barbarians (po)
_____. Flame of Life (n)
_____. Men, Women, and Children (fic)
_____. Storm: New Poems (po)
Charles Hubert Sisson. In the Trojan Ditch (po, trans)
Sacheverell Sitwell. The Netherlands (e, trav)
Ian Crichton Smith. Goodbye, Mr. Dixon (n)
_____. Notebooks of Robinson Crusoe (po)
Stevie Smith. Collected Poems (pub)
C.P. Snow. In Their Wisdom (n)
Muriel Spark. The Abbess of Crewe: A Modern Morality Tale (n)
Jon Stallworthy. The Apple Barrel: Selected Poems, 1956-1963 (po)
_____. Hand in Hand (po)
David Storey. Life Class (dr)
Ronald Thomas. Selected Poems, 1946-1968 (po)
_____. What Is a Welshman? (po)
Anthony Thwaite. New Confessions (po)
John Tolkien. Bilbo's Last Song (po, pub)
Charles Tomlinson. The Way In and Other Poems (po)
William Trevor. Elizabeth Alone (n)
John Wain. Samuel Johnson (bio)
Arnold Wesker. Love Letters on Blue Paper (fic)
_____. The Wedding Feast (dr)
E.A. Whitehead. The Sea Anchor (dr)
Ted Willis. Death May Surprise Us (n)

1975

DEATHS
  Ray Coryton Hutchinson
  Julian Huxley
  Robert Sherriff
  Arnold Toynbee

WORKS
  John Antrobus. Mrs. Grabowski's Academy (dr)
  Alan Ayckbourn. Bedroom Farce (dr)
  Beryl Bainbridge. Sweet William (n)
  Howard Barker. Claw (dr)
  _____. Stripwell (dr)
  Arthur David Beaty. Electric Train (n)
  Edw. Bond. The Fool (dr)
  Martin Booth. Snath (po)
  John Bowen. Florence Nightingale (dr)
  John Braine. The Pious Agent (n)
  Howard Brenton. Government Property (dr)
  Christine Brooke-Rose. Thru (n)
  Charles Causley. The Animals' Carol (po)
  _____. Collected Poems, 1951-1975 (pub)
  _____. Their Heads Made of Gold (fic)
  Agatha Christie. Curtain: Hercule Poirot's Last Case (n)
  Jack Clemo. Broad Autumn (po)
  Alex Comfort. Coming Together: Poems Chiefly about Women (po)
  David Compton. George Davenport (dr)
  Rhys Davies. Honeysuckle Girl (n)
  Len Deighton. Yesterday's Spy (n)
  Margaret Drabble. The Realms of Gold (n)
  Maureen Duffy. Capital (n)
  _____. Evesong (po)
  Lawrence Durrell. Monsieur; or, the Prince of Darkness (n)
  Maurice Edelman. Disraeli Rising (n)
  Michael Frayn. Alphabetical Order (dr)
  Gillian Freeman. The Marriage Machine (n)
  Roy Fuller. From the Joke Shop (n)
  Tom Gallacher. Hallowe'en (dr)
  _____. A Laughing Matter (dr)
  Rumer Godden. The Peacock Spring (n)
  Steve Gooch. Strike '26 (dr)
  Winston Graham. Woman in the Mirror (n)
  Robert Graves. Collected Poems, 2 vols (pub)
  William Haggard. The Kinsman (n)
  _____. The Scorpion's Tale (n)
  John Hale. In Memory of Carmen Miranda (dr)
  Wilson Harris. Companions of the Day and Night (n)
  _____. Genesis of the Clowns (n)
  John Heath-Stubbs. Indifferent Weather (po)
  Reyner Heppenstall. Reflections on the Newgate Calendar (his)
  Molly Holden. The Country Over (po)
  Geoffrey Household. Red Anger (n)
  Brian Stanley Johnson. See the Old Lady Decently (n, pub)
  John B. Keane. Matchmaker (dr)
  Emanuel Litvinoff. Blood on the Snow (n)

David Lodge. Changing Places: A Tale of Two Campuses (n)
Frank Marcus. Beauty and the Beast (dr)
John Masters. The Field-Marshal's Memoirs (n)
John McGahern. The Leavetaking (n)
Aubrey Menen. Fonthill: A Comedy (n)
Stanley Middleton. Distractions (n)
John Mole. A Partial Light (po)
_____. Scenarios (po)
Iris Murdoch. A Word Child (n)
Sean O'Faolain. Foreign Affairs (fic)
John Osborne. The End of Me Old Cigar (dr)
Gilbert Phelps. The Low Roads (n)
Harold Pinter. No Man's Land (dr)
_____. Pinter Plays 1 (dr, pub)
Stephen Poliakoff. Join the Dance (dr)
Anthony Powell. Hearing Secret Harmonies (n)
J.B. Priestley. The Carfitt Crisis (n)
Simon Raven. The Survivors (n)
Peter Redgrove. Sons of My Skin (po)
Alan Ross. Open Sea (po)
David Rudkin. Penda's Fen (dr, pub)
Alexander Scott. Selected Poems, 1943-1974 (pub)
Tom Scott. Musins and Murgeonins (po)
John Peter Scupham. Prehistories (po)
Sydney Goodsir Smith. Collected Poems (po)
C.P. Snow. Trollope: His Life and Art (bio)
Cecil P. Taylor. The Killingworth Play (dr)
_____. Pilgrim (dr)
Donald Michael Thomas. Love and Other Deaths (po)
William Trevor. Angels at the Ritz (fic)
Auberon Waugh. Brief Encounter (n)
Arnold Wesker. The Journalists (dr)
E.A. Whitehead. Old Flames (dr)
Hugo Williams. Some Sweet Day (po)
John Stuart Williams. Banna Strand (po)
Ted Willis. The Left-Handed Sleeper (n)
Charles Wood. Jingo (dr)
David Wright. A South African Album (po)

1976

DEATHS
Agatha Christie
Richard Hughes
Colin MacInnes
Gilbert Ryle
Willian Sansom

WORKS
Dannie Abse. Pythagoras (dr)
John Antrobus. They Sleep Together (dr)
Alan Ayckbourn. Just Between Ourselves (dr)
Howard Barker. Wax (dr)
Samuel Beckett. Ends and Odds (dr)
_____. Fizzles (fic)
_____. Footfalls (dr)

_____. I Can't Go On: A Selection from the Works of Samuel Beckett (ed)
_____. That Time (dr)
Edward Bond. A-A-America (dr)
_____. Stone (dr)
John Bowen. Which Way Are You Facing? (dr)
Howard Brenton. Weapons of Happiness (dr)
Brigid Brophy. Beardsley and His World (e)
David Compton. No Go Area (dr)
_____. One Possessed (dr)
_____. What Are You Doing Here? (dr)
David Edgar. Destiny (dr)
_____. Events Following the Closure of a Motorcycle Factory (dr)
_____. Saigon Rose (dr)
Michael Frayn. Clouds (dr)
_____. Donkeys' Years (dr)
Tom Gallacher. The Sea Change (dr)
Steve Gooch. Our Land Our Lives (dr)
John Hale. Love's Old Sweet Song (dr)
_____. Lovers and Heretics (n)
James Hanley. A Dream Journey (n)
Roger Howard. Contemporary Chinese Theatre (e)
_____. The Great Tide (dr)
_____. History of the Tenth Struggle (dr)
_____. Klong 1, Klong 2, and the Partisan (dr)
_____. The Mao Play (dr)
Christopher Isherwood. Christopher and His Kind (auto)
John B. Keane. Death Be Not Proud (fic)
_____. The Good Thing (dr)
Frank Marcus. Anatol (dr)
Iris Murdoch. Henry and Cato (n)
John Osborne. Watch It Come Down (dr)
Stephen Poliakoff. City Sugar, and Hitting Town (dr, pub)
J.B. Priestley. Found, Lost, Found: or, The English Way of Life (n)
_____. The Happy Dream (bio)
David Rudkin. Ashes (dr, pub)
_____. The Sons of Light (dr)
Johnny Speight. The Thoughts of Chairman Alf (dr)
Tom Stoppard. Dirty Linen, and New-found-land (dr, pub)
David Storey. Mother's Day (dr)
_____. Saville (n)
Cecil P. Taylor. Aladdin (dr)
_____. Bandits (dr)
_____. Goldberg (dr)
William Trevor. The Children of Dynmouth (n)
Derek Walcott. Sea Grapes (po)
_____. Selected Verse (po)
Arnold Wesker. The Plays of Arnold Wesker (ed)
Ted Willis. Man-Eater (n)
Charles Wood. The Script (dr)

1977

DEATHS
 Christopher Murray Grieve ("Hugh Macdiarmid")
 John Pudney

Terence Rattigan
Cecil Woodham-Smith

WORKS
　Alan Ayckbourn. Three Plays (dr, pub)
　Samuel Beckett. Far to End Yet Again and Other Fizzles (fic)
　John Bowen. The Fortunate Conspiracy (dr)
　Maureen Duffy. The Passionate Shepherdess: Aphra Behn, 1640-1689 (bio)
　John Fowles. Daniel Martin (n)
　John LeCarre. The Honourable Schoolboy (n)
　Frank Marcus. From Morning to Midnight (dr)
　Peter Nichols. Privates on Parade (dr)
　John Tolkien. The Silmarillion (n, pub)
　E.A. Whitehead. Mecca (dr)
　Angus Wilson. The Strange Ride of Rudyard Kipling (bio, e)

1978

DEATHS
　F.R. Leavis

WORKS
　Desmond Bagley. The Enemy (n)
　Beryl Bainbridge. Injury Time (n)
　James Graham Ballard. The Best Stories of J.G. Ballard (fic, pub)
　Deidre Blair. Samuel Beckett (bio)
　Basil Bunting. Collected Poems (pub)
　Anthony Burgess. 1985 (n, e)
　Robert Conquest. Kolyma. The Arctic Death Camps (his)
　Jonathan Cott. Forever Young (e, nar)
　Donald Davie. The Poet in the Imaginary Museum. Essays of Two Decades
　　　　　(e, pub)
　John Fowles. The Magus. A Revised Version (n)
　P.N. Furbank. E.M. Forster: A Life (bio)
　Graham Greene. The Human Factor (n)
　Arthur Koestler. Janus. A Summing Up (e)
　Robin Maugham. Conversations with Willie. Recollections of W. Somerset
　　　　　Maugham (nar, bio)
　Ian McEwan. The Cement Garden (n)
　Flann O'Brien. A Flann O'Brien Reader (fic, pub)
　Harold Pinter. The Proust Screenplay. A la Recherche du Temps Perdu
　　　　　(trans, fic)
　Stephen Spender. The Thirties and After. Poetry, Politics, People.
　　　　　1933-1970 (e, auto)
　Virginia Woolf. Letters, 1923-1928 (pub)

1979

DEATHS
　Jean Rhys

WORKS
　Alfred Alvarez. Hunt (n)
　Kingsley Amis. Jakes Thing (n)
　Beryl Bainbridge. Young Adolf (n)
　Anthony Burgess. Abba Abba (n)

_____. Man of Nazareth (n)
David Cecil. A Portrait of Jane Austen (e, bio)
Joseph Conrad. Congo Diary and Other Uncollected Pieces (nar, e, pub)
Len Deighton. SS-GB (n)
Lawrence Durrell. Livia. Or, Buried Alive (n)
Brian Finney. Christopher Isherwood (bio)
Terry Gilliam and Lucinda Cowell. Animations of Immortality (e)
Robert Graves and Alan Hodge. The Reader over Your Shoulder, rev ed (e)
General Sir John Hackett. The Third World War: August 1985 (e, fic)
E.J. Hobsbawn. The Age of Capital (his)
David Jones. The Dying Gaul (e, pub)
Norman Lewis. Naples '44 (his, nar)
Bryan Magee. Men of Ideas (e, pub)
Eric Newby. The Big Red Train Ride (trav)
John Pearson. The Sitwells. A Family's Biography (bio)
William Plomer. Electric Delights (e, pub)
Frank T. Prince. Collected Poems (pub)
V.S. Pritchett. The Myth Makers (e)
_____. Selected Stories (fic, ed)
Giles St. Aubyn. Edward VII. Prince and King (bio)
E.F. Schumacher. Good Works (e, pub)
John Shawcross. Sideshow (his, e)
Charles Hubert Sisson. The Avoidance of Literature (e)
Muriel Spark. Territorial Rights (n)
Sunday (London) Times. Suffer the Children. The Story of Thalidomide (e)
William Trevor. Lovers of Their Time (fic)
Frank Tuohy. Live Bait. And Other Stories (fic, pub)
John Wain. The Pardoner's Tale (n)
Derek Walcott. The Star-Apple Kingdom (po)
John Willett. Art and Politics in the Weimar Period (his)
Virginia Woolf. Letters, 1929-1931 (pub)

Index

A

Abbey Theatre, 214, 286
Abbotsford Club, 151, 176
Abercrombie, Lascelles, 190, 218, 222, 223, 232, 241, 251
Abse, Dannie, 233, 261-263, 266, 268, 271-272, 276-277, 279, 289, 291, 294, 298, 301, 307
Academy, 179, 219
Adam, James, 117
Adam, Robert, 99, 117, 125
Adams, Sarah Flower, 132, 156, 162
Adamson, Robert, 165, 188, 213, 218
Adcock, Fleur, 246, 282, 288, 296, 303
Addison, Joseph, 77, 90, 92-94, 96
Adelard of Bath, 10
Adelphi, 233, 261
Adventurer, 107, 108
Advocates' Library, 83
AE, 178, 203, 208, 213-214, 221, 224, 228, 232, 236, 239, 243, 246-247
Aelfric, 7-9
Aethelbert of Kent, 3
Aethelred, 8
Aethelstan, 7
Aethelwold, 7-8
Ainger, Alfred, 153, 192-193, 213-215
Ainsworth, William Harrison, 132, 151, 155-158, 162, 179, 191
Ainsworth's Magazine, 157, 165
Akenside, Mark, 96, 105, 110, 115-116
Alcuin of York, 5-6
Aldington, Richard, 201, 240, 243-244, 263, 269, 279
Aldiss, Brian, 235, 269, 272-273, 275-277, 279, 282, 284, 286, 288-289, 291-292, 294, 296, 301, 303
Alexander, Sir William, 40, 54, 58, 67
Alfred, 6
Alison, Sir Archibald, 125, 149-150, 165, 178
Allen, Grant, 204
All Soul's College, Oxford, 24
All the Year Round, 170, 180
Alvarez, Alfred, 240, 266, 289, 296, 298, 303, 309
Ambler, Eric, 219, 249-250, 251-252, 254, 264, 267, 271, 275, 279, 282, 288, 292, 298, 303
Amis, Kingsley, 231, 260, 267-269, 273, 276, 279, 281, 288-289, 296, 298, 301, 303, 309
Amory, Thomas, 84, 109, 123
Anderson, Patrick, 226, 244, 258-259, 267
Andreas, 5
Anglicus, Bartholomeus, 15
Anglo-Saxon Chronicle, 6
Annales Cambriae, 7
Anne, Queen, 89
Annual Register, 110
Anstey, Christopher, 97, 114, 132
Anti-Jacobin, 128
Antrobus, John, 245, 303, 306-307
Appius and Virginia, 42, 71
Arbuthnot, John, 76, 88, 90, 93, 95, 100-101, 103
Archer, William, 201

Arden, John, 241, 275, 281, 282, 284, 288-289, 296
Armstrong, John, 105
Arnold, Sir Edwin, 188
Arnold, Matthew, 142, 163, 165,167, 170, 172, 176, 178-180, 183, 185, 197
Arnold, Thomas, 126, 148, 154, 157, 159
Arthur and Merlin, 17
Ascham, Roger, 31, 36-37, 41
Ashby, George, 26
Ashendene Press, 204
Asser, 6-7
Association of Poets. . .Novelists, 231
Athenian Gazette, 83, 85
Athelston, 18
Athenaeum, 147
Athenaeum Club, 144
Atterbury, Francis, 74, 86, 100, 103, 124
Aubrey, John, 62, 86, 96, 136
Auden, Wystan Hugh, 217, 247, 249-251, 255, 258, 261, 264, 269, 271, 276, 284, 286, 290, 292, 301, 303
Austen, Jane, 117, 135-137, 139, 181
Austin, Alfred, 201
Austin, John, 149, 174
Awdeley, John, 39
Ayckbourn, Alan, 252, 303, 306-307, 309
Ayer, Alfred Jules, 220, 249, 254, 271
Aytoun, William, 160

B

Bacon, Francis, 39, 50, 54, 56, 60-62
Bacon, Roger, 14, 17
Bage, Robert, 99, 120, 121, 123, 125, 127, 130
Bagehot, Walter, 145, 178, 183, 186-189
Bagley, Desmon, 309
Bagnold, Enid, 198, 230, 234, 248, 251, 256, 264, 266, 269, 276, 282, 288
Bailey, Nathaniel, 96
Bailey, Philip James, 138, 155,159, 163, 167, 170, 178, 198, 212
Baillie, Joanna, 111, 124, 128,135, 142, 152, 164

Bain, Alexander, 139, 167, 171, 179-180, 182, 192, 213
Bainbridge, Beryl, 246, 288, 290, 298, 301, 303, 306, 309
Baker, Sir Samuel White, 142,165, 182, 184, 202
Baldwin, William, 36
Bale, John, 29, 36, 39
Balfour, Arthur James, 162, 188, 197, 202, 204, 219, 226, 230, 232, 237, 241
Ballad of Chevy Chase, 111
Ballad Society, 188
Ballard, James Graham, 309
Balliol College, Oxford, 16
Bank of England, 85
Bannantyne Club, 143, 172
Bantock, Gavin, 252, 284, 290, 292, 294, 298, 301
Barbour, John, 19
Barclay, Alexander, 27, 30-32, 37
Barclay, John, 53
Barclay, Robert, 79
Baretti, Guiseppe M.A., 111
Baring, Maurice, 184, 200, 212, 220, 223, 235, 258
Barker, George Granville, 224,245, 248, 252, 254, 255, 257, 260, 263-264, 272, 279, 284, 286,290, 292, 296, 298, 301
Barker, Howard, 259, 306-307
Barnard, Edward, 86
Barnes, Barnabe, 41, 47, 49, 56
Barnes, William, 130, 159, 171, 195
Barnfield, Richard, 42, 48-50,62
Barri, Giraldus de, 12-14
Barrie, Sir James Matthew, 171, 200, 203, 205, 211-215, 218,220, 227, 230, 250
Barrow, Isaac, 63, 71, 76, 78-80
Barrow, Sir John, 113, 139, 161-162
Barstow, Mrs. Montagu, 215
Battle of Brunanburh, 7
Battle of Malden, 8
Bawden, Nina, 235, 267-269, 271-272, 276-277, 281-282, 286, 288, 290, 294, 298, 303
Baxter, Richard, 58, 70, 82, 84,86
Bayly, Ada Ellen, 168, 213
Beattie, James, 101, 116-117, 132
Beaty, Arthur David, 229, 261,268, 271, 275-276, 279, 282, 284,296, 306
Beauchamp, Kathleen Mansfield,197, 233

INDEX 313

Beaumont, Francis, 44, 55-57, 59-60, 69
Beckett, Samuel, 216, 251, 264,266, 267, 272-273, 275, 277, 284, 292, 294, 301, 307-309
Beckford, Peter, 103, 120, 133, 135
Beckford, William, 110, 121-122,152, 158
Becon, Thomas, 38
Beddoes, Thomas Lovell, 131, 142-143, 162-163
Bede, 4-5
Beef-Steak Club, 186
Beer, Patricia, 234, 275, 281, 288, 296, 301
Beerbohm, Sir Max, 182, 205-206, 208, 214, 217, 219, 221, 223,229, 232, 234, 239, 257, 271
Behan, Brendan, 231, 271, 273, 279, 281-282
Behn, Aphra, 67, 79, 81, 83
Bell, Clive, 190, 225, 239, 240,282
Bell, Martin, 228, 294
Bellerby, Frances, 259, 262, 273, 294, 303
Belloc, Hiliare, 180, 212, 216,218, 221, 223, 236, 254, 267
Benedict, 10
Benlowes, Edward, 71
Bennett, Arnold, 178, 212, 217-221, 223, 226, 233-234, 237, 241-242
Bentham, Jeremy, 106, 118, 123-124, 138, 148-149
Bentley's Miscellany, 153, 156-157
Beowulf, 4
Beresford, Anne, 240, 288, 290,298
Berkeley, George, 81, 92-93, 100-101, 105, 108
Berners, John Bourchier, 26, 33-35
Berry, Francis, 226, 245, 249, 257, 260, 266, 277, 286, 296
Besant, Sir Walter, 152, 192, 194, 197, 211
Betjeman, John, 216, 245, 250,254, 257, 268, 271, 273, 276, 286,296, 298, 303
Betterton, Thomas, 65, 77, 83, 88, 92, 96
Bevis of Hampton, 17
Bible, Authorized Version, 57
Bibliographical Society, 201
Bickerstaffe, Isaac, 112, 113-115, 136
Bingham, Joseph, 91
Binyon, Laurence, 179, 203, 225, 233, 256

Birrell, Augustine, 163, 212, 215, 245
Biscop, Benedict, 3-4
Black, David, 255, 276, 281, 286, 288, 292, 298, 303
Black, William, 156, 181-183, 188, 207
Blackburn, Thomas, 226, 264, 268, 271, 273, 277, 283, 296
Blackmore, Sir Richard, 93
Blackmore, Richard Doddridge, 145, 175, 177, 179, 182, 185, 187, 190, 196, 210
Blackstone, Sir William, 97, 112-113, 119
Blackwood, Algernon, 218
Blackwood's Edinburgh Magazine, 139
Blair, Deidre, 309
Blair, Eric, 213, 263
Blair, Hugh, 95, 118, 121, 130
Blair, Robert, 86, 104-105
Blake, William, 109, 121, 124,126-128, 143, 146
Blessington, Marguerite Power, 149
Blickling Homilies, 8
Bloomfield, Robert, 130
Blunden, Edmund, 205, 239, 259, 303
Blunt, Wilfrid Scawen, 155, 189, 225, 232
Boar's Head Inn, 149
Bodleian Library, 56
Bohn, Henry George, 156
Bohn's Antiquarian Library, 161
Bokenham, Osbern, 25
Bold, Alan, 256, 284, 286, 288, 292, 296, 301, 303
Bolingbroke, Viscount, 79, 95,100-102, 106-108
Bond, Edward, 246, 286, 290, 296, 301, 306, 308
Book of Common Prayer, 37, 239
Book of Homilies, 36, 40
Book of St. Albans, 28
Booth, Martin, 257, 288, 290, 292, 294, 296, 298, 301, 303, 306
Borde, Andrew, 35
Borrow, George, 131, 156, 158,164, 169, 173, 190
Bosley, Keith, 250, 292, 298, 301
Boswell, James, 103, 114-115, 122, 125, 127
Bottrall, Ronald, 216, 243, 246, 252, 258, 262, 268, 301, 303

Boucicault, Dion, 141, 156, 162, 171, 175, 185, 199
Bowdler, Thomas, 139
Bowen, Elizabeth, 198, 233, 240, 258, 251, 255, 258, 262, 269, 283-284
Bowen, John, 234, 303, 306, 308-309
Bowyer, William, 117
Boyer, Abel, 76, 89, 91, 97, 99
Braddon, Mary Elizabeth, 173
Bradley, Andrew Cecil, 214
Bradley, Francis Herbert, 160, 186, 193, 202, 225, 234
Bradley, Henry, 214
Bradshaw's Monthly Railway Guide, 156, 277
Brady, Nicholas, 86
Bragg, Melvyn, 252, 284, 286, 292, 294, 296, 298, 303
Braine, John, 231, 272, 275, 279, 290, 294, 299, 306
Brakelond, Jocelyn de, 14
Brasenose College, Oxford, 31
Brenton, Howard, 256, 292, 294, 306, 308
Breton, Nicholas, 35, 47, 50, 53-54, 62
Brewer's Dictionary, 180
Bridges, Bp. John, 45
Bridges, Robert, 158, 183, 186, 194, 200, 202-204, 207-208, 215, 223-225, 227, 235, 240, 241
Bridie, James, 197, 241, 244-245, 250, 257, 260, 262, 264
Brinkelow, Henry, 35
British Association for the Advancement of Science, 149
British Broadcasting Company, 232
British Broadcasting Corporation, 237
British Humanities Index, 227
British Institute of Industrial Art, 243
British Magazine, 110
British Museum, 108
Briton, 112
Brock, Edwin, 237, 275-276, 279, 292, 294, 299, 301, 303-304
Brome, Richard, 61, 64-65, 67, 71-73
Bronte, Ann, 141, 160-162
Bronte, Charlotte, 138, 160-161, 163, 165, 167, 169, 171
Bronte, Emily, 139, 160, 162
Brooke, Henry, 89, 101, 103, 111, 117, 121
Brooke, Rupert, 196, 221, 226,228
Brooke-Rose, Christine, 272, 274, 277, 283, 286, 290, 294, 306
Brophy, Brigid, 240, 267, 271,279, 281, 283, 288, 292, 301, 308
Brougham, Henry Peter, 119, 145, 155, 179, 181
Broughton, Rhoda, 155, 178, 195, 215, 230
Brown, George Douglas, 211
Brown, George MacKay, 230. 268, 275, 284, 286, 290, 292, 296, 299, 301, 304
Brown, John, 170, 172, 192
Brown, Thomas, 88
Brown, Thomas Edward, 183, 190
Browne, Michael Dennis, 253, 294, 304
Browne, Sir Thomas, 54, 68-69, 72, 81, 95
Browne, Thomas Alexander, 145,197, 199, 226
Browne, William, 46, 58, 68
Browning, Elizabeth Barrett, 133, 145, 150, 154, 159, 163, 169, 171-173
Browning, Oscar, 153, 223-224, 227, 233
Browning, Robert, 136, 150, 152-153, 156-157, 160, 163, 167, 175, 179, 181-183, 185, 187-188, 189, 193-194, 196, 198
Brownjohn, Alan, 240, 268, 277, 288, 292, 294, 296, 299
Bruce, George, 219, 257, 284, 288
Bruce, James, 124
Bryce, James, 154, 175, 197, 206, 211, 213, 223, 232
Brydges, Sir Samuel E., 111, 133, 135, 137, 153
Buchan, John, 185, 224, 226-227, 229, 233, 236, 243-244, 246,254
Buchanan, George, 214, 246, 249, 251, 254, 264, 266, 274, 276, 277, 284, 294, 296, 299
Buchanan, Robert, 156, 177, 184, 186, 190, 192, 194, 198, 203, 204, 211
Buckingham, 2nd Duke, 77
Bullock, Michael, 228, 251, 277, 281, 292, 296, 299, 301, 304
Bulwer-Lytton, Edward G.E., 131, 146-154, 156-158, 160, 162, 163, 165, 170-173, 180-181, 183
Bulwer-Lytton, Edward R., 148,171,

INDEX

194, 200-201
Bunting, Basil, 210, 264, 270,284, 286, 294, 309
Bunyan, John, 62, 72, 76-77, 79-81, 83
Burgess, Anthony, 227, 271, 274,278-279, 281, 290, 296, 299, 304,309-310
Burgoyne, Sir John, 97, 117, 122, 125
Burke, Edmund, 99, 109, 115, 117-120, 122, 124-128
Burnand, Sir Francis Cowley, 152, 177-178, 190, 227
Burnet, Gilbert, 68, 79-81, 87,94, 97
Burnet, Thomas, 81
Burnett, Frances E.H., 195
Burney, Charles, 118
Burney, Frances, 107, 119-120, 127, 137, 156
Burns, Jim, 248, 288, 292, 299, 301
Burns, Robert, 110, 122-123, 125, 127, 129
Burton, John Hill, 134, 160, 166, 173, 175, 190
Burton, Sir Richard, 142, 167, 194, 199
Burton, Robert, 43, 60, 67
Bury, Richard de, 27
Butcher, S.H., 189
Butler, Alban, 109
Butler, Joseph, 84, 98, 102, 107
Butler, Samuel, 57, 74-75, 79-80
Butler, Samuel, 151, 182, 187-190, 194, 196, 211-213
Byron, Lord, 123, 133-134, 136-140, 143-144
Bywater, Ingram, 155, 187, 219,225

C

Caedmon, 4
Caine, Sir Thomas H.H., 165, 194, 196, 199-200, 203, 206, 211, 214, 218-219, 224, 242
Caird, Edward, 152, 179, 193, 198, 202, 213
Caird, John, 190
Caius College, Cambridge, 38
Calderon, George, 178, 219, 222-223, 226, 231
Calverley, Charles Stuart, 173
Calves' Head Club, 101
Cambridge Camden Society, 155
Cambridge University, 15

Cambridge University Press, 44
Camden Society, 154
Camden, William, 37, 55, 58, 61-62
Campbell, Colin, 94-95, 98
Campbell, Donald, 253, 299
Campbell, Roy, 211, 234, 241, 244, 252, 259, 262, 264, 272, 275-276
Campbell, Thomas, 118, 129, 134, 144, 157, 159
Campion, Thomas, 49, 53, 56, 60
Canaway, William Hamilton, 235, 274-275, 278-279, 281, 284, 286, 288, 292, 296, 301, 304
Canning, George, 144
Canute, 9
Capell, Edward, 114, 121
Capgrave, John, 26
Carew, Thomas, 50, 65, 67
Carey, Henry, 101, 104
Carliell, Robert, 60
Carleton, William, 126, 150-151, 155, 179
Carlton Club, 149
Carlyle, Jane, 130, 177, 193
Carlyle, Thomas, 126, 144-146,152-153,. 155-156, 158, 160, 164,170, 185, 190, 191
Carroll, Lewis, 149, 176, 207
Carter, Elizabeth, 110
Cartwright, William, 57, 66, 68, 70
Cary, Henry Francis, 116, 133,137, 159
Cary Joyce, 197, 216, 244-245,249, 253-260, 262, 266-267, 270, 272, 274, 275, 276
<u>Castle of Perseverance</u>, 25
Caudwell, Christopher, 217, 250, 251, 253
Causley, Charles, 227, 249-251, 261, 264-265, 267, 272, 274,278, 290, 292, 304, 306
Cavendish, George, 67
Cavendish Laboratory, 184
Caxton, William, 23, 27-28
Cecil, David, 310
Centlivre, Susannah, 76, 92, 94-95, 97
Chalkhill, John, 81
Chalmers, Thomas, 150
Chamberlayne, William, 60, 72-73, 77, 83
Chambers, Sir Edmund, 177, 213, 233, 241, 268
Chambers, Ephraim, 99

Chambers, Robert, 131, 159, 173, 181
Chambers's Encyclopaedia, 171
Chambers's Journal, 149
Champion, 103
Chapman, George, 39, 48-50, 54-55, 57-59, 64-65, 67
Chapone, Hester Mulso, 117
Charles I, 62
Charles II, 73
Charterhouse, 19
Chartists, 153, 162
Chatterton, Thomas, 107, 113, 115, 118
Chaucer, Geoffrey, 18-20, 22, 27
Chaucer Society, 179
Chesterton, G.K., 184, 213-214, 218-220, 222, 224-225, 244-245, 248
Chestre, Thomas, 24
Chettle, Henry, 47, 49, 52-53, 55
Child, Francis James, 193
Childers, Erskine, 213
Chillingworth, William, 66
Chippendale, Thomas, 108
Chitty, Sir Thomas Willes, 236
Christ Church, Oxford, 36
Christian Mission, 176
Christie, Agatha, 199, 236, 250, 261, 288, 304, 306-307
Chronicle of Mont St. Michel, 9
Chronicles and Memorials of Great Britain and Ireland, 169
Chronicon ex Chronicis, 47
Church of Scotland, 39
Church, Richard William, 137, 159, 180, 187-189, 194, 199, 200
Churchill, Charles, 100, 111-113
Churchill, Winston, 184, 207-208, 210, 216, 218-219, 233, 241, 245, 259, 261, 271, 284
Churchyard, Thomas, 32, 40, 43, 45, 54
Cibber, Colley, 77, 86, 90, 99, 103, 109
Cilverwel, Nathaniel, 71
City Mercury, 78
Clanvowe, Thomas, 22
Clare, John, 125, 141-142, 146, 152, 175
Clarendon, Earl of, 56, 78, 89, 96, 110
Clark, Andrew, 217
Chesney, Sir George Tomkyns, 150, 181, 186, 204
Chester Plays, 18
Chesterfield, 4th Earl of, 85, 116-117, 199
Clark, John Willis, 150, 195, 206, 211, 220
Clark, Leonard, 215, 257, 258, 261, 267, 288, 294, 296, 299, 304
Clarke, Austin, 205, 227, 231, 235, 238, 240, 244, 249, 251, 255-257, 259, 264, 266-267, 270, 272, 276, 279, 281, 286, 288, 290, 294, 296, 301, 303
Clarke, Marcus Andrew, 184
Clavell, John, 63
Clayton, Richard H.M., 217
Cleland, John, 91, 106-107, 124
Clemo, Jack, 226, 261, 265, 278, 288, 296, 306
Cleveland, John, 68
Clifford, William, 159, 188, 189
Clive, Caroline Archer, 167
Cloud of Unknowing, 18
Clough, Arthur Hugh, 140, 162, 172, 173, 180
Cobbe, Frances Power, 142, 167, 175, 182, 191, 214
Cobbett, William, 112, 139, 144, 147-148, 152
Cobbett's Political Register, 131, 152
Cobbett's State Trials, 134
Cobbing, Bob, 230, 284, 286, 288, 290, 292, 294, 296, 299, 301, 304
Cockburn, Henry Thomas, 119, 165-166, 168
Cockton, Henry, 156
Coke, Sir Edward, 37, 52, 63, 65
Cole, Barry, 248, 288, 290, 292, 294, 296, 299, 301
Coleman, George (elder), 100, 111, 114, 119, 121, 126
Coleman, George (younger), 112, 123, 127-128, 132, 152
Colenso, John, 137, 166, 172-173, 192
Coleridge, Hartley, 127, 150, 162, 164
Coleridge, Mary Elizabeth, 172, 202, 206, 217, 220
Coleridge, Samuel Taylor, 116, 126-131, 136, 138-139, 145, 151
Coleridge, Sara, 153
Collier, Jeremy, 70, 86, 91, 98
Collier, John Payne, 124, 161, 176, 192
Collingwood, Robin, 198, 145, 249, 251, 256, 259

INDEX 317

Collins, Arthur, 83, 92, 96, 101, 111
Collins, John Churton, 162, 188, 191, 211, 214-215, 218
Collins, Wilkie, 144, 164, 166,169, 171, 173, 177, 179-180, 182-183, 189, 191, 198
Collins, William, 96, 104, 106-107, 109-110
Collinson, Laurence, 235, 266, 272, 288, 301
Colvin, Sir Sidney, 159, 191, 196, 203, 208, 227, 231, 237
Combe, William, 103, 118, 135, 141-143
Comedie of Mucedorus, 50
Comfort, Alex, 230, 250, 255-261, 265-266, 278-279, 306
Comic Almanack, 152
Common Conditions, 43
Companion, 147
Compton, David, 234, 286, 306, 308
Compton, Burnett, Ivy, 201, 222, 235, 240, 243, 245, 248, 253,255, 265, 270, 275, 279, 291
Congreve, William, 77, 84-86, 88,97
Conington, John, 145, 179
Conn, Stewart, 248, 278, 283, 288, 290, 292, 294, 296, 299, 301
Connolly, Cyril, 213, 248, 251,258, 262, 267, 281, 284
Connor, Tony, 241, 279, 284, 290, 296, 299, 301, 304
Conquest, Robert, 227, 270, 279, 292, 309
Conrad, Joseph, 168, 204-207, 210, 212-214, 216-217, 222-224, 226-227, 229, 231, 233-236, 310
Conran, Anthony, 242, 276, 278,281, 284, 286, 292, 304
Constable, Henry, 39, 47, 58
Contemporary Review, 176
Con-Test, 109
Cook, Eliza, 163, 166, 180, 198
Cook, James, 99, 114, 118-119, 121
Cooper, Lettice, 206, 235, 238-241, 243, 245, 248-249, 251, 260, 267, 272, 276, 279, 296, 301
Cooper, William, 220, 264-267, 271, 274, 278, 296, 301
Copland, Robert, 34
Coppard, Alfred, 187, 231-232, 235, 239, 248, 260, 272
Copyright Act, 91, 157
Corbet, Richard, 44, 65, 69-70
Corelli, Marie, 167, 195, 202, 204-205, 210, 212, 227, 231, 234
Cornhill Magazine, 170
Cornington, John, 177
Cornwell, David J.M., 242
Corpus Christi College, Cambridge, 18
Cory, William Johnson, 170
Coryate, Thomas, 43, 57, 59
Cotgrave, Randle, 57
Cott, Jonathan, 309
Court of Sapience, 26
Court of Star-Chamber, 67
Courthope, William John, 157, 181, 194, 204, 227, 230
Covent Garden Journal, 107
Covent Garden Theatre, 100, 134
Coventry, Francis, 107
Coverdale, Miles, 28,34
Coward, Noel, 208, 241, 243, 245, 255
Cowden-Clarke, Mary, 159, 188
Cowden-Clark, Charles, 188
Cowell, Lucinda, 310
Cowley, Abraham, 59, 63-64, 66,68-69, 72, 74, 76
Cowley, Hannah, 104, 118, 120-121
Cowper, William, 100, 119-121, 125, 129-130
Cox, G.W., 164
Cox, William Trevor, 238
Crabbe, George, 108, 120-121, 133, 135, 149
Craftsman, 98, 102
Craigie, Mrs. P.M.T., 178, 216
Crashaw, Richard, 57, 69-71
Creighton, Anthony, 274
Creighton, Mandell, 158, 186, 192, 197, 205, 211
Cremorne Gardens, 187
Criterion, 232, 252
Critical Review, 109, 139
Criticisms on the Rolliad, 121
Crockford's Clerical Directory, 169
Crockford's Gambling Club, 146
Croker, John Wilson, 120, 132, 149, 169
Croker, Thomas, 128, 144, 145, 147, 155, 166
Croly; George, 120, 143, 147, 160, 171
Crosby Hall, 26
Crowe, William, 123
Crowne, John, 67, 75, 78, 80-83, 85, 87
Croyland History, 49
Cruden, Alexander, 102

Cuckoo Song, 17
Cudworth, Ralph, 59, 79, 83, 100
Cumberland, Richard, 100, 115-116, 124, 127, 135
Cunningham, Allan, 121, 143, 145, 147, 157
Cunningham, John, 99, 106, 114, 116
Cunninghame-Graham, Robert, 165, 207, 210, 212-213, 225, 241, 249
Curzon, George, 201
Curzon, Robert, 135, 163, 166-167, 183
Cynewulf, 5-6

D

Daily Courant, 89, 101
Daily News, 160
Daily Telegraph, 167
Daily Universal Register, 122-123
Dale, Peter, 251, 275, 279, 290, 294, 304
Dame Sirith, 16
Dampier, William, 71, 86-87, 89, 94
Daniel, 5-6
Daniel, Samuel, 39, 47-50, 54, 56, 58, 60
Darley, George, 127, 143, 145-146, 160
Darling, Frank, 213, 251, 253
Darwin, Charles, 134, 155, 157, 159-160, 171, 173, 175, 179, 181-182, 185-186, 190-191
Darwin, Erasmus, 100, 124-126, 128, 131
Dasent, Sir George, 138, 171-172, 205
D'Avenant, Sir William, 54, 63, 65-66, 70, 72, 76-77
Davidson, John, 168, 199, 202-203, 205-206, 208, 219
Davie, Donald, 231, 272, 283, 292, 294, 304, 309
Davies, John, 40, 53-54, 56-57, 59, 62, 64
Davies, Sir John, 41, 49-50
Davies, Rhys, 213, 238, 240-241, 243-245, 248-251, 254-256, 258-260, 262, 265, 268, 270, 272, 274, 276, 288, 297, 306
Davies, William, 181, 218-219, 223, 235, 254, 281
Davison, Francis, 53, 57, 60
Davison, Walter, 53, 57, 60
Davy, Sir Humphry, 147
Davys, John, 36, 48-49, 54

Day, John, 52, 54-55
Day, Thomas, 121
Day-Lewis, Cecil, 214, 235, 243, 245-246, 248, 253, 257, 260-261, 265, 267-268, 272, 276, 283-284, 286, 289, 298
Debrett, John, 131
Dee, John, 33, 40, 43, 55
Defoe, Daniel, 73, 86, 88-90, 96-97, 100
Dehn, Paul, 222, 263, 266, 278, 284
Deighton, Len, 240, 279, 281, 283, 286, 288, 290, 294, 297, 299, 304, 306, 310
Dekker, Thomas, 41, 52-54, 56-57, 60-61, 63-64
De la Mare, Walter, 183, 212, 214, 220, 223-224, 231-233, 235, 237, 241, 242, 249-250, 253, 258, 265, 270-271
Delany, Patrick, 108
de la Ramee, Mary Louise, 155, 218
DeMorgan, William, 155, 216-220, 222, 225, 227
Denham, Sir John, 58, 68-69
Dennis, John, 72, 85-86, 88, 90-91, 93, 101
Deor's Lament, 8
DeQuincey, Thomas, 122, 143-144, 146, 150-151, 159, 163, 166, 170
DeVere, Aubrey, 137, 157, 196, 206, 212
Diaper, William, 93
Dibdin, Charles, 127
Dibdin, Thomas, 118, 131, 135, 142, 144, 152, 154, 161
Dicey, Albert Venn, 194
Dickens, Charles, 136, 152-154, 157-163, 165, 167, 171, 175, 180
Dickens, Monica, 226, 254, 257-259, 261, 263, 267, 270-271, 274, 278, 283, 286, 290, 294, 304
Dickinson, Patrick, 225, 258-259, 261, 266, 270, 276, 283, 294, 301
Dictionary of National Biography, 192
Digby, Kenelm, 130, 143, 149, 189
Digby, Sir Kenhelm, 53, 68, 75
Dilke, Sir Charles, 158, 179, 184, 199, 221
Disraeli, Benjamin, 132, 145, 149-153, 159-161, 165, 180, 190
Disraeli, Isaac, 113, 125, 136-137, 144, 157, 162

INDEX

Dives and Pauper, 22
Dixon, Richard, 150, 187, 193, 210
Dobell, Sidney, 144, 164, 167-168, 184-185
Dobson, Henry Austin, 155, 183,187, 189, 193-195, 197, 199, 201,203, 205, 212, 213, 231
Dodd, William, 108
Doddridge, Philip, 89, 105-107
Dodgson, Charles, 149, 180, 182, 186, 189, 193, 199, 207
Dodington, George Bubb, 121
Dodsley, Robert, 89, 99, 101, 104-106, 110, 113
Domett, Alfred, 135, 182, 187, 196
Dominican Friars, 15
Donne, John, 42, 57, 61, 63-64,67, 70, 73
Doomsday Book, 9
Dorrington, Edward, 98
Doughty, Charles, 158, 197, 216,218-219, 223, 227, 230, 236
Douglas, Lord Alfred, 180, 208,219, 234, 248, 258
Douglas, Gavin, 27, 30-32, 37, 122
Douglas, George Norman, 178, 222, 223, 226-227, 230-231, 233,238, 240, 245, 259
Doves Press, 155
Dowden, Edward, 158, 185, 187,195, 224
Dowling, Basil, 220, 255, 258, 263, 290, 297, 299, 301
Dowson, Ernest, 178, 205, 210
Doyle, Arthur Conan, 170, 196, 199-200, 203, 205, 210, 212, 223, 241
Drabble, Margaret, 252, 281, 283-284, 288, 292, 299, 304, 306
Drayton, Michael, 39, 46-50, 53-54, 56, 60, 62-63
Dream of the Rood, 6
Drinkwater, John, 191, 223-224,228, 231, 233, 242, 250
Drummond, Henry, 164, 193, 203,206
Drummond, William, 45, 58, 61, 70-71
Drury Lane Theatre, 78, 136
Dryden, John, 63, 70, 72-86, 88
Duck, Stephen, 90, 102, 109
Duff, James, 145
Duffy, Sir Charles, 138, 190, 199, 207, 213
Duffy, Maureen, 245, 279, 283,286, 290, 292, 297, 301, 306, 309
Dugdale, Sir William, 54, 71-72,74, 76, 78, 82

DuMaurier, Daphne, 217, 243-245, 249, 251, 254-255, 257-259,263-266, 268, 272, 275-276, 288,292, 297, 299
Dunbar, William, 26, 30-31, 33
Dunn, Douglas, 256, 292, 297, 299, 304
Dunn, Nell, 248, 281, 288, 304
Dunsany, Edward, 187, 215-216,218-220, 223, 225, 228, 233, 250, 272
Dunton, John, 90
D'Urfey, Thomas, 71, 79-80, 86, 96-97
Durrell, Lawrence, 222, 248,257, 259, 261, 263, 266-267, 270,272, 274-276, 281, 290, 294, 297,299, 301-302, 304, 306, 310
Dyer, John, 86, 98, 103, 110

E

Eadgar, 7
Eadmer, 10
Eadmond Ironside, 9
Eadmund, 7
Eadred, 7
Eadward the Confessor, 9
Eadward the Elder, 6
Eadward the Martyr, 8
Eadwig, 7
Ealdhelm of Wessex, 4-5
Earle, John, 63
Early English Text Society, 175
East India Company, 52
Economist, 158
Eddington, Sir Arthur, 245
Edelman, Maurice, 221, 265, 267-268, 272, 275, 278, 281, 283, 288, 292, 299, 306
Eden, Emily, 128, 159, 171, 177, 179, 182
Eden, Richard, 32, 37-39, 42
Edgar, David, 261, 297, 299, 304, 308
Edgeworth, Maria, 114, 127-128, 130-132, 136, 139, 143, 145,162
Edgeworth, Richard Lovell, 128
Edinburgh Review, 109, 240
Edward I, 16
Edward II, 17
Edward III, 18
Edward IV, 25
Edward V, 27
Edward VI, 36
Edward VII, 211

Edward VIII, 249
Edwards, Richard, 32, 40-41, 43
Edwin of Northumbria, 3
Egan, Pierce, 116, 136, 142, 144, 162
Egoist, 225, 229
Eliot, Sir Charles, 174, 211, 217, 231, 242
Eliot, George, 140, 160, 167, 169, 171-173, 177-181, 184, 189
Eliot, T.S., 197, 228-230, 232, 239, 242, 244-246, 248-249, 253-258, 261, 263, 265-268, 271-272, 275, 279, 283-284, 292
Elizabeth I, 38
Elizabeth II, 266
Elliott, Ebenezer, 120, 147, 160, 162
Ellis, George, 108, 119, 133, 137
Ellis, Havelock, 170, 199, 203, 206-207, 218, 223, 252
Elphinstone, Mountstuart, 119, 157, 170, 196
Elton, Oliver, 172, 208, 223, 230, 239, 258
Elyot, Sir Thomas, 29, 34-36
Empson, William, 216, 240, 242, 248, 251, 265, 270, 278
Encyclopaedia Britannica, 114, 118, 123, 131, 220, 240
England's Helicon, 52
England's Parnassus, 52
English Association, 216
English Dialect Society, 183
English Opera House, 126
English Place-Name Society, 233
English Review, 218
Englishman, 93-94
Enright, D.J., 230, 267, 270-271, 276, 279, 284, 290, 297, 299, 300
Essays and Reviews, 172
Esto Perpetua Club, 121
Etherege, Sir George, 65, 75-76, 79, 84
Eton College, 24
Eusden, Laurence, 95
Evans, Sir Arthur, 164, 193, 204-205, 207, 211, 232, 255
Evans, Sir John, 143, 172, 175, 182, 191, 218
Evans, Mary Ann, 140, 189
Evans, Sebastian, 148, 207, 219
Evelyn, John, 74, 75, 78, 90, 139
Ewing, Juliana, 156, 183, 194
Examiner, 92
Examiner, 134, 189

Exeter Book, 8
Exeter Hall, 149
Exodus, 5, 16

F

Fabian Essays, 199
Fabian Society, 194
Fabyan, Robert, 31-32
Falconer, William, 112
Fantosme, Jordan, 13
Faraday, Michael, 155
Farquhar, George, 79, 87-91
Farrar, William, 170
Fascisulum Morum, 17
Feinstein, Elaine, 241, 286, 294, 297, 299, 302, 304
Female Spectator, 104-105
Fenner, Dudley, 45
Ferguson, Sir Samuel, 135, 150, 182, 190, 195-196
Fergusson, Robert, 117
Ferrier, James, 134, 154, 157, 167, 175, 177
Ferrier, Susan, 120, 140, 144, 149, 166
Field, Nathaniel, 57, 59, 64
Field, Richard, 45
Fielding, Henry, 91, 100, 102, 104, 106-108
Fielding, Sarah, 92, 105, 112, 114
Figaro in London, 149
Finlay, George, 159
Finney, Brian, 310
Finnisburg, 5
Firbank, Ronald, 195, 226-229, 233-234, 236
First Part of Sir John Oldcastle 52
Firth, Sir Charles, 210
Fish, Simon, 33
Fisher, Edward, 69
FitzAylwin, Henry, 13
Fitzgerald, Edward, 134, 164-166, 171, 189, 192
Flatman, Thomas, 78
Flecker, James, 193, 217, 222, 224, 226, 230, 232, 235
Flecknoe, Richard, 72, 75, 79
Fleet Street Prison, 162
Fletcher, Giles (elder), 36, 47, 57
Fletcher, Giles (younger), 45, 56, 61
Fletcher, John, 43, 55-57, 59-62, 67, 69, 71
Fletcher, Phineas, 44, 62, 64, 70

INDEX   321

Florence of Worcester, 10
Florio, John, 53
Floris and Blaunchefleur, 15
Foote, Samuel, 96, 108, 111-113,
  116, 118
Ford, Ford Madox, 183, 211-213, 215,
  217-217, 222, 224-226, 234-236,
  238, 240, 249, 251-252
Ford, John, 63-66
Ford, Richard, 127, 160, 169
Forster, E.M., 188, 215, 217-218,
  220, 222, 232, 234, 238-239,246,
  249, 253, 256, 261, 265, 267,271,
  284, 293, 297
Forster, John, 136, 162, 170,172,
  175, 180, 182, 186
Fortesque, John, 21, 25-27
Fortesque, Sir John, 208
Fortnightly Review, 176
Fowler, F.G., 216, 222
Fowler, H.W., 216, 222, 234, 236,
  284
Fowles, John, 236, 281, 286, 292,
  304, 309
Fox, George, 61, 84-86, 91
Foxe, John, 32, 36, 38-41, 45
Franciscan Friars, 15
Fraser, Alexander, 140, 168, 204,
  214, 225
Fraser's Magazine, 148, 192
Frayn, Michael, 245, 294, 297,306,
  308
Frazer, Sir James George, 166,196,
  199, 207, 210, 223, 240, 249,255
Freeman, Edward, 143, 164, 168,174,
  178, 191-192, 195, 200, 201
Freeman, Gillian, 240, 270-271,275,
  278, 281, 284, 292, 294, 306
French Academy, 65
Frere, John, 115, 155-157, 160
Friend, 134
Froude, James, 139, 168, 178, 182,
  195, 197, 203-205
Fry,Christopher, 217, 259, 263-265,
  268, 270, 274, 278, 294
Fuller, John, 250, 278, 288, 290,
  292, 294, 299, 302, 304
Fuller, Roy, 222, 249, 254, 256,
  258-259, 261, 263, 267-268, 272,
  275, 278-279, 281, 284, 290,294,
  299, 302, 304, 306
Fuller, Thomas, 55, 65-71, 73-74
Fulwell, Ulpian, 41
Furbank, P.N., 309

G

Gaimar, Geoffrey, 12
Gallacher, Tom, 246, 306, 308
Galsworthy, John, 178, 214, 216-
  217, 220, 222-224, 228, 230-232,
  234, 236, 238-240, 242-246
Galt, John, 119, 141-144, 155
Gardiner, Samuel, 147, 174, 184,
  193, 195, 200, 203, 212
Garnett, Richard, 152, 173, 187,
  198, 206-207, 214, 216
Garrick Club, 149
Garrick, David, 95, 103-104, 106,
  114, 116-117, 119
Garter, Thomas, 43
Garth, Sir Samuel, 74, 87, 96
Gascoigne, George, 33, 40, 42-43
Gascoyne, David, 226, 244, 249,251,
  257, 264, 271, 284, 294
Gaskell, Elizabeth, 135, 162, 164,
  166-167, 169-171, 174-176
Gasquet, Francis, 160, 198, 216,
  228, 232, 240
Gay, John, 81, 91, 93-95, 98-100,
  102
Gem, 147, 149, 217, 252
Genealogical and Heraldic History,
  145
Genesis, 4, 16
Genest, John, 150
Gentleman's Journal, 84, 85
Gentleman's Magazine, 100, 225
Geoffrey of Monmouth, 10, 12, 31
George I, 94
George II, 98
George III, 111
George IV, 135, 141
George V, 220
George VI, 249
Gerard, John, 35, 50, 57
Gerhardi, William, 204, 232-233,
  243, 246, 249, 254, 260
Germ, 163
Gervase of Tilbury, 14
Geystes of Skoggan, 40
Gibbon, Edward, 102, 111, 118-120,
  123, 126-127
Gifford, William, 109, 126-127, 145
Gilbert, Sir Humphrey, 43
Gilbert, William, 52
Gilbert, William S., 152, 177, 180-
  181, 183, 221
Gildas, 3
Gill, David, 246, 286, 294, 304
Gill, Eric, 191, 228, 238-239, 254

Gilliam, Terry, 310
Gilpin, William, 97, 121, 124-125, 128, 130, 132
Girton College, 179
Gissing, George, 168, 190, 194-195, 198-202, 207-209, 211, 213-216
Gladstone, William, 134, 154, 164, 170, 180, 184-187, 189, 207
Glanvill, Joseph, 66, 74, 80
Glanville, Brian, 242, 266, 268, 271, 274-275, 278-279, 281, 283-284, 286, 288, 292, 294, 299, 302, 304
Glen, Duncan, 245, 286, 288, 292, 294, 297, 299, 304
Glasse, Hannah, 106, 115
Globe Theatre, 50, 58
Glover, Richard, 93, 102, 108, 112, 122
Godden, Rumer, 217, 249, 251, 253-254, 256, 258-259, 262, 264, 270, 272, 274, 278, 281, 290, 292, 306
Godley, Alfred, 168, 196, 200-201, 205, 208-209, 212, 223, 235-236
Godly Queen Hester, 39
Gododdin, 3
Godwin, William, 109, 126, 129, 132, 152
Golagros and Gawain, 31
Golding, William, 221, 268, 270-271, 274-275, 283, 285, 288, 297
Goldsmith, Oliver, 99, 110-118
Gooch, Steve, 258, 306, 308
Googe, Barnabe, 30, 40, 43, 48
Gore, Catherine, 129, 149, 152, 157-159, 172
Gore, Charles, 165, 208-210, 227, 230, 244
Gospels, 8
Gosse, Sir Edmund, 162, 185, 189, 192, 194, 198, 209, 214-215, 217-218, 222, 228, 238
Gower, John, 17-21, 23
Grace Dieu, 23
Graham, Winston, 247, 259, 264, 267, 278, 281, 297, 302, 306
Grammer Gurton's Needle, 42
Granger, James, 115
Grant, James, 142, 160, 162, 183, 190, 196
Granta, 198
Granville-Barker, Harley, 187, 211, 215, 220, 233, 259
Graves, Richard, 94, 116, 118, 122, 124, 132

Graves, Robert, 204, 227-228, 235, 238, 240, 244, 247, 251, 254, 257-259, 262-263, 265, 270, 272, 275, 279, 283, 285-286, 290, 294, 297, 299, 304, 306, 310
Gray, Thomas, 95, 104, 106-108, 110-111, 116
Great Bible, 35
Great Exhibition, 164
Great Fire, 75
Green, Henry, 215, 237, 240, 253-254, 257-258, 260, 262, 266, 301
Green, John, 153, 184, 186-187, 191, 193
Green, Mary Anne, 139, 160, 163, 169, 204
Green, Matthew, 102
Green, Thomas, 152, 191, 193-194
Greene, Graham, 214, 240, 244, 247-249, 251, 254, 256-257, 262, 264-265, 267, 271-272, 274-275, 278, 283, 285, 292, 297, 299, 302, 304, 309
Greene, Robert, 39, 45-48
Greenwood, Walter, 213, 245, 247, 249-251, 253, 288
Greg, Sir Walter, 185, 235, 238-239, 243, 275
Gregory I, 3
Gregory, Lady Augusta, 165, 214-216, 219, 222-223, 232, 234, 244
Greville, Sir Fulke, 37, 56, 63, 65, 71
Grey, Sir George, 167
Grieve, Christopher Murray, 201, 308
Griffin, Gerald, 131, 147, 156, 157
Grigson, Geoffrey, 215, 253, 257, 260, 267, 288, 292, 297, 302, 304
Grimald, Nicholas, 38
Grose, Francis, 122
Grosvenor Gallery, 186
Grote, George, 126, 160, 176, 181-182, 186
Grove, Sir George, 188
Grub Street Journal, 100, 102
Guedalla, Philip, 198, 225, 230, 232-233, 237, 243, 255, 257
Guardian, 93
Guild of the Trinity, 31
Gunn, Thom, 240, 268-269, 272, 278, 280, 288, 297, 304
Gunning, Susannah Minifie, 103, 112, 114, 120, 126, 130
Gurney, Thomas, 107

INDEX 323

Guthrie, Thomas Anstey, 168, 192-195, 199-202, 210, 216, 246
Guy of Warwick, 17

H

Habington, William, 54, 65, 67, 74
Hackett, Sir John, 310
Haddan, A.W., 182
Haggard, H. Rider, 168, 195, 197, 200, 215, 235
Haggard, William, 217, 275, 279, 283, 288, 290, 302, 306
Hakluyt, Richard, 37, 44-46, 59
Haldane, John B.S., 201, 234, 238, 239, 244, 251, 254, 269, 282
Haldane, Richard, 168, 197, 213, 231-232, 238
Hale, John, 236, 304, 306, 308
Hale, Sir Matthew, 56, 79, 93, 102
Hales, Thomas de, 15
Hall, Edward, 35
Hall, John Clive, 230, 265, 286, 302
Hall, Joseph, 42, 50, 55, 69, 72-73
Hallam, Arthur Henry, 151
Hallam, Henry, 118, 140, 146, 153, 170
Halliwell-Phillipps, James, 141, 162, 166, 172, 191, 198
Hamilton, Anthony, 93
Hanley, James, 211, 290, 299, 302, 308
Hardicanute, 9
Hardy, Thomas, 155, 181-184, 187, 191-192, 196, 198, 200, 203, 205-206, 208, 212-213, 216, 218, 220, 224-225, 229, 232, 235, 238-239, 242
Hare, Julius, 127, 147, 156, 160, 167
Harington, James, 72
Harington, Sir John, 49
Harleian Society, 179
Harold I, 9
Harold II, 9
Harris, Frank, 168, 210, 220-222, 228, 242
Harris, Theodore Wilson, 230, 276, 278-279, 281, 283, 285, 288, 290, 294, 297, 299, 306
Harrison, Frederic, 148, 173, 185, 196, 198, 204-206, 210, 212, 215, 217, 223, 233
Harrowing of Hell, 16
Hartley, David, 90, 106, 109

Hartley, Leslie, 204, 244, 258, 260, 267, 270, 272, 276, 278, 283, 286, 290, 292, 294, 297, 298-299, 302
Harvey, Gabriel, 35, 47-48, 50, 63
Harvey, William, 43, 63, 70, 72
Havelock the Dane, 16
Hawes, Stephen, 27, 31, 33
Hawkins, Sir Anthony Hope, 174, 245
Hawkins, Capt. Sir John, 41
Hawkins, Sir John, 96, 118, 123-124
Hawkins, Sir Richard, 60
Haydon, Benjamin, 160
Hayward, Abraham, 130, 165, 170, 183-184, 193
Hayward, Sir John, 40, 50, 58, 62-63, 66
Haywood, Eliza, 85, 107, 108-109
Hazlitt, William, 119, 139-142, 144-146, 148
Hazlitt, William Carew, 151, 178, 186, 206, 224
Hearne, Thomas, 89, 98
Heath-Stubbs, John, 228, 256-257, 260, 263-264, 269, 274, 280, 290, 294, 306
Hell-Fire Club, 105
Helps, Sir Arthur, 136, 161-162, 167, 179, 181, 185
Henley, William Ernest, 162, 198, 200-202, 207, 209, 213
Henry I, 10
Henry II, 12
Henry III, 14
Henry IV, 21
Henry V, 23
Henry VI, 23, 26
Henry VII, 28
Henry VIII, 31, 32
Henry of Avranches, 15
Henry of Huntingdon, 12
Henryson, Robert, 24, 31, 48, 60
Henty, George, 208
Heppenstall, Rayner, 221, 250, 253-254, 257, 260, 267, 280, 292, 306
Hepplewhite, George, 123
Heralds' College, 27
Herbert, Edward, 44, 61, 69-70
Herbert, George, 47, 64-65, 71
Here Prophecy, 13
Her Majesty's Theatre, 90
Herrick, Robert, 46, 69-70, 78
Hewlett, Maurice, 172, 207, 210, 214, 218, 220-221, 227, 230-234
Heylyn, Peter, 52, 71, 74, 76-77

324   INDEX

Heywood, John, 29, 34, 36, 38, 43, 55
Heywood, Thomas, 42, 50, 52-53, 55, 57, 61, 64-67
Higden, Ranulf, 18
Hill, Geoffrey, 243, 290, 297
Hinde, Thomas, 236, 266, 272, 278, 280-281, 283, 285-286, 290, 295, 299, 304
Historical Manuscripts Commission, 179
History of Richard the Third, 34
Hoadly, Benjamin, 106
Hobbes, John Oliver, 178, 201, 209-211, 216
Hobbes, Thomas, 45, 68, 70-72, 79-80
Hobsbaum, Philip, 243, 283, 285-286, 293, 299
Hobsbawn, E.J., 310
Hoccleve, Thomas, 19, 22-25
Hodge, Alan, 310
Hodgson, Ralph, 181, 224, 279
Hodgson, Shadworth, 149, 176, 180, 188, 208, 222
Hoff, Harry Summerfield, 220
Hogarth, David, 173, 205, 214, 221, 237, 239
Hogarth, William, 108
Hogg, James, 115, 133, 135-137, 140, 143-144, 146, 151-152
Holbrook, David, 233, 278, 280-281, 286, 288, 293
Holcroft, Thomas, 105, 120, 125, 126
Holden, Molly, 237, 283, 290, 297, 299, 302, 304, 306
Hole, Samuel, 140, 161, 171, 180, 182, 201, 203, 211, 214
Holland, Philemon, 37, 53, 56, 64, 66
Holland, Richard, 25
Holloway, John, 230, 267, 271, 276, 278, 280, 283, 285, 287, 290, 295
Holme, Constance, 190, 225, 229, 231, 269
Home, John, 109
Hood, Thomas, 129, 145, 157-159
Hook, Theodore, 123, 146, 148, 153-154, 156
Hooker, Richard, 37, 48, 50, 52
Hope, Anthony, 174, 203, 208, 245
Hope, Thomas, 140
Hope Theatre, 58
Hopkins, Gerard Manley, 158, 198, 228, 242, 262, 288
Hopkins, John, 39
Hopkins, Matthew, 69
Horizon, 252, 263
Horman, William, 32
Horne, Richard, 132, 158, 160, 164, 171, 193
Hort, Fenton J.A., 202
Hospitallers of St. John of Jerusalem, 10
Houghton, William, 190, 218, 220-224
House of Commons' Journals, 117
Household, Geoffrey, 210, 250-251, 253, 264-266, 270, 274, 276, 281, 285, 287-288, 290, 297, 299, 302, 306
Household Words, 163, 170
Housman, A.E., 170, 205, 232, 245, 249, 252-253, 287
Housman, Laurence, 176, 234, 239, 275
Howard, Edward, 153
Howard, Roger, 251, 297, 308
Howell, James, 48, 68, 72, 75
Hoyle, Edmund, 77, 104, 111, 115
Hudson, William, 214
Hudson's Bay Company 77, 179
Hugh of Rutland, 13
Hughes, Richard, 210, 232, 237, 240, 243, 251, 254, 278, 307
Hughes, Ted, 241, 272, 276, 278, 280-281, 288, 295, 299, 302
Hughes, Thomas, 142, 169, 171-172, 183, 203
Hulme, Thomas Ernest, 234
Hume, David, 92, 103-104, 106-108, 110, 118-119
Humphreys, Emyr, 229, 260, 263, 265-266, 270, 273, 275, 280, 285, 290, 297, 304
Hunt, Leigh, 121, 138, 140, 145, 151-152, 156, 159-161, 164, 170
Hurd, Richard, 96, 106-107, 112, 116, 134
Hurdis, James, 123
Hutcheson, Francis, 85, 98, 105, 109
Hutchinson, Lucy, 133
Hutchinson, Ray Coryton, 217, 242, 244-245, 248-249, 251, 254, 259, 263, 266, 273, 278, 283, 293, 297, 306
Huth, Henry, 137, 178, 181, 184, 185, 187
Hutton, Richard, 145, 181, 197,

INDEX

203, 206, 209
Huxley, Aldous, 203, 230-233, 235, 237, 239, 242-244, 247, 249-250, 252, 255-256, 259, 262, 264, 269, 271, 274, 280, 281
Huxley, Sir Julian, 196, 233, 240, 244, 253, 263, 273, 306
Huxley, Thomas, 145, 174, 179, 181, 183, 196, 201-204
Hyde, Douglas, 171, 203, 209, 216, 262
Hymns Ancient and Modern, 172

I

Idler, 201
Inchbald, Elizabeth, 106, 122, 125, 127, 133, 142
Indicator, 140, 142
Inge, William, 171, 229, 232, 268
Ingelow, Jean, 141, 174, 178, 206
Innes, Hammond, 224, 250, 252-255, 260-266, 269, 271, 274, 276, 280, 285, 297, 302, 304
Intelligencer, 74-75
Isherwood, Christopher, 214, 239, 247-248, 250-253, 259, 265, 266, 280, 287-288, 295, 308

J

Jacobs, William, 174, 205, 207, 211, 225, 256
Jaggard, William, 50
Jacob's Well, 24
James I (England), 53
James II (England), 82
James I (Scotland), 24
James, George, 129, 147, 149-150, 153, 171
James, Henry, 158, 185, 187-191, 196, 198, 200, 207-209, 211-214, 222, 224-225, 227-228
James, Montague, 173, 234, 243, 248
Jameson, Anna, 150
Jamieson, John, 134
Jeans, Sir James, 242
Jebb, Sir Richard, 186
Jellicoe, Ann, 237, 283, 287, 289, 295
Jennings, Elizabeth, 236, 270, 278, 283, 287, 295, 299
Jenyns, Soame, 89, 108, 110, 118, 123
Jerome, Jerome, 218
Jerrold, Douglas, 132, 147, 149, 160, 169
Jewsbury, Geraldine, 136, 160, 162, 164, 171, 189
Jockey Club, 107
John of Bromyard, 21
John of Salisbury, 10, 12-13
John, Augustus, 266
Johnson, Brian Stanley, 245, 281, 283, 287, 293, 297, 301-302, 306
Johnson, James, 123
Johnson, Lionel, 178, 204-205, 207, 212, 219, 223
Johnson, Richard, 42, 47, 50, 55, 57, 73
Johnson, Samuel, 91, 100-103, 105-110, 113-117, 119, 121-123
Johnstone, Charles, 111
Jones, David, 204, 250, 265, 275, 293, 303, 304, 310
Jones, Henry, 164, 189, 192, 194, 199-200, 203-205, 207, 218, 224, 225, 240
Jones, Sir William, 122
Jonson, Ben, 42, 50, 52-54, 56-60, 62-67, 71
Jonsonus Virbius, 66
Joseph of Arimathie, 18
Joseph of Exeter, 13
Jowett, Benjamin, 138, 172, 202
Joyce, James, 191, 217, 223, 225, 227-228, 232, 237, 239-240, 247, 249-250, 253, 255, 275
Joyce, Patrick, 146, 180, 191, 213, 225
Juliana of Norwich, 21
Junius (Letters), 116

K

Kames, Lord, 85, 111-112, 120
Kavanagh, Julia, 144, 164, 170, 187
Kavanagh, Patrick Joseph, 242, 275, 289, 290, 295, 299, 304
Keane, John Brendan, 238, 275-276, 285, 293, 306, 308
Keats, John, 127, 136-138, 140-142
Keble College, Oxford, 180
Keble, John, 125, 146, 161, 177, 180
Kelly, Hugh, 103, 114-115, 117-118
Kelly's Directory, 129
Kelmscott Press, 199
Kemble, Frances, 134, 159, 192, 202

Kemble, John, 133, 150, 155, 163, 169
Kemp, Margery, 24
Kemp, William, 52
Ken, Thomas, 66, 75, 82, 85, 92
Kennedy, Margaret, 205, 234, 242
Kennelly, Brendan, 248, 281, 283, 285, 287, 289-290, 293, 295,297, 299, 302
Kensington Palace, 56
Ker, William, 167, 207, 215, 233
Keyes, Sidney, 231, 256-257, 260
Keynes, John Maynard, 192, 229, 249, 259, 263
Killigrew, Henry, 66
Killigrew, Thomas (elder), 66
Killigrew, Thomas (younger), 96
Killigrew, Sir William, 54, 75-76, 85
King Alisaunder, 17
King Darius, 40
King Horn, 16
King, Thomas, 121
King, William, 74, 83, 87, 91-93
King, Archbp. William, 70, 84, 89, 99
King's College, Cambridge, 24
Kinglake, Alexander William, 134, 159, 174, 200
Kingsley, Charles, 140, 162, 164, 166-169, 171, 174-176, 181,183, 185
Kingsley, Henry, 148, 171, 173-174, 176-178, 186
Kinsella, Thomas, 238, 266, 271-274, 276, 278, 280, 287, 289, 293, 300, 302, 304
Kipling, Rudyard, 176, 196, 198, 200-201, 203, 205, 209, 211-212, 216, 221, 229, 238, 242, 245-246, 248
Kirkup, James, 233, 261, 265-266, 269, 273, 275, 280-281, 285,290, 293, 295, 297, 300
Kit-Kat Club, 88
Knack to Know a Knave, 48
Knights Templars, 10
Knolles, Richard, 53
Knowles, James, 121, 137, 141,145, 147, 150, 153, 173
Knox, John, 30, 36, 38-39, 42, 45
Knox, Ronald, 197, 224, 228, 238-239, 244, 248, 253, 259, 263-264, 270, 272-273
Knox, Vicesimus, 107, 119, 124,142
Knyvett, Sir Henry, 49

Koestler, Arthur, 215, 253-254, 257, 259-260, 265, 290, 300,304, 309
Kottabos, 179, 197
Kyd, Thomas, 38, 48-49
Kyrle Society, 187

L

Lamb, Lady Caroline, 122, 138,143-144, 146
Lamb, Charles, 117, 129, 131-135, 146, 148, 150-151
Lamb, Mary, 133, 135
Lambeth Homilies, 14
Lamentable Tragedies of Locrine,49
Lancaster, Joseph, 132
Landon, Letitia, 153
Landor, Robert, 120, 144, 147,161-162, 179
Landor, Walter Savage, 117, 129, 136, 144, 151, 153, 155, 161,166, 175
Lane, Edward, 154
Lang, Andrew, 158, 182, 189-194, 196-198, 200-203, 207-209, 211-212, 216, 219-223, 233
Langland, William, 18-20, 22
Langtoft, Peter, 17
Larkin, Philip, 231, 259-261, 265, 269-270, 283, 295, 304
Latham, Simon, 58
Laud Troy Book, 22
Law, William, 82, 95, 97-100, 103, 108, 111
Lawless, Emily, 159, 196, 201,212, 224
Lawrence, D.H., 194, 222-233, 235, 237-244, 247, 249, 253, 264,270, 273, 280, 285, 287
Lawrence, George, 146, 169, 171, 186
Lawrence, T.E., 197, 237, 247
Layamon, 14
Leader, 163, 177
Leaf, W., 193
Leander Club, 173
Lear, Edward, 136, 161, 181, 197
Leavis, F.R., 204, 242, 244, 249, 262, 266, 270, 309
LeCarre, John, 242, 276, 280-281, 285, 290, 297, 304, 309
Lecky, William E.H., 154, 172-174, 176, 180, 188, 205, 209, 213,219
Lee, Nathaniel, 71, 78-81, 84
Lee, Sir Sidney, 170, 195, 208,212,

INDEX 327

215-216, 221-222, 226, 235-236
LeFanu, Joseph, 137, 153, 174-175, 182-183
Lefroy, Edward, 195
LeGallienne, Richard, 177, 224,237, 260
Lehmann, John, 217, 265, 276, 281, 285, 297, 305
Leland, John, 30, 36-37, 92, 94
Lennox, Charlotte, 96, 108, 115, 132
Lerner, Lawrence, 235, 275, 281, 290, 293, 305
Lessing, Doris, 229, 264-266, 269, 275-276, 280-281, 283, 285, 293, 297, 300, 302, 305
L'Estrange, Sir Roger, 59, 80, 84, 89
Lever, Charles, 133, 153, 156,158-161, 163-166, 174-176, 182
Lewes, George, 138, 160, 168, 170-171, 173, 183, 187
Lewis, Alun, 226, 256-257, 259,262
Lewis, Charlton T., 189
Lewis, C.S., 207, 246, 249, 252, 254, 256, 269, 276, 281
Lewis, Sir George, 133, 147, 163, 168, 173-174
Lewis, Matthew Gregory, 117, 127, 129, 139
Lewis, Norman, 310
Lewis, Percy Wyndham, 195, 228-229, 237-240, 242, 244, 247, 249-250, 253, 266, 269-272
Libel of English Policy, 24
Liber Eliensis, 10
Liber Exemplorum, 16
Liberal Magazine, 143
Library, 198, 230
Liddon, Henry, 178
Lillo, George, 85, 100-103
Lilly, William, 70
Lily, William, 33
Lindisfarne Gospels, 4
Lindsay, Lady Anne,116
Lindsay, Sir David, 28, 33-34, 37-38, 44
Lingard, John, 116, 133, 141, 164
Linnean Society, 123
Literary Club, 113
Literary Magazine, 109
Literature, 206
Litvinoff, Emanuel, 226, 255-256, 262, 275, 291, 300, 302, 306
Livings, Henry, 240, 285, 291,293, 297

Livingstone, David, 136, 169, 176, 183-184
Locke, John, 64, 83-85, 90
Locke, William, 174, 216, 241
Locker, Frederick, 142, 169, 178, 189, 204
Lockhart, John, 126, 141-144, 147, 153, 166
Lodge, David, 247, 276, 280, 285, 295, 307
Lodge, Sir Oliver, 164, 220, 227, 235, 242, 254
Lodge, Thomas, 38, 43-46, 48-49, 53, 58, 61-62
Logue, Christopher, 236, 280, 287, 289, 293
London Bridge, 14, 149
London Hay Market, 75
London Library, 156, 177
London Magazine, 100, 122, 141,147, 268
London Monument, 79
London Prodigal, 54
London University, 147
London Working Men's College, 166
Longley, Michael, 252, 285, 291, 293, 300, 302
Lounger, 122
Lovelace, Richard, 59, 70, 72
Lovelich, Henry, 24
Lover, 94
Lover, Samuel, 128, 153, 155, 157, 179
Lover's Message, 7
Lowbury, Edward, 224, 247, 260, 270, 278, 285, 291, 293, 302,305
Lowndes, William, 151, 155, 158
Lowry, Malcolm, 219, 246, 261,272, 280
Lubbock, Percy, 188, 231, 233,240, 261, 284
Ludlow, Edmund, 86
Lupton, Thomas, 43
Luttrell, Henry, 141
Luttrell, Narcissus, 94
Lyall, Sir Alfred, 152, 192, 199, 202, 209, 213, 216, 221, 226
Lyall, Edna, 168, 192, 194-195, 213
Lyceum Theatre, 151
Lydgate, John, 19, 23-25, 28, 30-31
Lyell, Sir Charles, 128, 148, 154, 160, 163, 174, 185
Lyly, John, 37, 43-48, 50, 54
Lyra Apostolica, 153
Lytell Geste of Robyn Hoode, 29

Lyttelton, George, 91, 111, 114, 116

M

Macaulay, Dame Rose, 190, 230, 233-234, 247, 264, 271, 273
Macaulay, Thomas Babington, 130, 157-158, 163, 168, 170, 171
MacBeth, George, 243, 269, 280-281, 283, 285, 287, 289, 291, 293, 295, 297, 300, 302, 305
MacCaig, Norman, 220, 257, 260, 270, 273, 277, 280, 285, 287, 291, 293, 295, 297, 302, 305
Macdiarmid, Hugh, 201, 236-238, 242-244, 247, 252, 257, 261, 270, 273, 275, 280-281, 283, 285, 287, 289, 291, 293, 295, 302, 305, 308
MacDonagh, Donagh, 274
MacDonald, George, 144, 168, 170, 174, 176, 215
Machen, Arthur, 174, 213, 216, 226, 233-234, 260
MacInnes, Colin, 225, 264, 291, 293, 307
Mackay, Mary, 167, 234
Mackenzie, Sir Compton, 192, 223-226, 238-240, 243, 250, 261, 282-283, 285, 287
Mackenzie, Henry, 105, 116-118, 148
Mackintosh, Sir James, 113, 125, 138, 148-149, 151
Macklin, Charles, 86, 110, 120, 128
Macleod, Fiona, 167, 203-204, 211, 215
Macmillan's Magazine, 170, 217
Macneice, Louis, 217, 240, 248, 250, 252-255, 258, 261-263, 266, 269, 273, 278, 281-283, 285, 287
Macpherson, James, 102, 111-112, 118, 127
Madden, Didgson, 207
Magdalen College, Oxford, 25
Magee, Bryan, 310
Magnet, 218, 254
Mahon, Derek, 255, 285, 291, 295, 300
Maine, Sir Henry, 142, 172, 181, 185, 193, 195, 197
Maitland Club, 147
Maitland, Frederic, 163, 197, 204, 207-208, 211, 213, 216
Major, John, 26, 31-32, 37
Mallet, David, 90, 97, 103, 113
Mallock, William, 187

Malone, Edmund, 103, 119, 124, 136
Malone Society, 216
Malory, Sir Thomas, 26, 28
Malthus, Thomas, 113, 129, 132, 138, 141, 151
Manchester Guardian, 142
Mandeville, Bernard, 77, 90, 94, 101
Mandeville, John, 19
Manning, Henry, 185
Mannying, Robert, 17
Mansel, Henry, 141, 163-164, 170, 172, 181
Mansfield, Katherine, 197, 222, 228, 230, 232-235, 259
Map, Walter, 11, 13-14
Marcus, Frank, 238, 283, 285, 307, 309
Mariner's Mirror, 220
Marischal College, 47
Markham, Gervase, 41, 48-49, 55, 59, 64-66
Marlowe, Christopher, 40, 46-48, 50, 52, 54, 65
Marmion, Shackerley, 53, 66-68
Marriage of Wit and Science, 41
Marriage of Wit and Wisdom, 43
Marryat, Frederick, 125, 147, 151, 155-157, 159, 162
Marston, John, 42, 50, 53-55, 65
Marston, John Westland, 140, 157, 163-164, 169, 177, 180, 199
Marston, Philip, 163, 181, 185, 193, 196-197, 200
Martin, Sir Theodore, 138, 160, 176, 185, 188, 193, 196, 219
Martineau, Harriet, 131, 150-151, 153-155, 157, 163, 166, 186
Martineau, James, 132, 189, 192, 195, 198, 200, 210
Marvell, Andrew, 60, 70, 78-80, 83
Mary I, 37
Mary II, 83
Masefield, John, 187, 214, 216, 220-221, 223, 226, 228, 232, 234, 238, 240-241, 246, 248, 250, 252, 254, 256, 269, 282, 288
Massinger, Philip, 44, 60-61, 63-67, 71-72
Masson, David, 171
Masters, John, 225, 265-267, 269-270, 273, 275, 277, 280, 283, 285, 289, 295, 300, 305, 307
Mathias, Thomas, 126
Matthew's Bible, 35
Maturin, Charles, 120, 134-135,

INDEX 329

138-141, 144
Maugham, Robin, 309
Maugham, W. Somerset, 184, 207, 226, 229, 231-232, 236, 242,247, 258, 263, 265, 284
Maurice, John, 132, 154, 161, 166, 182
Mavor, Osborne Henry, 197, 264
May, Thomas, 48, 62-63, 69-70
May, Sir Thomas Erskine, 137,167, 172, 195
Mayhew, Henry, 136, 172, 196
McCarthy, Justin, 148, 185, 188-189, 222
McEwan, Ian, 309
McGahern, John, 246, 282, 287, 307
McGough, Roger, 250, 289, 293, 297, 302, 305
McTaggart, John, 177, 206, 211,216, 221, 231, 235, 238
Medwall, Henry, 28-29
Memoirs of a Cavalier, 97
Memoirs of Captain Carleton, 99
Menen, Salvatore A.C., 222, 262, 263-264, 266, 269, 271, 275,280, 285, 307
Mercator, 93-94
Mercer, David, 238, 283, 289, 295
Mercurius Librarius, 80
Mercurius Politicus, 95-96
Mercurius Publicus, 73
Meredith, George, 146, 164, 168-169, 171-173, 175-177, 181, 185, 187, 189-190, 193, 195, 197-198, 200, 203-204, 206, 208, 212, 219, 220-221
Meres, Francis, 50
Merivale, Charles, 134, 164, 166, 175, 177, 202
Merivale, Herman, 155, 192-194, 196, 198, 216
Merriman, Henry, 173, 198, 201, 203, 206-207, 213
Merry Devil, 55
Merton College, Oxford, 16
Metaphysical Society, 179, 190
Metham, John, 25
Metropolitan Tabernacle, 172
Meynell, Alice, 161, 185, 202,206, 208, 212, 221, 228, 231-232, 234
Michel, Dan, 18
Microcosm, 122-123
Middleton, Christopher, 236, 258-259, 280, 285, 293, 295, 300, 305
Middleton, Conyers, 81,104,106-107

Middleton, Stanley, 229, 274,277-278, 280, 282-283, 287, 291,293, 297, 300, 302, 305, 307
Middleton, Thomas, 41, 55, 57-63, 71-72, 74, 119
Miles, Henry Downes, 217
Mill, James, 116, 140, 142, 147, 152
Mill, John Stuart, 133, 145, 158, 162, 171, 173, 176, 178, 180,183
Miller, Hugh, 131, 157, 161, 167-169
Milman, Henry, 124, 138, 148, 156, 167, 179
Milne, Charles Ewart, 213, 252, 254-255, 258, 261, 264-265, 267, 274, 280, 289
Milton, John, 55, 62-66, 68-73, 76-78, 81
Mind, 186
Minot, Laurence, 18
Mirror, 115
Mirrour for Magistrates, 39-40
Misogonus, 39
Mitchel, John, 139, 160, 168, 180, 185
Mitford, Mary, 123, 144, 152, 154, 165, 167
Mitford, William, 122
Moir, David, 147
Mole, John, 255, 278, 295, 300, 305, 307
Molly Maguires, 158
Monboddo, Lord, 94, 117, 119, 129
Monitor, 109
Monro, Harold, 246
Monsarrat, Nicholas, 220, 247-250, 253, 257-262, 265, 267, 270-271, 275, 277-278, 280, 282-283, 285, 287, 291, 302
Montagu, Charles, 82
Montagu, Elizabeth, 115
Montagu, Lady Mary Wortley, 83,95, 112
Montague, Charles, 178, 232, 238-239
Montague, John, 240, 274, 277-278, 283, 287, 289, 295, 300, 302,305
Montgomerie, Alexander, 38, 50, 56, 60
Montgomery, Robert, 133, 147-148, 167
Monthly Review, 106, 159
Moore, Edward, 93, 108
Moore, Francis, 88
Moore, George, 165, 193, 195, 198,

203-204, 208, 212, 214, 217, 223, 225, 227, 234, 242, 245, 265
Moore, George Edward, 183, 214, 232, 268, 273
Moore, John, 99, 119, 122, 126-127, 130, 131
Moore, Thomas, 119, 131, 136, 139-140, 144-146, 148-149, 152, 161, 165
More, Edward, 107, 109
More, Hannah, 105, 117-119, 123, 135, 150
More, Henry, 58, 68-69, 71-73, 75-76, 82
More, Sir Thomas, 27, 31-35
Morgan, Charles, 203, 240, 244, 249, 254-255, 261, 263, 266, 273
Morgan, Robert, 231, 289, 291, 293, 297, 300, 302, 305
Morgan, Lady Sydney, 121, 133, 137, 146, 170
Morgann, Maurice, 119
Morier, James, 120, 136, 140, 144, 162
Morley, John, 154, 178, 181-182, 184, 187-189, 191, 200, 211, 214, 225, 228, 233
Morning Advertiser, 126
Morning Chronicle, 115, 173
Morning Herald, 120, 179
Morning Post, 116, 250
Morris, Sir Lewis, 150, 181, 186, 189, 193, 196, 200, 216, 217
Morris, William, 151, 170, 178-179, 182, 185-186, 195, 197-200, 204-208
Morte Arthur, 22
Morte Arthure, 19
Morton, John, 135, 161, 200
Morton, Thomas, 113, 127-129, 154
Motherwell, William, 128, 146, 150, 152
Motteaux, Peter, 90
Moxon, Joseph, 81
Muggleton, Lodowicke, 71
Muir, Edwin, 196, 228, 234, 236-237, 239, 247-249, 253-254, 257, 260, 263, 266, 269, 271, 275, 277
Mulcaster, Richard, 33, 44, 57
Mulock, Dinah, 169
Mum and the Sothsegger, 22
Munby, Arthur, 146, 165, 176, 190, 212, 220
Munday, Anthony, 37, 46, 48, 53, 64
Mundus et Infans, 32

Munro, Hector, 180, 221-223, 225, 227, 246
Munro, Hugh, 140, 175, 188, 194, 204, 215
Murdoch, Iris, 229, 268-269, 271, 273-274, 278, 280, 282-283, 285, 287, 291, 293, 295, 297, 302, 305, 308
Murphy, Arthur, 98, 111, 113, 133
Murray, George, 177, 218, 224, 246, 254, 260
Murray, Sir James, 153, 184, 194, 226
Murray, Lindley, 105, 127, 129, 132, 145
Murry, John Middleton, 198, 232, 234, 236-237, 243, 246, 269, 272
Myers, E., 193
Myers, Frederic, 158, 178, 191, 193, 211
Myers, Leopold, 190, 232, 236, 240, 248-249, 254, 257
Myres, J.N.L., 249

N

Nairne, Carolina, 161
Nanteuil, Samson de, 11
Napier, John, 36, 58-60
Napier, Sir William, 147
Nashe, Thomas, 40, 46-53
Nation, 157, 163
Nation and Athenaeum, 231
National Gallery, 154
National Portrait Gallery, 168
National Review, 193
Nature, 179
Neal, Daniel, 100
Neale, John Mason, 139, 161, 166, 177
Nennius, 5
Nesbit, Edith, 169, 209, 212, 215, 218-219, 221, 234
New College, Oxford, 20
New Interlude for Children, 39
New Monthly Magazine, 137, 194
New Sporting Magazine, 149
New Statesman, 224, 243
New Style Calendar, 107
New Theatre, 94
New Writing, 249, 254
Newbolt, Sir Henry, 173, 207, 215, 221, 230, 251
Newby, Eric, 310
Newdigate Prize, 133
Newgate Calendar, 117

INDEX
331

Newgate Prison, 120
Newman, John Henry, 130, 150,157, 160, 162, 164-165, 168, 171,175, 177, 179, 181, 184, 199
Newnham College, 186
News, 74-75
Newton, Sir Isaac, 68, 82, 90, 98
Newton, John, 113
Nice Wanton, 39
Nichols, John, 105, 120, 127, 131, 136, 139, 145
Nichols, Peter Richard, 237, 289, 293, 297, 300, 305, 309
Nicholson, Norman, 225, 258-263, 268-269, 275, 287, 289, 300, 305
Nineteenth Century, 187
Noctes Ambrosianae, 143
Noel, Roden, 151, 184, 191, 195, 203
Norris, John, 89
North Briton, 112
North, Sir Thomas, 34, 38, 41, 43, 43
Northern Homily Cycle, 17
Norton, Thomas, 39
Notes and Queries, 163
Noyes, Alfred, 189, 219, 224, 232, 264, 273

O

O'Brien, Flann, 309
Observator, 80, 82
Observer, 125
O'Casey, Sean, 189, 236-237, 239, 246, 248, 253-254, 256, 259, 263, 269-270, 274, 277, 282
O'Connor, Frank, 213, 243-244, 250, 252, 254, 258-261, 265, 273, 275, 277, 282-283, 288, 293
O'Donovan, Michael Francis, 213, 288
O'Faolain, Sean, 210, 244, 246, 248-250, 254, 261, 273, 278, 287, 295, 307
O'Flaherty, Liam, 206, 236-237, 240, 243-244, 247, 250, 262, 271, 302
Ogden, C.K., 234
O'Keefe, John, 105, 119, 121, 125, 150
Old Testament, 194
Old Vic Theatre, 139
Oldham, John, 71, 80-81
Oldmixon, John, 78, 91, 93, 97-98, 104
Oliphant, Margaret, 146, 163, 174,
190, 192, 198-200, 206-207, 209
Opie, Amelia, 115, 132-133, 150, 165
Original, 152
Orrery, 5th Earl of, 112
Orwell, George, 213, 246-250, 252-255, 259-261, 263-264, 268, 291
Osborne, John, 240, 273-274, 278, 282, 285, 287, 291, 295, 297, 300, 305, 307-308
Osborne, Thomas, 105
Osbourne, Lloyd, 204
O'Shaughnessy, Arthur, 158, 181-182, 184, 190
Otway, Thomas, 71, 78-81
Ouida, 155, 178, 180-184, 191-192, 218
Overbury, Sir Thomas, 44, 58
Owen, Robert, 116, 136, 163, 169
Owen, Wilfred, 202, 228, 230, 243, 282, 287
Owl and the Nightingale, 14
Oxford and Cambridge Magazine, 168
Oxford Gazette, 75
Oxford University, 12
Oxford University Press, 83

P

Pain, Barry, 175, 211, 213, 222-224, 239
Paine, Thomas, 102, 118, 125-127
Painter, William, 40
Paley, William, 104, 122, 124, 131, 133
Palgrave, Francis, 123, 150-151, 154, 164, 172
Palgrave, Francis Turner, 144, 173, 191, 206
Palgrave, William, 145, 176, 183, 197
Pall-Mall Gazette, 176, 189
Paltock, Robert, 107
Pantheon (London), 125
Paris, Matthew, 15-16
Park, Mungo, 129
Parker, Matthew, 42
Parkinson, John, 63, 67
Parkinson, Thomas, 40, 70
Parliamentary Intelligencer, 73
Parnassus Plays, 52
Parnell, Thomas, 80, 95-96
Parrot, 105
Pater, Walter, 155, 184, 195, 197, 202-204, 206
Paternoster Play, 20

Patmore, Coventry, 143, 167-168, 172-173, 187-188, 196, 199, 201, 205
Pattison, Mark, 136, 172, 193, 199
Payn, Thomas, 148, 166, 175, 188, 192, 194-195, 204, 207, 209
Payne, Basil, 238, 280, 298, 302, 305
Peacham, Henry, 42, 55, 61, 68
Peacock, Reginald, 21, 24-25
Peacock, Thomas Love, 122, 138-140, 143, 147, 149, 173, 177
Pearl, 18
Pearson, John, 73
Pearson, John, 310
Peckham, John, 17
Peele, George, 38, 44-46, 48-49, 51
Penn, William, 68, 76-77, 85, 95
Pennant, Thomas, 98, 114, 116-117, 119-121, 128
Penny Cyclopaedia, 150, 159
Penny Magazine, 149, 159
Pentonville Prison, 157
Pepys, Samuel, 64, 89, 145
Percy Society, 156
Percy, Thomas, 99, 112-113, 135
Peter of Peckham, 16
Peterborough Chronicle, 12
Petty, Sir William, 84
Phelps, Gilbert, 226, 268, 270, 274, 277, 282, 298, 302, 307
Philips, Ambrose, 92
Philips, John, 78, 90-91
Phillip, John, 40
Phillippe de Thaun, 10
Phillipps, Edward, 73
Phillipps, John, 72
Philosophical Society, 69
Phoenix Nest, 48
Pickering, John, 40
Pierce the Ploughman's Creed, 21
Pimlyco, 56
Pindar, Peter, 102, 121-122, 140
Pinero, Sir Arthur Wing, 167, 191, 195-198, 200-202, 204-205, 208-209, 212, 217, 219-220, 223-224, 246
Pinter, Harold, 241, 277-278, 280, 282, 285, 289, 291, 293, 307, 309
Piozzi, Hester Lynch Thrale, 122
Piramus, Denis, 12
Pitman, Sir Isaac, 154
Pitt, Christopher, 103
Planche, James, 127, 145, 150-151, 157, 189

Plomer, William, 310
Poema Morale, 12
Poetry Review, 222
Pole, Reginald, 34
Poliakoff, Stephen, 267, 307, 308
Pollock, Sir Frederick, 159, 186, 192, 197, 215, 223, 250
Pomfret, John, 88
Poole, John, 122, 145-147, 182
Poor Robin's Almanack, 74
Pope, Alexander, 83, 92-95, 97-104
Popple, William, 101
Pordage, Samuel, 64, 81, 84
Porson, Richard, 110, 123, 128, 129, 131, 134
Porter, Jane, 118, 132, 134-135, 163
Potter, Beatrix, 177, 213-214, 256
Pound, Ezra, 194, 219-221, 223, 227-230, 235, 243, 247-248, 252, 262, 264-265, 268-269, 271, 291, 293, 298, 303
Powell, Anthony, 215, 243, 246, 265-266, 270, 273, 277, 280, 283, 287, 298, 303, 307
Powys, John Cowper, 182, 206, 209, 226-228, 232, 234, 236, 241, 243, 244, 246-248, 251-252, 254, 261, 265-266, 269-271, 277, 281-283
Powys, Llewelyn, 193, 239, 242, 248, 250, 252-253
Powys, Theodore, 185, 234-239, 242-244, 260, 267
Preston, Thomas, 41
Price, Richard, 109
Pride of Life, 22
Priestley, J.B., 203, 236, 238, 241-242, 245-246, 252-253, 259, 277-278, 280, 283, 285, 287, 289, 291, 307, 308
Priestley, Joseph, 101, 114, 117, 132
Primrose League, 193
Prince, Frank T., 310
Prior, Matthew, 75, 82-83, 88, 91, 95-97
Pritchett, Victor S., 210, 241, 251, 256, 260, 265, 271, 278, 282, 293, 295, 303, 305, 310
Procter, Adelaide Anne, 145, 170, 174-175
Procter, Bryan, 142
Prynne, William, 52, 64, 74, 76
Public Advertiser, 107, 128
Public Ledger, 110

INDEX

Pudney, John, 219, 246, 248, 252, 256-258, 260-262, 264-266, 268, 273, 275, 278, 289, 293, 298, 300, 303, 305, 308
Pugin, Augustus, 136, 157-158, 161, 165
Pullen, Henry, 181
Punch, 156
Punchinello, 149
Purchas, Samuel, 42, 58, 60, 62
The Puritan, 55
Purvey, John, 21
Pusey, Edward, 130, 168, 191
Pusey House, 194
Puttenham, Richard, 46
Pye, Henry James, 124

Q

Quaritch, Bernard, 197
Quarles, Francis, 47, 65, 68
Quarterly Review, 134
Quiller-Couch, Sir Arthur, 174, 211, 221, 223, 227, 229-230, 236, 241, 253, 257

R

Radcliffe, Ann, 113, 124-126, 128, 143
Raigne of Edward III, 49
Railway Timetables, 153
Raine, Kathleen, 218, 257, 260, 263, 266, 271, 277, 285, 291, 298, 303
Ralegh, Sir Walter, 37, 46-47, 49, 52, 57-59
Raleigh, Sir Walter, 172, 211, 214, 218, 221, 232, 234
Ramsay, Allan, 82, 97-98, 110
Randolph, Thomas, 63, 65-66, 70
Ranelagh Gardens, 104, 132
Rashdall, Hastings, 169, 205, 218, 229, 234
Rattigan, Terence, 221, 262, 266, 268-269, 274, 282, 309
Rauf Collyer, 42
Raven, Simon, 237, 275, 277, 280, 283, 285, 287, 289, 291, 295, 298, 300, 305, 307
Ravenscraft, Edward, 81
Rawlinson, George, 170
Ray, John, 62, 77, 82, 90
Raymond of Pennafort, 15
Read, Sir Herbert, 202, 229, 236-237, 239, 242, 245-248, 254, 257, 260, 268, 289
Reade, Charles, 137, 165-167, 169-171, 173-174, 177, 180-184, 189, 193
Reade, William, 154, 174, 183-185
Redgrove, Peter, 244, 277-278, 282, 287, 291, 295, 298, 300, 307
Reeve, Clara, 99, 119, 122, 133
Reeve, John, 71
Reeves, James, 219, 249, 263, 266, 273-274, 277, 283, 289, 293, 300, 305
Regent's Park, 137
Regius Professorship, Cambridge, 35
Reid, Forrest, 185, 222, 243, 249, 258, 260
Reid, Thomas, 92, 113, 122-123, 127
Reid, Thomas Mayne, 139, 164, 177, 193
Review of English Studies, 235
Review of Reviews, 199
Review of the Affairs of France, 90, 93
Reynard the Fox, 27
Reynolds, Frederick M., 150
Reynolds, John H., 142
Reynolds, Sir Joshua, 97, 115, 125
Rheims-Douai Bible, 44, 56
Rhys, Jean, 204, 287, 309
Ricardo, David, 116, 139, 143
Rich, Barnabe, 44
Rich, Edmund, 15
Richard I, 13
Richard II, 20
Richard III, 27
Richard Cour de Lion, 17
Richard the Redeless, 21
Richards, I.A., 202, 234, 236, 241, 274, 277, 300, 305
Richardson, Dorothy, 182, 226-229, 231, 234, 236, 238, 243, 248, 252, 272
Richardson, Ethel, 180, 259
Richardson, Henry Handel, 180, 219, 221, 236, 240, 253, 259
Richardson, Samuel, 83, 103-104, 106, 108, 111
Richmond, Legh, 135
Ripley, George, 26
Ritchie, Ann, 153, 178, 184, 219, 224, 229
Ritson, Joseph, 107, 121, 131, 132
Roberts, Michael, 212, 245, 249, 255, 261
Robertson, Thomas, 147, 175-181

334 INDEX

Robertson, William, 96, 110, 115, 119, 125–126
Robin Hood's Garland, 77
Robinson, Lennox, 195, 219, 229, 230, 235–237, 239, 241, 273–274
Rochester, Earl of, 69, 80
Rogers, James, 143, 177, 185, 194, 199
Rogers, Samuel, 112, 125, 135,137, 143, 167
Rogers, Woodes, 93
Rolfe, Frederick, 171, 208, 212, 215, 224, 247
Rolle, Richard, 17–18
Romanes Lectures, 200
Roscoe, William, 108, 127, 133–134, 148
Roscommon, Earl of, 64, 80–81
Rose Theatre, 47
Rosebery, Earl of, 161, 200, 209,211, 240
Rosenberg, Isaac, 199, 223, 226, 228, 263
Ross, Alan, 231, 255, 261, 269,274, 280, 285, 289, 298, 300, 303,307
Ross, Sir James, 155
Rossetti, Christina, 148, 174, 177, 183, 191, 203, 206
Rossetti, Dante, 146, 164, 173,181, 191
Rossetti, William, 147, 176, 178, 188, 197, 221, 229
Round, John, 166, 201, 205, 212, 221, 239
Round Table, 220
Rowe, Nicholas, 78, 88–92, 94–95
Rowlands, Samuel, 41, 50, 52–56,58, 63
Rowley, Samuel, 53, 68
Rowley, William, 45, 64–66
Rowse, Alfred Leslie, 213, 251,256, 258–260, 265, 276, 280, 283,287, 289, 298, 300, 303
Rowton House, 201
Roxburghe Book Club, 147
Royal Academy of Arts, 114
Royal Botanic Gardens, 156
Royal Exchange, 40, 75, 154, 159
Royal Historical Society, 179
Royal Society, 74–75
Royal Society of Literature, 143
Rudkin, James David, 248, 305, 307–308
Rudolph, Thomas, 54
Ruff, William, 157
Rugby School, 40

Ruggle, George, 59
Ruskin, John, 140, 158, 163, 165–166, 169, 171, 174, 176–178, 182–183, 195, 201, 210
Russell, Bertrand, 182, 214, 221, 231, 254, 262, 293
Russell, Countess, 208
Russell, George William, 178, 247
Russell, Lord John, 125, 141, 144, 166, 171, 187
Russell, William Clark, 158, 185, 187, 192–193, 221
Rutherford, Mark, 148, 191, 195, 197, 202, 206, 224
Ryle, Gilbert, 210, 263, 269, 307
Rymer, Thomas, 67, 79, 84, 90, 93

S

Sackville, Charles, 66, 89–90
Sackville, Thomas, 34, 38, 40, 55
Sadler's Wells Theatre, 113
St. Aubyn, Giles, 310
St. Dunstan's Hospital, 226
St. Godric of Durham, 9, 12
St. James's Gazette, 189
St. James's Square, 73
St. Mary of Bethlehem, 15
St. Mary of Bethlehem Hospital,78
St. Mary's Hospital, 14
St. Paul's Cathedral, 17, 75
St. Paul's, Covent Garden, 65, 127
St. Paul's School, 31
St. Peter's Church, 145
St. Stephen's Chapel, 151
Sainte-More, Benoit de, 12
Saintsbury, George, 159, 192,197, 206–208, 211,217, 230, 232, 245
Saki, 180, 227
Salmon, Thomas, 96
Salvation Army, 188
Samber, Robert, 99
Sanderson, Robert, 90
Sandys, George, 43, 60, 66–68
Sansom, William, 222, 258, 260, 262–266, 269, 271, 273–274,278, 282, 287, 293, 298, 303, 305, 307
Sassoon, Siegfried, 195, 217, 223, 226, 229, 237, 239, 242–243, 246–247, 251, 256–257, 259, 264,277–278, 288
Saturday Review, 167
Savage, Richard, 99, 104
Savile, George, 64, 82–83, 85, 107
Savile, Henry, 36, 46, 56, 58, 60

INDEX 335

Sayers, Dorothy, 202, 247, 256, 263, 270, 272
Scannell, Vernon, 231, 262, 268, 273, 277-278, 280, 285, 293, 295, 298, 303
Schumacher, E.F., 310
Scott, Alexander, 230, 262-263, 266, 269-270, 273-274, 291, 298, 300, 307
Scott, Hugh Stowell, 173, 213
Scott, Michael, 13, 15, 27, 29, 61
Scott, Michael, 124, 147, 151-152
Scott, Reginald, 45
Scott, Robert, 178, 216, 222, 224
Scott, Tom, 228, 268, 272, 282, 291, 307
Scott, Sir Walter, 116, 128-129, 131, 133-149
Scottish Text Society, 192
Scriblerus Club, 93
Scrutiny, 244, 267
Scupham, John Peter, 245, 300, 303, 307
Sedley, Sir Charles, 67, 76, 82, 88
Seeley, Sir John, 151, 176, 188, 193, 204-205
Selborne Society, 194
Selden, John, 44, 58-59, 61, 64-65, 67-69, 71, 74, 83
Selden Society, 196
Select Society, 108
Senior, Nassau, 124, 153, 171, 174-175, 179, 182-183, 188
Settle, Elkanah, 69, 81-82, 84, 97
Sewell, Ana, 187
Shadwell, Thomas, 68, 76, 78-79, 83-84
Shaffer, Peter, 236, 274, 284-285, 295
Shaftesbury, Earl of, 77, 87, 92-93
Shakespeare Folio, 61, 64, 74, 82
Shakespeare, William, 40, 46-57, 59
Sharp, William, 167, 198-200, 205-206, 215
Shaw, George Bernard, 168, 196, 200-201, 208, 212, 214, 218, 221-222, 225, 227-229, 231, 235, 239, 242, 247, 253, 263, 280
Shawcross, John, 310
Sheldonian Theatre, 76
Shelley, Mary, 128, 140, 144, 146, 152, 164
Shelley, Percy Bysshe, 125, 135, 138, 140-143
Shenstone, William, 94, 104, 109, 112
Sheraton, Thomas, 107, 125, 131-133
Sheridan, Frances, 97, 111-112, 114
Sheridan, Richard Brinsley, 107, 118-119, 129, 138
Sherlock, Thomas, 99
Sherlock, William, 67, 83, 84, 91
Sherriff, Robert, 205, 241-243, 262, 264, 270, 306
Sherwood, Mary Martha, 117, 131, 138, 140, 164
Shirley, James, 49, 59, 62, 64-65, 67-68, 73, 75
Shirley, John, 19, 25
Short, Charles, 189
Shorthouse, Joseph, 191
Sidgwick, Henry, 154, 182, 184, 193, 195-196, 200, 210
Sidney, Algernon, 86
Sidney, Sir Philip, 38, 44, 46, 49
Silkin, Jon, 241, 264, 269, 274, 278, 284, 287, 298, 303, 305
Sillitoe, Alan, 238, 273-274, 276-277, 279, 285, 287, 289, 291, 295, 298, 300, 305
Simon of Durham, 11
Simpson, Norman, 229, 277, 284, 287, 291
Sinclair, Catherine, 155
Sion College, 61
Sir Clyomon and Sir Clamides, 50
Sir Gawain and the Green Knight, 19
Sir Perceval of Gales, 18
Sir Thomas More, 49
Sisson, Charles Hubert, 225, 268, 270, 279, 285, 287, 289, 291, 305, 310
Sitwell, Dame Edith, 196, 226, 232, 235-236, 238, 242, 246-247, 254, 257-258, 262, 264, 268, 270, 273, 282
Sitwell, Sir Osbert, 201, 235, 237, 291
Sitwell, Sacheverell, 206, 249, 251, 255, 262, 300, 305
Skeat, Walter, 152, 175, 177, 181, 182, 189, 191, 204, 222
Skelton, John, 25, 31-33, 41
Sloane, Sir Hans, 91
Smart, Christopher, 97, 108, 112, 116
Smedley, Francis, 139, 164-165, 168, 175

Smiles, Samuel, 136, 169, 171, 173, 182, 185, 190, 197, 214
Smith, Adam, 97, 111, 118, 124
Smith, Alexander, 148, 166-167,169, 174, 176, 178
Smith, Edmund, 92
Smith, Florence Margaret, 212, 296
Smith, Horatio, 119, 136-137, 146, 162
Smith, Ian Crichton, 238, 270, 277, 279, 285, 291, 293, 295, 298, 300, 303, 305
Smith, James, 136-137
Smith, John, 73
Smith, John Thomas, 113, 147, 150, 160
Smith, Stevie, 212, 249, 252, 263, 280, 287, 296, 305
Smith, Sydney, 134
Smith, Sydney Goodsir, 226, 255, 260-262, 265-266, 268, 270, 276-277, 285, 291, 293, 307
Smith, Thomas, 124, 154, 158
Smith, Sir William, 136, 157, 159, 172, 202
Smith, William Robertson, 160, 191-192, 203
Smollett, Tobias George, 96, 105-111, 114-116
Snow, C.P., 215, 245-247, 255, 261, 263, 265, 269, 272, 274, 276,282, 291, 295, 300, 305, 307
Society for Promoting Christian Knowledge, 86
Society for Pure English, 224
Society for the Protection of Ancient Buildings, 187
Society of Antiquaries, 42, 53, 95
Society of Dilettanti, 100
Society of Doctors' Commons, 31, 170
Society of Friends, 69
Somerville, Edith, 169, 200, 217, 219, 262
Somerville, William, 78, 101, 103-104
Song of Canute, 12
Song of Ingeld, 5
Song of Lewes, 16
Southerne, Thomas, 73, 85, 105
Southey, Robert, 117, 131, 133-137, 139, 142, 144-146, 148, 150, 158
South Sea Company, 92
Southwell, Robert, 39, 48-49, 55
Spalding, John, 125

Spark, Muriel, 228, 273-274, 276-277, 279, 282, 286, 291, 295, 298, 300, 305, 310
Spectator, 92, 93, 94, 147
Speculum Christiani, 19
Speculum Laicorum, 17
Speed, John, 57
Speight, Johnny, 231, 293, 303,308
Speke, John, 174
Spence, Joseph, 142
Spencer, Herbert, 141, 165, 168, 172-175, 181, 194, 186, 189,194, 197, 213
Spender, Stephen, 219, 239, 242, 247-248, 251-253, 256, 260-261, 263, 265, 267-268, 270, 282, 286, 298, 309
Spenser, Edmund, 37, 41, 43, 46-47, 49-50
Sprat, Thomas, 65, 73, 76, 93
Sprigg, Christopher St. John, 217, 250
Stallworthy, Jon, 247, 274, 279, 282, 289, 293, 295, 305
Stanhope, Philip, 132, 150, 153, 173, 181, 185
Stanley, Arthur, 137, 159, 167-168, 173-174, 179, 181, 183,190
Stanley, Sir Henry, 156, 183,188, 214
Stanley, Thomas, 72
Starkey, Thomas, 34-35
Stationers' Company, 38
Steel, Flora Annie, 206
Steele, Sir Richard, 77, 89-90, 92, 94, 97, 99
Steevens, George, 102, 114, 117, 130
Stephen, James, 170, 200, 201
Stephen, Sir James, 124, 163, 165, 170
Stephen, Sir James Fitzjames, 147, 174-175, 184, 193, 203
Stephen, Sir Leslie, 149, 182,184, 186, 188, 190, 192, 206, 208, 211, 213-215
Stephens, James, 223
Sterne, Laurence, 93, 111, 113-114
Sternhold, Thomas, 39
Steuart, Sir James, 114
Stevenson, James Hall, 112
Stevenson, Robert Louis, 163, 177, 188-193, 195-199, 201-204, 206-207
Stewart, Dugald, 108, 125-126,130-131, 146

INDEX 337

Stillingfleet, Edward, 65, 73-74, 82, 87
Stirling Club, 154
Stirling, James, 141, 176, 191, 219
Stoker, Bram, 207
Stoppard, Tom, 250, 287, 308
Storey, David, 245, 280, 284, 289, 293, 295, 300, 303, 305, 308
Stowe, John, 33, 39-42, 44, 50, 54
Strachey, Giles Lytton, 189, 223, 229, 231-232, 239, 243-244
Strawberry Hill Press, 110, 128
Stretton, Hesba, 177
Strickland, Agnes, 127, 156, 164, 176, 184
Strickland, Elizabeth, 156, 164
Strutt, Joseph, 106, 119, 128, 131
Stubbes, Philip, 44
Stubbs, William, 145, 169, 175, 181-182, 184, 186, 195, 211
Stukeley, William, 82, 97, 103, 110, 113
Sublime Society of Beef Steaks, 101
Suckling, Sir John, 56, 66-69
Sunday (London) Times, 310
Surrey, Earl of, 32, 36, 38
Surtees, Robert Smith, 132, 138, 154, 158, 160, 161, 166, 170, 172, 175-176
Sweet, Henry, 159, 184, 186, 201, 211, 219, 222
Swift, Jonathan, 76, 84, 89-94, 97-103, 105, 114
Swinburne, Algernon, 153, 173, 176-178, 182, 184-186, 188, 190-192, 195-197, 199, 201, 206, 209, 215, 219
Symonds, John, 155, 184-185, 188, 190, 192, 198, 202
Symons, Arthur, 176, 196, 209, 258
Synge, John Millington, 181, 214, 215-216, 218-219, 221, 280

T

Tabard Inn, 85
Tale of Gamelyn, 18
Talfourd, Sir Thomas, 152
Tate Gallery, 206
Tate, Nahum, 71, 81, 84, 86, 88, 94
Tatler, 91, 92, 148-149
Tattersall's Auction-Room, 114
Taverner's Bible, 35
Taylor, Ann, 120, 132-133, 135, 177
Taylor, Cecil P., 240, 307-308
Taylor, Sir Henry, 130, 146, 151, 153, 157, 161, 174, 195
Taylor, Jane, 121, 132-133, 135, 138, 144
Taylor, Jeremy, 57, 63, 69-73, 76
Taylor, Tom, 138, 160, 168, 170, 189
Temple, Sir William, 63, 76-78, 80, 84, 87
Tennant, William, 136
Tennyson, Alfred Lord, 134, 146, 148, 151, 157, 161, 163--164, 167-168, 171-172, 175, 179-180, 182-183, 186, 189-192, 194-196, 199, 201
Tennyson, Frederick, 133, 146, 167, 200, 207
Test, 109
Thackeray, William, 135, 154-166, 169, 172-175
Thatched House Club, 137
Theatre, 95-96
Theobald, Lewis, 83, 98, 101, 104
Theodore of Tarsus, 4
Thirlwall, Connop, 128, 147, 152, 185
Thomas, 12-13
Thomas of Kent, 17
Thomas, Donald Michael, 247, 291, 298, 303, 307
Thomas, Dylan, 225, 257, 253, 255, 257, 260, 267-270
Thomas, Philip Edward, 187, 213, 220-221, 224, 227-230, 232, 249
Thomas, Ronald, 224, 260, 267-268, 270, 274, 279, 282, 284, 287, 291, 300, 305
Thompson, Francis, 170, 202, 205, 207, 216-217, 220
Thoms, William, 132, 154, 159, 194
Thomson, Sir Charles Wyville, 187
Thomson, James, 88, 98-103, 105-106
Thomson, James, 151, 185, 191-192, 194
Thoresby, John, 19
Thurlow, Edward, 137
Thwaite, Anthony, 241, 268, 273, 282, 289, 300, 303, 305
Tickell, Thomas, 82, 93-94, 97, 103
Ticknor, George, 163
Times (London), 123
Times Literary Supplement, 212
Titus and Vespasian, 22
Tolkien, John, 201, 233, 251, 264, 269-270, 272, 301, 305, 309

Tomkis, Thomas, 55, 59
Tomlinson, Charles, 237, 274,287, 293, 300, 305
Tomlinson, Henry, 183, 223, 229, 231, 238, 242, 273
Toplady, Augustus Montague, 118
Torrens, William, 136, 161, 202-203
Tory Party, 83
Tottel, Richard, 38, 48
Tourneur, Cyril, 42, 52, 55, 57,62
Townley, James, 111
Toynbee, Arnold, 198, 226, 247,262, 265, 268, 306
Tracts for the Times, 151
Tradescant, John, 59
Trafalgar Square, 147
Tragedy of Mr. Arden of Feversham, 47
Traherne, Thomas, 78
Traill, Henry, 157, 192, 194,200-202, 210
Transatlantic Review, 234
Travers, Walter, 46
Trelawny, Edward, 125, 149, 170, 190
Tremayne, Sydney, 222, 260, 262-265, 270, 280, 291, 303
Trench, Richard, 133, 157, 161,163, 165, 195
Trevelyan, George Macaulay, 186, 218, 220, 222, 225, 237, 242,258, 279
Trevelyan, George Otto, 154, 175-176, 180, 186, 190, 220, 223,239
Trevisa, John de, 18, 20-21
Trevor, William, 238, 303, 305,307, 308, 310
Trimmer, Sarah, 123
Trinity College, Cambridge, 36
Trinity Homilies, 14
Trollope, Anthony, 137, 161-162, 168-170, 173-176, 178, 180, 184-188, 190-191
Trollope, Frances, 120, 150, 154
True Chronicle History of. . . Cromwell, 53
True Tale of Robin Hood, 64
Tucker, Abraham, 114
Tuohy, Frank, 310
Tupper, Martin, 135, 150, 159,198
Turberville, George, 35, 41-42, 56
Turner, Sharon, 129
Turner, Walter, 198, 229, 233, 243, 248, 250, 259
Tussaud's Wax Museum, 131

Tusser, Thomas, 38
Tyburn Gallows, 121
Tyndale, William, 28, 33-34
Tyndall, John, 141, 172, 174-176, 178, 180, 183-184, 191, 202
Tyrrell, George, 172, 207-209,212-214, 217-220, 225
Tyrwhitt, Thomas, 99, 114, 118, 122
Tytler, Patrick, 124, 147, 155, 162

U

Udall, Nicholas, 37
Unitarian Church, 116
University College, Oxford, 15
Urquhart, Sir Thomas, 57, 71, 73, 84
Usk, Thomas, 20

V

Vale Press, 205
Vanbrugh, Sir John, 75, 86, 90, 98-99
Vancouver, George, 129
Vauxhall Gardens, 170
Victoria, Queen, 153, 178, 193
Victoria and Albert Museum, 164
Vinegar Bible, 95
Viner, Charles, 104
Vitalis, Ordericus, 11

W

Wace, 10, 12-13
Wager, Lewis. 40
Wain, John, 235, 268, 270, 272-274, 276-277, 280, 282, 286-287, 289, 293, 295, 298, 300, 305, 310
Wakefield, Gilbert, 109, 123,126, 128, 131
Walcott, Derek, 241, 303, 308,310
Waley, Arthur, 198, 231, 236, 239, 252, 256, 265, 271, 284
Wallace, 27
Wallace, Alfred, 143, 166, 180, 186, 199, 208, 214, 224
Wallace, Edgar, 185, 216, 238,242
Wallace, William, 158, 185, 200, 204, 206, 208
Waller, Edmund, 54, 62, 69, 82
Wallis, John, 72
Walpole, Horace, 95, 110, 112-115,

INDEX
339

128-129
Walpole, Hugh, 193, 221-223, 225, 227, 229-230, 235-236, 239, 242-243, 246, 253, 255
Walpole, Spencer, 155, 188, 199, 215, 217
Walsh, William, 74, 89-91
Walter of Bibbesworth, 15
Walton, Brian, 71
Walton, Izaak, 47, 67, 70-72, 75, 77, 79, 81
Walton, John, 23
Wanley, Humfry, 86
Wanley, Nathaniel, 79
Wapull, George, 43
Warburton, Rowland, 132, 161, 171, 200
Warburton, William, 86, 102, 106, 107, 112, 119
Ward, Edward, 76, 86, 90, 100
Ward, Mary, 164, 194-195, 198, 202, 204, 206, 208, 216, 222, 230
Ward, William, 159
Warner, Rex, 215, 251, 159, 274, 277, 282
Warner, William, 38, 45, 49, 55-56
Warren, John, 152, 177, 179, 190, 202, 204
Warren, Samuel, 133, 254-155, 187
Warton, Joseph, 97, 105, 109, 121, 130
Warton, Thomas (younger), 99, 105, 109, 113, 117, 119, 122, 124
Watchman, 127
Waterton, Charles, 145
Waiter's Club, 140
Watkins, Vernon, 216, 255, 259,262, 269, 276, 280, 288, 291
Watson, Henry, 37
Watson, Richard, 44-48
Watson, Bp. Richard, 102, 118, 128, 138
Watson, Thomas, 38, 44, 47
Watson, Sir William, 169, 202, 204-206, 217, 223, 247
Watt, Robert, 145
Watts, Isaac, 78, 91, 94, 96, 106
Watts-Dunton, Walter, 149, 195,207-208, 225
Waugh, Alec, 207, 229, 241, 245-247, 250, 255, 272, 303
Waugh, Auberon, 248, 279, 282,286, 291, 300, 307
Waugh, Evelyn, 213, 228, 239, 242, 245, 247, 252, 256, 259-260,262, 264, 267-268, 271, 273, 276, 279,

286
Webb, Mary, 190, 228, 235, 237
Webster, John, 43, 54-56, 58, 61
Wellington, Duchess of, 272
Wells, Charles, 130, 143, 145,188
Wells, H.G., 177, 205-209, 211-217, 219-223, 225, 227, 230, 233-234, 237-238, 242-243, 246, 253, 255, 259, 287
Wesker, Arnold, 244, 276-277, 279-280, 287, 295, 301, 305, 307-308
Wesley, Charles, 91, 123
Wesley, John, 89, 116, 124
West, Dame Rebecca, 201, 229, 233, 241, 250, 252, 256, 263, 273, 274
Westminster Palace, 31, 151
Westminster Review, 144
Westminster School, 39
Weyman, Stanley, 167, 202, 212, 217, 239
Whately, Richard, 123, 141, 143, 146, 174
When Holy Church Is under Foot, 15
Whetstone, George, 43
Whewell, William, 126, 151, 154, 160, 165-166, 177
Whig Examiner, 92
Whig Party, 83
Whistler, Laurence, 222, 241, 245, 247, 250, 252, 255-256, 258,263, 272, 279-280, 282, 289, 291,293
Whitaker's Almanack, 179
White, Gilbert, 96, 124, 126-127
White Hart Inn, 198
White, Joseph, 117, 145, 147, 152, 156
White, Terence, 216, 246, 265, 269, 274, 282
White, William Hale, 148, 224
Whiteboys Society, 111
Whitefield, George, 94, 115
Whitehall Palace, 86
Whitehead, Alfred North, 172, 221, 236-238, 241, 246, 260
Whitehead, Charles, 132, 149, 151, 153, 157, 173
Whitehead, Edward Anthony, 245, 298, 301, 305, 307, 309
Whitehead, William, 94, 107, 109-110, 112, 122-123
White's Chocolate House, 86
Whittington, Richard, 21-23
Whole Duty of Man, 73

Who's Who, 163
Whymper, Edward, 155, 182, 202,221
Whyte-Melville, George, 142, 166, 172-173, 175, 181-183, 186-189
Widsith, 4
Wife's Lament, 5
Wilberforce, William, 128
Wilde, Oscar, 166, 191, 201-203, 205, 208, 210, 216
Wilkes, John, 98, 128
Wilkinson, Sir John, 154
Willett, John, 310
William I, 9
William II, 9
William III, 83
William IV, 148
William of Malmesbury, 10-11
William of Newburgh, 14
Williams, Charles, 195, 242, 250-253, 257-258, 262
Williams, George Emlyn, 215, 252, 279
Williams, Helen Maria, 112, 124, 126, 129, 131, 138, 141, 146
Williams, Hugo, 256, 286, 293,301, 307
Williams, Isaac, 154
Williams, John Stuart, 230, 280, 289, 295, 307
Willis, Edward Henry, 228
Willis, Robert, 195
Willis, Ted, 228, 301, 305, 307-308
Wilmot, Robert, 47
Wilson, Angus, 224, 263-264, 267, 272-274, 279, 282, 284, 289, 293, 295, 303, 309
Wilson, Sir Arnold, 193, 239, 254-255
Wilson, Sir Daniel, 138, 161, 165, 201
Wilson, John, 122, 136, 138, 166
Wilson, John, 62, 75, 84-85
Wilson, Robert, 45-46, 48
Wilson, Thomas, 33, 37, 44
Winchelsea, Countess of, 74, 89, 93, 96
Winchester College, 21
Wireker, Nigel, 13
Wisden, John, 175
Wiseman, Nicholas, 167
Wither, George, 45, 58-61, 68, 76
Wolcot, John, 102, 140
Wolfe, Charles, 139
Wollstonecraft, Mary, 110, 125,128
Wood, Anthony, 64, 78, 84, 85

Wood, Charles, 245, 295, 301, 307-308
Wood, Ellen, 137, 173-174, 185, 188, 196
Woodes, Nathaniel, 44
Woodham-Smith, Cecil, 206, 264, 267, 309
Woolf, Leonard, 226
Woolf, Virginia, 191, 226, 228-229, 233, 235-236, 238-239, 241, 243, 245, 247, 251-252, 255-256, 261, 309-310
Wordsworth, William, 115, 126-133, 135, 137, 141, 143, 152, 158,163
World, 108-109
World's Classics, 212
Wotton, Sir Henry, 41, 61, 67, 70
Wren, Christopher (younger), 107
Wren, Percival Christopher, 235
Wright, David, 230, 263, 267, 269, 274, 286-287, 393, 307
Wright, Thomas, 135, 153-154, 156, 158-159, 174, 187
Wulfstan, 9
Wyatt, Sir Thomas, 30, 35-36, 38
Wycherley, William, 67, 77-79, 90, 95, 99
Wycliffe Bible, 21
Wycliffe, John, 18-20
Wynnere and Wastoure, 18
Wyntoun, Andrew, 23, 127

Y

Yarrell, William, 121, 153, 158, 168
Yeats, William Butler, 176, 196, 199, 202, 204-205, 207, 209,211, 213-215, 217219, 221-223, 225-226, 228-231, 233, 235-236, 238-239, 241, 245, 247, 250-253, 255, 264-265, 267, 273, 277, 287
Yellow Book, 203, 206
Yonge, Charlotte, 143, 166-169, 176-177, 181, 189, 198, 211
York Plays, 20
Yorke, Henry Vincent, 215, 301
Yorkshire Tragedy, 55
Young, Andrew, 194, 221, 264, 274
Young, Arthur, 103, 117, 120, 125, 141
Young, Edward, 81, 93, 96-98, 104, 111-113
Ywain and Gawain, 18

Z

Zangwill, Israel, 175, 202-203,
  205, 207, 218, 236
Zoological Society, 145

About the Author

SAMUEL J. ROGAL is a member of the English Department at Mary Holmes College in West Point, Mississippi. He is the author of several books including *The Paragraph* and *The Student Critic.*

A Chronological Outline of Bri

9780313214776.3